FASCIST IDEOLOGY

Fascist Ideology is a comparative study of the expansionist foreign policies of Fascist Italy and Nazi Germany from 1922 to 1945. One of the most extensively debated features of Fascist Italy and Nazi Germany was their propensity for aggressive, large-scale territorial expansion. From the initial goal of revising the post-1918 territorial settlement to its culmination in the Second World War, territorial expansion became a defining characteristic of the two regimes' ideologies and policies, and played a crucial role in their eventual collapse in 1943–5.

Fascist Ideology provides a comparative investigation of fascist expansionism by focusing on the close relations between ideology and action under Mussolini and Hitler. With an overview of the ideological motivations behind fascist expansionism and their impact on fascist policies, this book explores the two main issues which have dominated the historiographical debates on the nature of fascist expansionism: whether Italy's and Germany's particular expansionist tendencies can be attributed to a set of generic fascist values, or were shaped by the long-term, uniquely national ambitions and developments since unification; and whether the pursuit of expansion was opportunistic or followed a grand design in each case.

This book is a fascinating study of the expansionist visions of Hitler and Mussolini and it enlightens our understanding of the dynamics and evolution of the fascist policies of Italy and Germany to the end of the Second World War.

Aristotle A. Kallis is Tutor in the Departments of Politics and History at the University of Edinburgh.

FASCIST IDEOLOGY

Territory and expansionism in Italy and
Germany, 1922–1945

Aristotle A. Kallis

London and New York

First published 2000
by Routledge
11 New Fetter Lane, London EC4P 4EE

Simultaneously published in the USA and Canada
by Routledge
29 West 35th Street, New York, NY 10001

Routledge is an imprint of the Taylor & Francis Group

Typeset in Baskerville by Taylor & Francis Books Ltd
Printed and bound in Great Britain by Clays Ltd, St Ives plc

British Library Cataloguing in Publication Data
A catalogue record for this book is available from the British Library

Library of Congress Cataloging in Publication Data
Kallis, Aristotle A., 1970–
Fascist ideology: territory and expansionism in Italy and Germany, 1922–1945/
Aristotle A. Kallis.
p.cm.
Includes bibliographical references and index.
1. Fascism–Italy–History. 2. Italy–Foreign relations–1922–1945. 3. Nationalism–
Italy–History–20th century. 4. National socialism–Germany–History. 5. Germany–
Foreign relations–1933–1945. 6. Nationalism–Germany–History–20th century. I.
Title.
DG571.K34 2000
320.53'3'0943–dc21   99–087416

ISBN 0–415–21611–7 (hbk)
ISBN 0–415–21612–5 (pbk)

CONTENTS

ACKNOWLEDGEMENTS

This book draws on my research for the degree of Ph.D. at the University of Edinburgh. Therefore, my primary academic debt is to a number of scholars who provided me with invaluable support and vital guidance during my postgraduate studies. I am indebted, first of all, to my supervisors, Dr Jill Stephenson and Professor Malcolm Anderson, for their constructive feedback, their willingness to read drafts at very short notice, and their unceasing encouragement. At certain stages I sought the advice of a number of other scholars, and I am grateful to them for their eagerness to sacrifice precious time in responding to my requests. Mr Chris Black went far beyond the call of duty to read the final draft of my thesis, providing me at the same time with extremely useful hints that helped me in the preparation of this book. Dr Henry Palairet offered useful criticism and suggestions for Chapter One. Professor John Dimakis at the University of Athens was always willing to discuss my work from its inception to its later stages.

My warmest thanks are also owing to a number of people who helped me in different ways during the period of research and writing. At the Department of Politics of the University of Edinburgh, the warmth and personal concern of all members of staff, but especially of Professor Russell Keat, Dr Mary Buckley, Professor Alice Brown and Dr Richard Freeman, were an immense source of support in my everyday academic experience. The staff of the Main Library of the University of Edinburgh, and especially Scott Summers, were especially helpful and accommodating to my often excessive demands. Thanks are also due to Dr Simon Dixon at the University of Glasgow for his kindness; to Dr Stuart Wallace at the Centre for Continuing Education for offering me the opportunity to teach the subject of fascism to a particularly engaging audience of mature students; and to David White for a series of highly engaging conversations on the nature of fascist ideology back in 1996–7.

My research was significantly assisted by two generous grants, from the Voudouri Foundation and from the Sofia Saripolou Trust of the National Kapodistrian University of Athens. A parallel research project of interwar Greek foreign policy, funded by the Foundation of the Hellenic World in 1998, helped me to develop aspects of the last chapter of the book on the Second World War.

ACKNOWLEDGEMENTS

Researching and writing proved far more solitary undertakings than I had anticipated or, indeed, hoped for. This is why I owe a particular debt to a whole list of personal friends, without whose encouragement at crucial stages and moments of crisis this work would have never seen the light of day. It would be impossible to mention them all, but their support and love in so many different ways and instances were an unremitting source of cumulative strength that sustained my efforts to complete this work. A special thanks, however, is due to George Pavlakos, who has constantly reminded me of our common academic and personal goals; and to my partner, who provided me with a more sound perspective on life and work alike, a great deal of emotional support, and invaluable help in the painstaking process of proofreading.

Back in 1996, my grandmother, who had been born in the dying moments of the nineteenth century, asked me why I had become engrossed in the study of something so unreservedly negative and spiteful as fascism. I uttered something about the constructive remembering of the past, the need to try to understand what you reminisce without being enchained by animosity. She could not read, but I am sure that she would have loved to see this work completed. My parents, on the other hand, never asked such questions. Instead, they supported my choices in every way imaginable without a mere hint of reservation, in spite of the numerous sacrifices that they entailed for them. Without their kindness, understanding and generosity this book would have still been a distant, unfulfilled dream for me. To them, and to the memory of my grandmother, this work is dedicated.

For the contents of this book, and for any error of fact or judgement, I alone am responsible.

ABBREVIATIONS

ANI	Associazione Nazionalista Italiana
CGII	Confederazione Generale d'Industria Italiana
DBFP	Documents of British Foreign Policy
DDI	Documenti Diplomatici Italiani
DDF	Documents Diplomatiques Français
DDP	Deutsche Demokratische Partei
DGFP	Documents on German Foreign Policy
DKG	Deutsche Koloniale Gesellschaft
DNVP	Deutschnationale Volkspartei
DVP	Deutsche Volkspartei
FZ	*Frankfurter Zeitung*
NSDAP	Nationalsozialistische Deutsche Arbeiterpartei
OO	*Opera Omnia di Benito Mussolini*
PO	Politische Organisation (NSDAP)
PNF	Partito Nazionale Fascista
PPI	Partito Popolare Italiano
PSI	Partito Socialista Italiano
SA	Sturm Abteilung
Scritti	*Scritti e Discorsi di Benito Mussolini*
SPD	Sozialdemokratische Partei Deutschlands
SS	Schutzstaffeln
VB	*Völkischer Beobachter*

INTRODUCTION

More than fifty years after the end of the Second World War, interwar fascism still remains an extremely slippery terrain for research. Notwithstanding the numerous works on, and interpretations of, various aspects of the fascist phenomenon, fascism remains a 'conundrum' for historians and political scientists alike.[1] Lack of conceptual clarity, competing methodological approaches and failure to generate a solid theoretical framework for research have contributed to a conspicuous absence of a lasting consensus about what 'fascism' really represents. Undoubtedly, recent developments in research have produced a more sophisticated methodology and a reasonable distance from the rigidity of many pioneer interpretations. The postwar 'moral' obligation to castigate fascism as an aberration – of national histories, of the whole European civilisation, of capitalism and industrialisation, of modernity, of the human *psyche*[2] – has subsided, thus allowing for an acknowledgement of fascism's complexity, ambiguity and seductiveness. The plurality of approaches, however, neither produced unequivocal answers to the most fundamental questions about the nature of fascism, nor fostered any tendencies for consensus building in key areas of research. We are still left with a plethora of mystifying questions that resist clear-cut responses: about the nature of fascism, about the utility of a *generic* definition or a *comparative* approach to it, about its geographical and historical boundaries, about its ideological significance, about its place in national and European history, about its relevance to our past and future.

For a comparative study of the expansionist policies of the Italian and German 'fascist' regimes, the challenge of conceptual and methodological clarity embraces all the above complex issues, but is also magnified by a series of other questions intrinsic to a general theory of foreign relations. It is not coincidental that research on the two regimes' expansionist policies has generated heated controversies and passionate exchanges. Emphasis on the dissimilar characteristics, structures and conditions of the two regimes appears to have rendered comparison and synthesis obsolete, if not methodologically questionable. Even for many of those interpretations that still subscribe to a generic notion of 'fascism', expansionism is often regarded as that vital *differentia specifica* which draws the final frontier of comparability.[3] The extreme racialist *Weltanschauung* of

1

the Nazi regime with all its well-documented excesses (anti-Semitism, total war, genocide) has frequently served as the basis of the argument that the German case is *singular* and, therefore, defies categorisation. Rather than fostering the impression of similarity, expansionism has become a major liability for the comparative approach to generic 'fascism'.

On a more theoretical level, the study of fascist expansionism has stumbled upon a series of controversies about the process of foreign policy making. The growing popularity of the 'primacy of domestic affairs' thesis has cast its shadow upon the relation between *ideology* and *action* in foreign policy. Emphasis on the latter's role as a diversion from domestic deadlocks or as an effective mechanism for consensus building (the social imperialist thesis) has obscured the relative autonomy of foreign policy making, especially in regimes whose leaders showed such an obstinate interest in the formulation of foreign policy. In turn, this has undermined the value of ideology in shaping foreign policy strategies and in guiding actions in this field. Differences of opinion about whether the expansionist policies of the two regimes were ideological, opportunistic or diversionary have again served to underline their dissimilarities; and thus torpedo the validity of comparison. In general, research has treated the Nazi regime more seriously than its Italian counterpart. The destructive force of Nazi policies, the brutality in implementing them and the rigidity of the regime's expansionist objectives have fostered an interest in the ideological aspects of Nazi territorial policies.[4] Such an interest is more limited in the case of the Italian expansionist policies, whose 'flexibility' and constant re-orientation have been widely seen as reflections of an unprincipled, non-ideological handling of foreign affairs. The examples of A.J.P. Taylor, I. Kirkpatrick and D.M. Smith are indicative of a historiographical trend which had its roots in the polemical accounts of G. Salvemini but was subsequently pushed to extremes in its depiction of Mussolini's regime as the apotheosis of propaganda without substance or conviction.[5] However, the uncertainty about the role of ideology in shaping fascist foreign policies simply reproduces the lack of consensus that underlies the theory of foreign relations in this field – a lack of consensus about the ideology–action relation that originates no less from the elusiveness of the notion of *ideology*, upon which such a theory is conceptualised.

In this sense, the comparative stance of this study, and its focus on Italy and Germany as legitimate case studies for the analysis of fascist expansionism, are far from self-evident choices. To state the obvious, namely that only the Italian and German interwar regimes nourished expansionist millenarian ideologies *and* possessed the material capabilities to implement them in an aggressive style, is completely different from claiming that fascist expansionism was derived from a fascist ideological commitment to territorial expansion or that such a commitment was a generic element of the fascist worldview. Before embarking on such a course, however, it is vital to consider two pivotal methodological prerequisites: first, why it is meaningful to re-establish the validity of a generic concept of 'fascism', which in itself legitimises a comparative approach to its different – and idiosyncratic – manifestations; and second, why the scope of such an approach should be limited to these two countries – Italy and Germany – and to that specific span of time, the interwar period.

The validity of a comparative approach to fascism: Italy and Germany

In one of his last writings, Tim Mason criticised the lack of a 'longer historiographical perspective' in the recent studies on National Socialism. The 'decline of the Fascist paradigm', he argued, and the emphasis on the singularity of the Nazi regime have obscured the fact that 'National Socialism was a peculiar part of something larger'.[6] In a similar vein, Ernst Nolte concluded one of his most ambiguous and controversial essays by berating the futility of the recent trend in historiography to 'demonise' National Socialism, presenting it as 'unique, singular' and unparalleled in every respect.[7] Notwithstanding the dubious methodological and historical validity of his analysis,[8] Nolte expressed a reservation towards the direction of research on National Socialism that was essentially shared by Mason: namely, that focus on the genocidal and destructive aspects of National Socialism 'makes critical distance [from fascism] more difficult'.[9]

Where the two approaches radically diverge, however, is in their prescriptions for the broadening of the research focus. While Nolte's main objective was to relativise the destructive force of National Socialism by locating precedents and antecedents outside the context of the fascist regimes, Mason called for constructive comparisons in the framework of a generic 'fascist' paradigm. The significance of his analysis, however, lies also in his suggestions for the content and samples of such a comparative approach. Mason does not express nostalgia for the traditional definitions of generic 'fascism' (for example, the 'totalitarian' approach). The revival of the 'fascist' paradigm for him has to be constructed upon a new conceptual basis that would guarantee the soundness and validity of comparison. In this respect, there is only one candidate for a comparative analysis of National Socialism: the underexplored reservoir of Italian fascism. Nolte's comparisons with such disparate cases as Pol Pot's Cambodia and the slaughter of the Armenians are 'extraneous to any serious discussion of Nazism; Mussolini's Italy is not'.[10]

In the face of the unpopularity of comparative analysis, there have been systematic attempts to provide the kind of comparison that Mason suggested. The Italian and German regimes have become the focus of some comparative approaches to fascism in the 1980s and 1990s. S. Payne's work,[11] R.A.H. Robinson's studies on European fascism[12] and, more recently, A. De Grand's, R. Eatwell's and R. Bessel's comparative analyses[13] have placed the discussion of a generic concept of 'fascism' on a more sound theoretical platform. Bessel's effort, especially, divulges through its title the challenge and power of the suggested comparative approach: namely, that there is as much to learn about the nature of fascism from the similarities as from the differences in the ideology and policy of the 'fascist regimes'. R. Griffin's authoritative study *The Nature of Fascism* (1994) has built confidently upon this dual significance of comparison. Griffin constructs a clear and elaborate 'ideological minimum' for a fascist paradigm (a 'palingenetic' form of extreme nationalism in the form of a 'third way' between liberalism itself and socialism), and then tests its validity against the different representations of this minimum in the various fascist movements and regimes.[14] In spite of a debatable broadening of focus to extra-European and post-1945 phenomena, the author devotes most space to the Italian and German fascisms, thus acknowledging their primary relevance to any discussion of a generic concept of 'fascism'.

In the field of foreign policy, the limits of the comparative sample have somehow been determined by history itself in a *de facto* manner. Of all potentially 'fascist' regimes only the Italian, German and Japanese systematically pursued expansionist policies. It was, however, the earlier convergence between the former two, and their closer political co-operation in promoting the goal of a new territorial map in Europe, that has focused the attention on the Italian and German cases. E. Wiskemann's work has underlined the significance of the German–Italian alliance for the implementation of the fascist 'new order'.[15] In a similar vein, J. Petersen's study has examined the origins of the two regimes' politico-ideological convergence in 1933–6 and provides insight into the nature of the Axis alliance, while F.W. Deakin has focused on the significance of the alliance during the Second World War.[16] Yet, for these comparative – and many other singular – studies, Axis expansionism reflected the triumph of Nazi ideology and policies over a weaker Italian regime that was dragged to aggression and war against its initial political intentions. In this respect, the work of M. Knox is unique in its analysis of the expansionist penchant of the Italian and German regimes.[17] Knox has pinpointed the origins of this common propensity in comparable ideological traditions of indigenous nationalism (myth of the nation, glorification of national history, cult of violence and war, and so on), in the personal visions of the two leaders, as well as in the idiosyncratic circumstances of the interwar period in the two countries. He has also formulated a common theoretical framework which helps to incorporate expansionism into the internal logic of the two regimes. The political and ideological relevance of expansion is established here in two ways: first, horizontally, as a common denominator between the two regimes' *Weltanschauungen*; and second, vertically, combining the propensity for territorial expansion with the desire for 'conquering' (that is, transforming in a radical direction) the domestic system. Knox's thesis, granting equal gravity to the ideological value and political functionality of expansion in the Italian and German cases, provides a strong defence for the value of a comparison between them. At the same time, however, it does not explore the link between the two regimes' propensity for expansion and the generic 'fascist' values that underpinned or radicalised it. Such a radicalisation, according to Knox, emanated from the need to speed up the process of domestic consolidation and to free the two leaders from the last remaining vestiges of the old order. This assertion is undoubtedly correct, in the sense that successes in foreign policy provided the two fascist leaderships with the necessary prestige and political self-confidence to challenge traditional institutions and establish their primary role in foreign policy decision making. However, radicalisation resulted from a spectacularly high level of consolidation of fascist power and not from a need to achieve it. Even in Italy, where the preservation of the institutional role of the Crown and of social allegiances to the Catholic Church survived the strengthening of Fascist power, there is little evidence that the regime's shift to an aggressive foreign policy accelerated the process of domestic transformation. Obviously, in the extraordinary circumstances of a major military conflagration, both regimes (and especially Nazism) initiated experiments with new forms of rule that would have been barely conceivable in a semblance of peace. In the end, though, the interpretation of fascist expansionism presupposes a clarification of the relation between *ideology* and *action*. Knox's highly sophisticated comparative analysis seems to cope better with the long-term ideological legacies of each fascist regime than with the generically 'fascist' ideological determinants of the radicalisation of fascist expansionism in the late 1930s. In this sense, his interpretive stance is somehow reminiscent of the traditional justification for a comparison between Fascist and Nazi expansionism – namely, that we should examine them together simply because they seem comparable, served similar political functions or were pursued concurrently.

This study aims to examine fascist expansionism in each regime on two levels: first, as *ideology*, both in its links with long-term traditions in the two societies since unification and in its relevance to specific 'fascist' values; and, second, as a process of *translating intentions into action* through the influence of domestic and international factors. The unique expression of expansionism as both thought and action under the two regimes sets them apart from other quasi-fascist cases, where expansion remained a utopian ideology or was practised outside the framework of a coherent ideological system. In this sense, comparison provides an opportunity to test two main hypotheses – first, whether the two regimes' idiosyncratic propensity for territorial expansion *and* their expansionist policies were underpinned by specifically 'fascist' ideas; and, second, whether the ideology and practice of territorial expansion by the two fascist regimes displayed a degree of programmatic coherence and commitment to the realisation of a concrete long-term vision.

Ideology and action: a puzzling relation

The dualism between ideology and action constitutes a pivotal element of the fascist systems, not only in the sphere of foreign policy but generally in every aspect of fascist thought and policy. Yet, the nature of this dual relation in fascism has traditionally been an area of heated controversy and debate. Again, the origins of this controversy lay in a general lack of consensus about the role of ideology in the process of foreign policy making. In spite of many attempts to present the ideology–action problem in fascist regimes as a special feature of 'fascism', this debate remains part of a wider discussion on domestic and foreign policy making. Perceiving fascist foreign policy as an extreme expression of this theoretical problem might satisfy intentions to mythify or demonise fascism as a completely unique phenomenon; it does not provide, however, a constructive methodological point of departure for understanding fascism itself. The intricate relation of ideology and action is not the exclusive privilege of the study of fascist foreign policies; it is, in fact, not even limited to the theory of foreign policy in general. Instead, it remains a philosophical and political riddle in all systems and spheres of policy, domestic and foreign.[18] Fascism enters the debate as an aspect – however unique – of the wider problem, in the same way that fascism is in itself an aspect of our wider social, political and intellectual history.

Two different debates – the first about the programmatic or opportunistic/diversionary character of fascist foreign policies, the second about the continuities of fascist expansionist policies with previous national aspirations – have dominated our perceptions of the fascist phenomenon. We may dismiss their crude polarisation and cut across their artificial barriers, but we can neither disregard it nor refrain from using their terminology as a point of reference. With regard to the 'programmatic' or not substance of fascist foreign policy, the existing literature has treated the two regimes rather differently. The Nazi regime has been regarded as more ideological and consistent in its expansionist pursuits.[19] Hitler's fanatical exposition in *Mein Kampf* and his unwavering commitment to rearmament and reckless activism have formed the basis of the so-called intentionalist approach. H. Trevor-Roper's rigid conception of Hitler's ideology as a 'blueprint for power'[20] was followed by K. Hildebrand's and A. Hillgruber's notion of a 'stage-by-stage' plan for territorial expansion.[21] G. Schubert located the ideological origins of Hitler's foreign policy in the 1920s, a view shared by G. Stoakes who regarded the period 1919–25 as pivotal for the evolution of Hitler's worldview.[22] Even more flexible intentionalist arguments, such as A. Bullock's distinction between 'consistent aims' and 'opportunistic methods', underlined how such ideological aims underpinned the regime's foreign policy making and were never contradicted by tactical vacillations.[23] However, the intentionalist orthodoxy has been challenged from a variety of viewpoints. A.J.P. Taylor's classic and controversial interpretation rejected any ideological substance in Nazi foreign policy, arguing instead that expansionist goals were shaped according to traditionally German objectives and were pursued in reaction to inauspicious international developments.[24] H. Rauschning and H. Mommsen share the conviction that Nazi foreign policy originated from an unprincipled and blind pursuit of absolute power, devoid of any particular objective or strategy.[25] Mommsen also underlined the social imperialist function of territorial expansion, especially in appeasing the radicalism of the Nazi party's old fighters, while T. Mason echoed a similar argument when he described Hitler's foreign policy as a reaction to domestic pressures in a 'barbaric variant of social imperialism'. According to Mason, these internal deadlocks prompted a radicalisation in the Nazi expansionist policies which culminated in the invasion of Poland as a desperate move to divert attention from the terminal crisis of the German economy in 1939.[26]

By contrast, the 'traditional' interpretation of the Italian Fascist foreign policy has underlined the opportunistic, non-programmatic and diversionary character of Mussolini's expansionist plans.[27] Total rejection of the notion of a programme forms the basis of G. Salvemini's classic accounts, which emphasise both the improvising and the propagandistic nature of the *Duce*'s foreign policy making.[28] D. Mack Smith, who dismissed Mussolini as a 'cloud-cuckoo-land' amateur and presented his whole policy as fraudulent, has echoed similar views.[29] More moderate was the analysis of E. Di Nolfo, who nevertheless detected no clear ideas in the regime's foreign policy in the 1922–30 period.[30] Social imperialist connotations pervade G. Rochat's extensive writings on Fascist military policy, stressing that expansionist ventures were aimed at increasing the regime's domestic security.[31] In a similar vein, F. Catalano linked the radicalisation of the regime's foreign policy from 1935 onwards with the mounting economic crisis which hit the country later than other European countries.[32] However, a growing number of historians have attempted to overcome the absence of a Mussolinian *Mein Kampf* and to trace an ideological consistency in the regime's foreign policy which could unify the relatively quiescent 1920s with the aggressive expansion in the 1930s and the decision to enter the war in 1940. G. Rumi dated the origins of a programme in the early 1920s, while M. Knox and P. Alatri agreed on the existence of a general *disegno finale* (living space in the Mediterranean) which was formulated in the mid-1920s.[33] Although most of these approaches acknowledged a high degree of continuity between liberal and Fascist expansionist goals, they attacked the idea that Fascist foreign policy changed objectives and style in the 1930s.[34] Instead, they underlined an internal continuity and consistency in Mussolini's revisionist objectives, rejecting the notion that the radicalisation of Fascist expansionism in the 1930s was the exclusive result of Nazi influence or mounting domestic deadlocks.

The second historiographical debate, focusing on the degree of ideological and political continuity between pre-fascist and fascist aspirations and actions, proved in many ways even more controversial. After an initial period dominated by the tendency to discredit fascism completely, to present it as an aberration due to short-term anomalies and to place the whole fascist chapter in a historic parenthesis,[35] research turned to the idea that a certain degree of continuity existed between the emergence of fascism and pre-1918 historical trends in the two societies. Unsurprisingly, in a postwar period dominated by endeavours to reconcile Italian and German societies with the 'uncomfortable' fascist experience and to reconstruct feelings of national pride in a more positive, constructive direction, references to such a continuity hit raw nerves. In general, this argument appeared to insinuate that fascism was much more an integral part of long-term indigenous ideological and political developments than most were willing to admit. With regard to foreign policy, this new interpretive angle explored the hypothesis that fascist expansionism could be linked to a continuity of aggressive expansionist traditions, evident in Italy and Germany since the last quarter of the nineteenth century.[36] This revisionist approach to the problem of how to historicise fascism reached its peak in Germany in the 1960s with the so-called 'Fischer controversy'.[37] The idea that Nazism might have simply exaggerated intentions and aspirations which had dominated German policies since Bismarck had a tremendous impact on German historiography, generating acrimonious debates (for example, the Fischer–Ritter exchange) but also opening up new directions in the research on the course of German history. In Italy, the notion of continuity between Liberal and Fascist foreign policy has been an even more sensitive suggestion, given the ideological tendency of anti-Fascist tradition to present Fascism as an ephemeral aberration of national history. When the Australian historian R.J.B. Bosworth alluded to a clear line of continuity between Liberal and Fascist expansionist aspirations, there was an angry reaction and criticism from a series of Italian historians in defence of the singularity of Fascism.[38] The legacy of 'liberalism' in post-unification Italy and the country's 'victory' in 1918 rendered a revisionist retrospective analysis of long-term authoritarian structures and aggressive expansionist intentions much more difficult than in Germany, where the Wilhelminian *Reich* had been discredited after the First World War. The 'orthodox' interpretation of the historical transition to Fascism, articulated by distinguished Italian historians such as R. Vivarelli, has treated Italy's 1915 intervention in the European conflict as a *legitimate* expression of her long-term 'great-power' aspirations.[39] It was the 'failure of liberalism', as Vivarelli claimed, that created the conditions for a fundamental discontinuity in Italian history, opening up a political faultline which Fascism manipulated and widened in the interwar years. The apparent continuities between the anti-liberal character and aggressive hyper-nationalism of the *intervento* movement in 1914–15 and the expansionist discourse of Fascism were greatly played down in favour of treating Mussolini and his movement as a major historical deviation.[40]

At the same time, the revisionist historiography on Nazi Germany tended to be rather dismissive of the aggressive motivations behind Fascist Italy's policies. In his customary exaggerated style, A.J.P. Taylor presented Hitler's expansionist worldview as a routine re-articulation of post-unification German nationalism (see Chapter 6), but had very few (and largely disparaging) things to say about Mussolini's foreign policy. For Taylor, Fascism was a travesty that could hardly be compared to the destructive madness of Nazism.[41] This argument was perfectly in line with the attempts of various Italian historians to employ a variant of the 'continuity' thesis in a totally different direction, to draw a definite line between the traditions of Italian and German nationalism. F. Chabod's study of Liberal foreign policy found discontinuities where Fischer had encountered causality: the liberalism of the patriarchs of modern Italian nationalism and politics (Mazzini and Cavour, for example) was hardly comparable with Bismarck's conservatism and Wilhelminian authoritarianism-militarism.[42] In his controversial interview with M. Ledeen, R. De Felice found in the Fascist 'movement' a set of 'positive' goals which were progressively distorted by the excesses of the 'regime-model' of Fascism. Although long-term continuity was regarded as irrelevant to the understanding of why Fascism emerged and seized power, it could nevertheless shed light on why Fascism failed to follow Nazism on its path of unbounded aggression and destruction. The 'radical' political model of fascism, as epitomised by Nazism, was alleged to have faltered on the Italian traditions of liberalism, individualism and 'kindness'.[43] Ironically, the findings of the revisionist historiography on German history were partially endorsed in order to rebuff similar inferences for modern Italy and Fascism.

The plan of the study

It becomes obvious that any notion of an ideologically conditioned and programmatic foreign policy has to be established against three major objections. The first is that expansion as a policy option had little to do with the general fascist worldview and was mainly the result of long-term *national* aspirations which fascism simply emulated and pursued further. The second is that the two fascist leaders were not in a strong position domestically which would enable them to shape and dictate foreign policy according to their beliefs and visions. The third is that fascist expansionist policies were dictated by short-term developments and traditional aspirations, thus lacking both internal cohesion and long-term objectives upon which they eventually converged. The following analysis of territorial expansion in Fascist Italy and Nazi Germany is structured according to these three separate aspects of the ideology–action problem. On the level of ideology, fascism is analysed as a 'nationalism plus' phenomenon, which blended radical elements of each country's nationalist tradition with a specific novel commitment to a fascist *new order*. In this sense, a conjunction of comparative analysis of fascism with a parallel scrutiny of national history in the *long durée* is needed. Chapter 1 examines the ideological traditions in the Italian and German post-unification societies and shows how fascist ideology achieved an ideological fusion of pre-existing radical traits in a new synthesis (updated with the experience of the Great War) with an increased emphasis on action and a determination to unite reality with utopia. Chapter 2 studies the expansionist ideologies of the two fascist movements–regimes as coherent systems of thought, combining a number of generic, *abstract* underlying features (historic living space, elitism, cult of violence, unity of thought and action) with idiosyncratic, *concrete* articulations of expansionism according to long-term autochthonous traditions and aspirations.

On the level of foreign policy making, Chapter 3 analyses the domestic framework of foreign policy decision making. It lays emphasis on the leader-oriented character of the two fascist systems, and assesses the evolution and dynamics of the triangular political struggle between fascist leaderships, traditional elites and fascist parties to inform and shape the foreign policies of each regime. Chapter 4 examines the practical forms of the two regimes' expansionist foreign policy (revisionism, colonialism, irredentism) and explores the transition from limited *border* policy to the more aggressive and ambitious expansionist rationale of the second half of the 1930s. In the context of this analysis, three separate issues are addressed: the continuity between pre-fascist and fascist expansionist policies, the continuity between early and later fascist expansionism, and the correspondence between fascist ideology and action. On the same theme of radicalisation, Chapter 5 examines the importance of the exclusive political–diplomatic relation between the two fascist regimes for the evolution of their more radical expansionist policies in the second half of the 1930s. It examines the process of fascism's internationalisation, and analyses how both rivalry and co-operation between the two fascist regimes contributed to the radicalisation of their expansionist objectives and policies. The account of fascist foreign policies in these chapters is neither chronological nor exhaustive. Instead, emphasis is placed on a series of key decisions of each regime which serve as case studies for examining developments in the above three main areas (decision making, ideological consistency and cumulative radicalisation within the Axis alliance).

Finally, Chapter 6 concentrates on the Second World War as the culmination of fascist expansionism. Here the emphasis is on the period between the summer of 1939 and 1942, when the two regimes' radical expansionist ambitions entered the most crucial stage of parallel implementation. Again, the analysis investigates the ideological/non-ideological character of decision making, the programmatic relevance of the decision to wage war to the overall framework of each regime's expansionist policies, and the way in which ideological intentions interacted with structural factors (domestic organisation, material capabilities, co-operation within the Axis alliance). Although 1941–2 signified the relegation of what was intended to be an ideological campaign to desperate war making, the chronicle of fascism's trajectory to defeat and eventual collapse during 1943–5 is briefly reviewed.

1

ITALIAN AND GERMAN EXPANSIONISM IN THE *LONGUE DURÉE*

Without doubt, the fascist phenomenon has dominated the postwar debate about the course of modern Italian and German history.[1] The domestic and international impact of fascist policies drew attention to the conditions which facilitated the appeal of fascism in Italy and Germany, and to the factors which contributed to the radicalisation of its ideology and political practices.[2] Despite the differences in the level of economic development, as well as in the social and political structures of the two countries, the fact that they shared the experiences of late state formation and belated modernisation may shed new light on their similar historical trajectory in the interwar years. Without discounting these significant differences in the economic and social conditions between Italy and Germany, it seems that the 'late-comers' theory has provided a better starting point for the understanding of the similar long-term propensity of the two systems for territorial expansion than the theories of uneven economic or political development.[3] According to this theory, expansion was a means of both accelerating the pace of domestic development, enhancing the international prestige of the 'late-comers' in their pursuit of 'great power' status, and breaking free from the limitations (political, economic, geographical) that their belated arrival had placed upon them. Instead of focusing on the differing long-term socio-economic features of the two systems (as modernisation theory does, making a sharp distinction between the more advanced German society and the essentially backward, agrarian Italian equivalent[4]), the 'late-comers' thesis places emphasis on the similar motivations generated by the common desire of the two newly unified states to establish their position as *political* 'great powers' in the European system.

There are, however, questions particular to each country's historical trajectory that the above theory cannot answer convincingly without recourse to specific *national* developments and to the impact of external factors on national politics. Although pre-1918 Italian and German expansionism was motivated by similar aspirations (great power status, completion of unification, social imperialism) and forces (emergence of radical nationalist organisations, deterioration of international relations, opportunities offered by the First World War), these factors were crystallised and subsequently affected national histories in a host of different ways. Given that the appeal of fascism in the two societies owed most of its strength to the way in which fascism processed, and responded to, national past (see Chapter 2), it is interesting to examine first how these pre-1918 developments shaped Italian and German nationalism (and its expansionist discourses, in particular). The following analysis briefly reviews the arguments that lend validity to the 'late-comers' thesis, paying particular attention to the symbolic significance of *territory* for the two states as a result of the specific pattern of their state-formation (aggressive territorial reconstitution of a historic nation). It accounts for the *radicalisation* of the expansionist ideologies and policies of the two countries in the years immediately preceding the First World War, offers a brief analysis of the various prewar expansionist arguments, and finally examines the impact of the First World War in relation to its ideological legacy and political influence upon the nationalist/expansionist discourse in the two societies.

'Late-comers' and the symbolic significance of territory

Unification and the importance of territory

The patterns of state formation followed by Italy and Germany in the second half of the nineteenth century present two crucial similarities. First, they drew their legitimacy from a liberal nationalist tradition which had pursued the goal of national unification as the platform for domestic development and international power. In Italy, the Mazzinian principle of self-determination in 1848 had given rise to the vision of a 'new' republican, democratic Italy as the heir to the glorious Roman empire, with a historic mission in the Mediterranean area.[5] In Germany, the Frankfurt parliament of 1848 had emphasised the urgency of national unification in order to abolish the authoritarian structures of the German states, to provide an efficient basis for social and economic modernisation, and to create a German state as a great power in the political vacuum at the heart of Europe. The second similarity concerned the specific political motivations behind the process of state formation. In both countries, this process was instigated by one state that had achieved political and economic power, as well as a certain diplomatic position in the European system. Prussia in Germany exploited its political prestige amongst the smaller German states and its great military potential to achieve its goals on its own, while Piedmont in Italy took advantage of the antagonisms among the European powers in order to offset its military incapacity, which had hampered its aspirations in 1848–9.[6] In order to provide legitimacy to their expansionist plans and to their struggle against foreign dominators, both states invoked the principle of self-determination and gradually put forward the ideal of national unification.

On the international level, the great power ambitions of the two 'late-comers' were inevitably conceptualised in the pre-existing pattern of territorial domination, in Europe and overseas. Nationalism entailed a perception of power that could only be measured in comparison with other states of high international standing. These states – primarily Britain and France – had long ago developed a network of colonial possessions that offered them protected markets, raw materials and prestige greater than Italy and Germany. This had been a time-consuming process, and the two new states had to copy the old imperial states under great pressure of time and with severely limited political or geographical flexibility. In this respect, the 'late-comer' theory offers valuable insight into the importance and the problems of expansion for the new Italian and German states in the nineteenth and early twentieth century. On the one hand, the late experience of state formation in Italy and Germany meant that the two unified states had to abbreviate a whole process of social, political and economic development – that had taken centuries in the case of their main competitors, Britain and France – into a few decades. Only this would enable them to compete on equal terms with them for the attainment of their great power aspirations. They also had to adhere to an already existing pattern of competition amongst states (economic, political), to a restrictive concept of the European balance of power, and to a geographically limited sphere of potential expansion. The pressure of time meant that they had to hasten for the few remaining territories (the best lands had already been appropriated by the British and French, and also by the Dutch, Portuguese and Spaniards) before even having resolved the problems of domestic economic development and decided on the priorities of expansion. On the other hand, they were aware that they had started from a territorially underprivileged position and with a growing domestic pressure for establishing a commanding role in the international system. Territory became a *sine qua non* for the political ascendancy of the new states and for the prestige of the domestic ruling forces against the growing challenges from both left and radical right.[7]

The prestige factor gradually overshadowed the economic significance of expansion, in the sense that the remaining options were not necessarily the most economically or geographically beneficial ones for the states, but had to be exploited for reasons of international competition.[8] Political pressure for expansion meant that economic and social needs had to be adapted afterwards to the – often limited – opportunities offered by the seized territories. At the same time, economic infiltration, both in European and overseas territories (informal imperialism) was often seen as something more than a goal in itself. It was also a form of political investment for future expansion in those areas, when circumstances would be favourable. Economic exploitation of colonies was often a very costly enterprise, with little support from industrial and economic interests in the metropolis, and became the subject of severe criticism.[9] Criticism was, however, mainly directed against ineffectual or limited expansion, not against expansion as such. Failure in one field simply increased the appeal of the

13

other forms of expansion. With the exception of the socialist left, territorial aggrandisement remained high on every other political agenda. The plethora of expansionist arguments that emerged after unification in Italy and Germany reflected a symbolic significance of territory which was more important than the political or economic considerations behind expansion.

Thus, we arrive at a widely disregarded common element which underlay the idiosyncratic expansionist tendencies of the two states and remained a constant long-term factor in the ideology of Italian and German nationalism. The process of Italian (1859–70) and German (1866–71) national unification had not taken place in a geographical or political vacuum. In both cases, it involved the incorporation of populations inhabiting territories under foreign rule. It rested upon political control of *territories* and this, in turn, presupposed territorial *conflict*. Ultimately, unification entailed the expansion of Piedmont and Prussia at the expense of international 'enemies' and against the opposition of domestic antagonists. At the same time, because the concept of an Italian or German 'nation' had predated state formation, it was extremely difficult for the new states to claim a real 'nation-state' status once they had opted for the 'small' territorial solutions.[10] In the 1870s the two states declared their territorial 'satiation' in Europe, despite growing awareness that the ethnically incomplete unifications had increased the popularity of irredentism and had produced a stronger pressure for expansion outside the European system. In this way, however, they did nothing to allay a growing feeling that, although the 'nation' was the basis of state formation, the state had abdicated its responsibility to incorporate all populations and territories which formed part of this 'nation'. Voices advocating expansion and an ethnically and territorially 'complete' unification proliferated and became increasingly vocal.[11] The pressures upon the governments for tangible manifestations of national prestige and the need to combat the post-unification disillusionment in the two countries strengthened the link between domestic and foreign policies. Territorial concessions came to be seen as the ultimate political and economic solution to domestic grievances. The fact that these aspirations were temporarily diverted to colonial antagonism did not preclude a return to territorial conflicts in Europe, should more auspicious circumstances arise. After 1900, with the gradual disintegration of the European balance of power, these suppressed ambitions were once again on the agenda and eventually led to a war that was essentially a territorial struggle on the continent.

The emergence of radical nationalist organisations

This long-term symbolic significance of territory in post-unification Italian and German history lends considerable credence to the 'late-comers' theory. However, explaining the radicalisation of the expansionist policies of the two countries in the years up to the First World War requires the examination of another crucial development: the emergence and mobilisation of radical

nationalist organisations. The process through which the ideological developments on the radical nationalist right affected the conduct of foreign affairs in
the two countries was a highly complex one. On an ideological level, the
transformation of the nationalist movements in Italy and Germany into
imperialist organisations, with beliefs in the transcendental power of the nation
and a growing aggressive tone in their territorial programmes, largely predated
the political emancipation of the two movements. In Italy, the turning point in
the ideological transformation of the nationalist right was the foundation of the
Italian Nationalist Association (*Associazione Nazionalista Italiana*, henceforward
ANI) in 1906. The new organisation aimed to give political expression to the
'new' nationalist ideology that had made its appearance after the traumatic
defeat of the Italian armed forces at Adowa, Ethiopia in 1896,[12] in an attempt to
restore faith in the capacity of the new Italian state to acquire the prestige that
its glorious past justified.[13] The ANI became an umbrella organisation for the
various nationalist groups, covering a wide spectrum from radical ideologies of
imperialism to the liberal exponents of irredentism. It attempted to provide a
synthesis of the different nationalist ideologies into a uniform programme for
domestic rejuvenation and international ascendancy, and thus to justify its
political function as the main representative of a nationalist renaissance in
contrast to the 'old' bankrupt official nationalism of the Italian state. In
Germany, such an umbrella organisation did not theoretically exist, with a
number of new groups emerging in the first decade of the twentieth century and
a fairly even distribution of membership figures among them.[14] However, the
central role occupied by the Pan-German League (*Alldeutsche Verband*) in the
representation of the radical nationalist viewpoint since the 1890s rendered it a
mirror of the ideological developments in the whole German radical nationalist
movement.[15] The intensification of the aggressive character of the organisation
under the leadership of Heinrich Class reflected the emergence of a new trend in
German nationalism. This trend supported a confrontational foreign policy
against the other European states, a revival of the imperial glories of the
German nation and an extensive territorial agenda for expansion, mainly in
Europe but also overseas.[16]

The radicalisation of expansionist arguments: irredentism, continental expansion versus colonial expansion, conquest versus economic infiltration

The radicalisation of territorial politics in the years prior to the First World War
dramatically affected the way in which expansion was conceptualised in Italian
and German society. Although traditional arguments for territorial aggrandisement (irredentism, colonial expansion, economic infiltration, 'living space')
continued to dominate the debate in the two countries, their content underwent
a long-term transformation. The shift to confrontational policies was reflected in
the radicalisation of previously moderate arguments (irredentism) and in the

priority given to continental expansion and territorial conquest (as opposed to overseas expansion and informal imperialism). We shall now turn to these separate expansionist arguments and examine the process of their radicalisation, their contribution to the aggressive spirit which led to the First World War, and their legacy to the post-1918 expansionist ideologies in the two countries.

Irredentism

The historic origins of irredentism lie in the liberal nationalist ideology of the nineteenth century. The term (derived from the Italian *irredenta*, meaning literally 'unredeemed territories') signified the desire of an ethnically homogeneous yet scattered population to be incorporated in the same political unit, the nation-state, on the basis of national self-determination. Clearly, the dream of a complete unification of the Italian and German peoples presupposed a political vacuum in central and eastern Europe, namely the absence of strong states occupying territories and controlling peoples claimed by the 'new' states. This was not the case, however. Powerful neighbouring states (France and the Habsburg empire in the case of Italy, the same two plus Russia in the case of the German Reich) placed territorial restrictions upon the plans of Cavour and Bismarck for a complete national unification. This led to a political compromise which had two characteristics. On the one hand, it did allow the establishment of the Italian and German states as nation-states, representing politically the Italian and German historic nations in the European system. On the other hand, the ethnically incomplete unifications prompted the formation of national *irredenta* outside the frontiers of the two states. In this sense, the post-unification irredentist claims of Italian and German nationalism reflected an attempt to resume the interrupted process of national and territorial unification by non-aggressive, liberal means (see Chapter 2).

In the last decades of the nineteenth century, irredentism acquired a new popularity within the wider nationalist discourse of the two countries. In Italy, the Mazzinian vision of a unified Italian state, based on self-determination, survived in various nationalist organisations which emerged in the three last decades of the nineteenth century. The story of all these organisations (Pro-Italia Irredenta, 1877; Dante Alighieri, 1889; Trento e Trieste; Pro Patria and others[17]) followed a similar pattern until the turn of the century. Largely confined to intellectual circles, with a relatively small membership and a non-aggressive character, they advocated the ideological and ethical priority of irredentism over all other forms of territorial politics (such as colonialism). Anti-Austrian sentiments – inheritance of the bitter *Risorgimento* struggle since 1848 – made the irredentist claims to Trento and Venezia Giulia politically more important than the claims to the south-eastern coast of France.[18] The early alignment, however, of the Italian state with the Triple Alliance (along with Germany and Austro-Hungary) rendered territorial expansion at the expense of the Habsburg Empire impossible.[19] Italian governments from 1876 onwards endeavoured to play down the importance of irredentist agitation in the country, while taking active steps to limit the influence of nationalist organisations, especially in the north-eastern provinces.[20] It has been argued that the shift of attention to Africa (implemented mainly by the Minister of Colonies Manzini and the Italian Premier Crispi in the last quarter of the nineteenth century) was a substitute for the impracticality of irredentist claims.[21] Such an assertion, however, is anachronistic, since irredentist ideology did not occupy a prominent position on the expansionist agenda before the first decade of the twentieth century. Before that time, even irredentist organisations acknowledged the political necessity of the alliance with Austria.[22] In the same vein, official Italian foreign policy aimed to uphold the European balance of power, accepting the political necessity of a strong state at the heart of Europe (Habsburg Empire) at the expense of the principle of self-determination which underlay the formation of the Italian state.[23]

Similarly, the formation of the Pan-German League in 1893 reflected – as its title suggests – the ideological popularity of the irredentist argument in post-unification Germany, but was initially confined to an aspiration not involving *immediate* political action. The right of all the German *Volk* to belong to the same state was a demand shared not only by nationalist organisations, but also by liberal and non-conservative circles of the German society.[24] This right, however, did not amount to a questioning of the European territorial map, especially since expansion could be pursued in other, less aggressive forms, in colonies or through economic infiltration in Europe. Until the first years of the twentieth century there was a flexibility in the ideologies of *Lebensraum*: economic or territorial, living space could be claimed anywhere without subverting the overall territorial settlement. Thus, irredentism remained marginal to the territorial debate in Germany until the beginning of the twentieth century.

Increasing European instability, in conjunction with nationalist mobilisation in the two countries during the decade before the war, transformed the context of irredentist ideology and provided it with a new political significance. In Italy, the 'new' nationalist movement rejected the mediocrity of the post-unification Italian system and advocated instead an expansionist policy as part of a rejuvenating process and a completion of the *Risorgimento*. The policies of the Italian governments after the defeat at Adowa in 1896 remained focused on the task of domestic reform, renouncing irredentism as 'sentimental rhetoric', incompatible with the country's strategic interest in strengthening the Triple Alliance.[25] This dogma did not change significantly even after the vehement nationalist reaction to the annexation of Bosnia-Herzegovina (formally an Ottoman territory) by the Habsburg Empire in 1907, when the Giolittian administration was severely criticised for playing down any Italian claim for territorial compensation.[26] The chasm, however, between the 'legal' and 'real' Italy (*Italia legale* and *Italia reale*, government and people) was growing constantly.[27] The ideological synthesis in the framework of the ANI provided the conceptual platform for incorporating the liberal irredentist argument into a wider programme of territorial aggrandisement. Especially after the annexation of Bosnia-Herzegovina, the imperialist wing of the ANI acknowledged the political utility of irredentism. A small liberal irredentist group, under the leadership of Sighele, joined the ANI, aiming to preserve its ideological autonomy in the context of this anti-Giolittian nationalist conglomeration.[28]

By 1910, however, the incompatibility between the aggressive imperialist wing and the narrow 'liberal' irredentism of Sighele's Irredentists prepared the ground for a final struggle for the soul of the ANI. The Libyan campaign (1911–12), which Giolitti authorised in the aftermath of the Second Moroccan Crisis (1911) in order to claim the last remaining north African colony, marked a turning point in the fate of irredentist ideology in Italy. The Irredentist group within the association reacted against this broader imperialist campaign that treated the *irredenta* as part of a historic claim for the restoration of Italian rule in the Mediterranean. Yet, by the Congress of Rome in 1912 the Irredentists had been completely marginalised, first ideologically and then politically, following the withdrawal of Sighele from the Association.[29] Consequently, anti-Austrian irredentism survived in the new Italian nationalist ideology, but only after having made two irreversible concessions.[30] First, the programme of the ANI reduced it to one of several elements of territorial policy, thus facilitating the synthesis of colonial, imperialist and liberal expansionist goals. Second, by its absorption into the militant expansionist spirit of the ANI, irredentism assumed confrontational implications which facilitated its conceptualisation in terms of international territorial rivalries. This in turn made possible its adoption as official foreign policy of the Italian state in 1915, as part of an aggressive expansionist programme in contrast to the initial liberal inspiration of the concept.[31]

Similar tendencies characterised the irredentist ideology of the German *völkisch* nationalist movement which revolved around the Pan-German League. The proposition that the unification of 1871, involving the concept of a *Kleindeutschland* ('minor Germany', excluding Habsburg territories inhabited by Germans), was territorially incomplete acquired a new political significance in the decade before the war.[32] Of course, the main current of German irredentism, namely the union with the German population of the Habsburg empire, was politically unrealistic in the context of the Triple Alliance. However, the deterioration of European international relations after 1905 – starting with the First Moroccan Crisis – provided three further stimuli to the development of a stronger irredentist element in German nationalist ideology. First, the limited gains from colonial expansion re-focused territorial policies on the European continent, thus providing ideological currency for the ideas of a central European union (*Mitteleuropa*), in economic or even annexationist terms.[33] Second, the collapse of Russian–German relations led to ruthless policies of Russification of the German minorities of the Tsarist empire, thus provoking the interest of the German nationalist movement in the fate of Germandom outside the frontiers of the Reich. Third, the irresponsible and self-centred policies of the Habsburg empire infuriated German nationalists to the degree that they even wished for a quick war, in order to cause the collapse of the Dual Monarchy and thus redeem the German territories and populations of the *Ostmark*.[34]

In the remaining years before the outbreak of the war, the idea that the existing German state was a *Vorstaat*, a transitional stage in the process of state formation,[35] was coupled with the economic and defensive necessity of territorial expansion in central and eastern Europe. As in the case of Italy, the overlapping of irredentist claims with imperialist plans for the economic and political domination of vast areas of the continent provided a synthetic ideological platform for aggressive territorial expansionism. Irredentism was placed in the wider context of a *Lebensraum* (living space) policy, echoing the millenarian obsessions of the *völkisch* nationalist movement for the historic mission of *Grossdeutschland*. As in Italy, the radical nationalist organisations in Germany accomplished a remarkable ideological preparation for combining the claim for colonial expansion with irredentist objectives, in order to achieve both national development and international prestige. They plucked irredentism out of its liberal context and reintroduced it as a prerequisite for national power in competition to other European states. This meant that irredentism acquired a political role in international rivalries and was directed in an aggressive manner against the territorial integrity of those states still holding the *irredenta* within their frontiers.

What expansion? Continental versus colonial expansion, formal versus informal imperialism

Throughout the period between the 1880s and the First World War, ideological and political controversies emerged about the most beneficial type of expansion. These controversies involved official government policies, organisations not affiliated to a political party and public opinion in the two countries. The dilemma between continental and colonial expansion permeated the expansionist debate in Italy and Germany, and produced a rough polarisation which survived the First World War. This was understandable, since on a theoretical level the two expansionist arguments represented different perceptions of national prestige and different philosophies about how expansion could aid the goal of national development. The advocates of colonialism regarded overseas expansion as combining territorial expansion and economic growth without destabilising effects for the European balance of power. They also supported the idea of colonial possessions as a symbol of great power status, thus enabling the 'late-comers' to achieve equality of standing with the other European great powers.[36] For them, European stability was a prerequisite for the fruitful advance of national goals, and they hoped that colonial expansion would, in the long run, deliver more substantial politico-economic benefits than any expansion in the continent. On the other hand, the so-called 'continentalists' supported the

19

reverse argument: expansion in Europe and the political acceptance of the 'late-comers' as equals by the major powers of the continent was the necessary precondition for a successful expansionist policy overseas.[37] According to the exponents of this view, the state should look for material resources, 'elbow room' and political prestige in Europe before embarking on a world policy. They did not advocate the undermining of the stability of the continental system, but believed that the real struggle amongst European nations would be eventually transferred from the colonies back to the continent. It was, therefore, vital to guarantee their strong politico-economic position in Europe, to win a he-gemonic role in European affairs, with the acquisition of colonies as a complementary objective. Furthermore, the Mediterranean and central Europe had historically been the cradle of the Italian and German civilisations respectively (see Chapter 2), the area where they had established their vast empires in the past and from where they had acquired their strength. In this sense, continental expansion possessed a historic and symbolic significance, reminiscent of the hegemonic role that the two nations had exercised in Europe and the Mediterranean in the past.

This theoretical controversy was coupled with another controversy, this time about the character of expansion. There was tension between economic infiltration and territorial conquest, that is, between *economic* and *political* control over territories.[38] Again, this controversy originated from different perceptions of how territory would benefit domestic well-being and national prestige. Economic infiltration promised the creation of an informal empire, in Africa, Asia and south/central Europe alike, which could provide immediate material solutions to domestic needs, and help the expanding industrial sectors against foreign competitors. More importantly, however, it could also enhance the political strength of the state without risking a costly military confrontation for territorial control. On the other hand, the advocates of annexation focused on three different aspects. First, they stressed the importance of territory as 'space' for the problems of emigration and overpopulation.[39] Second, they asserted that Italy and Germany, as 'late-comers', could not compete on equal terms with the other great European powers on the economic level because they lacked the resources and economic network which only political control over territories could furnish. Third, they underlined the significance of territory in terms of national defence (in Europe) and living space, two elements that were considered by them as prerequisites for the survival and flourishing of the nation.

These confrontations between different expansionist programmes were evident in the official foreign policies of the Italian and German states. They explain to a great extent the plurality of expansionist strategies, the oscillations of the governments and the divisions in the radical nationalist camp in the period up to the First World War. Domestic and international developments of the last decade before 1914, however, had an impact upon the ideology and practice of expansionism in the two countries. Three major changes may be identified. First, the view that espoused colonial expansion as substitute for the territorial stalemate in Europe was gradually reversed. The strength of alliances and the prestige of each nation in the continental system became the primary factors which could guarantee power, security and the preconditions for expansion abroad. In Italy, this trend was manifested in two different developments. On the one hand, the focus of Italian colonialism shifted from the distant regions of south-eastern Africa to the Mediterranean basin, towards the northern coast of Africa, the Aegean Sea and its islands. Strictly speaking, this was still expansion in colonial terms, an attempt to divert the pressure for territorial conquest away from the European system. Yet, it was also expansion in an area crucial for Italy's strategic position in Europe, indispensable for the control of the Adriatic and for winning relative advantage against Britain and France in the Mediterranean basin. On the other hand, after 1908 the domestic consensus for Italy's participation in the Triple Alliance suffered a severe blow. The renewal of the treaty in 1912 was not actually criticised by the radical nationalist groups (the sole exception were the Irredentists, whose anti-Austrian orientation was unyielding), but this consent reflected less of an unqualified support for the spirit of the Alliance, and more a grudging realisation that, at that time, there was no diplomatic alternative open to the Italian government.[40]

In Germany, a similar trend became predominant immediately before and after the second Moroccan crisis. The priority of continental expansion over colonialism had long been advocated by the radical nationalist organisations.[41] In the context of this logic, the Second Moroccan Crisis indeed had a colonial function, reflecting Germany's long-standing aspirations in the Congo basin.[42] Yet, this was not the primary consideration which ignited the incident. The diplomatically isolated Reich attempted to stir up colonial antagonism in north-west Africa in order to break the British–French front and consolidate its political position in the European system against its main rivals. The crisis, however, had exactly the opposite effect. It increased tension between Germany and the other European states, and strengthened the continental, annexationist arguments as the prerequisite for national prestige, security and strength of the Reich.[43] In the Moroccan Crisis of 1911, the Navy (a consistent advocate of expansion overseas) proved incapable of securing the international interests of the nation. The Army, on the other hand, traditionally intent on directing German expansion to the continent, grasped the opportunity of this alleged failure in order to press for more funds and a primary role in foreign policy making.[44] The clamour for a military confrontation increased, the *Weltpolitik* (world policy, denoting expansion overseas) objectives lost their appeal, and an aggressive form of continental foreign policy gained the upper hand.[45]

The second major change pertained to the shifting character of Italian and German expansionist policies. The previous balance between economic infiltration and annexationism was disturbed by the growing need for prestige and the difficulties related to economic expansion itself. The domestic crisis of the two systems (predominantly due to the criticisms by the new radical nationalist movement and to left-wing mobilisation) in the years immediately preceding 1914 caused a substantial loss of government legitimacy and necessitated impressive victories which the subtlety of informal imperialism did not provide. This, in conjunction with the objective difficulties for the 'late-comers' in catching up with the position of the other great powers in areas of economic confrontation, gradually discredited economic infiltration as an alternative to territorial conquest. Italy and Germany continued their efforts at informal expansion, the former mainly in the Balkans and Asia Minor, the latter in central and southern Europe as well as in northern Africa.[46] Yet, the symbolic significance of territory gradually gained currency. Arguments in favour of living space, for demographic, economic and defensive reasons prevailed in the expansionist discourse of the two countries. The decision of Giolitti to sanction the campaign for the acquisition of Libya provides evidence for this shift towards annexationism. Far from being a colonial enthusiast, but aware of the need to manifest Italy's power in a tangible manner, the architect of Liberal Italy succumbed to the growing emotive attraction of territorial expansion, regardless of the minimal tangible benefits promised by the venture.

The example of the Libyan campaign highlights the third change in Italian and German expansionist politics in the period immediately before the First World War, namely the loss of the practical character of the expansionist objectives. Both the Libyan campaign and the Tangier crisis reflected an unconditional hunger for territory in strategic and prestige terms, in complete defiance of material considerations.[47] The *ex post facto* arguments for settlement prospects and economic opportunities in the areas claimed reflected less and less the genuine motives behind the decisions to expand. This was not simply the result of the 'late-comers'' limited margins for expansion in a world almost completely occupied by the traditional great powers. It was mainly the outcome of the growing impression that geopolitical advantage and prestige were the keys to power in a highly competitive international system. Understandably, economic infiltration could not satisfy this illusion; nor could the degree of usefulness of a territory for settlement or economic development overshadow the need for territorial expansion in any possible direction and at every opportunity.

The experience of the First World War: inflated territorial ambitions and frustrated hopes

The deterioration of international relations and the ensuing radicalisation of expansionist ambitions notwithstanding, the July 1914 crisis found the Great European Powers without a set of definitive ideas about how to proceed in the event of a wider military conflict.[48] In Italy, the liberal political establishment was torn between the country's formal allegiance to the Central Powers (especially as the Triple Alliance had been renewed in 1912) and the anti-Habsburg implications of the long-term irredentist ambitions of Italian nationalism ever since unification. The outbreak of the war was met with a rare instance of consensus between nationalists (old and new) and socialists on the basis of a policy of neutrality. Soon, however, the disparate expectations of the different political groups were exposed, shattering the initial atmosphere of domestic unity. While Giolitti and his entourage continued to underline the long-term benefits of a policy of diplomatic *quid pro quo* with Austria, in the autumn of 1914 the ANI shifted its position to a staunchly interventionist programme against the Central Powers, in anticipation of military gains in Dalmatia and the Brenner.[49] At the same time, a certain sector of the PSI (Partito Socialista Italiano, Italian Socialist Party), with Benito Mussolini as its spokesman, grew increasingly frustrated with the non-interventionist stance of the official party leadership. For Mussolini, the initial socialist opposition to what was termed as a war of the 'plutocratic powers' had been thwarted by the eagerness with which the German SPD had endorsed the rationale of military confrontation in August 1914. If the united socialist front was no longer an option, he argued, then Italy's entry into the conflict would accelerate the dynamics of, and demand for, domestic reform. This was a prospect that he personally welcomed as the first step towards a wider revolutionary transformation of Italian (and European) society. His divergence from the official PSI line resulted in his expulsion from the party and helped solidify the social appeal of the growing movement in favour of intervention, known as *intervento*.[50]

As the interventionist forces gathered momentum steadily throughout the autumn and early winter of 1914, the Italian government was forced to reconsider its initial policy of loyalty to the Triple Alliance and initiate parallel contacts with the Entente Powers in anticipation of a more advantageous territorial bargain than the vague and modest promises of Austria for postwar colonial compensations. Amid mounting agitation from the *intervento* forces, it became clear to the Italian political establishment that the negotiations with Britain and France would yield more tangible and generous territorial promises that the Central Powers were not willing to match.[51] The ensuing Treaty of London (which was secretly agreed between the Italian government and the Entente Cordiale)[52] signified the re-orientation of Italian foreign policy away from the policy of territorial 'satiation' in Europe and towards continental irredentism. Under the conditions of the Treaty, Italy would satisfy her long-standing irredentist territorial ambitions in the coast of the Adriatic and Alto Adige (South Tyrol) as the prize for her military contribution to the defeat of the Central Powers. The Entente also offered vague promises of colonial compensation in Africa, a long-coveted prerequisite of Italy's 'great power' status. The temptation was too strong to resist, and on 23 May 1915 Italy declared war on Austro-Hungary. The 'radiant days of May' (a jubilant phrase coined by the poet Gabriele D'Annunzio, who had become a prominent figure of the *intervento* movement) constituted the first major defeat of Giolittism and underlined the growing social appeal of the 'new' radical nationalist agenda, both amongst the population and the political elites of Liberal Italy.[53]

Italy's 'Great War', described as the last war of independence in a direct reference to the vision of completing the *Risorgimento*, proved an uphill struggle. After an initial period of stalemate in the Italian-Austrian front, the Regio Esercito (Italian Army) faced a humiliating and highly traumatic defeat at Caporetto in October 1917.[54] What had been authorised as an offensive campaign for expansion in pursuit of the goal of a complete Italian 'nation-state' was soon transformed into a defensive war inside Italy's national territory. In a last-ditch attempt to rally the national forces and boost the plummeting morale of the population, the Italian government offered to reconsider the antiquated organisational system of its armed forces and to promise far-reaching social reforms. The gamble paid off, and in the remaining period until the November 1918 armistice the Italian forces managed to reverse the effects of Caporetto, emerging narrowly victorious by the end of the conflict. The sombre mood of 1917 gave way to a jubilant atmosphere of pride that nurtured expectations from a thorough territorial settlement in the peace negotiations. The eventual 'victory' was greeted as the ultimate vindication of the *intervento* mentality and bolstered hopes that the world would now recognise Italy as a truly great power in the European system.[55]

In Germany, the enthusiastic endorsement of the war by the majority of the population and all political parties (including the SPD) fuelled expectations of massive territorial gains in both the west and the east. The publication of Bethmann Hollweg's September Programme (a comprehensive blueprint for Germany's vast territorial goals at the expense of France, the Low Countries and Russia) was used by Fischer as evidence of the long-term expansionist ambitions of post-unification German foreign policy. Fischer's exhaustive references to pre-1914 warlike declarations from prominent figures of the military, political and industrial establishment of the Second Reich underlined the continuity of a specific radical nationalist discourse in German society, especially after the 1890s, which gradually endorsed the option of war as the only solution to the country's encirclement and failed attempts to pursue her great power plans in a peaceful diplomatic manner.[56] However, the definitive character of Wilhelminian expansionist policy should not be overstated. After some modest advances in the western front, the military stalemate of 1915–16 prompted far-reaching reconsiderations by both left and right. A growing section of the SPD (which soon seceded from the party to form the Independent SPD) came to oppose the military conflict, reacting to the increasing death toll of the operations in the west and to the devastating effects of the Allied blockade on the German population.[57] By contrast, the formation of the Fatherland Party in 1917 gave expression to the most radical expansionist ambitions of the German nationalist right, demanding a reorientation of the war against the crumbling Russian empire.[58] By the end of 1917 the Reichswehr had achieved impressive advances in the eastern front, taking advantage of the power vacuum created in Russia after the first revolution of 1917 and of the ill-guided decision of the new leader, Kerensky, to continue the war. By the time the Bolsheviks seized power autonomously and began negotiations for a swift peace with Germany, the vast military gains of the German army in the east nurtured even more radical territorial ambitions. The Treaty of Brest-Litovsk (1918) sanctioned the shattering defeat of the Russian empire and allowed Wilhelminian Germany to relish the prospect of a gigantic German empire, stretching into Ukraine, the Baltic and the Black Sea, following the historic path of the Teutonic Knights.[59]

The sense of triumph, however, was as short-lived as it was intoxicating for German nationalism. Reverses in the west, coupled with the impact of the Allied blockade on supplies and domestic morale, brought Imperial Germany to her knees by the autumn of 1918. The devastating news that Germany had agreed to surrender unconditionally and that Kaiser Wilhelm II had abdicated following the revolution of November 1918 came at a time when Germany had just achieved an impressive expansion in the east and was still fighting on foreign territory in the western front.[60] The political establishment of Wilhelminian Germany sanctioned the establishment of a republican system in order to appease the Entente powers and achieve more favourable conditions of peace. A bewildered public opinion, deluded by wartime propaganda about the alleged invincibility of the German forces, turned its frustration and wrath on the forces of revolution, blaming them for the collapse of the domestic front and the thwarting of Germany's territorial expansion in the east. A young officer of the Reichswehr, Adolf Hitler, summed up the mood of the nationalist camp in his invectives at the 'betrayal' of November 1918.[61] As revolution spread throughout the country, reaching a climax in the short-lived 'Red rule' of Bavaria, the radical nationalist forces despaired at the instant collapse of what they perceived as a costly but deserved and justifiable territorial aggrandisement.

In general, the experience of war generated new opportunities and justifications for what each of the two countries regarded as legitimate territorial expansion. For Italy, the irredentist claims against the Dual Monarchy, although previously sacrificed for the sake of the stability of the Triple Alliance, appeared at the forefront of the Italian expansionist aspirations. This altered priorities to such an extent that the Italian state considered that any postwar territorial solution without substantial frontier adjustments in the north (Brenner) and east (Dalmatia, Istria) would be incomplete, humiliating and unjust. Germany, on the other hand, entered the war with plans for eastward and westward expansion alike without having indisputably decided on geographical priorities. In contrast to the traditional Prussian policy, especially after 1815, of expansion in central and eastern Europe, Wilhelminian foreign policy never established clear geopolitical priorities, deeply divided between *Weltpolitik* and continental expansion. In this sense, the German First World War campaigns in the east re-established the priority to eastern expansion, but did so to an extent which went significantly beyond traditional Prussian ambitions and plans. The collapse of the Tsarist empire and the subsequent treaty of Brest-Litovsk established the eastern territories as Germany's living space *par excellence* and as a vast area of opportunity for German large-scale expansion. For both countries, war, the territorial aspirations invested in the campaign, the conquests and losses, all created new opportunities, new necessities and new priorities for the two late-comers' future expansion. This transformation affected postwar political decision-making but, most significantly, forged a new territorial utopia which fascism could effectively manipulate and radicalise as a *leitmotif* for future expansion.

2

FASCIST IDEOLOGY AND
TERRITORIAL EXPANSION

The concept of 'fascist ideology' has become the focus of a heated controversy among researchers of fascism. The debates about the nature of fascism ever since the 1960s have undoubtedly contributed to the elaboration of the most fundamental questions of definition; yet, after more than half a century, the quest for interpretive consensus appears perhaps more elusive than ever.[1] Attempts to devise a *generic* ideological minimum of fascism have stumbled upon two major objections. On the one hand, a number of historians have categorically rejected the notion that a specific *fascist* value system underpinned the decisions and actions of the fascist movements/regimes. On the other hand, even amongst those who accept the ontological value of fascist ideas, there is widespread scepticism about the validity and utility of a *generic* model of 'fascist ideology'. The comparative grand theories of R. Griffin (palingenetic ideology of a 'third way'), S. Payne (new form of right-wing authoritarianism), R. Eatwell (new radical right) and G.L. Mosse (third way) – to mention only a few generic interpretations[2] – have been criticised for their inflexibility and alleged failure to account for the fundamental differences in the ideas and practices of the wide sample of 'fascist' movements/regimes in recent history. Contrary to the emphatic suggestion of the 'genericists' that indigenous fascism can be best understood horizontally (in comparison to similar ideological/political phenomena of other countries), critics underscore the significance of dealing with 'fascist' cases within the framework of distinctive national traditions and long-term developments.

These objections are only compounded when one explores the specific relation between fascism and territorial expansion. Even the highly sophisticated comparative model of Griffin rejects the notion that expansionism should be considered a *generic* attribute of fascist ideology and practice, confined as it is to only two case studies of fascism (Fascist Italy and Nazi Germany).[3] At the same time, the tendency to view fascism as a 'demonic' repudiation or aberration of national history might have served the instinctive need to castigate it morally, but it has also obscured the relevance of its ideas and politics to the secular ideological and political traditions of post-unification Italian and German nationalism.[4] On a comparative level, the debate has been dominated by an emphasis on the unique elements of Nazi expansionist policies (terror, racism, and especially anti-Semitism) that set apart the German from the Italian – and all the other potentially 'fascist' – cases. While *Lebensraum*-oriented expansion has been widely seen as central to the Nazi worldview,[5] Italian Fascism has been alleged to lack clear expansionist visions and the determination to pursue aggressive policies, leading to an eventual enslavement to the dynamism of Nazi territorial ambitions.[6] The Italian Fascist leadership has consistently been portrayed as unable to produce a systematic ideological ethos for their regime, as being simply determined to exploit the emotive power of expansion to consolidate its domestic position.[7]

Therefore, the analysis of the expansionist tendencies of these two regimes should revolve around two somewhat different questions: first, was their expansionism ideologically motivated and consistent with a set of fundamental beliefs; and, second, to what extent was it underpinned by specific *fascist* values or inhered in long-term *national* attributes which fascism inherited and pursued rather than pioneered. The central premise of this book is that, while territorial expansion should not be regarded as a generic element of fascist ideology *per se*, the expansionist tendencies of the Italian and German fascist regimes were underpinned and prescribed by a combination of common 'fascist' ideological themes and long-term 'national' traditions. The result of this ideological osmosis was an idiosyncratic variety of expansionism, both interlaced with national history in the *longue durée* and unintelligible without reference to specifically 'fascist' common values. The following analysis attempts to define such a common 'minimum' for the ideologies of the Italian and German fascist regimes which underpinned their inclination towards territorial expansion. This minimum projected expansion as a necessity for, and a right of, the two countries in three different yet complementary ways. Expansion was a *national* necessity, pursuing the vision of a complete national unification and aspiring to create a homogeneous state which would encompass all ethnically kin peoples and their territories. It was a *natural* necessity, prescribed by a set of generic 'fascist' values (activism, violence, elitism), in the context of the eternal struggle among nations and civilisations for a 'place in the sun'. Finally, and by far most importantly, it was a *historic* necessity, derived from the alleged superiority of the two peoples and their destiny as creators and defenders of European civilisation. Beyond this nucleus of comparable ideological attributes, the analysis underlines how each regime formulated its expansionist ideology and programme in accordance with national traditions and interests, fusing pre-existing ideological trends and the different experience of the First World War into a new synthesis with a significantly more pronounced propensity for activism.

Fascist ideology and the analysis of the past: the 'self-historicisation' of fascism

Fascist ideology and the liberal past

One of the most common criticisms levied at the concept of 'fascist ideology' has been its negative, reactionary, 'anti-' character.[8] This charge, implying the lack of an original, autonomous and long-term perspective, has been based on the perception of fascism as an ideology of crisis, defined by its oppositional attitude to established beliefs rather than on a novel conceptual core. The 'negative' character of fascism originated from the context of interwar crisis and polarisation which defined its negative, confrontational, myopic principles and credos. It was also condemned to limited originality, since the 'space' for ideological novelty had long been occupied by other major ideological trends.[9] This assumption, however, should not reduce fascist ideology to a mere 'anti-', destructive reaction to short-term crisis. For all its negations – and they were numerous[10] – fascism offered a novel interpretation of the past (descriptive aspect) and provided a long-term normative platform for the future (prescriptive aspect), prioritising goals and justifying methods and practices.[11] The 'negative' experience of the recent past, both on the national and international levels, was incorporated in the fascist vision as the necessary stage of collapse before renaissance. In this sense, the 'anti-' and 're-' elements of fascist cosmology were dovetailed in a *biological* perception of history as a process of birth, triumph, collapse and rebirth.

It is interesting to examine how fascist ideology positioned itself in the context of the short-term and long-term developments of the post-unification national histories of Italy and Germany. This task involved, first of all, the invention of a symbolic watershed, a chronological point or period which pushed the old, decadent forces to a state of collapse and generated the rejuvenating dynamism of the fascist movements. In Italy, this turning point coincided with the period between the emergence of the *intervento* (1914–15) and what the Fascists perceived as the real collapse of liberalism in 1918–20.[12] During that period, the ideological mentors of Italian fascism located the origins of the Fascist postwar *raison d' être* in three separate developments. The first, and the only positive one, was the formation of the *intervento* bloc as a national reaction to the inertia of the liberal 'oligarchy'[13] (see Chapter 1). Mussolini saw in the events of 1914–15 the first political expression of the revolutionary qualities of 'new' Italy: the vision of a great nation, both territorially and politically, redeemed in its internal life and ready to embark on a 'permanent revolution'.[14] This vision was not limited to the reconfiguration of the national spiritual forces prior to the war, but was solidified by the collective experience of the battlefield.[15] The eventual overturning of the liberal ideology of *parecchio* in May 1915 signified the triumph of the new era of imperialism, national grandeur and idealistic activism in its historic antithesis to the 'liberal *vecchiaia*'. War in itself became the source of an apocalypse, a new secular religion of the

29

nation, based on the revelation of its unique destiny which permeated Fascism's later ultra-nationalist millenarianism.[16] Prominent members of the *intervento* movement, among them Giuseppe Papini and Curzio Malaparte, saw the First World War as the symbolic beginning of a long struggle for the 'new' Italy's domestic transformation and international ascendancy.[17] Even the traumatic Italian defeat at Caporetto in 1917 was depicted as an essential act of martyrdom on the way to spiritual catharsis.[18] This was the nadir in the decay of the 'old' Italy, both militarily and spiritually, as well as the beginning of a truly 'national' war. The experience of fighting to liberate Italian lands, to repel enemy forces and avenge the defeat united people of all regions and social strata in what Mussolini called in December 1917 'the brutal apprenticeship of the trenches'.[19] It also revealed to the soldiers their collective identity as defenders of the common cultural and historic ideal of a reborn Italy. The experience of war succeeded, according to Mussolini, where the *Risorgimento* had failed, in instilling a common sense of national pride in the Italian people, displacing the previous diverse regional identities by the ideal of 'citizen-soldier' (*cittadino-soldato*) of the nation.[20] What followed Caporetto, he added, showed to the world that Italians could wage a brave national war, that they were indeed the worthy inheritors of the historic Roman civilisation and that the process of 'making the Italians' had entered its final, decisive stage.[21] The task of the Fascist 'revolution', as he stressed in numerous occasions during the 1920s, was to unite the nation under the authority of a new, all-encompassing state.[22] In Fascist Italy, there would be no division between regions, between north and south; there would be only Italians united 'at the heart of the fatherland'.[23]

Linked to this positive development were the other two negative origins: the postwar peace settlement and the rapid decline of the Giolittian system after 1918. The unsatisfactory territorial gains from the treaties of Versailles, Trianon and Rapallo (see Chapter 4) provided the *intervento* movement with a new point to rally its disparate ideological and social forces. The so-called 'minimalist' solution to Italy's territorial claims in the Adriatic (excluding Fiume and other parts not inhabited by ethnic Italian majorities) was regarded by the Fascist leadership as an artificial, arbitrary denial of the status that the country had achieved through her participation in the First World War.[24] The resurrection of the Italian nation during, and because of, the war warranted the annexation of vast areas, established as historically and geographically Italian.[25] This claim was significantly more than naked imperialism, it was argued. It was the ultimate consecration of the Italian victory which emerged from the apocalyptic vision of a 'new' Italy.[26] Yet, for the Fascists the war was not over in 1918.[27] Liberalism, they argued, proved itself incapable of responding to the new realities, especially in its incompetent representation of the nation at the peace negotiations. The myth of *vittoria mutilata* (mutilated victory) and the violent suppression of the *dannunzianismo* in Fiume were further manipulated by the leadership of the *Fasci* to propagate the imagery of liberal collapse.[28] Mussolini commented sarcastically that the liberal *vecchiaia* had failed to grasp that the war and the 'immense

Italian victory' had established the country as a power with a universal mission and an imperial destiny.[29] Against the defeatism and lack of ambition of Giolittism, on the one hand, and the corrupt internationalism of the socialists, on the other, Fascism developed its own ideological identity as a *terza via* between the decadent ideologies of the left and the right[30] or even as a 'fourth way', rejecting old-fashioned models of authoritarianism.

In Germany, the 'turning point' was partly in the experience of the Great War itself,[31] but mainly in the developments of the immediate postwar period: the 1918 Revolution, the Versailles Treaty and the establishment of the Weimar Republic. As in the case of Italy, the peace settlement became the focal point of nationalist criticism against the liberal system. However, the institution of the Republic was the epitome of what German radical nationalism opposed: it represented liberal incompetence, socialist subversion, class divisiveness and international conspiracy against the German *Volk*. In the interviews with early Nazis of the Abel collection, anti-Weimar feeling was one of the major factors in the NSDAP members' decision to join the party in the 1920s. At the same time, after the experience of the 1918 revolution and left-wing agitation in the interwar period, they combined their rejection of the Republic with a deep-seated hatred of socialists and an equally fundamental anti-Semitic prejudice. The overwhelming majority of the respondents tended to identify all these negative elements with the reality of the Weimar Republic, thus investing their political opposition to liberalism with nationalist and irrational ideological beliefs in the purity and unity of the German *Volk*.[32] This criticism was further strengthened by the moderate attitude of Weimar politicians towards the prospect of treaty revisions, and reached its climax during the campaign against the Young Plan in 1929.[33] The grievances of the German nation in 1918–24, and then during the economic crisis of 1929–33, were exploited in Nazi rhetoric to project a positive message of national endurance, in contrast to the decaying, contaminated Weimar system.[34]

The 'new' German nationalism of the 1920s succeeded in transforming the negative experience of the interwar period into a positive apocalypse, from which the nation's heroic destiny and its inevitable *Neugeburt* would emerge. At a time when the traditional nationalist forces (most notably the DNVP, Deutschnationale Volkspartei) were moving towards a positive, if somewhat uneasy commitment to the Republic, the forces of 'new' Germany (the Nazi ideologues, but also radical nationalist thinkers like Oswald Spengler, Ernst Jünger, Moeller van den Bruck and Jung) called for the 'annihilation' of the Weimar experiment.[35] The experience of war itself, the national grandeur it instilled into the *Volk*, the territorial dream it temporarily realised, all contributed, they claimed, to the generation of a new national conscience. This process was delayed by the conspiracy of 1918 (Revolution, the 'stab in the back' or *Dolchstoss*), but could be resuscitated out of the ruins of the Republic.[36] The legacy of the 'new' nationalism was presented as antithetical to the old perceptions of 'liberal' nationalism, and to the 'jingoism' of the traditional politicians.[37] It was a

31

political religion, based on the *Lebensnotwendigkeit* of the nation, the unique destiny of the German *Volk* and the generational conviction that a cycle of national history had been initiated by the war.[38]

Fascism in post-unification national history: a syncretic ideology

The second task of fascism's short-term historicisation involved a critical assessment of the policies and worldviews which dominated the post-unification history of the two countries. This assessment rested upon a clear separation between those elements which diverted the nation from its destiny, on the one hand, and those which contributed to the revelation of the nation's role of grandeur for the future. The fascists could justify an original and historically crucial role for their movements by making a sharp break with a past which, by 1919, had been widely held as responsible for the unfortunate course of national history. This served a dual function. It made fascism ideologically intelligible by presenting it as the synthesis, continuation and reinvigoration of constructive, but unexploited forces of post-unification history.[39] It also avoided the danger of a total rejection of the past as futile. Instead, fascist ideology presented the five or six decades after unification as a period of national 'soul-searching', as a necessary apprenticeship which, through both its ventures and failures, paved the way for the fascist rebirth.[40]

The attempt to devise a history of 'proto-fascism' and to distance it from the context of the overall criticism of the pre-1914 policies was indeed a complex process. In Italy, Mussolini attacked the pusillanimous and humiliating liberal policies concentrated on the key figures of the Giolittian system: Giolitti, above all, but also Vittorio Emanuele Orlando (who occupied the position of Prime Minister between 1917 and 1919) and Francesco Saverio Nitti (who succeeded him in 1919) for their mishandling of the territorial negotiations after the war and their inability to grasp the changing nature of nationalist feeling in the country.[41] However, the *Duce* replicated the rhetoric of the ANI in excluding Crispi from the context of his anti-liberal polemics. Crispi, as the man responsible for the most prestige-oriented imperialist policy in modern Italian history, the man charged with the cost of the most opprobrious failure of Italian expansionism (Adowa in 1896), was resurrected in Fascist propaganda as the 'bearer' of the great-power conscience of modern Italy.[42] He was credited with the invention of a truly 'Italian' – as opposed to the 'Prussian' or 'western' – style of imperialism.[43] Mussolini also praised his intuition in pushing Italy towards the Mediterranean and Africa. This policy reflected the nation's universal imperial destiny and was a necessity dictated by the country's underprivileged economic, commercial and demographic conditions.[44]

The abandonment of Crispi's vision, however, by successive liberal politicians was not simply seen as a fatal miscalculation of Italy's real needs and objectives. According to G. Gentile, Crispi was the torch-bearer of the *Risorgimento* tradition, the only true heir to the Mazzinian dream of 'new' Italy and the ultimate exponent of the 'Roman myth'.[45] The romantic, spiritual ideal of a new universal empire, based on the legacy of the Eternal City, the traditions of Mazzini, Garibaldi and Gioberti, were the true guiding principles behind Crispi's 'cultural imperialism'.[46] Mussolini did not interpret these policies as imperialistic in the conventional sense of the word. They were inspired, he argued, by an ideal of egalitarianism among peoples under the spiritual and cultural domination of Rome.[47] They echoed Italy's moral and historic right to equality with the other great European nations, in political and territorial terms. In its opposition to Crispian policies after 1896, liberalism and Giolittism were presented as rejecting the long-term objectives and legacies of the *Risorgimento*. In this sense, they were historic aberrations, a parenthesis that was sealed off by the *intervento* movement and the final victory of Fascism in 1922.[48]

On the other hand, the Fascists had been significantly more reluctant to acknowledge ideological debts to the 'new' Italian nationalist movement which came to be identified with the ANI. Undoubtedly, the PNF had its own ideological mentors within its ranks: Mussolini himself, the revolutionary syndicalists,[49] the Futurists,[50] even Gabriele D'Annunzio, the poet who had actively participated in the *intervento* movement and organised the ill-fated occupation of Fiume in September 1919.[51] The ANI represented a kind of nationalism that was pro-monarchical, 'dynastic' and highly 'ideological'; both qualities unacceptable to Fascism's early republicanism, anti-intellectualism and activism.[52] In contrast, the revolutionary aspects of syndicalism and squadrism tended to focus on the need for domestic transformation which was antithetical to most nationalists' social conservatism and old-fashioned nationalism. At the same time, the ANI was widely regarded by the revolutionary wing of the PNF as part of the same 'old' nationalist tradition which Fascism opposed. Despite the respect for the father figures of Enrico Corradini (editor of the Florentine journal *La Voce* and co-founder of the ANI's newspaper *Idea Nazionale* in 1911), Giovanni Papini and Giuseppe Prezzolini (two important figures of the Florentine scene of the *novecento*), the new stars of the ANI, mainly Luigi Federzoni and Alfredo Rocco, had been charged with a certain 'restorationism' and ideological rigidity, alien to Fascism's revolutionary *élan*. Even when the PNF emerged as the strongest nationalist force in 1921, or even after the March on Rome, the prospect of a merging of the two poles of the *Destra Nazionale* was viewed with considerable scepticism, if not hostility, among extreme groups of the PNF.[53] Reservations about fusion were also expressed in the ANI camp, the spokesmen of which pointed to the ethical ambiguity and ideological poverty of Fascism.[54] Yet, in the sphere of foreign policy, the lack of a clear vision in early Fascist expansionist rhetoric facilitated the assimilation of many nationalist themes in the programme of the PNF. The two parties shared a number of novelties and experiences which set them apart from the 'old' Italian national-ism: the cult of war, the belief in a new hierarchy based on individual merit, the vision of a strong, expansionist Italy, the idea of an Italian 'mission' and, most of all, the struggle of *intervento*.[55] In the sphere of foreign policy, the PNF had long subscribed to the ideological myths of the ANI, but at the same time it imposed upon them an idiosyncratic emphasis on action, in contrast to the ANI's intellectualism and obsession with programmes. With the fusion of 1923, Fascism completed its rewriting of post-unification national history. Both politically and ideologically, it emerged as the culmination of all those suppressed energies of the past with a unique dual task: to rectify the recent mistakes, and to fulfil the long-term visions of the *Risorgimento*, of Crispi and the *intervento*.[56]

A similarly selective treatment of the past characterised the attempts of Nazi ideologues to historicise their movement. The *Dolchstoss* rhetoric relieved the Second Reich of the main responsibility for the humiliating postwar settlement. Of course, it was an undeniable truth that Wilhelminian Germany had failed to win the First World War. The reasons for this lay not in the qualities of the German *Volk* (which was superior, destined to dominate and of the highest racial stock, as Hitler repeatedly stressed[57]), but in the political handling of foreign affairs by the Wilhelminian *Honorationenpolitiker*.[58] Hitler was not prepared to demolish the reputation of pre-1914 Germany. That task would entail a rejection of the significance of unification, and of the special role of Bismarck in achieving it. Nazism needed these two elements in order to construct its own myth of national reawakening.[59] The *Führer* was eager, however, to put the blame on the policies of Bethmann Hollweg which had isolated Germany from the other Great Powers (Britain, France and Russia) and pushed the Reich into a two-front war with no overall strategy and no concrete territorial objectives.[60] The war in itself was not the sole responsibility of the Second Reich. The conspiracy of the 'plutocratic' nations of the west (Britain and France) against Germany's ascendancy had confined the Reich to a suffocating diplomatic encirclement which dictated a policy of self-defence. It was, therefore, a struggle for national survival and not crude imperialist aspirations which changed the 'peace-loving' nature of the Second Reich.[61] The Wilhelminian politicians, however, had 'done everything by halves'[62] and thus failed to prepare the nation for the war, both militarily and psychologically. Their experiments with 'alien' forms of internal organisation (liberalism, parliament, racial tolerance) had fatally undermined the strength of the *Volksgemeinschaft* and had led to a decline that became even more traumatic after 1918.

The criticism of the Second Reich for its share of responsibility for the events of 1914–18 was not peculiar to the NSDAP. Both the Wilhelminian *völkisch* nationalist organisations and the various radical nationalist groups and ideologues in the 1920s pointed to Germany's domestic and international weaknesses.[63] The need for radical change, 'rejuvenation', *Neugeburt*, had formed the focal point of the interwar nationalist rhetoric.[64] In the difficult years between 1920 and 1928, when the NSDAP was caught between putschism and diminishing electoral support, independent mentors of the 'new' nationalism (Spengler, Jung, Jünger and Moeller van den Bruck, to name but a few[65]) carried out a magnificent ideological preparation for the forthcoming 'salvation'. Even Hitler himself initially perceived his role as a 'drummer' (*Trommler*), a prophet for a future *Führer*.[66] In this respect, the Nazi movement and its ideology became the platform of a synthesis of *völkisch* ideals of national unity, rebirth and greatness with the added element of historic urgency which pervaded the atmosphere of crisis in the 1920s. Where the NSDAP differed from the other forces of the nationalist opposition, however, was in its complete self-exemption from the stigma of the liberal system. The Nazi leadership emerged from the ruins of 1918 as a truly 'new' spiritual elite, a negation of the forces of national destruction (liberalism, socialism, Jews), and of the 'old' institutionalised nationalism.[67] In this respect, the Nazi self-historicisation involved an unqualified rejection of post-Bismarckian choices. As in the case of Italy, the disaster of war was viewed as a 'god-sent gift', from which the apocalyptic vision of 'new' Germany originated.[68] Hitler's theory of territorial expansion emerged from the experience of 1917–18, in an attempt to remedy those conditions which had led to encirclement, defeat and loss of territory.[69] Furthermore, the degree of suffering that the negative elements of the old system inflicted upon the *Volk* strengthened and justified Nazism's 'anti-' character as a precondition for a true national renaissance. Destruction and endurance in German history highlighted the 'transcendental' necessity of the existence of the German *Volk*. This belief invested Nazism's task of rebirth with a historic obligation to the nation itself, consisting in rescuing and completing the dream of unification but also defending the superiority of the national culture against the forces of 'corruption' and 'collapse'.

The fascist myth of national unification: the 'mission' of completing the process of nation-state building

The connection made by the fascist ideologues to the process and goals of national unification formed the basis of what has been termed the 'palingenetic nature of fascism', that is, the revival of old national myths of grandeur in an effort to regenerate a society in deep crisis.[70] Attacks on the concepts of 'territorial saturation' and 'pacifism' resonated with the belief that unification was incomplete, and this fatally undermined the process of domestic unity and national ascendancy. Proto-fascism rejected the complacency of the post-unification generations and advocated the completion of unification as the spiritual *sine qua non* of national regeneration. This was a message that, according to the radical nationalists, neither Italian liberal politicians nor the *Honorationen-politiker* of the Wilhelminian–Weimar systems could comprehend. Their historic deviation from the true goals of unification remained a source of domestic and external weakness for the two countries and peoples, culminating in what was perceived as a disastrous postwar heritage. The triumph of fascism with the March on Rome of 1922 and the *Machtergreifung* of 1933 validated the perception of liberalism as a historic aberration in terminal decay. It also confirmed the historic role of the two regimes in returning the unification process to its ideological origins and in reinventing it, this time freed from the forces of corruption.

In this sense, fascism married its revolutionary activism with the idealism of national utopia and the necessity to expand in order to complete the mystic union of the whole nation within the national territory. This was not a re-negotiation of the past, but a conscious effort to reset the clock of national development and restart unification from point zero.[71] It also mirrored a psychological reluctance to accept past failures (the thwarted visions of Crispi and Bismarck) as historic facts. In this respect, fascism may be seen as an alternative process of unification,[72] in contrast to the political reality of unification as experienced after 1861 (in Italy) and 1871 (in Germany). Fascist ideology contrasted the ideological core of the unificatory vision (one state for the whole nation, nationalisation of the people, common struggle for greatness) to the decadent experience of the post-unification period. The myth of national rebirth expressed the aspirations of new politicised forces (the middle and lower classes), which had emerged after unification and now claimed a special role in the process of national ascendancy.[73] Representatives of these social groups interpreted the problems of the unified state not as the ideological bankruptcy of unification as an ideal, but as the outcome of political inertia, pragmatism and compromise by political leaders. The gap between the vision and the reality of unification, it was argued, was one of a mismatch between ideas and actual developments, thus underscoring the ideological sterility of liberalism. It was, therefore, fascism's historic role to reunite the initial idealism of the *Risorgimento* and the *Vereinigung* with a determination to achieve their goals. Fascists perceived the *raison d'être* of their movements as the ultimate culmination, not the negation, of the unificatory visions of the nineteenth century. Liberalism, as the dominant force of the past century, attempted to give political expression to these visions, but had failed. Now, fascism, portrayed as the only meaningful political form of the twentieth century, would have its turn.[74]

The fascist vision of national unification presented itself as the ultimate heir to the ideological legacy of the patriarchal figures of the struggle for national unity. In Italy, the prophecies of Mazzini, Oriani and Gioberti for the nation's superior historic mission and universal significance were adopted by Fascist ideology as a proof of the limited relevance of the modern Italian state to the dream of the *Risorgimento*.[75] The *Risorgimento*, according to Gentile, was not simply a static concept, an act that might or might not be accomplished. It was a permanent struggle for renaissance and grandeur, in which the conquest of Rome and Venice were landmarks but not termini.[76] The liberal attempt to present unification as completed reflected a conservative philosophy of history and showed its ideological irrelevance to the 'revolutionary' and idealistic principles that inspired the *Risorgimento*.[77] The failure to carry out the promises of 1848–60 had its roots in the marginalisation of Mazzini and Garibaldi by a liberal 'oligarchy' which held a pragmatic and limited vision of the 'new' Italy.

Mussolini was always at pains to criticise the notion that the *Risorgimento* had been a liberal accomplishment. For him, the Garibaldian revolutionary and universalist vision, on the one hand, and the Mazzinian idealism (represented as the heritage of Dante), on the other, had been the two foundations of the modern Italian state.[78] The liberals entered the game later and they usurped the ideological and political credit for unification, with the disastrous consequences of Giolittism and postwar humiliation. In his co-operation with the philosopher Giovanni Gentile, Mussolini saw the unity of ideals and actions which reflected the complementary roles of Mazzini and Garibaldi, against liberal introversion and lack of vision.[79]

Hitler, too, perceived his task as a continuation of Bismarck's artificially interrupted and distorted vision of national grandeur. This goal was significantly more difficult than the defence of Mazzini and Garibaldi by the *Duce*, since the architect of the German nation-state shared responsibility in the fate of post-unification Germany in the 1870s and 1880s.[80] Bismarck had been very reluctant either to pursue a policy of colonial expansion or to promote the territorial goal of *Grossdeutschland* (that is, the completion of unification with the inclusion of Austria into the Reich[81]). His dismissal in 1890, however, marked the end of an era and initiated the downward slide of the Second Reich. Hitler did not fail to criticise the shortcomings of Bismarckian Germany, but he was always respectful of the role and the vision of Bismarck himself.[82] He was the 'prophet', the 'precursor of Great Germany', the man who realised the destiny of the German *Volk* and initiated the difficult process of its renaissance.[83] The elements of 'moral decay', inherent in his Reich, finally managed to overpower him, leaving the task of forming a complete state and a mature nation unfinished.[84] Yet, here lay the historic significance of the Nazi movement, which was to draw the Bismarckian effort to its logical conclusion. The Nazi regime was destined to fulfil the last stage of unification, namely to create one people and one Reich, as well as to unite the German state with its historic birthplace of central Europe which remained 'unredeemed'.[85] The negative experience of the past taught Hitler to avoid compromises and not to waste any valuable time. German unification was historically incomplete and this would eventually drag Germany into chaos, unless it was complemented immediately. Any hesitation would exacerbate the problems and lead to a repetition of the post-Bismarckian disaster.[86]

In general, the fascist myth of unification recast the traditional radical nationalist claim of uniting all ethnically kin populations and their territories with the fatherland. Having successfully amalgamated previous nationalist themes into their ideological system, the two fascist movements emerged in the 1920s as the torchbearers of the struggle for the rebirth of their nations, in pursuit of the nationalist utopia of completing the process of unification. This notion provided the first tangible argument in defence of territorial expansion beyond the existing boundaries of the two countries. However, in contrast to conventional irredentist arguments, fascist ideology did not prescribe the reconstitution of the nation-state on the basis of an ethnic utopia. The completion of unification had immense territorial and, above all, spiritual value but was regarded as the necessary *sine qua non* for greatness, the beginning – rather than the terminus – of national 'palingenesis'. This was an essentially open-ended project, underpinned and fuelled by two further abstract ideological motivations. The first was the conception of history as a constant struggle in social Darwinist terms for the survival and triumph of the fittest. The second pertained to the self-perception of everything fascist (leadership, nation, culture) as an *elite force*, entrusted with a mission to legitimise the spreading of its values. To these two pivotal elements we shall turn now.

Beyond national unification: justifying the right to expand

Fascist expansionism, 'constant struggle' and the ideology of 'violence'

If fascism's analysis of the past provided ideological support for the claim of Italy and Germany for international leadership, post-1918 political realities seemed to impede the realisation of this destiny. Both fascist leaders capitalised on this gap between the historic right of their nations to dominate and the artificial thwarting of this destiny by internal and external foes in the recent past. They based their appeal on the promise to rectify this historic aberration by exploiting the dynamism which the Italian and German nations *de facto* possessed, based on their alleged spiritual superiority and 'widest range of capacities'.[87] Expansion, as Hitler repeatedly emphasised, was the historic right of the 'talented' people to possess space equivalent to the quality of their activities, but the reality was diametrically different, with less talented people possessing 'a greater and often unexplored extent of living space'.[88] Neither of the two leaders, however, made any secret of the difficulties that this promise entailed. The rise of the two 'young' nations to prominence would continue to be subverted by the selfishness and greed of the 'old', 'plutocratic' powers.[89] History in itself, according to fascist ideology, was the outcome of a permanent struggle for survival and domination. In the long term, only the most competent would excel. Struggle, even in the form of violent confrontation, was both inevitable and desirable for the fulfilment of the fascist prophesies.

This was the point where expansion ceased to be simply *one* option for foreign policy making and became a necessity for the existence and the legitimate aspirations of the two nations. The belief that history was decided by constant struggle, and the conviction that fascist all-round excellence was destined to prevail, offered a new significance to the spreading of the fascist idea through force. In this sense, expansionism was not simply a political form of control and subordination of populations or a policy of ruthless exploitation (as in the case of British and French imperialism). It was rather the natural extension of a higher moral, cultural and biological order. The ethical–religious connotations are obvious. Fascism was destined to expand as a force of salvation and rebirth.[90] The media for this new order were the two nations with the strongest universal cultural tradition. As Hitler argued in 1938, Italy and Germany were so powerful internally that they were designed to turn this dynamism outwards, in an expansion of values that was a natural and moral inevitability.[91]

The cult of violence in fascist ideology had two separate aspects.[92] The *spiritual* aspect of violence was perceived as a force of national renovation, as an imperative step in the re-education of the individual in order to 'remake his content' and transform him into a genuine *uomo fascista*.[93] Fascism, Mussolini argued, was the negation of liberalism, because the former 'attacks' and progresses while the latter only 'defended' and sank into inertia.[94] Fascism's task was to mobilise the Italian people both for the 'works of peace' and the ineluctable 'labours of war'.[95] One of his favourite themes was the 'morality' of violence and its spiritual importance as expression of human will. In a speech he gave at Udine just a month before the March on Rome, he stressed that violence was a legitimate instrument of the State, crucial for the spiritual preparation of the Italian people for their future glory.[96] In the opening speech to the Fascist Congress of 1925 he went even further, claiming that violence was more moral than any form of compromise or negotiation.[97] Force was lawful and preferable to inertia, so long as it was pervaded by a worthy objective and was not blind.[98] In December 1924, speaking about his regime's foreign policy in front of the Italian Deputies, he once again underscored the morality of violence and asked the Italian people to be prepared for an 'armed peace' (*pace armata*).[99] Only through the spiritual strength of violence and will could the Italian people be transformed into a real nation of warriors, building upon the experience of the First World War.[100]

In Germany, on the other hand, war and violence were significantly more embedded virtues in the militarist framework of society.[101] Exponents of radical nationalist ideology saw in war the means to 'transcend' decadent bourgeois morality and to continue the process of transformation that had been initiated with the First World War.[102] The overwhelming majority of the respondents to the Abel interviews accepted the necessity of using violence, and almost half of them exercised it wholeheartedly as a moral means to promote the Nazi new domestic order.[103] Nazism endorsed and systematised the notion of a *Volk* in a state of constant mobilisation, modelled on the example of the armed forces.[104] The 'military' structure of the Nazi organisations, the spirit of 'comradeship' they inspired in their recruits and the opportunities they offered for activism were regarded by the Abel Nazis as the most important factors in their decision to join the NSDAP.[105] Violence and war became the ultimate expressions of the will to dominate, as well as the devices that offered concrete, effective form to fascist political activism. All these amounted to a perception of violence and war as both a means and an end in itself; a means for realising national destiny, and a goal in its ethical and educational value for the people.[106]

The *external* aspect of violence, that is, its use *against* others and its destructive potential, was regarded by fascist ideology as less fortunate but no less inevitable or legitimate. Mussolini saw confrontation as a historic necessity, since life itself was punctuated by antitheses and clashes. It was not a pleasant 'sport' or an entertainment to exercise violence, he noted in 1924, but in the end fundamental conflicts could be resolved only through force and war.[107] In this respect, the use of violence by an elite was moral and legitimate, not only in a natural sense (the strongest had to prevail), but also politically (in order to bring the necessary readjustments to the 'new order').[108] This was an argument consistent with the squads' emphasis on violent action and their 'dogmatic, violent negation of the present', as Mussolini described it in the Doctrine of Fascism. Fascism, he continued, did not believe in pacifism and perpetual peace, as these derived from the renunciation of struggle and from cowardice in the face of sacrifice.[109] War was regarded as the 'most ferocious necessity', but it also possessed qualities which determined the 'whole progress of humanity'.[110] The nation, he added in 1934, must be militarised and must prepare for war by subjecting all other considerations and needs to military priorities.[111] Similarly, Hitler repeatedly stressed his aversion to violence as such, but claimed that its use had been sanctioned by higher historic priorities. The right of the German *Volk* to transform its inner superiority into international supremacy was questioned by a plethora of *Feinde*. If Germany wished to become again a great power (and, as an elite, she had the obligation to do so), she had to fight against the desire of her enemies to annihilate her.[112] The Nazi 'new world' would come to life only through struggle and destruction, the latter directed against the forces of national and universal decay.

Fascism and elitism: elite 'leaders', elite 'nations', elite 'civilisations', and fascism's 'mission' of expansion

It has been one of the most perplexing ideological paradoxes of fascism that it strove to stress its egalitarian, meritocratic and classless elements[113] while at the same time not concealing its elitist character. Unfortunately, even the few systematic accounts of fascist elitism focus on the National Socialist movement.[114] It is crucial to understand that these elitist theories were at the root of serious tension between 'elites' and 'non-elites' which inevitably resulted in the dominance of the former over the latter. In this sense, the 'triumph' of fascism reflected the dynamism of the fascist elites, as well as their self-assigned 'mission' to dominate and lead those groups that had been excluded from the fascist definition of elite.

Fascist elitism owed its ideological substance to the previous elitist theories of social transformation. People like Michels and especially Pareto had spoken of a pattern of constant circulation of elites in society and viewed the triumph of one elite group as evidence of its superior qualities. In this sense, Pareto argued, fascism represented a victory of a historic set of ideas and mentalities which were destined to prevail and become generic.[115] At the same time, elitism evolved out of fascism's interpretation of history in essentially social Darwinist terms. The two fascist movements introduced themselves as the reincarnation of the highest elements of the *Risorgimento* and the *Vereinigung*, the bearers of the task to fulfil the prophecies of national reawakening and excellence. On a more general level, the fascist movements had allegedly emerged as a political, ideological and ethical elite through their successful struggle against the 'old' forces of national and universal decay. Perseverance in difficult times led to their eventual victory and thus justified their self-historicisation as the new dynamic force, destined to guide the nation towards a future utopia.

The interrelation of the elitist fascist theories with the propensity for aggressive expansion becomes evident when we analyse the ideological conceptualisation and legitimation of this elitist self-perception. Fascist elitism was articulated on three progressively wider levels: an elite *leadership*, an elite of *nations*, and an elite of *races* or *forms of civilisation*.[116] The social Darwinist production of the elites (as leaders, nations and races or cultures) gave fascism a sense of historic significance and a determination to continue its struggle for the attainment of its allegedly superior historic objectives. Expansion, therefore, was the outward manifestation of fascism's transcendental power, of the fascist will to power and of the claim to ethical supremacy.[117] Domestic conquest was the primary task of the fascist elite as the 'leadership' of the nation. The two fascist movements shared a biological interpretation of hierarchy as the outcome of a permanent struggle between old and new forces. Elites performed their historic functions, but they were destined to decay or defeat by stronger and 'younger' groups in a circulation of elites.[118] The events of 1922 and 1933 (the acquisition of power) not only legitimised the transcendental role of the historic fascist leadership, but also proved the superiority of its vision and morality.

However, the establishment of the fascist leadership as the spiritual aristocracy of the nation inevitably created a gap between the elite and non-elite elements within the national community. Notwithstanding the 'open' meritocratic character of the two movements, the fascist regimes gradually imposed a new hierarchical structure. The privilege of moral and political authority was the monopoly of the enlightened fascist 'minority' and this was potentially the source of an inferiority complex for the majority excluded from the elite group. Mussolini described the Fascist leadership as 'few but the greatest force of the nation', while Hitler justified the principle of authoritative leadership as legitimate if based on genuine spiritual values.[119] To allay these sentiments of discrimination, fascist ideology introduced the idea that the whole 'fascist' nation was *de facto* an elite among the community of nations. This transfer of elitist sentiment to the level of the nation performed two important functions. First, it established an egalitarian concept of nation, based on a community of people who shared the same qualities and pursued common objectives for the benefit of the collectivity.[120] Second, it translated the notion of historic hierarchy to the international system by asserting the superiority of the new elite of 'young nations', i.e. the Italian and German nations.[121] The two nations had purport-edly manifested their ability to produce the highest forms of universal civilisation in history.[122] The alleged Roman and Christian origins of the modern Italian state and the heritage of the Holy Roman Empire of the German nation attested to the long-standing spiritual superiority of the two peoples. Ironically, this belief was strengthened by the grievances of the post-unification period. In spite of international 'conspiracies' and the tyranny of the decadent 'old' nations,[123] Italy and Germany displayed an admirable determination to survive and a will to excel, which attested to their transcendental power as precursors of a new historic era. The victory of fascism terminated the cycle of national decay and brought the two nations back onto their destiny. The nations of Italy and Germany, according to the words of Hitler, 'stand young not on new territory, but on historic soil'.[124] Their classification as elite nations stemmed not simply from the power of destiny, but from the ability of fascism to provide allegedly tangible evidence of this historic superiority.

Both leaders placed particular emphasis on the demographic vitality of the population. Mussolini's persistent efforts to promote a combination of food- and birth-increase policies in the second half of the 1920s aimed to ensure a demographic boom, which was regarded a necessary evidence of the nation's renewed vitality under Fascism. Women were seen as the bearers of a new generation of warriors, and should therefore be confined to their domestic functions as wives and mothers in order to contribute best to this national goal.[125] Italy, he argued in 1923, should avoid the fate of France, whose demographic decadence was regarded as evidence of political and spiritual decline.[126] The same example was used by Hitler in *Mein Kampf* as an example of what Germany should avoid in order to reclaim her international position and historic significance. In 1937 he celebrated what he called 'fifteen years…of strong life' after a period of painful decay, evident in the strength, progress and numerical expansion of the German *Volk*.[127]

Civilisations and races as 'elites': racialism, anti-Semitism and fascist ideology

The third level of the fascist elite ideology again rested upon the perception of the fascist nation as a superior force. This time, however, the implications of this transcendental privilege were extended much further, presenting fascism as an elite force of civilisation in a historic, universal sense. The universal tendencies of fascism had their origins in the elitist theory of the fascist nation, but were politically indispensable in the context of the historic antithesis between socialism and fascism.[128] Both leaders, individually and in unison after 1936, repeatedly declared that Bolshevism represented a lethal menace both to individual nations and to the whole existence of 'European' civilisation. Fascism represented, therefore, a dual defence. First, it should safeguard the elite character of the nation against the international forces of corruption. Second, it had to defend the European culture, which both Italian and German fascist ideologies perceived as the historic achievement of their respective nations.[129]

This universal 'mission' of fascism portrayed the fascist nations as the elite, or the most superior form, of civilisation. Before 1936–8, each of the two regimes had attempted to monopolise this title for itself and its respective nation. The dual heritage of Rome and Catholicism formed the basis of Fascism's claim to universality and cultural superiority. Nazi ideology, on the other hand, presented the Teutonic past and the legacy of the Holy Roman Empire as evidence of Germany's destiny to dominate and defend Europe (see below). After the rapprochement between Italy and Germany, the two fascist leaderships presented the historic task of the struggle against Bolshevism as a joint undertaking.[130] However, in the execution of their universal project, the two regimes exhibited considerable differences which merit attention. A fundamental difference between the two fascist ideologies was the way in which the concept of *nation* was defined. Italian fascism, as well as its nationalist precursors, stood for a voluntarist idea of nation-formation.[131] The *nazione* comprised all those individuals who shared an Italian cultural ideal, those who placed their allegiance to the Italian state and tradition above any other loyalty, religious or ethnic.[132] In this sense, the nation was not a biological or historic reality, but the result of a continuing process of cultural education and integration.[133] Undoubtedly, there was an extremist minority in the Italian Fascist movement which advocated a semi-biological, unalterable inherent national identity (the writer and member of the Gentilian school of philosophy Julius Evola, and the *ras* of Cremona Roberto Farinacci). Their ideas, however, did not gain wide currency, even in such fertile ground as the anti-Semitic or anti-Slav groups within the Fascist party.[134] Even in the early years of the movement, only occasionally did unruly *squadri* target Slav groups in north Italy, and such actions remained isolated incidents of uncontrolled minorities rather than systematic regime policies of discrimination.[135] By contrast, Nazi ideology was monolithic in its acceptance of the biological origins of national identity. An individual was either German by blood or could never become so, even if they chose to adopt the cultural elements of *Deutschtum*.[136] This rigid axiom explains Hitler's conditional espousal of Germanisation policies in the conquered areas. In principle, he had repeatedly rejected the rationale of Germanisation of 'alien' peoples, even if they possessed linguistic and cultural elements of German culture.[137] On the other hand, he authorised SS schemes for the re-Germanisation of *specific* populations (Polish, Rumanian, Russian) who, although they did not speak German any more, were considered by the Nazi regime as 'ethnically German' in terms of 'blood' derivation.[138] The scientific ethos of German post-unification society penetrated the irrational nucleus of nationalist mythology, thus providing it with what appeared to many as unquestionable empirical credibility.

The above different definition of 'nation' also explains why the two regimes diverged in the definition of their *racial* doctrines. In Italian Fascist ideology, the distinction between race as a cultural product and race as a biological condition was never clear.[139] As defender of European civilisation and the white race, the Italian nation was superior to the other European 'races' (*stirpe*) because of its higher cultural idea and history.[140] Until 1935, however, Mussolini was highly critical of Hitler's biological racism, stressing that race was meaningless due to the common biological origins of all white peoples.[141] As he stated in the 1932 *Doctrine of Fascism*, the nation 'was not a race, nor a geographically individualised region, but stock *(schiatta)* historically perpetuating itself'.[142] Against this ideological backdrop, it is difficult to comprehend the introduction of anti-Semitic policies by the PNF after 1936. From an ideological point of view, the 'Manifesto of the Race' and the subsequent anti-Semitic legislation do not stand up to any serious criticism.[143] The Italian Jews were a small and integrated group in the national community, with a high representation in the PNF hierarchy, as Italo Balbo (Governor of Libya and member of the 1922 *quadrumvirate*) kept repeating to his *Capo* at the Grand Council in 1938–39.[144] The shift in the policy towards them reflected a change in Mussolini's definition of race: from now on, Jews were *de facto* a biological category. Although there is no evidence that the Nazi leadership had exercised pressure for the introduction of the racial laws, Mussolini adopted an anti-Semitic legislation which bore little relevance to the original ideology of Italian Fascism. Not surprisingly, the legislation found unqualified supporters in Julius Evola, Roberto Farinacci and the painter-writer Ardengo Soffici (a member of the Florentine avant-garde scene in the beginning of the century), who had always made their anti-Semitic beliefs clear. Surprisingly, even Giuseppe Bottai (former Minister of Corporations and since 1936 in charge of national education) – by no means a fervent anti-Semite – backed the legislation, although his support was more a sign of loyalty to Mussolini and did not endorse its violent side-effects.[145] Yet a sizeable minority of leading Fascist figures, including Italo Balbo, the President of the Senate Luigi Federzoni and the Vice-President of the Chamber Giacomo Acerbo, did speak out against the rationale of the laws, questioning their utility and their relevance to Fascist ideology, and asking for wide exemptions.[146] The cultural nature of the PNF's elitism did not rule out the partial integration of Jews into Italian society, through renouncing their religion and culture. The legislation, rigid in doctrine, was loosely and selectively implemented, falling short of the extremes of Nazi anti-Semitic policies.[147] Especially in the periphery of the Italian *Impero*, implementation of the legislation depended heavily upon the views of the local Fascist administration. The example of Libya is indicative. Balbo – as Governor of the colony – remained reluctant to abide by the regime's official anti-Semitic line. Mussolini continued to criticise his lack of enthusiasm and to press for a more systematic application of the racial laws, but he did not take active steps to curb his Governor's liberal interpretation of the legislation. As a result, the Jewish community in Libya remained relatively insulated from the implications of the anti-Semitic legislation until Balbo's death in June 1940.[148]

Italian racism did reflect a biological basis in the treatment of the Ethiopian peoples. The importance of the racial legislation in Ethiopia after 1936 went far beyond the rise of anti-Semitism in Italy. In many ways, the experience of managing a proper, extensive colonial empire after the formal occupation of Ethiopia in 1936 may be seen as the reason behind the inception of all racist legislation by the Italian Fascist regime.[149] Its logic, however, was reminiscent of the conventional 'white man's burden' colonial justification rather than of any rigid eliminationist doctrine; the black race was both culturally and biologically inferior to the 'Aryan' race, and therefore its subjugation to white rule was legitimate and its separation from the white peoples essential. Here, cultural re-education would have had limited effect, because the black peoples were incapable of adopting the 'superior' moral and cultural qualities of European civilisation.[150] Some integration was again possible; the regime planned to grant a 'special' kind of Italian citizenship to the people of the northern provinces of Libya in return for their acceptance of their subordinate status. Such flexibility, however, could not conceal the underlying belief in the 'biological' shortcomings of the black race.[151] Fascism's universal task, it was alleged, was to civilise the inferior races and to defend the purity of western civilisation from racial miscegenation, which could harm the intellectual qualities of the white race; but not to eradicate them altogether.[152]

German racism, by contrast, was significantly more rigid, in the sense that it regarded culture as a reflection of the biological characteristics of a nation or a race. The Germanic *Kultur* was superior, because the Nordic race was by nature the elite of all other races, as well as the elite of white peoples.[153] The problem lay with those of the 'inferior' races who were allegedly feeding from, and poisoning, the blood of the German *Volk*.[154] Since their biological faults rendered any attempt at integration both unfeasible and dangerous, they had to be eradicated for the sake of Germany and western civilisation. Therefore, Nazi racial elitism was directed against Jewish, Slav and Latin peoples (sometimes not excluding even Italians, as Mussolini himself often noted with considerable irritation[155]), against black peoples and Indians,[156] as detrimental to the sanity of the German race. What transformed the Jews from *one* possible target to the most hunted victim of Nazi racism had indeed a lot to do with the Nazi *Weltanschauung*. According to Hitler's thought, the Jews lacked a national and cultural identity, a common history and their own place (*Boden*) in the world. They were also equated in his worldview with the internationalist conspiratorial project of world communism.[157] Alfred Rosenberg, the chief Nazi ideologue of anti-Semitism, had since 1918 spoken of the 'Jewish menace' for Germany and the whole of Europe, advocating a systematic policy of exclusion and expulsion. His major works, *Myth of the Twentieth Century* and *Pest in Russia*, reflected a systematic attempt to lend scientific validity to an irrational prejudice and thus bring it to the forefront of popular nationalist feeling. At the same time, Heinrich Himmler's idea of a racially reorganised and purified German society contained the seeds of an eliminationist, mystical attitude to anti-Semitism which was reproduced in the SS organisations and was allowed significant latitude in the last years of the Nazi regime.[158]

However, Nazism was not the only source of the anti-Semitic eliminationist ideology which led to the persecution and annihilation of the European Jews in the 1930s and 1940s. Other factors, which had been assimilated – rather than produced – by Nazism facilitated the radicalisation of anti-Semitic tendencies within the German society. The survival or revival of atavistic notions of 'purity' and 'wholeness', the discarding of the philosophy of the Enlightenment, and the belief in the ideal of a 'blood community' and the rejection of cultural concepts of nationhood were long-lasting legacies of German radical nationalism since unification. By the turn of the century, the Jewish 'threat' had been invested with more far-reaching qualities: the Jews were morally, politically, culturally, racially, even economically 'deviant'. Anti-Semitic hatred was still abstract and divorced from action (that is, physical elimination), but it had become so central to the 'cognitive model' of German nationalism that constituted an unquestionable element of social attitudes, passed on uncritically from one generation to the other.[159]

This again was not an exclusively German phenomenon. In the first half of the twentieth century, a number of other European societies often ran amok with anti-Semitic obsessions, originating from a resurgence of extreme nationalist sentiment.[160] Yet, where German society had already begun to diverge was in its combined belief in the elite character of Germandom and in the 'racial'-biological source of its superiority. The institutionalisation of the Jewry as the scapegoat for every social, economic and political setback was strengthened by the widespread phobia towards communism and Bolshevism, which were regarded as a Jewish scheme for international domination. The 1918 revolution and the subsequent left-wing agitation throughout the period of the Weimar Republic bolstered popular beliefs in the alleged international conspiracy of the Jews against the German nation. At the same time, the atmosphere of crisis in interwar Germany was further compounded by the two economic crises and the threat of a communist revolution which, unlike in Italy, had not abated by the time of the seizure of power.[161] The publication of the fabricated *Protocols of the Elders of Zion* in the early 1920s acted as a confirmation of the suspicions about Jewish intentions which were rife in large sections of German society. Nazi anti-Semitic ideology appealed to all these irrational fears and presented the Jewish 'threat' as a lethal challenge to the 'mission' of the German nation. The Abel interviews highlight that strong anti-Semitic beliefs were reflected in the discourse of half the respondents. However, a significant additional number came to an endorsement of anti-Semitism through resentment for defeat, the 1918 revolution and the Weimar Republic, which they were ready to accept as indications of a international Bolshevik-Jewish conspiracy.[162] The Nazi regime subsequently radicalised these perceptions by investing them with grotesque pseudo-scientific metaphors; Jews were described as a 'malignant poison', 'bacillus infecting the life of peoples', 'the race-tuberculosis of nations', 'pest', 'bacteria invading the body of the *Volk*' and 'rotten'.[163] The morbid biological account of national life as a 'closed' organism rendered all alien influences or interventions to its reproduction parasitic and contagious. Only complete eradication could guarantee the health of the *Volksgemeinschaft* and of the whole European civilisation. In this sense, defence of the nation was not enough. Expansion through force and destruction for the removal of the cultural and biological threat was perceived as a historic necessity consigned to the German nation. Nazi Germany as an elite nation, race and *Kultur* had the historic duty to salvage Europe from cultural and racial annihilation.[164] This was a struggle to defend the ultimate nationalist 'utopia'; that of national purity and wholeness.[165]

Choosing targets: fascist expansionism and the notion of living space

So far we have concentrated our analysis on the generic ideological factors in the fascist worldview which produced and explained the general propensity of the Italian and German regimes for territorial expansion. However, fascist ideology also needed a conceptual formula which could focus the general tendency to territorial expansion upon a more concrete and intelligible set of expansionist goals. In this respect too, fascist ideology continued its function of annexing pre-existing themes and currents into its mythical core of elitism and violent activism.[166] Hence, the idea of *living space* was gradually put forward as the pivotal object of fascist expansion and the ultimate measure of fascism's success in revitalising the national community and in promoting its historic universal mission.

The notion of spatial expansion comprised two different levels of justification and legitimisation. The first, *abstract* level focused on space as agriculturally usable land suitable for migration and resettlement of the excess population of the metropolis. It was related to demographic factors and underscored the need to find an effective relation between territory and population through expansion in underdeveloped, thinly-populated areas. It was also put forward as a technique to bring about a fairer redistribution of natural resources in the world among the alleged demographically strong and culturally prominent nations. The second, *historic-ideological* level of justification of spatial expansion centred on the notion of space as a specific geographical entity, determined by the historic ties of a nation with its adjacent territories. This was an essentially irredentist argument, but not in its limited ethnic sense or its traditional emphasis on populations. It was rather an argument which used the historic precedent of a nation's control over a given territory in order to justify its right to 'redeem' it at a much later stage in history, even in defiance of the principle of popular self-determination. This fascist notion of historic irredentism was directly derived from the ideological concept of elitism. It linked the acquisition of these territories with the fascist universal project and justified the subjugation of the populations inhabiting them to the professedly more 'advanced' fascist nations as a natural necessity.

The production of an ideology of spatial expansion in these terms by the two fascist movements was the result of a long process of absorbing and digesting diverse ideological currents into a new synthesis. The idea of living space *per se* was by no means a fascist conceptual innovation. It had previously informed the expansionist programmes of various nationalist movements in the two countries which lingered from the nineteenth to the twentieth century and continued to be influential until the First World War. However, the fascist notion of space went significantly further than its ideological predecessors. It was transformed into an ultimate ideological symbolism of fascist expansion, bridging the traditional nationalist goal of completing national unification with the fascist millenarian aspirations for a new international order.[167] In this sense, it is important to monitor how the notion of space was shaped in Italian and German fascist ideologies, acknowledging debts to previous nationalist movements and thinkers but also highlighting how it became the symbolic manifestation of all fundamental priorities and principles which informed the worldviews of the two regimes.

Italy: the idea of spazio vitale *and the Mediterranean project*

The idea of space in demographic and historic terms was introduced in Italian nationalism by the 'new' radical generation of nationalist thinkers who made their appearance felt in the first decade of the twentieth century. The need for space as agricultural land for Italy's excess population and as solution to the problem of emigration had been a crucial element of legitimisation for Italy's colonial policies since the 1880s, giving rise to the ideology of migrationist colonialism in parts of Africa (see Chapter 1). However, the new radical nationalist ideology of the *novecento* movements linked the objective demographic and economic rationale of spatial expansion with a metaphysical notion of historic greatness and imperial destiny. The influence of leading figures of the Italian Nationalist Association (ANI) – most notably, Enrico Corradini – on Mussolini's expansionist ideas has been acknowledged by a plethora of works on the intellectual basis of Fascist ideology.[168] Corradini's conception of Italy as a 'proletarian nation' was the first synthesis of the abstract and the historic aspects of space ideology. Italy as a young nation, he argued, had been entitled to a very limited share of the world's resources by the established 'plutocratic' great powers. This reality was unacceptable not simply for economic and demographic reasons but also as an insult to Italy's past grandeur and historic significance. In this sense, the legacy of the Roman empire redirected the modern Italian people to the Mediterranean basin in search of both living space and a new period of national greatness.[169]

However, there were limits to the appeal of Corradini's ideas in pre-1914 Italian society. For a start, in spite of the ANI's consolidation after 1908, the movement continued to be regarded as an intellectual, elitist organisation, divorced from action and with limited impact upon *popular* nationalist perceptions.[170] Furthermore, Corradini's influence on the ideological profile of the ANI had already started to wane by 1910–12, when the more conservative attitude to foreign policy – epitomised by Federzoni and Rocco – gained the upper hand in the organisation. The ideas of imperialist nationalism and Africanism which inspired Corradini's vision of spatial expansion became less relevant to the nationalist 'border readjustment' agenda of Adriatic expansion which underpinned the opposition of the ANI to liberal policies during and after the First World War.[171] Finally, Corradini's emphasis on the primacy of a foreign policy conceived in imperialist, palingenetic terms was not shared by a large section of the radical nationalist movement. Prominent figures of the *novecento*, such as Papini and Malaparte, continued to view foreign policy and expansion as a means subjected to the goal of a revolutionary social transformation, rejecting the traditionalist Roman inspiration of Corradini's project.[172]

In this sense, Mussolini's revival of the principle of space in the post-1918 period, albeit not conceptually novel, was politically significant in that it popularised a previously elitist concept and transformed it into the fulcrum of a radical mass ideology of expansion. After 1919, he underlined the importance of acquiring more living space as a demographic necessity for the expanding Italian people. In the Second Declaration of San Sepolcro (1919) he contrasted Italy's meagre territory and natural resources with the vast lands of the British empire, calling for a forward policy of expansion in order to rectify this dangerous disproportion between 'plutocratic' and 'proletarian' nations.[173] A year later, in a major speech delivered at Trieste, Mussolini justified the demographic reasons behind the Fascist demand for expansion, calling for a more equitable ratio of territory to people for postwar Italy.[174] Although after the acquisition of power he sponsored an ambitious, if ineffective, policy of increasing agriculturally usable land (through land reclamation) and production (through the 'battle of grain'), he believed that neither the exploitation of the existing territory alone nor the control of births were effective solutions to the demographic and food problems of postwar Italy.[175] Spatial expansion was the right and the proof of a demographically and culturally flourishing people, as he explained in September 1928. In the same speech, titled 'the Number as Force', he described any population decrease as a prelude to the decay and cultural annihilation of a nation.[176] Expansion, therefore, for demographic-economic reasons was an open-ended process, intending to accommodate the existing excess population and to provide the necessary space for the – hopefully – expanding population of a regenerated Italy.[177]

At the meeting at San Sepolcro in March 1919, Mussolini also spoke of the need to expand in order to give Italy a 'place in the world' amongst the great powers.[178] In contrast to the ANI's pessimism about the prospects of the Latin peoples in their competition with the Nordic and Slavic races, the Duce professed his faith in Italy's future by prescribing the acquisition of living space as the necessary precondition for domestic recovery and international ascendancy.[179] The significance of acquiring new territory was not simply economic but also symbolic. Apart from completing the process of unification which had been initiated with the *Risorgimento*, spatial expansion would build upon Italy's gains after the war and consolidate her position among the great powers by using territorial aggrandisement as the currency of great power status.[180] The state should strive to expand its territory, he argued in 1929, for the welfare of its thriving population and for the everlasting glory of the whole nation in its struggle for greatness.[181]

To this abstract notion of *spazio vitale*, which appeared to justify interminable expansion without specific objects, Mussolini gradually added a more concrete historic and geopolitical focus. The June 1919 Programme of the *Fasci di Combattimento* made vague references to a 'foreign policy calculated to improve Italy's position' and to safeguard her vital strategic interests.[182] However, by that time Mussolini had already started developing the idea of a Mediterranean *mare nostrum*, extending from the Adriatic to the north African lands, as historically belonging to Italy. Again at San Sepolcro, he explained that Italy's claim to great power status was derived from history. The Mediterranean basin was her historic living space, he argued, threatening to oust the British and limit the influence of France in the region if they attempted to impede Italy's rightful expansion in the region.[183] The June 1919 Programme of the *Fasci* expressly stated Fascism's opposition to the 'plutocratic powers' in the region which threatened Italy's interests and impeded the will of the Italian people to dominate the region.[184] The heritage of the Roman past directed the forces of the new Italy to its historic birthplace, the 'sea of Rome', in order to commence the third Italian universal civilisation.[185] Emphasis on the official Italian claims to Dalmatia at Versailles was justifiable only as a means to ensure the country's land frontiers first and a prelude to expansion in the whole Mediterranean region, including both European and colonial lands.[186] The heritage of the first (Roman empire) and the second (Papacy) civilisation of Rome rendered modern Italy universal *par excellence*, with a mission to 'spread our gospel to other lands where Italians always lived'.[187] By 1922, the fusion of the abstract notion of *spazio vitale* with the historic irredentist notion of *mare nostrum* had been essentially completed. In his last major speech before the March to Rome in October 1922, the Duce spoke of the Fascist myth of the nation as a positive utopia, combining the significance of territory with the spiritual and historic qualities of the Italian people. 'It is not simply a matter of size', he added with reference to territorial expansion, but of the totality of national forces derived from the glorious Italian history and the spiritually rejuvenated 'new' Italian nation.[188] Less than a year later, this time from his responsible position as Prime Minister, he justified the violent occupation of the island of Corfu by blaming the Greek government for not appreciating that 'Corfu had been Venetian for four hundred years' before becoming part of the modern Greek state.[189]

As for the geopolitical dimension in Mussolini's vision of Mediterranean expansion, it originated from the growing awareness of the multiple external obstacles to Italy's territorial ambitions in the region. It was not just the British and the French who forestalled Italy's access to her historic *spazio vitale*. Other lesser powers, according to Mussolini, had been allowed to enjoy privileges which had been denied to Italy in the past and especially after the peace settlement. Spain controlled one major exit point from the Mediterranean and had direct access to the vast resources of the Atlantic ocean.[190] At the same time, he argued, the new state of Yugoslavia, in itself a creation of the Peace Treaties, pursued a policy of expansionist greed against vital Italian interests in the Adriatic sea, impeding the realisation of Italy's historic claims over Dalmatia and jeopardising her strategic position in an area crucial to her national defence.[191] In this respect, expansion in the Mediterranean was also a prerequisite for the country's rise to international prominence as it would ensure favourable strategic conditions for Italy's struggle against the other contenders for her historic living space. This geopolitical notion, crystallised in Mussolini's thinking before the March on Rome, was subsequently enriched with the idea of Italy's geographic 'imprisonment' in the Mediterranean and the necessity of securing access to the oceans.[192] The product of this ideological fusion was a concept of *spazio vitale* which dictated expansion into crucial control points of the wider Mediterranean and Red Sea areas, in order to alter the balance of power in the region and establish Italy's strategic advantage. Such arguments became more pronounced in Mussolini's more radical expansionist discourse in the 1930s and especially from 1935 onwards (see Chapter 4). In his major programmatic speech at Milan in November 1936, Mussolini justified Italy's vast aspirations in the Mediterranean basin as 'a struggle for life and death', in contrast to Britain's interest in the region as simply a sea route to the Indian Ocean. Italy, he added, was an island surrounded by the Mediterranean with no other exit to the world. If her world power ambitions were to be taken seriously, control of her land and maritime *spazio vitale* was the geopolitical and historic key to greatness.[193]

The doctrine of Italy's right to expand in the Mediterranean was further strengthened by Mussolini's notion of a spiritual and cultural hierarchy of races (*stirpe*). His references to 'thinly populated areas' surrounding the Mediterranean did not simply amount to a demographic justification for Italy's claim to a fairer share of territory in proportion to her population.[194] In a permanent struggle between cultures, Italian civilisation possessed a historic heritage which rendered her the *de facto* spiritually dominant force in the Mediterranean. Prior to the March on Rome, Mussolini had made ample use of the myth of Rome as a metaphor of Fascist Italy's historic universal legacy.[195] In his Trieste speech in September 1920 he described Rome's universal task as 'yet unfulfilled', alluding to Fascism's responsibility as the true heir to Italy's glorious past.[196] In February

1921 he spoke of Rome as the historically dominating force in European culture, while a year later he went as far as equating Fascism with the Roman past, thus legitimising modern Italy's right to expand in the Mediterranean.[197] The African lands were underdeveloped because the peoples inhabiting them lacked the demographic and cultural momentum to exploit their resources and prosper, both in numbers and political power.[198] The tendency to imperial expansion was a 'natural law' for the strongest peoples, as he noted in the *Doctrine of Fascism*, published in 1932; it was the expression of the vitality of one people and the acceptance of inferiority on the part of the subjugated populations in the conquered areas.[199] At the same time, even in Europe there was a fierce struggle between the various 'racial masses', as he termed them, for domination. Racist undertones were evident in Mussolini's discourse long before the official shift of the regime towards apartheid and anti-Semitic policies from 1936 onwards. As early as in September 1920, speaking to the people of Trieste, he described the Slav peoples as 'inferior' and 'barbaric', unworthy of their territory but extremely dangerous in their continued demographic and territorial expansion in central and south Europe.[200] Seven years later, he demanded that the Italian population reach at least the sixty million level in the near future through the intensified emphasis of the regime on marriages and births. According to his argument, this was a historic imperative in order to compete with the rising tide of Slav and non-white peoples in Europe and in the colonial empires.[201] The demographic and spiritual regeneration of the Italian people was the *conditio sine qua non* for greatness and for fulfilling the historic mission of dominating the Mediterranean *mare nostrum*. With the introduction of racial legislation, first in the *Impero* and then in the Italian mainland, Mussolini's notion of 'race hierarchy' acquired even more rigid qualities. In October 1938 he justified the racial policies of his regime as a historic necessity, arguing that only in this way could the Italian 'racial mass' be protected and dominate the struggle for the shaping of future Europe. Italy's historic and geopolitical *spazio vitale* in the wider Mediterranean region had to be either reclaimed from other countries and populations or asserted in fierce competition with other powers.[202] In this sense it became a metaphor for superiority and vitality, blending the abstract Fascist ideas of elitism, violent activism and historic mission with a specific historic and geopolitical focus of expansion.

Germany: the quest for Lebensraum in the east

The idea of living space (*Lebensraum*) has been widely acknowledged as the most consistent ideological current in Hitler's expansionist vision. The conquest of *Lebensraum* in the east for agricultural settlement has been described by a number of historians as the unalterable basic tenet underpinning his foreign policy ideas since the early 1920s.[203] By the time Hitler wrote *Mein Kampf*, the idea of spatial expansion for the acquisition of living space had already been equated in his mind with the notion of *Drang nach Osten*. As a continental power, Germany could only acquire sufficient *Lebensraum* at the expense of the Soviet Union, in order to nourish her growing population, expand her natural resources and strengthen her ability for self-defence.[204] Hitler annexed an economic argument to his analysis: neither colonies nor foreign trade could enhance the country's natural resources and improve living conditions for the German people. Only further spatial expansion could provide a just and lasting solution to the problem.[205] Fate, he added, was assisting Germany's need for eastern expansion by handing Russia to Bolshevism and thus weakening the spiritual power of the country and its leadership.[206]

As it emerged from *Mein Kampf* and later from his *Second Book*, Hitler's *Lebensraum* ideology coalesced a plethora of pre-existing German radical nationalist currents and personal preoccupations into a new and outwardly coherent synthesis. The romantic idea of *Blut und Boden*, namely the mystical union between blood and soil, had traditionally been a constant theme of *völkisch* nationalism and gained significance in the post-1918 period.[207] During the Wilhelminian period, various ideologies of living space made their appearance, emphasising the agricultural benefits of spatial expansion, the need for economic autarky and the possibility of resettling excess population in the conquered areas.[208] The ideal of Pan-Germanism, as expressed by the *Alldeutscher Verband* (Pan-German League), presupposed the conquest of the 'historic living space' of the German *Volk* in eastern and central Europe (see Chapter 1). At the same time, cultural and racial justifications for the expansion of the German nation in Europe abounded in pre-1918 radical nationalism, albeit with far less popular appeal than during the Nazi period. The *Alldeutscher Verband* spoke openly of the biological and cultural 'inferiority' of the Slav races, while after 1908 anti-Semitic references became more widespread in the organisations' declarations. The geopolitical notion of *Lebensraum*, as systematised by Friedrich Ratzel by the 1890s, justified expansion in social Darwinist terms, in the context of an eternal struggle between cultures and peoples.[209] Even such a highly-respected liberal figure as Max Weber advocated the need 'to win the greatest elbow room' so long as *free* territory and economic regions still existed. Although Weber's idea differed from the *völkisch* notion of aggressive *Lebensraum* expansion, it did accept the inevitable struggle between peoples for a 'space in the sun' and saw expansion, both in spatial and economic terms, as the vital element in Germany's international ascendancy.[210]

However, there was a significant qualitative difference in the pre-Nazi ideologies of *Lebensraum* and Hitler's concept of 'living space'. As we have already seen, until the 1920s *Lebensraum* formed only part of the legitimisation of Germany's expansionist ambitions, caught in the political dilemma between continental and overseas expansion (*Weltpolitik*; see Chapter 1). It had also absorbed different ideological undercurrents – such as migrationist elements, social Darwinism, historic justifications and racist connotations – but lacked a systematic integration of these diverse ideas into a coherent argument which could project spatial expansion as an all-embracing solution to Germany's domestic and international problems. In this sense, Hitler's contribution to the notion of *Lebensraum* was twofold. First, he amalgamated and radicalised pre-existing ideological, economic, historic, racist and geopolitical principles into a congruous system of thought which prescribed eastern expansion as the fundamental answer to Germany's grievances and the door to world power. Second, like Mussolini, he popularised the previously marginal and vague idea of living space by placing it in the forefront of the political programme of the Nazi mass movement.

Having said that, the production of the elaborate ideology of spatial expansion found in *Mein Kampf* and later in his *Second Book* followed a long process of integration and systematisation in the early 1920s.[211] The DAP Programme of 1920, to which Hitler's contribution should not be exaggerated, restated the conventional irredentist argument of uniting 'all Germans' and added only vague references to 'land and territory', including colonies, as solution to the country's space problem.[212] The absence of any allusion to eastern expansion originated from Hitler's initial obsession with the Versailles treaty, as a result of which he regarded – apart from France – 'England [sic] and America' as the 'absolute opponents' of the Reich.[213] There are various indications that in the 1919–21 period he was not averse to the idea of an alliance with Russia[214] against the main powers guaranteeing the Versailles settlement. The demographic aspect of *Lebensraum* permeated his references to spatial expansion in 1920–1, underscoring the unfavourable ratio of population to land in the post-Versailles Germany, but the prescription of spatial expansion lacked a concrete geographic character.[215] In contrast, Hitler had already developed the two central ideological themes of his worldview, anti-Semitism and anti-Bolshevism. The myth of an 'international Jewish conspiracy' underpinned his earlier anti-Semitic comments in 1920 and induced him to speak of a fundamental historic struggle between nationalism and internationalism (epitomised by the Jews), in which Germany would lead the fight against the latter.[216] At the same time, Bolshevism was also accused of internationalist and expansionist ambitions, allegedly promoting the ideal of a vast Russian empire in eastern and central Europe. By 1920 Hitler had fused the two concepts into one single enemy (Bolshevism was perceived as the vehicle for Jewish international domination) and for that reason excluded the possibility of an alliance between Germany and a Bolshevik Russia. He did not, however, rule out a collapse of the Bolshevik regime which would pave the way for a *rapprochement*.[217]

The identification of Russia with Bolshevism and the Jews in Hitler's mind was completed in 1922. By that time, the end of the Civil War in Russia had consolidated the Bolsheviks in power and had caused massive destruction to the country and its population. The 'ruined civilisation' of Russia, he said in July 1922, had been the result of the Jews' destructive influence and their absolute lack of constructive abilities.[218] This was also an indication of the fate that awaited any other European country if it succumbed to communism – a theme he constantly reiterated in the 1930s and especially after the Spanish Civil

War.[219] Bolshevism, he argued in February 1925, was the new religion spreading from the east towards Europe like a 'world pest', aided by its spiritual supporter, namely Jewry.[220] This convergence of his central racial prejudice (anti-Semitism) and his fundamental ideological antithesis (anti-communism) upon Russia re-orientated his foreign policy programme against the Soviet Union with the cumulative vehemence of a metaphysical struggle. The elitist self-perception of National Socialism and Nazi Germany as the vanguard of the historic struggle against Bolshevism and international Jewry for the protection of European civilisation established Russia as the symbolic alliance of all enemy forces to the German universal mission.

To this racial-ideological nucleus of anti-Russian sentiment, Hitler added a historic dimension which linked the Teutonic and imperial past of the German 'race' with its need for living space. In *Mein Kampf*, he reiterated that the central tenet of the National Socialist foreign policy was the 'securing of land and soil *rightfully belonging to the German Volk*'. The historic living space of the German people lay not in the west or in the colonies, as the Wilhelminian *Weltpolitik* had erroneously assumed, but in the east, linking the route of the Teutonic knights with the triumph of Brest-Litovsk in 1917 (see Chapter 1).[221] Again, racial considerations shaped his perception and analysis of German history. He argued that the creation of the vast Russian empire could not have been the work of the 'inferior race' of the Slavs; it was rather the achievement of 'Germanic organisers and rulers' who formed the basis of Muscovite Russia and established themselves as the intellectual and political elite of Russia throughout the centuries.[222] However, after the 1917 Revolution, 'a brutal dictatorship of foreign [Jewish] rule' had seized control of the country, destroying the constructive work of the Germanic race.[223] In attacking the Soviet state, therefore, Germany not only defended the west against the 'poison' of bolshevism, but also marched again over the traces of history to rescue her past achievements and make constructive use of the space and resources which inferior and incompetent races had reduced to ruins.[224] Nazi foreign policy would pick up the thread left by the Holy Roman Empire and the Germanic crusaders, spreading towards the east and establishing what Hitler described as the 'Germanic empire of the German nation'.[225]

In this sense, the concept of *Lebensraum* in Hitler's programme of spatial expansion performed an integrative and symbolic function similar to that of the *spazio vitale* in Mussolini's expansionist discourse. In the abstract sense of space for settlement, it expressed demographic and economic arguments about the importance of territory for the progress of a nation. It also comprised a geopolitical nucleus, underscoring Germany's precarious geographical position in the centre of the European continent and emphasising the need for living space in order to stave off the danger of external attack.[226] However, the exact geographical focus of Nazi spatial expansion was defined by the combination of ideological, racial and historic factors. The universal mission of Nazi Germany as defender of European culture, the protection of the elite character of the

German *Volk* and the historic legacy of the past converged upon the territories of the Soviet Union. By fusing the notion of historic irredentism with the anti-Semitic, anti-Slav and anti-communist traditions of the German radical right, Hitler produced a symbolic justification for territorial expansion which could rally a wide variety of forces in interwar German society. He also succeeded in integrating the idiosyncratic anti-Bolshevik feelings and fears caused by the 1917 Russian revolution into the pre-existing *völkisch* prejudice against the Jews and the Slavs. In this way he added a sense of political urgency and contemporary relevance to Germany's historic drive towards Russia and brought previously abstract or passive racial feelings to the focus of popular nationalist sentiment.[227]

If the integrative and figurative function of the ideology of living space was common in the two fascist regimes' expansionist policies, differences in the nature and importance of the various justifications should be neither discounted nor overemphasised. The rigidity of the concept of race in Hitler's *Weltanschauung* cannot be compared either with Mussolini's endorsement of racism after 1936 or with Italian Fascism's emphasis on a hierarchy of cultures. Conversely, the element of historic irredentism was much more prominent in Mussolini's universalist project (based on the heritage of ancient and medieval Rome) than in the Hitlerite ideological-racial-historic notion of eastward expansion. The idea of *mare nostrum* and the claim to world power were much more akin to a nationalist utopia, if significantly more far-reaching in scope and radical in methods. Hitler's vision, by contrast, performed a significantly wider function of synthesis in the context of a much more fragmented nationalist agenda. It reconfigured the geographic priorities of German expansionism and purged it from remnants of previous currents (Wilhelminian policy, *border* policy, *Weltpolitik*).[228] It is important, however, to note that the Nazi ideology of living space owed its dynamism and appeal to the cumulative effect of *all* its constituent elements. Anti-Semitism *alone* cannot adequately explain Hitler's vision of eastern expansion – as the Head of the SA (Sturm Abteilung), Ernst Röhm, put it, 'the problem was the Jews, not the *eastern* Jews';[229] nor can exclusive emphasis on anti-Bolshevism or the legacy of Brest-Litovsk. Similarly, Mussolini's active pursuit of a Mediterranean empire cannot be understood as the sole consequence of the importance of historic irredentism in fascist ideology. Geopolitical and defence considerations played an important part in his decision making, in the same way that his social Darwinist perception of history created the ideological momentum for active spatial expansion at the expense of other nations. Any attempt to over-determine the two regimes' ideology of living space as the primary outcome of a single factor discards the metaphorical and composite character of living space in fascist ideology, as the point where history, elitism, constant struggle, demography, national security and world power ambitions intersected.

Expansionist ideology in practice: the unity of thought and action in fascism

If the above visions of large-scale spatial expansion were derived from ideological convictions and aspirations which were not exclusive to fascist ideology, their prioritisation by the two fascist regimes owed its dynamism to a specifically *fascist* resolve to take them at face value and promote them in their totality through a constant activism.[230] In the worldviews of the Italian and German fascist movements, action was not simply the vehicle for the implementation of ideas and programmes. It was also an ideological goal in itself, the political externalisation of national virility, of the will to power and prominence. Like violence, which may be seen as an indispensable part of fascist activism, action was the necessary precondition for the spiritual mobilisation of the nation and the transition to the fascist 'new order'. It was a lasting legacy of fascism's revolutionary origins and a powerful weapon against normalisation and stagnation.[231] However, it was also a source of experience, processed by the fascist worldview to produce a more accurate account of national needs and interests. Expansion as action was indeed prescribed by fascist ideology, but it was clearly the *expression* of ideas as well as a generator of new options which *produced* ideas. The experience of the First World War fostered the fascist belief in the power of activism to reveal the inner qualities of the nation and a *leitmotif* for its future.[232] The consequent unity of thought and action in the fascist worldview was a reflection of the equal significance given to both elements as complementing each other in serving the long-term aspirations of the nation. It was also a sign of fascism's determination not simply to mediate between the real and the utopian, but to use the latter *in toto* as the sole guiding principle for policy making, unrestrained by other ideological beliefs and geared to uniting reality with vision.

In Italy, the short incubation period of the Fascist movement before 1922 resulted in a scarcity of policy statements on the part of its historic leadership. Mussolini did not perceive this as a disadvantage for his party: his only programme was to govern and make Italy great again, both domestically and internationally.[233] He was also very emphatic in his rejection of the traditional notion of ideology as divorced from action. Ideas, he said, had not saved Italy from decay.[234] The only remedy was a people with a will to power, with the strength to fight and exploit the superior inner qualities of the nation.[235] Only the strength of will could 'open the doors of power' and find solutions to every problem.[236] In the *Doctrine of Fascism*, Mussolini and Gentile described Fascism as both a faith and a doctrine in the making, an ideal with an evolving content realised through action and the laws of the omnipotent Fascist state.[237] Words and ideas were good and essential, he noted in 1925, but action was even more crucial.[238] At the same time, Fascism, as a renovative force and a *terza via* (third way), was a movement which did not slavishly copy existing programmes and ideas of the past. Instead, it was a historic force that would *produce* a doctrine as a result of its activities.[239] Since old ideals had failed to restore the prestige of the

Italian nation, Fascism would follow its own path, rejecting the limitations of existing principles and forging its ideological character according to the results of its activism. According to the sociologist Camillo Pelizzi (an important intellectual figure of the regime, who served as leader of the *Fascio* in Britain until 1938), Fascism based its historic success on the conjunction between pure idealism and uncompromising action.[240] The latter element guaranteed the revolutionary character of the movement, eliminating the option of political compromise which had kept utopia divorced from reality for so long. Even if Fascist ideas were not particularly original in themselves, the determination of Fascism to pursue them in an absolute manner was indeed innovative.[241]

For Mussolini, the priority of serving the interests of the nation overshadowed all other ideological aspects of Fascist foreign policy. Since short-term interests were constantly changing in a very fluid international system, the *Duce* declared his determination to cut across ideological and political principles in order to achieve the most effective service to Italy.[242] In his conduct of foreign affairs he had always endeavoured to exorcise two main enemies: normality and any restriction on his freedom of action. Normality was the negation of the revolutionary spirit of transcendence, something inconceivable as long as the 'old order' was still alive and resisting. As for freedom of action, he fought stubbornly, even after the outbreak of the Second World War, to retain his regime's political autonomy, to keep all his options open and to avoid hasty commitments. He often declared his willingness 'to swim against the stream',[243] following an equivocal policy towards allies and enemies, ideologies and principles. Ideals possessed an ultimate value only with reference to the achievement of long-term visions. In the short term, political flexibility and uncompromising action were not regarded by the Fascist leadership as weakness, but rather as a *sine qua non* in the revolutionary fight against predictability and stagnation.[244] Since 1918, Mussolini had made clear his determination not to be impeded by 'forbidden' goals or means but to bring the vision of Italy as a world power to its logical, consummate conclusion.[245]

Hitler and the Nazi leadership did not go to such lengths in their deification of short-term activism. Unlike his Italian counterpart, the Führer had a long time at his disposal to study the experience of the past and reach a number of conclusions about how to achieve his goals more effectively than his predecessors. In his speeches, he presented the policies of his regime as stemming from a fairly concrete programme of priorities, which he had formulated before the assumption of power.[246] The unity between thought and action was the logical outcome of the ideologically conditioned emphasis on action as an expression of Nazism's superior qualities and dynamism. Hitler held a general idea of his long-term aspirations (expansion in the east, a racially reconstructed Europe). He also formulated some guidelines for the achievement of his vision: for example, his instinctive perception of Britain and Italy as indispensable allies.[247] Having said that, the Führer did not possess a blueprint for short-term action. In the conduct of foreign affairs, Hitler was very short on the detail of how he would achieve his grand long-term goals. He combined his belief in activism with a confidence in his political intuition, perceiving himself as a 'prophet' and gambler[248] with a strength originating from the transcendental belief in his visions and the importance of action. He was systematic enough in his domestic preparation (such as rearmament and introduction of conscription), and lucky enough in his timing to reap benefits which fostered confidence in his own instinct and judgement. Like Mussolini, Hitler declared his determination to fight for the salvation of his nation in defiance of any ideological principle.[249] Only action could provide the necessary expression of the ideological superiority of the regime and the nation. The inner qualities of the *Volk* would be revealed and become meaningful only through their externalisation. He also emphasised that the distinction between feasible and unfeasible national goals was nonsensical. In 1942, he spoke to his Minister of Munitions Speer about his aversion to the word 'impossible'. For him, the will to succeed, to act and provide solutions was the only formula for eventual success.[250] In this sense, the unity of ideas and action in Nazism becomes comparable to the Italian case in its dialectic nature. Action was the sharp edge of the fascist worldview and functioned as a force bridging the gap between reality and vision. It was the political and ethical vehicle for transforming the inauspicious present into a new reality that *could* realise the long-term aspects of the fascist 'new order'.

Both leaders repeated the themes of constant struggle, elitism and living space with a consistency throughout the lifespan of their regimes which should not be dismissed *a priori* as mere propaganda or bluff. They also declared their determination to unite utopia with reality by matching deeds with words and results with aspirations. Their position as charismatic leaders of the two movements established them as the living incarnation and ultimate expression of the fascist worldview. The transition of the movements to organised parties and finally to power necessitated the systematisation and clarification of those initial ideas which had informed the activities and aspirations of the two movements. The task of the two leaders was indeed formidable. They had to rally the disparate forces within their parties to a political programme of action which would combine and harmonise different views about the priorities and goals of fascism. Once in power, they had to translate fascist values into action and convince their fellow travellers that their decisions expressed the spirit of fascist ideology accurately and effectively. They also had to link expansionist policies with the wider fascist desire for a radical transformation of human life in all its expressions. The above ideological 'minimum' represented a consensus within the two movements as to the long-term priorities and character of foreign policy making. However, different views amongst fascist leading figures about the best way to achieve these goals persisted and remained in a dialectical relation with the leaders' own interpretations. At the same time, once in power, the two leaders became aware of the immense gap between what they perceived as 'ideal' conditions for accomplishing their visions and the existing internal and international situation.

These remarks bring us back to something mentioned earlier: that ideology produces predispositions, tendencies, options and priorities, but does not *determine* policy making. Action is also defined by domestic circumstances and limitations, by the struggle of domestic institutions and individuals to shape policy according to their own perceptions, by the interaction between states. Fascism did not become an ideological and political *fait accompli* because it did not expand in a vacuum. Rather, its nature and policies were shaped in constant interaction with, and in opposition to, other strong forces, domestic and international. The following chapters explore the impact of these opposing factors upon fascist policies and analyse the complex process through which fascist ideals struggled, but never managed, to attain their unity with action in reality.

3

FOREIGN POLICY DECISION-MAKING PROCESSES UNDER FASCIST RULE

The appointment of Mussolini and Hitler as heads of coalition governments in 1922 and 1933 respectively constituted a decisive development in the process of fusion in the Italian and German Right. In the previous chapter, we examined how such an osmosis took place on the ideological level, allowing fascism to emerge as an effective synthesis of traditional aspirations and a new sense of radicalism and activism. This process led to a gradual convergence between old and new Right upon a set of short-term goals for both domestic and foreign policy. In Italy, this had been manifested in the rallying dynamism of the *intervento* movement of 1914–15, but was strengthened through the inclusion of Fascists in the electoral lists of 1921. In Germany, the campaign against the Young Plan in 1929 produced a coalition between the industrialist and press magnate Alfred Hugenberg and Hitler which appeared to originate from agreement on a single issue (reparations' revisionism) but initiated a debate about the political role of Hitler and the NSDAP in the German Right. Although the implications of these developments did not become immediately apparent, a process of political fusion was set in motion which gradually legitimised Nazism as an alternative solution to the political crisis.[1] In this respect, the endorsement of the 'fascist solution' in 1922 and 1933 by the elite groups in the two societies, albeit neither predetermined nor inevitable,[2] was the conclusion of a calculated political rationale. The aim was to transform the political representation of the Right by harnessing the powerful appeal of fascism and injecting its dynamism into the existing institutional framework of the state.

This decision, however, instigated a new phase in the process of fusion, which this time involved the balance between traditional ruling groups and the fascist elites in the decision-making process. Agreement on a common agenda of short-term goals meant that the utilisation of Mussolini and Hitler was intended to remain confined within the framework of a 'caesarist' regime, in which the autonomy of the traditional groups would be enhanced and legitimised by the charisma of the two fascist leaders. Institutional rearrangements were not ruled out, but the emphatic separation of the two leaders from their more 'extreme' parties was aimed to reduce the ability of the former to intervene in the institutional debate with radical proposals and initiatives.[3] Such a calculation did seem logical, given that the number of fascist representatives in the two cabinets was initially very small (four in Italy, three in Germany), and the two Heads of State (King Vittorio Emmanuelle III and President Oskar von Hindenburg) possessed the constitutional prerogative to dispense with the fascist leaders at any time. However, by admitting the fascist leaders to power, the elite groups in Italy and Germany allowed fascism a significantly larger stake in the institutional debate over the form of decision making. Despite converging on ideological and political objectives, fascist and non-fascist elites held fundamentally different views on this debate; in other words, on how the state should be reorganised and what roles should be allocated to the different partners.

Therefore, the institutional form of the 'fascist' system was the outcome of three major factors. The first was the struggle between the new fascist elites and the traditional political, economic, military and bureaucratic groups. The second was the complex relationship between the fascist leaders and the fascist parties. The third was the clash between the diachronic features of the Italian and German domestic systems, and the desire of the fascist elites to implement new patterns of organisation that had little relevance to the existing ones. The outcome of this triangular political struggle (fascist leadership, traditional elites, fascist parties) was fundamental to the foreign policy decision-making process. Apart from whatever intentions and 'programmes' the two fascist leaderships possessed, the implementation of a foreign policy plan depended heavily on both the acquiescence of the political, military and economic groups and on the capacity of the material infrastructure to produce optimal conditions for the attainment of the pursued goals. At the same time, the political tension between the fascist leaderships and their parties was anything but minimised after the inclusion of the former and the exclusion of the latter from power sharing. This was of great importance, since the parties sponsored more radical approaches to both domestic and foreign policy issues, perceiving themselves as institutional alternatives to the existing states.

The following analysis aims to examine the progress of this triangular institutional struggle from the period of the *Machtübernahme* until the outbreak of the Second World War.[4] It assesses the changing influence of the various traditional elite groups (military, political, diplomatic), of the fascist leaderships and the fascist parties in the foreign policy decision-making process. It focuses on key decisions of the two regimes and highlights the role of each of the above agents in the formulation of foreign policy. The chapter first discusses how the 'minimum consensus' that the traditional elites granted to the fascist experiment lay down the foundations for a leader-oriented system but also initiated a fierce institutional battle between these elites, the fascist leaderships and their parties. The ensuing consolidation of fascist power is analysed on two levels: first, with regard to the declining influence of the traditional groups and, second, with regard to the marginalisation of the fascist party as *originator* of foreign policy. The analysis highlights the central role of the two fascist leaders in the decision-making process, a role which was established through the gradual relegation of traditional elites to a *functional* position in the decision-making process, and the curbing of the policy-making capacity of the fascist parties. However, the fascist systems that were developed in Italy and Germany were not simply the products of what the two leaderships might have perceived as the optimal state. The consolidation of the two leaders' positions in the fascist systems was not the inevitable consequence of any concrete 'fascist' theory of state or the outcome of the personal intentions of the leaders, but the end result of a long-term structural struggle in the essentially polycratic framework of decision making. In this sense, instead of speaking of the establishment of a 'fascist' state in Italy and Germany,[5] it would be more accurate to talk of a compromise between fascist concepts of 'state' and the resistance of traditional, long-term features of the two systems.

The concept of 'minimum consensus'

The concept of 'minimum consensus', that is, the support on the part of military, economic and political leading circles for certain domestic and international measures pronounced by the two fascist leaderships, in practice deprived the fascist acquisition of power in 1922 and 1933 of its revolutionary pretensions. Acquisition of power represented the successful revolution of the fascist movements, but also a revolution that took place in relative harmony with the interests and aspirations of the main actors of the *anciens regimes*.[6] This idiosyncratic blending of revolution with consent produced a complex dualism at the heart of the fascist regimes. On the one hand, the fascist revolution aspired to a dramatic break with the previous domestic and foreign policies, both in style and in objectives. On the other hand, however, the conditions which facilitated the *legal* seizure of power resulted in a complicated form of power-sharing between fascist leaderships and traditional elite groups. This meant that fascism possessed limited institutional freedom to proceed unilaterally with the implementation of its own concept of state or its wide expansionist plans. In Italy, Mussolini had to accept the institutional tutelage of the Crown, co-existence with the traditional military and diplomatic bureaucracies whose primary loyalty was to the House of Savoy, and the limitation of the party's influence upon the state machinery.[7] In Germany, Hitler faced similar political challenges: the dominant constitutional role of President Hindenburg under Article 48 of the Weimar Constitution,[8] the latter's insistence on keeping the military and diplomatic functions of the state under his supervision,[9] and the need to restrain the revolutionary or subversive activities of the Nazi party when these were directed against the institutional authority of the state.[10]

This situation presented the fascist leaderships in Italy and Germany with a similar problem: how to show moderation towards the traditional elites while appeasing the craving of the fascist parties for a more central political function and influence on policy making. From the viewpoint of the various traditional elite groups, the party constituted the unacceptable face of fascism. For them, the appeal of the 'fascist solution' adopted in 1922 and 1933 resulted exactly from the clear separation of the fascist parties from their leaders, who were regarded by the dominant groups as a moderating force within the two movements.[11] The two leaders' ability to exercise full control over their parties was unquestioned, and their mirage of moderation could very easily be interpreted as the prelude to a long-term trend towards political normalisation which could in turn be imposed upon the more radical fascist movements. Therefore, if fascist leaders and members of the two parties celebrated the seizure of power as the first step towards the fascist 'revolution' and the 'fascistisation' of the state, the 'minimum consensus' programme was intended to remove this very possibility while strengthening the crumbling legitimacy of the state. Mussolini's and Hitler's charismatic leadership would form the basis of an authoritarian caesarist regime which would transform decision-making procedures and strengthen the jurisdiction of each traditional group in its own sphere of responsibility. The new state would fulfil a long-standing claim of conservative forces, namely to remove the burden of political accountability to democratic institutions and public approval. Experienced politicians, such as Sonnino and von Neurath, welcomed the gradual removal of liberal forms of accountability after the fascist acquisition of power.[12] Internal reform of the state along authoritarian lines was based on the principle that the traditional groups would use their institutional autonomy to reassert their total responsibility for political and practical decisions in their respective fields.[13] In other words, policy would originate with the relevant expert groups and would be sanctioned by the charismatic leader as a symbol of plebiscitary approval.

This form of institutional fusion was, of course, compatible neither with the fascist leaders' ambitions for absolute power nor with the two fascist parties' plans for conquering the state and organising society in a totalitarian pattern. Consequently, from the first days of the Mussolini and Hitler cabinets the foundations of a fierce political and institutional struggle were laid down. What was essentially at stake was the balance of power among the three contenders within the state and their respective share of influence on the decision-making process. What was not apparent to the traditional ruling groups when the 'fascist solution' was decided was that the appointment of Mussolini and Hitler increased, rather than curtailed, the influence of fascism upon the institutional debate over reform of government. It produced a polycratic system in which rival conceptions of state and policy making were bound to clash with totally unpredictable consequences. It is, therefore, essential to examine the process of institutional rearrangement in each country separately, first with regard to the role of the various non-fascist elite groups and, second, with regard to the function of the PNF and the NSDAP in the fascist systems.

Foreign policy decision making, fascist leaderships and traditional elites: the emergence of a leader-oriented system

Italy: an authoritarian, etatist model

Long-term features of the system and Mussolini's early foreign policy (1922–4)

In Italy, the foundation of the modern Italian state reproduced the main constitutional framework of the Kingdom of Sardinia, preserving the predominance of Piedmontese bureaucracies in the post-unification institutions. The House of Savoy retained its constitutional prerogatives, namely the supreme command of the armed forces and a special relation with the traditional diplomatic group. Such institutional links perpetuated a tradition of primary allegiance of diplomatic and military elites to the Crown. The links, however, became increasingly weaker as liberal reforms of the state promoted the bureaucratisation of these groups and curtailed the political influence of the King upon policy making. The initial intervening power of the Crown in key appointments gradually waned, as did the monopoly of influential positions by the Piedmontese elite. Especially during the Giolittian period, the dynastic loyalty of diplomats and military officials became a feature of formal, rather than political, significance.[14] This resulted in a slight erosion of the aristocratic character of these groups as their transformation into 'national' institutions dictated their opening to other groups within the Italian society. Although the influx of members from different social (bourgeoisie) and geographic (central and south Italy) groups was not dramatic, it did re-proportion the share of the Piedmontese aristocracy and its political influence.[15]

The institutional links, however, between the monarchy and the diplomatic–military elites were never severed, insulating them from bureaucratic reform which took place after the turn of the century in the context of a general effort to modernise the Italian system.[16] This had a debilitating effect upon the effectiveness of the armed forces, which was painfully manifested in their performance in the First World War. Although the trauma of the defeat at Caporetto instigated a process of limited internal reform and change of leadership in the armed forces, there was no attempt to reassess the structure of the armed forces or to enhance their wounded prestige.[17] Their weakening link with the House of Savoy and loss of their aristocratic character affected their social standing negatively.[18] Unlike the armies of most other European powers, the Regio Esercito was not regarded as a channel to an attractive professional career. It remained a minor actor in foreign policy decision making, geared to peacetime functions of guaranteeing public order and security.[19] It was deprived of major political influence on key decisions of Liberal Italy, including the Libyan campaign of 1912 and the decision to enter the war in 1915.[20] After the end of hostilities, pressure for fundamental reforms was stubbornly resisted by traditional hierarchies within the armed forces, on the basis of their institutional autonomy from public scrutiny.[21]

Italian diplomacy, on the other hand, retained a similar institutional dualism (a state bureaucracy with traditional links to the Crown) but was more firmly integrated into the foreign policy decision-making mechanism of the state. Although the Foreign Ministry was less immune to attempts at administrative reform, the composition of its officials and its traditional structure were not seriously altered until the end of the First World War, in spite of changes introduced after the fall of Crispi in 1896 and, later, during the Giolittian period.[22] Again, the relation of the diplomatic corps with the monarchy became more formal and symbolic, but public perceptions of diplomacy as an elitist body, bound to the traditional foreign policy objectives of the House of Savoy, became more widespread. After the war, the handling of peace negotiations exposed Italian diplomacy to criticism from both the moderate left and the 'new' nationalist right. Reformist socialists, like Leonida Bissolati, renounced previous territorial claims (hence, their castigation as *rinunciatori*) in favour of lasting peace and international reconciliation, and criticised Italian governments for their expansionist, confrontational foreign policy.[23] The latter, including the ANI (*Associazione Nazionalista Italiana*, Italian Nationalist Association), D'Annunzio and gradually Mussolini, demanded a more ambitious foreign policy along the lines of a great power rhetoric, and unleashed their frustration after 1918 at the handling of the peace negotiations and especially the loss of Fiume. For them, the moderate gains at Versailles revealed the ineffective, antiquated character of Italian diplomacy and underlined the need for modernisation, that is, becoming more accessible to new social groups in Italian society. This call was mainly intended to strengthen the representation of the 'new', radical trend of nationalism at the expense of the aristocratic, elitist tradition of the diplomatic corps.[24] However, they also attacked the *rinunciatori* of the left: the first punitive expedition of the *Fasci* against socialists (January 1919) targeted Bissolati and his supporters for their alleged 'betrayal' of national interests.[25]

Thus, in the aftermath of the First World War, the impression that Italian diplomacy had been humiliated at Versailles resulted in its declining social prestige. This could only partly be rectified through the influx of new nationalist-minded candidates and through limited institutional reform. The new organisational pattern introduced by Count Carlo Sforza in 1920 effected internal changes in the structures of diplomacy but retained the separation of diplomacy from the state by strengthening the power of the Permanent Secretary of the Foreign Ministry.[26] This position was regarded by traditional diplomats as an institutional safeguard, ensuring their distance from the state and their special allegiance to the Crown. The dualism between state and monarchy was not altered in the institutional make-up of the Foreign Ministry, and the appointment of Mussolini was not interpreted as a challenge to this special status.

The Duce's approach to government has been characterised as etatist, namely aiming to strengthen the legitimacy of the state and the role of its various institutions.[27] This was a pivotal expectation from the 'minimum consensus' programme but was also sponsored and systematised by the moderate nationalist wing of the PNF. Alfredo Rocco and Luigi Federzoni, who occupied key positions (Ministers of Justice and Interior, respectively) in the Fascist cabinets, promoted a model of 'integral' state which promised increased power and prestige for the *Capo del Governo* by reducing the role of the Crown to a formal constitutional supervision.[28] Faced with the problematic dualism between monarchy and state, Mussolini endorsed the etatist project primarily as a means to provide a point of positive integration for the whole Italian population and to consolidate his personal power base against both the King and the traditional elites. This implication was missed or ignored by the diplomatic and military leaderships, who welcomed this etatism as a way to foster their influence on the decision-making process while retaining their independence through their privileged relation with the monarchy. In this sense, agreement between the Fascist leadership and the traditional hierarchies upon the concept of a 'strong state' ensured co-operation in the short term, but stemmed from radically different perceptions of authoritarianism which were bound to clash in the longer term.[29]

Although Mussolini manifested his ambition to supervise foreign policy developments by keeping the portfolio for himself, an impression of continuity in the decision-making process was upheld after the March on Rome.[30] With the exception of Sforza and Frassati, the overwhelming majority of high-ranking diplomats remained in their positions, in anticipation of a quick return of Giolitti to the government.[31] Salvatore Contarini maintained his critical post as Permanent Secretary to the Foreign Ministry, acting as an institutional check upon Mussolini's possible intrusions in the diplomatic jurisdiction. In the armed forces, the promotion of General Diaz and Admiral di Revel to the Ministries of War and Navy respectively served both as a vote of confidence for the new regime and as a guarantee of the exclusive jurisdiction of the military elites in their internal affairs.[32] For the first time, such high-ranking officials were elevated to ministerial status, indicating their intention to keep Fascism at arm's length from both military policy and absolute power. In return for their support to the Fascist leadership throughout the 1920s, all liberal plans for structural reform in the armed forces were thwarted, leaving the military hierarchies in command of the administration of the Regio Esercito and the Regia Marina.[33]

The first real test, however, was only a few months away from the March on Rome. In August 1923, a car carrying a League of Nations' arbitration team working on the delineation of the Greek–Albanian border was ambushed in northern Greece. All the passengers, amongst them the Italian General Tellini, were murdered by the rebels. As the incident had happened inside Greece's national territory, the Italian government held Athens responsible for the murder and issued a strong ultimatum, demanding a massive compensation, the immediate arrest of the culprits and tangible signs of apology from the Greek government. When Athens responded by stressing the unfeasibility of the first two conditions and complaining at the severity of the terms, Mussolini ordered the immediate violent occupation of Corfu in retaliation to the murder of Tellini.[34] The subsequent crisis was a tangible manifestation of the new activist style of foreign policy which Fascist participation in government had injected into the decision-making process. Mussolini succeeded in catching the diplomatic elite off guard: many senior diplomats, including Contarini, were away from Rome at the day that the Duce ordered the occupation of Corfu.[35] Subsequently, Contarini, Salandra (as the Italian representative in Geneva) and Romano Avezzana (as ambassador in France) played a crucial role in diffusing the crisis, restraining Mussolini's excessive demands and saving Italy's prestige in international affairs.[36] Yet, the Fascist leader had manifested his determination to act independently from the advice of his political experts; even at the height of the crisis, he repeatedly rejected the moderating counsel of Romano Avezzana to accept a diplomatic compromise.[37]

Much about the incident which resulted in Tellini's assassination remains unclear. There is sufficient evidence to lend credence to the Greek government's argument that the perpetrators had in fact originated from Albania and had crossed the border illegally to ambush the car inside Greece and thus inculpate the Greek side. In sharp contrast to the ignorance of the diplomatic elite, the Navy leadership had been actively involved since July in the preparation of a plan for the occupation of Corfu in response to *expected* 'provocative acts' by Greece.[38] The Minister of Navy, di Revel, endorsed the plan in order to underline the navy's crucial role for national security and for the country's great power aspirations in the Mediterranean. He also seized the opportunity offered by the occupation of Corfu to claim priority for the Regia Marina in the allocation of resources and funds for rearmament.[39] After the occupation and bombardment of Corfu the case was referred to international arbitration; not, however, to the League of Nations, but to the Conference of the Ambassadors. The reason for this decision was that the French and British governments preferred to deal with the issue in the more flexible manner of traditional secret diplomacy and thus diffuse the crisis without setting in motion the rigid mechanism of collective security in accordance with the Covenant of the League. Neither Britain nor France wanted to impair their relations with the new Italian regime, the former because it regarded Mussolini as a good bulwark to native socialism, the latter as a token of gratitude for the Duce's diplomatic support during the Ruhr crisis earlier in 1923 (when France had violently moved into the region in retaliation for Germany's failure to meet her reparations payments). The negotiations were long and difficult, disrupted by Mussolini's refusal to reconsider the amount of financial compensation demanded from the Greek government and by his erratic oscillation between intransigence and reconciliation. In the end, a compromise formula was agreed which enabled the Fascist regime to get away with aggression and receive the full compensation it had initially demanded in return for the immediate withdrawal of the Italian forces from Corfu. The result was presented by Fascist propaganda as an unqualified victory of Italian diplomacy and a superlative affirmation of the new style of foreign policy making.

The 'decade of good behaviour' (1925–35)

The ensuing period until the Ethiopian war has misleadingly been described as the 'decade of good behaviour'.[40] The term is justifiable only on the level of appearance as, after the Corfu incident, the Fascist regime did not officially commit any act of aggression in foreign policy, seemingly accepting its responsibility to contribute to European peace and stability. Although Mussolini manipulated institutional gaps to successfully establish his right to co-decide with the traditional diplomatic and military groups, the latter retained a primary responsibility for the handling of foreign affairs. The Palazzo Chigi averted the possibility of a choreographic celebration in Rhodes after the Treaty of Lausanne reaffirmed Italy's right to possess the Dodecanese Islands.[41] Furthermore, Italy's participation in the negotiations for the Locarno Treaty was effectively promoted by the Palazzo Chigi, in spite of Mussolini's reservations.[42] Even the signing of the Kellogg–Briand pact was accepted by Mussolini, notwithstanding his subsequent mockery of the pact's main principle of renouncing violence in international relations.[43] The traditional strategy of Italian foreign policy – co-operation with the western Powers, negotiations for colonial concessions in Africa, friendly relations with Yugoslavia, stability in Europe through multilateral arrangements – appeared to have been restored after the Corfu crisis.

However, the term 'good behaviour' grossly understates the gradual consolidation of Mussolini's personal role in foreign policy decision-making within a framework of co-decision with the diplomatic and military hierarchies. It has been established that the Duce's plans for an invasion of Turkey were not resisted by either the Palazzo Chigi or the Ministry of War. The first plan was studied by the army leadership at the beginning of 1924 with discouraging conclusions, but the Matteotti crisis re-focused the attention of the Fascist regime on domestic policy and the plan was dropped.[44] The second plan was organised in 1926 but was subsequently abandoned when Turkey responded to rumours of invasion with partial mobilisations.[45] At the same time, Mussolini received the political backing of the Palazzo Chigi for a more energetic policy in the Balkans. The signing of pacts with Rumania, Turkey, Greece and the revisionist Hungary in the second half of the 1920s underlined a priority shared by both Mussolini and the traditional diplomats for Italian infiltration in the Balkan–Adriatic region, both in political and economic terms.[46]

The handling of the Italian policy towards Yugoslavia and Albania revealed the declining grip of the diplomatic hierarchy over Mussolini. The traditional attitude of rapprochement with Belgrade, initiated by Carlo Sforza and endorsed by Contarini, clashed with the *Duce*'s intention to isolate Yugoslavia (which he perceived as the most dangerous obstacle to his plans for penetration in the Balkans[47]) through the conclusion of pacts with the other Balkan states. Until 1926, Contarini managed to blend the two opposing principles. He promoted a friendly policy towards Yugoslavia during 1924, but also supported Mussolini's plans for the *pénétration pacifique* of Albania, culminating in the Treaty of 1925.[48] For him, however, Albania was a secondary asset and not an antidote to Yugoslavia, and he hastened to remove the military implications of the Italo–Albanian alliance from the text of the treaty.[49] This was his last major success in restraining Mussolini; Contarini resigned in March 1926, allowing the Duce a significantly larger share of political freedom and enabling him to rehearse a more aggressive anti-Yugoslav policy after 1926, even to the point of contemplating a military campaign in 1927.[50]

The departure of Contarini had both personal and institutional implications for foreign policy decision making. His resignation terminated an anomalous situation, in which Contarini – representing traditional diplomatic interests – was bracketed by Mussolini (Foreign Minister) and Dino Grandi (one of the *quadrumvires* and Under-Secretary since 1925).[51] Contarini's successor, Bordonaro, lacked the political will of his predecessor, thus allowing Grandi larger institutional space for action. With the departure of Bordonaro for London, the position of Secretary General remained deliberately vacant, a development which eliminated a symbolic 'diaphragm' of the Foreign Ministry's independence from state intervention and was greatly resented by traditional diplomats.[52] At the same time, the pace of administrative reform accelerated. The appointment of Grandi as Under-Secretary in 1925 constituted an attempt to expand Fascism both in mentality and personnel within the Palazzo Chigi.[53] Since 1927, membership of the PNF became a prerequisite for retaining or acquiring influential diplomatic posts.[54] This was a direct assault on the bureaucratic, non-partisan character of Italian diplomacy but was unsuccessfully resisted by the diplomats. Meanwhile, the departure of older officials served the regime's plan to further erode the elitist, conservative composition of the diplomatic corps. The law of 1927 prompted the influx of new personnel in the Foreign Ministry a year later, the majority of whom either came directly from Fascist organisations or were more sympathetic to the philosophy of the regime. The so-called *ventottisti* formed the first generation of new officials in the process of constructing a 'Fascist' ruling class.[55]

The promotion of Grandi to the position of Foreign Minister in 1929 accentuated the impression of 'fascistisation' in the Palazzo Chigi and increased fears that the influence of the traditional diplomatic elites would be curtailed. This was not the case, however, in the short term. The intrusion of the *ventottisti* was mainly confined to the lower echelons of bureaucracy, while key positions – such as the General Directors and major Ambassadors – remained firmly in the hands of experienced diplomats like Raffaele Guariglia (Director of European Affairs), Vincenzo Lojacono (Head of the Ministry's Personnel) and Augusto Di

Rosso (who was appointed as Italian plenipotentiary to the League of Nation in 1927). The ability of the traditional diplomatic elite to adapt to the changing administrative structures without compromising their political priorities resulted in the gradual absorption of this new generation of officials to the spirit of responsible diplomacy. Membership of the PNF remained a formal concession to the party's totalitarian pretensions, devoid of any political consequence. As for Grandi himself, in many ways he was an unlikely candidate for the 'fascistisation' of Italian diplomacy and foreign policy. A representative of the moderate, etatist wing of the PNF and an opponent of the notion of an omnipotent hyper-party, he remained sensitive to Mussolini's demands for great power diplomacy and was by no means averse to an activist foreign policy which would include the option of going to war.[56] Yet he also showed an increasing reliance upon the professional expertise of the traditional diplomats, as well as a sense of realism which eventually clashed with Mussolini's more adventurous foreign policy initiatives. His policy of *peso determinante* (determinant weight) aimed to coalesce the Duce's vision of Italy as the arbiter of the European system with the diplomats' cautious style and focus on stability.[57] After 1930, Grandi became increasingly alarmed at the rise of the NSDAP in Germany and sought a reorientation of Italian foreign policy, promoting an understanding with France, in accordance with the priorities of the conservative diplomats.[58] He also displayed a determination to make Italy play an active role in the League of Nations, especially regarding the issue of disarmament, which caused repeated frictions between the Minister and the *Capo del Governo*.[59] Grandi's constructive approach to the Hoover plan for a proportional reduction of armaments was strongly criticised by Mussolini and contributed to his dismissal in July 1932.[60] According to the Duce, Grandi had 'gone to bed' with the western democracies, making Italy a prisoner of the League of Nations.[61]

By the time of Grandi's departure for the Embassy in London the Foreign Ministry had successfully digested the wave of the *ventottisti* and retained its influence on the shaping of foreign policy. However, a more subtle and potentially erosive procedure had already been set in motion, namely Mussolini's personal, parallel diplomacy. This practice was a projection of the Duce's authoritarianism and preference for personal rule in the field of foreign affairs. In 1925, Contarini painfully realised his superior's liking for secret diplomacy when he was informed of the activities of a personal emissary of Mussolini, Alessandro Lessona, in the conclusion of the Italo–Albanian pact of 1925, unbeknownst even to the most senior officials of the Palazzo Chigi.[62] Secret meetings between Mussolini's emissaries and German radical nationalists were mainly handled by the *Duce* himself, by-passing both his diplomats in Rome and the Italian Embassy in Berlin, with the Ambassador De Bosdari, who resigned in protest in 1926, repeatedly complaining about his marginalisation.[63] Plans for Italian–German co-operation in a war against France were constantly on top of Mussolini's secret agenda.[64] At the same time that Grandi followed a rapprochement with the Quai d'Orsay, where Ethiopia was for the first time mentioned as possible compensation for Italian friendship by Laval, Mussolini not only rejected his minister's efforts in this direction but also continued to contradict Grandi's official policy towards Yugoslavia and the disarmament negotiations.[65] The secret backing of Macedonian and Croat terrorist–separatist organisations in Yugoslavia contradicted the efforts for a *détente* with Belgrade.[66] Grandi himself was definitely aware of such dealings, but he was increasingly kept uninformed about the revisionist initiatives of his leader in Yugoslavia, Hungary and Germany.[67] In a similar vein, while Grandi was discussing with Briand the prospects of a disarmament pact, Mussolini commented sarcastically that 'words are nice things, but guns...ships, aircraft and cannon are even nicer'.[68] In this sense, paradoxically, the dismissal of Grandi was a blow to the traditional diplomats' control over foreign policy. At the same time, the formal abolition of the position of Secretary General in 1932 was only a symbolic reflection of the loss of the Foreign Ministry's institutional independence and the beginning of its relegation, first to a consultative and finally to a purely functional status.[69]

In the armed forces, the progress of 'fascistisation' was equally unimpressive until 1935, but the co-operation with Mussolini proved less problematic. The army's support for the regime during the Matteoti crisis[70] was of crucial importance and ensured the continuation of the military elites' primary jurisdiction in their internal affairs. In 1925 a traditional figure of the old military establishment, Marshall Pietro Badoglio, was appointed Chief of General Staff and proved instrumental in providing support for the regime's plans against Turkey in 1926 and against Yugoslavia throughout the late 1920s and early 1930s.[71] The Regio Esercito's operational plan (defensive against France, offensive in the Balkans) endorsed Mussolini's anti-French and anti-Yugoslav orientation. Indoctrination and internal organisations were mainly left to the military elites with only some superficial attempts at 'fascistisation'.[72] Mussolini's only notable initiative concerned his eventual rejection in 1927 of an initial plan for the creation of a powerful General Staff under Badoglio.[73] This decision thwarted any attempt to centralise military control, co-ordinate resources and promote a more powerful role of the military leadership in the shaping of foreign policy. The implications of this rejection were not felt immediately, but this decision would weaken the armed forces' influence upon, and resistance to, future aggressive decisions of the regime (see Chapter 6). If in 1932 Badoglio could successfully counter the plan for an invasion of Ethiopia by invoking logistical problems, a similar attitude would soon prove to be ineffective to arrest Mussolini's growing expansionist ambitions.

The Ethiopian campaign (1935–6)

The background to the decision to attack Ethiopia (see also Chapter 4) serves as an all-round case study for the understanding of the gradual changes in foreign policy decision making. After Grandi's departure, Mussolini (Foreign Minister) and Suvich (Under-Secretary) accentuated tendencies that were introduced after 1929. Fulvio Suvich, a traditional diplomat and fervent exponent of an anti-German line in foreign policy, repeatedly echoed similar complaints to those of Grandi before 1932: monopoly of important decisions by the Duce, lack of information about diplomatic initiatives, and less and less consultation in the shaping of foreign policy.[74] The resistance of the traditional diplomats to Mussolini's growing inclination towards an alliance with Germany was epitomised in Suvich's numerous memoranda in the first months of 1936. The Under-Secretary described sacrificing the independence of Austria as a 'colossal error' of judgement, and did not fail to point out to his *Capo* that Italian foreign policy suffered from lack of direction, upholding Locarno on the one hand and encouraging Germany's revisionism on the other.[75] Yet, the traditional diplomats' disagreements were by-passed through the Duce's dependence on parallel diplomacy. This was a tendency that was reciprocated by Hitler's eagerness to sidestep the equally unenthusiastic leadership of the Wilhelmstrasse in his dealings with the Italian regime for a 'fascist' alliance. Hermann Göring became the link of the Nazi leadership with the PNF through direct contact with Balbo and the Head of the party's Foreign Affairs Office, Renzetti.[76] After 1936, with the consolidation of the Axis alliance, he was assigned special responsibility by Hitler for the handling of the German–Italian affairs.[77] At the same time, the natural retirement of the old guard of Italian diplomacy in the early 1930s facilitated a deep personnel change in the Foreign Ministry. A second massive influx of new officials, coupled with radical changes in most embassies and directories of the Ministry in 1932, irreversibly eroded the continuity of Italian diplomacy.[78] The Palazzo Chigi again digested this second major reorganisation and salvaged its traditional spirit of a semi-autonomous bureaucracy. Yet, the absence of strong personalities, willing to retain their professional independence from the regime's demands, and Mussolini's growing tendency to conduct a personal diplomacy, all pushed the Italian Foreign Ministry a further step down in terms of political influence.

The unilateral introduction of conscription in Germany offered some ephemeral breathing space to traditional diplomats. Mussolini was forced to contemplate an agreement with France and to contribute to the creation of the Stresa Front with Britain and France against Germany's aggression in the spring of 1935.[79] Even regarding the thoughts for a campaign against Ethiopia, the impression of British and French support or *disinteressement* for a war in Africa was a source of some consolation.[80] The Ethiopian plan presented for the diplomats a much lesser evil to Mussolini's tendency to meddle with European stability; it entailed the abandonment of the Croat plan,[81] opened the way for a co-operation with France against Germany, and deflected Mussolini's activism to the *politica periferica*.[82] The Duce could also count on some support from the armed forces and even from the Crown for a limited operation against Ethiopia, which was widely regarded as a legitimate target of Italian expansionism, especially after the trauma of Adowa in 1896.[83]

Yet, this initial atmosphere of consensus was quickly shattered. In the summer of 1935, opposition by the western powers became evident, highlighting the potentially destabilising effect of the plan for the European system and the Stresa front in particular.[84] Eventually, the Palazzo Chigi bowed to the inevitable, but at least played a role in delaying the action and in averting a total rift with Britain and France. The complexity and delicacy of the ensuing situation did convince Mussolini to consult his diplomatic experts, especially in legitimising the aggressive action in the League of Nations and in minimising the extent of sanctions.[85] However, the initiative now rested with the Duce. Even at the height of the Ethiopian crisis, when Mussolini announced his decision to accept a 'satellite' status for Austria in January 1936, the exhortations of Suvich to reconsider this *volte-face* proved fruitless.[86] From now on, the Foreign Ministry would have to fight hard to retain some consultative authority in the face of Mussolini's personal foreign policy.

For the armed forces, the period of preparation for the Ethiopian campaign was a crude awakening to the regime's tightening grip on military issues. Mussolini's decision to hand responsibility for preparing the campaign to the more 'Fascist' Ministry of Colonies headed by Emilio De Bono,[87] forced Badoglio and the military leadership to hasten their contribution to the planning process. However, the overruling of the initial decision for a limited campaign in favour of a full-scale war involving more than 300,000 men raised voices of protest in the armed forces about the logistical impossibility of such action. Repeated memoranda by Badoglio, asking for more time and resources,[88] underlined the growing gap between Mussolini's expansionist aspirations and the more limited objectives of the military leadership. A further blow was the appointment of De Bono – and not Badoglio – in command of the operation, which started in October 1935.[89] De Bono's subsequent failure to deliver a swift military breakthrough in Ethiopia was a god-sent gift for the military leadership, paving the way to his substitution by Badoglio and the successful occupation of Addis Ababa in May 1936.[90] Yet, the prestige for the victory was not reaped by the armed forces. Instead, the *Impero* was presented by the regime as a 'Fascist' achievement. Mussolini carefully orchestrated a celebration for Badoglio's return to Rome which deliberately fell short of a 'national hero's' reception. Everybody stepped in to claim a share of the glory: the Crown participated actively both in the build-up to victory and in the celebrations for the declaration of the *Impero*, and even the Catholic Church sanctioned the campaign as a *mission civilisatrice*.[91] Yet, it was the cult of the Duce that received the lion's share of the popularity boost, even for the attainment of such a traditional goal of Italian foreign policy.[92] It was a meaningful reminder of Mussolini's power that the King had to share the title of the First Marshal of the Empire with the Duce, in spite of Victor Emmanuel's token role as head of the armed forces.[93]

Towards war: 1936–9

The ensuing three years (1936–9) reaffirmed the signs of a proceeding *mussolinismo* in the Italian Fascist system. The appointment of Count Galeazzo Ciano as Foreign Minister again had both an institutional and a personal significance. Since Ciano had pioneered a strongly pro-German approach to foreign policy and had criticised Suvich for not exploiting the German card during the Ethiopian campaign,[94] his promotion reflected Mussolini's victory over the policy of equidistance, sponsored by the traditional diplomats in the Palazzo Chigi. The dismissal of Suvich was accompanied by a third wave of new personnel in the Foreign Ministry. This time, an already weakened conservative diplomatic elite was outnumbered and capitulated to the new influx.[95] At the same time, Ciano's pro-German attitude clashed with the traditional lines of diplomacy, thus enhancing the gap between the Fascist leadership and the experienced officials of the Foreign Ministry. Administrative reforms after 1936 emphasised the shift of political weight from the traditional diplomatic hierarchies to the *Gabinetto* of the Ministry,[96] a change which reflected the growing political character of foreign policy-making and the marginalisation of professional expertise.

However, Ciano himself had more far-reaching plans for the Foreign Ministry. Although largely unpopular amongst party leading figures and despised by the older generation of Fascist *gerarchi*, he was the most prominent figure of a new generation of Fascists that epitomised the growing self-confidence of the regime. More importantly, Ciano, who had risen to political prominence as Minister of Popular Culture in 1933, was very sensitive to the propagandistic dimensions and functions of foreign policy. In this sense, his approach to the handling of foreign affairs was fundamentally more populist than the cautious, professional techniques of traditional diplomacy.[97] His appointment to the Palazzo Chigi signified Mussolini's determination to accelerate the process of 'fascistisation', after the less satisfactory experiments with Grandi and Suvich, and to inject an air of unconventionality in policy making that was alien to the perceptions of the conservative diplomatic elites. As Foreign Minister, Ciano entertained a close personal relation with the Duce, a relation that enabled him to play a more active role in the shaping of Fascist foreign policy and to be kept informed of Mussolini's plans and oscillations. This type of close communication had hampered the two previous patterns in the Palazzo Chigi since 1929 and provided the basis for a more effective integration of the Foreign Ministry into the 'Fascist' state.[98]

At the same time, Ciano was widely regarded – and definitely regarded himself – as a strong candidate to succeed Mussolini, in spite of reactions from senior Fascists (most notably De Bono, Farinacci and De Vecchi) at the Grand Council meeting of 21 March 1939, when a list of possible candidates was discussed.[99] His privileged relation with the Duce and the latter's unconditional support enhanced his political legitimacy and enabled him to create a personal authoritarian rule in the Ministry. In many ways, the Palazzo Chigi under Ciano was a miniature of the authoritarian character of the regime itself. The Foreign Minister could claim the exclusive right of interpreting Mussolini's intentions, consulting his favourite diplomats whenever he deemed it necessary and marginalising those officials who were less compliant at his own discretion. In this sense, the gap between Minister and diplomats was systematically widened, removing the latter's political role as group and reducing them to a purely functional status. Mussolini's tendency to conduct an independent foreign policy found a perfect institutional medium in Ciano's personal diplomacy until the summer of 1939, where for the first time the identity between the two men was shattered with regard to the policy towards Germany. By that time, however, Ciano's identification with the *Capo del Governo* had deprived him of his political influence over the Duce. His strong opposition to Mussolini's pro-German policy failed to form an alternative concept of foreign policy which could seriously challenge the Duce's omnipotence in the handling of foreign affairs (see Chapter 6).

As for the armed forces, the presence of Badoglio as Chief of the General Staff until December 1940 kept up appearances of continuity in the military leadership. However, Mussolini's increasing capacity to control new appointments throughout the 1930s had, by 1936, promoted a new generation of officials in the three arms: Alberto Pariani as Chief of the Regio Esercito and Under-Secretary of War, Mario Roatta as Commander of the forces in Spain and Pariani's deputy in the army, Giuseppe Valle as Chief of the Aeronautica (1930–9), and Rodolfo Graziani as Commander of troops in Libya and East Africa. This group of officials appeared more accommodating to the regime's demands and less willing to resist the propagandistic use of the armed forces by Mussolini. While the old Badoglian group maintained the traditional line of avoiding a conflict with Britain, the new Chief of the Army Staff Pariani drafted an operational plan in December 1937, based on the assumption of a German–Italian alliance against the western powers.[100] Success in Ethiopia nurtured a misplaced optimism about the armed forces' capabilities that even the setbacks in Spain could not overshadow. While Badoglio and, later in 1940–1, Graziani (by then Governor of Libya) voiced their concerns about the over-ambitious plans for military action, Mussolini was in a position to overrule the military experts and use the armed forces as a functional device of his foreign policy.

The Spanish Civil War exposed all the above developments. Unlike Ethiopia, Spain did not feature in any plan or traditional ambition of Italian foreign policy, except as a possible option in Mussolini's vision of Mediterranean domination. On logistical grounds, the military leadership opposed participation, pressing instead for some time of peace to recover from the Ethiopian campaign and to improve the fighting capability of the armed forces.[101] Ciano, however, ignored the cautious counsel of traditional diplomats and sponsored the idea of active military involvement with an enthusiasm that boosted Mussolini's Mediterranean ambitions.[102] Once the decision for limited participation had been made, everybody stepped in to prove themselves worthy

76

of their leader's trust. The issue was discussed summarily in the Grand Council and elicited unanimous approval. General Roatta, head of the SIM (*Servizio Informazioni Militare*, the intelligence service) played an important role in stepping up the pace of Italian intervention after December 1936 and organised the operations in Guadalajara and the air raids on Spanish cities.[103] As for Ciano, he showed a determination to make the Spanish Civil War a success not only for Italy's military intervention but also for a 'fascist' co-ordination. In his visit to Germany in October 1936, he pressed for closer co-operation between Italy and Germany, both in military and diplomatic terms.[104] The joint premature recognition of the Burgos government by the two regimes defied both military problems (defeat at Guadalajara, slow progress of Nationalist forces) and diplomatic advice, indicating the triumph of the Mussolini–Ciano line of activist foreign policy.[105]

The final stage in the relegation of military and diplomatic groups to a functional role with no serious political influence came with the consolidation of the Axis alliance. This marked a clear departure from traditional concepts of co-operation with Britain-France or 'equidistance' between western powers and Germany, and its warlike implications alarmed the military leadership and many traditional diplomats.[106] Yet, this opposition did not lead to a last ditch attempt to reverse this far-reaching reorientation of Italian foreign policy. Collective decision making had been substituted by the intuitive personal diplomacy of Mussolini and Ciano, who alone negotiated the military alliance with Germany, who alone closed the doors to British overtures in January 1939, and who alone acquiesced in the military treaty of the Axis alliance (known as the Pact of Steel; see also Chapter 5) in May 1939, while deliberately keeping ambassadors and diplomats uninformed.[107] The King found out about this pact after it had been signed,[108] but the fact that, although he did not formally ratify it, this was no prerequisite for the pact's validity shows the Crown's narrow margins of resistance and its waning institutional power of intervention. The Cavallero Memorandum, which Mussolini submitted to Hitler only days after the signing of the Pact of Steel, offered some assurances to the military leadership that the conflict might not be imminent. In it, the Duce insisted on the need for careful preparation for a future war after a respite of at least three years. Yet, even these additional *caveats* did not suffice to alleviate the unpopularity of the alliance amongst high-ranking military officials.[109] No effort was made by the leadership of the Regio Esercito to promote joint military or political talks in the context of the Axis. Even when Ciano reverted to an anti-German line after his meetings with the German Foreign Minister von Ribbentrop and Hitler in August 1939, no concerted action could be taken by diplomatic and military elites to ensure a permanent neutrality. In spite of private objections by prominent Fascist figures (such as Bottai and Grandi) to formalising the Axis alliance with the Pact of Steel,[110] there was no expressed opposition in the Grand Council or in the Council of Ministers meetings at the end of May.[111] Only Ciano spoke directly to a wavering Mussolini on a number of occasions during the autumn and winter of 1939, but even his special relation to the Duce did not suffice to avert Italy's entry into the war in the long run (see Chapter 6).

Germany: a 'parallel' state

Long-term features of the German system and Hitler's 'divide and rule' technique (1933–5)

In Germany, the traditional framework of foreign policy decision making presented a number of significant differences to the Italian model. First of all, the particular form of state that was entrusted to the Nazi executive in January 1933 had been regarded as a 'liberal' experiment, and one stigmatised by the events of 1918.[112] The obvious lack of legitimacy, which had plagued the Weimar Republic from the moment of its foundation but reached a terminal point in 1930–3, convinced the various traditional elite groups that the widespread need for change could not be promoted through some sort of identification with the present state, as was the case in Italy. Instead, the search for a new institutional arrangement entailed a clear break with the Weimar experience and a move towards an authoritarian solution with 'caesarist' features, in which the autonomy and primacy of the traditional elite groups would be reinstated and enhanced.

In the field of foreign policy making, the Weimar Republic attempted but failed to integrate the military, diplomatic and economic aspects of decision making into a co-ordinated and more transparent mechanism of state policy. Increasingly after 1930, the collapse of liberal institutions allowed the groups involved in these areas of decision making a much wider margin for manoeuvre and resulted in the strengthening of their direct political links to President Hindenburg. This reverted the system to a situation reminiscent of the pre-1918 period, in which the elite groups drew their legitimacy from their identification with the Head of State (then the Hohenzollern Kaiser, now the 'hero' of the First World War, Field-Marshal Hindenburg). The presidential dictatorship of the post-1930 period recreated an institutional gap between high politics and the parliamentary party system, a gap which the traditional military and diplomatic elites hastened to exploit in order to safeguard their primary role and autonomy in an authoritarian system.

The second major difference in Germany was the *de facto* traditional institutional strength and prestige of the armed forces and the diplomatic corps.[113] Unlike in Italy, the Reichswehr was regarded as a pillar of the German state. The militarist structures of the Prussian system survived to a great extent in the Bismarckian and Wilhelminian states, embodied in the role of the Emperor as both the head of state and supreme commander of the armed forces.[114] Nor in the Weimar years did this link seem to fade, given the pluralism of the system and the emphasis on the power of the Reichstag as the main pillar of the system. After the failed experiments of General von Seeckt with active revisionism in alliance with the Soviet Union in the early 1920s, the new Defence Minister, Groener, promoted a new concept of military policy, based on the principles of disarmament, peaceful revisionism and co-operation with the Western Powers.[115] In this sense, he attempted to integrate the armed forces into the Republican political framework, aligning military to diplomatic policy and subjecting the autonomy of the Reichswehr to the control of the state. This was a novel arrangement for the traditionally militaristic spirit of the German armed forces and was greatly resented by the majority of conservative officers, who kept flirting with ideas of war against Poland and France, rejecting in principle the 'inaction' of Weimar foreign policy. Groener's dogma could be upheld so long as the Republic enjoyed a minimum of political stability and an agreement of disarmament in the Geneva negotiations appeared a plausible prospect.[116] When both these conditions were thwarted by the early 1930s, the Reichswehr leadership distanced itself from the Republic's concept of revisionism and reverted to a more aggressive agenda based on the unilateral repudiation of the Versailles Treaty and emphasis on speedy rearmament.[117] In spite of its vastly reduced fighting power after 1918, the Reichswehr leadership retained its privileged political position in the foreign policy decision-making process and the power to influence decisions, not only in its immediate jurisdiction but also in general political and economic issues. The anomalous situation of the post-1930 period offered opportunities to people like von Schleicher to express their political ambitions with the consent of the Presidency, thus enabling the Reichswehr leadership to play a decisive role both in the 1930–3 period, and in the compromise that brought Hitler to power in January 1933.[118]

With regard to the diplomatic elite of the Wilhelmstrasse, the Weimar Republic was more of an interlude which did not affect the continuity of the Foreign Office's structures and attitudes. The Wilhelmstrasse bureaucracy drew its legitimacy not from any special constitutional link to the Head of State, as in Italy, but from its permanent character as a professional, non-partisan elite possessing an indisputable and unique expertise in foreign policy making. This identification with the permanent structure of the German state insulated the Foreign Office from the 'disgrace' of the Versailles Treaty which was almost exclusively debited to the Weimar politicians. Throughout the years of the Republic, the Wilhelmstrasse retained its traditional approach to foreign policy as a matter of professional, rather than public, jurisdiction. It also preserved its aristocratic composition in spite of the influx of new personnel in the early 1920s, mainly of bourgeois background. By the late 1920s the Wilhelmstrasse had successfully digested the newcomers, with the higher echelons of the Foreign Office remaining firmly in the hands of traditional officials.[119] The early attempts of the Republic to democratise the structures of German diplomacy had been abandoned in the face of more pressing problems for the very survival of the Republic. Although the diplomatic elite appeared to work together with Stresemann and Groener for a deal regarding disarmament, the commitment of the diplomats to the Republic's concept of peaceful revision was both half-hearted and ephemeral.[120] Long before Hitler came to power, the Wilhelm-strasse leadership, including the conservative Foreign Minister von Neurath, resented the burden of political accountability and the relative loss of political autonomy that this entailed.[121] Instead, they were drawn to the platform of 'minimum consensus', based on rearmament, use of military threat to achieve a unilateral revision of the Versailles Treaty, and an authoritarian system which could restore their primary influence upon foreign policy decision making.

The third major difference between Germany and Italy in the interwar period stemmed from the dissimilar stage of economic development experienced by each country. In spite of a plethora of surviving non-modern aspects in the German state, the Weimar Republic was an advanced capitalist society. This meant that, albeit not a great power in military terms after 1918, Germany was still a potential great power in the political and economic sense of the word. In this sense, the economic capacity of the system for supporting rearmament was significantly higher than in Italy, thus underlining the importance of industrial elites in the foreign policy decision-making process. The support of heavy industry for an authoritarian system after 1930 contributed significantly to the endorsement of the 'fascist solution'. Apart from subsidising to an extent the NSDAP before 1933, sectors of the industrial elite played a much more crucial political role in the events leading to the *Machtübernahme*, through their rejection of the policies of Brüning and Schleicher, their acquiescence in the participation of the NSDAP in the government and their importance for the success of the rearmament programme sponsored by the Reichswehr and guaranteed by Hitler.[122] Unlike in Italy, where foreign policy was traditionally based on great power diplomacy, prestige and a moderate use of the threat of force, the return of German foreign policy to concepts of unilateral revisionism did not rule out the actual use of force and thus established industry as a pivotal factor in rebuilding the country's military strength.

All these different factors dictated a fundamentally different approach to establishing a fascist state in Germany. For the Nazi leadership, an etatist model was neither available nor desirable as an option. For a start, the charismatic nature of Hitler's style of leadership, with its instinctive, mythical basis and its unsystematic approach to policy making could hardly be accommodated into the highly bureaucratised, rational structures of state administration.[123] This discrepancy became obvious from the first moment with the lapse of the Reich cabinet, but reached a terminal point by 1938, when access to Hitler became totally unreliable, in defiance of any form of government protocol and procedure.[124] Furthermore, Hitler's conception of the state as an ancillary – and not pivotal, as in Italy – institution of the Nazi system ruled out an identification between the state and the Nazi movement.[125] His distrust of the elitist, pragmatic mentality of the state bureaucracies led him into a different state model, combining the totalitarian representation of the *Volk* by the party, the centrality of the armed forces for promoting national interest, and the charismatic authority of the leader as the only source of legitimacy in the system.

In this sense, the consolidation of Nazi power entailed an institutional challenge to the autonomy and legitimacy of the state apparatus, but not the conquest of the state itself. It was rather operating on the basis of a 'parallel state', using duplication of state functions by party agencies as a political laboratory for the production of new institutions to replace the existing state.

This 'divide and rule' has been an item of heated historiographical dispute, as it is not entirely clear whether it was pursued intentionally by Hitler or resulted from administrative chaos and incompetence.[126] In the field of diplomacy, the Nazi leadership accepted Hindenburg's condition of keeping Neurath as Foreign Minister and respecting the institutional autonomy of the Wilhelmstrasse. From the first moment, however, Hitler actively encouraged the creation of party agencies which claimed expertise in certain fields of foreign policy. The Aussenpolitisches Amt was established to institutionalise Rosenberg's aspirations to become the guru of Nazi foreign policy.[127] In a similar fashion, Joachim von Ribbentrop's Dienststelle gave expression to its founder's alternative concepts of foreign policy making and became the vehicle for the consolidation of his personal influence over Hitler and the handling of foreign affairs.[128] The creation of the Auslandsorganisation (AO) created a parallel channel of communication between party officials and Nazi organisations or sympathisers abroad, providing an alternative source of information about international political developments.[129] Finally, Hitler developed a preference similar to Mussolini's for personal diplomacy, using von Papen for Austria, Göring for dealings with Italy, Spain (economic issues) and the Nazi Party in Danzig, and later Ribbentrop for secret negotiations with London and the Sudeten Party in Czechoslovakia.[130]

The operation of this multiple parallel mechanism reflects a deliberate strategy to undermine the authority of the Wilhelmstrasse, and this is attested to by Hitler's increasing reliance on the activities and advice of these agencies and special envoys at the expense of the diplomatic bureaucracy. Yet, the planning of this parallel mechanism was far from rational or successful. Rosenberg's disastrous trip to London in May 1933 reduced the influence of the APA (Aussenpolitisches Amt) to insignificant levels and led to a drastic cut in its funding by the party budget.[131] Ribbentrop's initiatives as Ambassador in Britain (1936–8) caused frequent disappointment both to the Nazi leadership and to himself for the failure to impress upon the British the need for a German–British alliance.[132] At the same time, party agencies and affiliated organisations operating abroad (National Socialist organisations in Danzig, Sudetenland and Austria) could often evade the supervision not only of the official German authorities but also of the Nazi leadership itself. As a result, the anarchic expansion of party activities caused a dual jurisdictional battle; between the party and the Wilhelmstrasse, and between the various party stars and agencies themselves. Rosenberg was happy to side even with Neurath against the prospect of Ribbentrop's appointment as State Secretary to the Foreign Ministry in 1937, while Joseph Goebbels's Propaganda Ministry kept antagonising Ribbentrop's Foreign Office after 1938 over control of the flow of information from and to foreign countries.[133] Hitler permitted the mushrooming of agencies but avoided unequivocal commitments to any particular one, because he was distrustful of any form of bureaucratisation of his charismatic power. In the end, his dealings regarding policy making remained confined to the level of personal relations, but his allegiance to Rosenberg initially, then to Neurath, Ribbentrop and finally to Himmler did not reflect an endorsement of the institutions each of them headed. The result was an institutional chaos, with agencies and bureaucracies competing to provide the best interpretation of Hitler's vague intentions. Such an uncoordinated polycratic system did strengthen the Führer's institutional role as supreme arbiter but did very little to formulate an alternative Nazi foreign policy mechanism which could carry out policies effectively.[134]

With regard to the armed forces, their centrality in the Nazi concept of state dictated a very different approach. The crucial significance of rearmament for Nazi expansionist plans, and the acknowledgement that technical expertise and infrastructure were exclusive privileges of the armed forces, led to a close co-operation and consensus between the Nazi Party and the Reichswehr leaderships which lasted until 1937. Agreement on a more active revisionism eliminated frictions and left a large political space for the Reichswehr leaders to formulate military policy, reaping the benefits of the regime's priority of funding for rearmament. There were only two potential challenges to the primary authority of the armed forces. The first, the SA, became a bone of contention in early 1934, but Hitler's growing irritation with Röhm's 'revolutionary' rhetoric made the SA purge of June 1934 a less magnanimous concession to Reichswehr demands for exclusive responsibility in military issues.[135] The second challenge, the SS (Schutzstaffeln), represented a less obvious danger initially, officially confined to the role of safeguarding domestic order. The Reichswehr's voluntary opt-out from domestic affairs in 1933 rendered such a cohabitation feasible, but the implicit ambitions of the SS to become an elite military force of Nazi Germany were initially missed by the traditional military leadership, thus allowing the SS space to flourish and eventually contest the authority of the army when the latter had lost most of its political authority.[136]

In many ways, the foreign policy initiatives of the Nazi regime between 1934 and 1936 were anticipated by the rationale of this military planning. The introduction of conscription in 1935 was regarded by the military leadership as a *sine qua non* for attaining the division figures set for the expansion of the army in 1933 and 1934 (see also Chapter 4).[137] Since the December 1933 rearmament programme, General Ludwig Beck, Chief of the General Staff since 1933, had spoken of the need to prioritise conscription in the context of a wider plan for the creation of a strong regular army against the prospect of a preventive war against Germany. Also, the remilitarisation of the Rhineland was presupposed both in Blomberg's plans for an effective defence policy against France and in Beck's March 1935 memorandum on the need to secure Germany's 'living space' against external attack.[138] There was agreement between the Nazi and the Reichswehr leaderships that these two steps should be prioritised and taken when the situation permitted it. However, identity of goals did not mean identity of strategies or planning. Even at this early stage, views about the timing of these actions diverged. Hitler had initially planned the introduction of conscription for the autumn of 1935, a mere six months earlier than the Reichswehr leadership's estimates of the optimal date from a military point of view.[139] Similarly, the sudden decision to remilitarise the Rhineland in March 1936 was the result of Hitler's astute opportunism, when he sensed that the Ethiopian crisis would impede the western Powers from actively opposing his unilateral violation of the Versailles Treaty. In fact, Hitler had no fixed thoughts regarding the timing of his major foreign policy initiatives; in the case of the Rhineland, he had not envisaged a favourable situation for remilitarisation before 1937 but seized opportunities offered by unforeseen international developments to promote a crucial goal of German revisionism much earlier and in the defiant, uncompromising style of a great power.[140] However, the failure of the armed forces' leadership to curtail the increasing autonomy of the Führer in deciding when and how to implement commonly agreed policies undermined its political role in the foreign policy decision-making process in the long term.

The challenge to the political influence of the Wilhelmstrasse upon foreign policy decision making was less subtle and more corrosive, originating in the Nazi leadership's deep-seated antipathy towards the diplomatic corps.[141] Hitler maintained a pattern of smooth co-operation with Neurath personally and allowed him ample political space to deal with the pressing issues of German foreign policy, especially the negotiations for disarmament at Geneva.[142] In spite of his previous efforts to achieve equality of status for Germany and a disarmament agreement amongst the Great Powers, Neurath endorsed Blomberg's argument in favour of withdrawal and played a crucial role in preparing Germany's simultaneous withdrawal from the League of Nations.[143] However, this initial reliance on the professional expertise of Neurath did not entail an overall respect for the political autonomy of the Wilhelmstrasse in general. In Hitler's non-bureaucratic style of policy making, there was space for Neurath, partly because the latter was a personal choice of Hindenburg and partly because the Führer could rely on Neurath's accommodating attitude in the face of the lack of a reliable party candidate for the effective handling of foreign affairs. In the same way that the armed forces aspired to use Hitler as a legitimising factor for their unilateral initiatives on rearmament and revisionism, Hitler himself acknowledged Neurath's potential to reassure international public opinion about Germany's increasing activism in foreign affairs. Indeed, Neurath met these expectations during both the conscription and the Rhineland crises, providing accurate predictions about the reluctance or inability of the Western powers to react and minimising the negative impact of German defiance of international agreements.[144]

The assault, however, on the political autonomy of the Foreign Office by the Nazi leadership started soon afterwards and it did not spare Neurath. Even before Hindenburg's death there were alarming indications of Hitler's tendency to ignore not only the reports of the diplomats but even the counsel of his Foreign Minister. In January 1934 he concluded a Non-Aggression Pact with Poland, a move which appalled Neurath and caused shock to the traditional diplomats as it seemed to thwart the utmost goal of German revisionism, the return of the Polish Corridor to the Reich (see Chapter 4). The July 1934 coup in Vienna, during which the Austrian Nazis attempted to overthrow the Dollfuss regime through a military insurrection, was another alarming indication of the uncontrolled meddling of Nazi groups in foreign policy decision-making. Although Neurath was under the impression that he had committed Hitler to a peaceful course of action towards Austria, plans for a military coup against Dollfuss were secretly promoted by the Austrian National Socialist party, headed by Theo Habicht, with the agreement of the Führer. The Foreign Office was aware of the subversive activities of party members in Austria, but Neurath seemed to have overestimated both the firmness of Hitler's conversion to a peaceful 'evolutionary' solution of the Austria problem and his capacity to control a chaotic party mechanism in Germany and abroad.[145] Hitler, led by the Austrian Nazi leadership to believe that the co-operation of the Austrian armed forces was guaranteed, allowed Habicht complete freedom of action without any consultation with his diplomatic advisors. The results were disastrous: the Austrian Chancellor was assassinated but the plans to seize power were thwarted by the non-co-operation of the Austrian army.[146] The brutality of the conspirators shocked international public opinion and resulted in a major diplomatic blow to the prestige of the Nazi regime. In the aftermath of the crisis, the Wilhelmstrasse did its best to alleviate the damaging diplomatic consequences of the putsch; but the event was an alarming indication of the Nazi leadership's ambitions to challenge the Foreign Office's monopoly in foreign policy decision making.

The introduction of conscription resulted from another sudden decision made by Hitler, in the company not of Blomberg or Neurath, but of Ribbentrop (then Hitler's special advisor on foreign affairs), and was then announced to the Defence and Foreign Ministers as a *fait accompli*. As with the case of Blomberg, Neurath's reservations concerned the timing and the danger of negative repercussions, but he accepted the inevitable and worked conscientiously to minimise the damage to German relations with the western powers. However, he also awoke to the realisation that his initial underestimation of Ribbentrop's potential was imprudent. Neurath had shown a certain willingness to establish constructive relations with the Nazi elites; in 1933, he informed the Wilhelmstrasse officials that they could join the party if they so wished. Yet, on a personal basis, Ribbentrop's consolidation through the establishment of his Dienststelle (summer 1934) and his increasing tendency to assume responsibilities without informing the Foreign Office was a step too far.[147] From 1935 onwards, Neurath used his privilege of having regular access to Hitler in order, first, to oppose Ribbentrop's ambitions to replace Bülow as State Secretary to the Foreign Ministry and, second, to make Ribbentrop's actions contingent upon the prior approval of the Wilhelmstrasse. He was fighting a losing battle, though. Ribbentrop's successful conclusion of the British–German Naval Agreement in the summer of 1935 enhanced his political leverage in the eyes of Hitler.[148] At the same time, Neurath's allies in the Foreign Office were becoming more scarce, not because of any extensive Nazification of German diplomatic and administrative personnel (the Wilhelmstrasse was still regarded by the party as a 'nest of conspirators' with only limited National Socialist representation amongst its ranks), but due to a natural combination of retirement and death. Filling the vacancies proved a formidable task for Neurath, because from 1935 Hitler had made personnel appointments subject to the approval of the Politische Organisation of the party.[149]

Neurath, however, could still claim victories. The decision to remilitarise the Rhineland unilaterally in early March 1936 (see Chapter 4) contradicted the Foreign Minister's previous policy of a negotiated solution, but at least Neurath was present at the conference at which the decision was taken.[150] Again, he did not ultimately oppose the move (as Blomberg and Beck did, fearing a military confrontation with France at the most critical stage for German rearmament[151]), convinced that no danger of military reaction existed at the time of the Ethiopian crisis.[152] He was definitely happy to be the Foreign Minister who had freed Germany from all the onerous restrictions of the Versailles Treaty. A few months later, the death of Bülow refuelled the bitter struggle between Neurath and Ribbentrop, as the latter restated his claim for the post of the State Secretary. Neurath was still in a position to carry the day with Hitler and avert the prospect of Ribbentrop's appointment even by threatening to resign.[153] His eventual choice, his son-in-law von Mackensen, came as a relief to the traditional diplomats but also underlined the scarcity of Neurath's available choices for filling the vacant places and the increasing influence of factors outside the Wilhelmstrasse upon the personnel policy of the Foreign Office.

Growing autonomy and self-confidence (1936–7)

Thus we arrive at the Spanish Civil War. The background to Germany's involvement exposed the extent to which gradual, subtle changes in the foreign policy decision-making process in the previous three years had resulted in a cumulative strengthening of Hitler's personal power at the expense of the traditional elite groups. In July 1936, a group of nationalist Generals organised a coup in the Spanish territories of Morocco against the Republican coalition which had won a majority in the elections earlier in that year. The conspirators soon crossed Gibraltar into mainland Spain and, under the leadership of General Francisco Franco, co-ordinated the effort to overthrow the republican regime and seize power. The crucial role of the NSDAP's Auslandsorganisation (AO) in dealing with both diplomatic and military issues of Germany's intervention has been established by the historiography on the Spanish Civil

War,[154] as has Göring's personal influence and pressure to intervene in order to benefit from Spain's rich raw material resources.[155] From the beginning, Neurath vehemently opposed any degree of involvement in the war or co-ordination with Italy for joint diplomatic–military action, while Ribbentrop pressed Hitler to accept Franco's and the AO's suggestions for a large-scale military intervention.[156] In this chaos of conflicting jurisdictions and policies, the role of Hitler as the ultimate initiator of policy was *de facto* acknowledged. Access to him became the most crucial and effective method of influencing policy making. The AO envoys succeeded in explaining their case in favour of military involvement at a meeting with Hitler at Bayreuth, with both the Minister of Aviation Göring and the Chief of Propaganda Goebbels endorsing the expediency of this course of action.[157] Obviously, this meant that the Foreign Office had lost not just its political primacy in foreign affairs but also the privilege of co-decision.

Neurath's relative success in curtailing the extent of German involvement in Spain and in thwarting a full-scale military intervention in retaliation for the bombing of the German warship *Leipzig* later in 1936 (against the initial wishes of the Nazi leadership for large-scale military retaliation[158]) should be placed in perspective. In this case, Neurath had failed to initiate or pursue a policy compatible with the objectives of German traditional diplomacy. He was excluded from consultations and only managed to intervene belatedly to alter practicalities, not the framework of the policy itself. His success owed almost everything to his personal relationship to Hitler and the considerable access to him which he still enjoyed; it did not reflect acceptance of any procedural obligation on Hitler's part to consult or inform the Foreign Office. So long as Neurath had Hitler's ear, the Foreign Office could exercise some influence on foreign policy decision making through him. If Neurath's access was curtailed by Hitler himself, then the whole German diplomatic service would be automatically cut off from decision making.

Subsequent developments confirmed the precarious position of both diplomatic and military elites, and their gradual relegation to a near-functional institutional status. For the armed forces' leadership, the gathering pace of Nazi aggression and independence in foreign policy making was a cause for alarm but did not result in any serious discussion of the long-term implications of the increasing rearmament programme. The Wehrmacht leadership was so absorbed in the practicalities of meeting increased targets of mobilisation in a shorter time-scale that they paid little attention to the goals that such a formidable military machine could serve.[159] There was still a high degree of agreement on the priorities of German foreign policy: Austria and Czechoslovakia were obvious targets, both in irredentist terms and for their importance in solving the labour and raw materials problems of German rearmament.[160] Yet, the implications of the offensive nature of military planning, entailing a higher risk of confrontation with Britain, were not taken at face value by the military leadership until the end of 1937. War as an option was not rejected altogether, but General Ludwig Beck understood it in a fundamentally different way; war would be only against France, possibly over Czechoslovakia which was a legitimate target of German expansion, but not before 1943, when the targets of the August 1936 programme of rearmament would have been attained.[161]

If the armed forces' leadership could still entertain an illusion of control over decision making, the Foreign Office had by 1937 given up most of its hopes. Hitler's tendency to bypass the Wilhelmstrasse increased, as did his reliance on the advice mainly of Ribbentrop and Göring. By implication, Neurath's access to the Nazi leadership was gradually curtailed, leading to the marginalisation of the institutional position of the whole Wilhelmstrasse. The 1936 German–Austrian Gentlemen's Agreement was signed without even consulting the Foreign Office, while Ribbentrop elicited Hitler's permission to negotiate a tripartite agreement with Italy and Japan without the prior knowledge and against the wishes of Neurath, who dreaded the anti-British implications of such a pact.[162] The prospect of concluding such a pact, and the consolidation of the Axis alliance, convinced not only Neurath but also other prominent non-Nazi figures of the government – such as the Minister of Economics, Hjalmar Schacht, who resigned in the autumn of 1937 – that the aggressive tone of Nazi foreign policy marked a qualitative departure from traditional principles and entailed a high risk of conflict with the western powers. The increasing fatalism with which the Foreign Minister viewed these developments, his frequent resignations and decreasing willingness to intervene as he had done in the past, were symptomatic of an awareness that political influence had eluded the Wilhelmstrasse. The Foreign Office might have succeeded in insulating its ranks from the intrusion of undesired figures (Ribbentrop, for example) until 1938, but the parasitic Nazi system allowed ample political space for Ribbentrop, Göring and Goebbels to use their direct access to Hitler in order to eclipse the political role of the traditional diplomatic group in the decision-making process.

In this sense, the Hossbach conference, which Hitler himself arranged in November 1937 in order to offer an exposition of his immediate foreign policy plans to leading military–diplomatic figures of the Nazi regime, had a limited importance as an overall programmatic statement, but was a catalyst in reflecting deep changes in the way foreign policy decisions were taken in the Nazi system, and in alluding to even more radical intentions for the near future. The prioritisation of Austria and Czechoslovakia as targets of Nazi expansion did not come as a real shock to the participants (Neurath, the Defence Minister Werner von Blomberg, the Chief of the Army Staff Werner von Fritsch, the Chief of Navy Admiral Erich Raeder, and Göring), because the former was regarded as a legitimate objective of German irredentism and the latter had figured prominently in the military planning of the Wehrmacht for German defence. Also, there was a seemingly reassuring commitment by Hitler to a significantly later date; optimal conditions for actions were expected in 1943. The difference lay in the choice of means and strategy. Instead of an evolutionary approach to *Anschluss* (which had been adopted in the aftermath of the abortive Vienna putsch of July 1934) and a defensive plan against a possible attack by France and/or Czechoslovakia, Hitler's exposition was underpinned by the doctrine of offensive action, focusing on the need to exploit a 'favourable situation which would not occur again' in terms of Germany's military advantage. The strategic prerequisites for this favourable solution were fairly absurd: civil war in France or a French–British–Italian war in the Mediterranean as a result of tension in Spain. However, the other importance of Hitler's account at the Hossbach conference regarded his inclusion of Britain in the camp of Germany's possible enemies, along with France. Here, the influence of Ribbentrop's anti-British rhetoric upon Hitler's medium-term strategy becomes evident; in particular, the allusions to a parallel action by Japan in the Far East and by Italy in the Mediterranean against British colonies echoed Ribbentrop's ongoing efforts for a tripartite alliance against the interests of the British empire (see also Chapter 4).[163]

The increased danger of a conflict with Britain alarmed the traditional military and diplomatic leaderships. Both Blomberg and Fritsch expressed strong reservations during the conference, while Neurath was mobilised after the discussion to seek the co-operation of the military in arresting Hitler's aggressive intentions.[164] However, the extent of reaction by the traditional military and diplomatic elites after the Hossbach conference can only partly be explained by these programmatic divergences. What mainly raised the stakes of opposition was the realisation that foreign policy decisions, even of such grave importance, were now taken by Hitler without even prior consultation with the Wehrmacht leadership or the diplomats about the practical aspects or the feasibility of his plans. Neurath had been more accustomed to this sort of marginalisation since 1936; but Fritsch, for example, who had struggled to check the influence of the Nazi party over the army, awoke to the realisation that rearmament and offensive military planning had reduced policy options to either war in the near future or peace by actively opposing Hitler's strategy.[165] The defiant manner in which the Führer drafted and announced his plans, 'rejecting the idea of discussion before the wider circle of the Reich cabinet', amounted to a *de facto* relegation of the military and diplomatic leaderships to the role of simply executing his programme. This places the function of the Hossbach conference in a different perspective. Hitler did not intend the discussion to be interactive; his intentions regarding Austria and Czechoslovakia were fixed, and co-decision was not part of his style of leadership. Instead, he used the occasion to test the participants' willingness to accept their institutional subordination to his primary, *exclusive* jurisdiction and to act as apolitical functionaries of a leader-oriented system.

By the end of 1937, the die had been cast. The hostile reaction of the conservative elite to the Nazi plans to raise the stakes of German foreign policy was not missed by Hitler and his immediate entourage. In this sense, the dismissal of Fritsch, Blomberg and Neurath was simply a matter of time and careful presentation. Rumours about General Fritsch's alleged homosexual inclinations, based on a report of the secret police, offered an excellent pretext for action. That such an accusation had been disproved (the report referred to another Fritsch) did not stop Hitler and Göring from exploiting it in order to achieve General Fritsch's discrediting and eventual dismissal. At the same time, von Blomberg's marriage with a former prostitute became the catalyst for his own downfall, despite the fact that the Nazi leadership had been aware of the matter long before January 1938 (and, in fact, Göring had disingenuously assured the General that no negative implications would result from it).[166] As in the aftermath of the 'Night of the Long Knives' in June 1934, Hitler appealed to the population's common sense of 'morality' to legitimise a ruthless and illegal political coup. Without doubt, the purge of the remaining leading conservatives (completed with the dismissal of von Neurath a few weeks later and his replacement by von Ribbentrop) demonstrated a peak of self-confidence for Hitler's instinctive leadership and his trust in the new generation of officials who were chosen to replace the old military and diplomatic guard. Ribbentrop had long before been a Foreign Minister-in-waiting, entertaining Hitler's personal support as special consultant on foreign matters. His exclusive responsibility for the secret German–Czech negotiations in 1936–7 and for the conclusion of the tripartite agreement with Italy and Japan were major initiatives without any involvement of the Foreign Office. In the armed forces, Hitler demonstrated his determination to control even the military planning of the Wehrmacht by taking over Blomberg's post as Commander-in-Chief of the Armed Forces. At the same time, Werner von Brauchitsch, the new Commander-in-Chief of the Army, and Wilhelm Keitel, head of the newly established Wehrmacht High Command (OKW), were more sympathetic to Hitler's aggressive policy and in any case represented a new technocratic, non-political attitude to policy-making that facilitated the Führer's plans to separate the political from the functional aspects of military and foreign policy.[167]

The triumph of the Nazi leadership: a different system of foreign policy decision making (1938–9)

The *Anschluss* in March 1938 was the first major achievement of the new Nazi style of foreign policy, but it does not offer the best example of how this new decision-making mechanism would operate. The reason was that the dramatic events leading to the incorporation of Austria into the Reich were precipitated by Schuschnigg's arbitrary decision to break his prior agreement with Hitler on 12 February 1938, when he visited Berlin. In accordance with the concessions he made under the pressure of Hitler's intimidating tactics, Schuschnigg was supposed to legalise the Austrian Nazis, co-operate with Germany in the shaping of his foreign policy, proclaim a general amnesty for all those arrested because of 'National Socialist activities' in the years since the 1933 ban on the Nazi Party, and appoint Arthur Seyss-Inquart (a lawyer who supported wholeheartedly the Nazi aspirations and had gradually become Hitler's and Göring's direct Trojan horse in Vienna) to the Ministry of Interior and Justice.[168] Instead, on 9 March Schuschnigg did a *volte-face* and called a plebiscite. The crisis caught the Nazi leadership by surprise to the extent that the new Foreign Minister, Ribbentrop, was in London throughout the time of the *Anschluss*.[169] The successful handling of the crisis was the result of Göring's autonomous role in dealing with Seyss-Inquart in Vienna and, ironically, of Neurath's professional advice and weight. Neurath offered his services to a hesitant Hitler in the absence of the Foreign Minister and, although he did not succeed in committing him to a non-invasion policy, he correctly predicted that no serious international repercussions should be expected.[170]

It was the Czech crisis of the summer and autumn of 1938 (see also Chapter 4) that illustrated the new division of labour between political, diplomatic and military groups in the Nazi system. Hitler's 'unalterable decision to smash Czechoslovakia by military action in the near future' was translated into a military plan by the new Wehrmacht leadership.[171] The only remaining bastion of the old military guard, General Beck, resorted to a last ditch attempt to change the course of German foreign policy by fighting against party involvement in the decision-making process.[172] Since the Hossbach conference, General Beck had endeavoured to bring traditional military figures (the Chief of the Army Staff Fritsch, and the Defence Minister Blomberg) into a political movement that could express the strong opposition of prominent political, diplomatic and military circles to the prospect of Germany's involvement in a major war.[173] Notwithstanding the purge of the military leadership, Beck continued to fight against the warlike implications of the Führer's new aggressive policy. During the Czech crisis, his reservations were shared not only by conservative figures like Neurath, Schwerin von Krosigk (Finance Minister) and Ernst von Weizsäcker (State Secretary to the Foreign Ministry since 1938), but also by Göring (responsible for the supervision of the Four-Year Plan) and Hitler's adjutant Wiedemann.[174] However, the objections of party figures such as Göring and Goebbels diverged from those of the traditional conservative elites in the armed forces and the Wilhelmstrasse. Göring was not averse to the idea of a general war, although he wished first to exhaust the function of diplomatic compromise and peaceful expansion in the pattern of the *Anschluss*. He was aware of German military and economic unpreparedness for an all-out war, and would have preferred to risk a major confrontation only after full mobilisation and fighting power had been achieved, especially after the conclusion of the air force rearmament programme.[175] He nevertheless viewed a German victory in a general war as possible even in 1938, and proceeded with the preparations for a showdown with Czechoslovakia.[176]

For Beck, however, the possibility of risking a war against a great coalition of western powers for the sake of what was for him a secondary target such as Czechoslovakia was inconceivable.[177] He was conscious that the whole strategic planning of the army rested on the assumption that a conflict with Britain and France should be avoided, if not altogether, at least until the early 1940s, thus allowing more time for the restructuring, expansion and rearmament of the German armed forces. His active objections reflected the traditional military view that the army should co-decide both the military and the political prerequisites for action, as opposed to Hitler's opinion that there should be a clear separation of jurisdictions. Contrary to Beck, the new leadership of the Wehrmacht, Keitel and Brauchitsch, had also come to accept Hitler's view and went on dutifully to translate Hitler's political instructions into military action.[178] They removed Beck's political arguments from his first memorandum in May 1938 before showing it to Hitler.[179] Therefore, while Beck expressed a political assessment of Nazi foreign and military policy, the adherence of Brauchitsch and Keitel to Hitler's strategy was irrelevant to their own personal and political beliefs. Having accepted Hitler's monopoly of authority in the handling of foreign affairs, any expression of disapproval would be incongruous. Interestingly, even Beck's vehement criticism excluded the person of Hitler, whose right to primary authority in the decision-making process was not questioned. The main targets were party appointees and members, both in the armed forces and the Foreign Office, who had surrounded the Führer and alienated him from his professional experts.[180] Hitler, however, could afford to discard Beck's protests now that he had the backing of the new military leadership for the execution of his plans. The resignation of Beck in the midst of the Sudeten crisis underlined the complete failure of the traditional elites to reinstate a degree of control over the foreign policy decision-making process.[181]

At the same time, Ribbentrop seized the opportunity offered by the Czech crisis for diplomatic activity in order to reassert his authority after his exclusion during the *Anschluss*. He played a significant role in reinforcing Hitler's aggressive intentions towards Czechoslovakia. He, like his leader, seems to have believed that Britain and France would not risk a major confrontation for the sake of Czechoslovakia, but he was prepared to follow an 'unwavering attitude' that could lead to a 'major war with the western powers'.[182] Ribbentrop had since 1936 been convinced that a German–British conflict would be inevitable, because 'Britain does not want a powerful Germany', and he pressed for an uncompromising line against the efforts of Halifax, Henderson and, later, Chamberlain to promote a peaceful solution.[183] Many conservative diplomats, including von Weizsäcker, had strong reservations about Ribbentrop's aggressive foreign policy ideas and reckless style, but were not willing to express their opposition or to act against the wishes of their chief.[184] In some ways, they had been content with the appointment of Ribbentrop to the position of Foreign Minister as his high profile with Hitler was expected to result in an improvement of the Wilhelmstrasse's status in the decision-making process after the last years of inactivity and marginalisation. Initially, Ribbentrop had chosen to rely on the existing professional personnel of the Foreign Office in a complex jurisdictional struggle against Goebbels's Propaganda Ministry and Göring's secret diplomacy.[185] When von Mackensen resigned in 1938, Ribbentrop proposed the conservative Ernst von Weizsäcker for the post of State Secretary; an unlikely choice by the star of Nazi diplomacy for an allegedly fascistised Foreign Office. Gradually from 1939 onwards, however, he marginalised the traditional groups by transferring personnel from his Dienststelle to key positions of the Foreign Office (like Martin Luther and Paul Schmidt).[186] He also initiated a process of administrative reform within the Office with two clear aims. The first was to create new bodies with enhanced responsibilities (like the Agency for News Analysis) in order to strengthen the Wilhelmstrasse position in its jurisdictional battle with the Ministry of Propaganda. The second was to instigate a process of creating a Ribbentrop Foreign Office within the Foreign Office, in other words, a small diplomatic elite comprising Ribbentrop's closest allies which would operate as the power base of Ribbentrop's personal diplomacy during the war years.[187]

The period from the Munich Agreement to the invasion of Poland offers ample confirmation of this decision-making pattern. The armed forces' leadership dutifully provided military solutions to execute Hitler's plans regarding the liquidation of the rump state of Czechoslovakia in March 1939.[188] Brauchitsch committed himself to a speedier indoctrination of the Wehrmacht, something that even Blomberg had been very hesitant about.[189] With the resignation of Beck, there was nobody in the armed forces to express the traditional army aspiration for co-decision-making in military planning. The Wehrmacht had reached formidable levels of fighting power, mobilisation and technological excellence, but it had also been reduced to a technocratic agency assigned to making political directives by the Nazi leadership practically feasible. The revision of the whole rearmament programme in 1938 with the so-called *Schnellplan* reflected a much earlier target for military preparedness, brought forward to 1939–40 as opposed to the 1943–5 date used at the Hossbach conference.[190] At the same time, the introduction of the Z-Plan for naval rearmament highlighted a deep change in the strategic assumptions of the Nazi leadership; war against Britain was becoming increasingly more probable, despite Hitler's desire to avoid it and his hopes that it could be averted even while the invasion of Poland was imminent.[191] For his part, Ribbentrop played a crucial role in producing a dramatic *volte-face* in European diplomacy that proved a catalyst for the decision to launch war in September 1939. The conclusion of the German–Soviet Non-Aggression Pact in August 1939 attained the strategic prerequisite for Hitler's aim to avoid a two-front war (see Chapter 6). Germany embarked on war with a foreign policy-making mechanism that confirmed the triumph of the autocratic, leader-oriented tendencies of the Nazi system. Power emanated from, and rested in, Hitler and those who were given the privilege of having access to him, providing plausible strategies for implementing their leader's ideas. The removal of decision-making responsibility from those involved in the execution of policy was by now complete.

Fascist parties and leaderships: totalitarianism versus authoritarianism

Against the backdrop of authoritarianism, epitomised in the cult of the Duce and in the *Führerprinzip*, the fascist parties represented an alternative source of power which was both instrumental for fascist consolidation and problematic for a leader-oriented regime. The PNF and the NSDAP sponsored a totalitarian conception of domestic life, a system in which the party would replace the state as the highest form of representing the nation and would thus raise claim to the totality and exclusivity of such a representation.[192] In the first years of their existence, the two parties maintained an identity between movement and leader, in the sense that the position of the latter theoretically depended upon the collective will of the party membership. Mussolini's resignation in 1920 after criticisms for his role in the Pacification Pact with the Socialists underlined the PNF's relative autonomy from its leadership which was not as yet regarded as permanent and unquestionable.[193] In Germany, until the late 1920s, Hitler's leadership was still an item of criticism, especially by the so-called 'left-wing' revolutionary members of the NSDAP who saw the growing authoritarian tendencies of the Führer as a negation of the collective character of the party.[194] The crisis came to a head in 1930, with Otto Strasser openly criticising Hitler for using the leadership principle to ban intra-party debate on ideological issues.[195]

The gap between leader and party increased in the last years before the acquisition of power. Mussolini's and Hitler's success in claiming to represent the whole parties and their ability to centralise authority over their supporters seemed to confirm the authoritarian model of leadership at the expense of the initial egalitarian and collective character of the movements. Even then, however, party officials aspired to a high degree of power-sharing with the leadership in a future fascist system, something that was an anathema to the traditional elites who had acquiesced in the 'fascist experiment' on the explicit understanding that this would involve the separation of the party from the allegedly responsible leader (see above). Thus, with their appointment as head of coalition governments, Mussolini and Hitler faced a complex dilemma: how not to thwart their parties' totalitarian aspirations and reward the support of the old fighters, without jeopardising their own positions of authority or offending the sensibilities of the traditional elites whose consent was pivotal for retaining power.

Italy: mussolinismo and the de-politicisation of the PNF

The complexity of the problem of how to deal with the party was different in each country. In Italy, the short period of Fascist incubation did not allow sufficient time for the crystallisation of the PNF's definite ideological character or the centralisation of Mussolini's power.[196] After the March on Rome, the party suffered from multiple political confusion and incompatible expectations. Moderates, such as Dino Grandi, and many members of the ANI favoured the

93

total integration of the party into the state structure and dismissed radical calls for an 'anti-state' function of the party.[197] The National Syndicalists, headed by Rossoni, rejected etatism, sponsoring instead plans for a radical reorganisation of Italian society on the basis of syndicalist corporatism.[198] Extremists, such as Farinacci and Malaparte, were against the idea of a strong state and advocated a totalitarian rule of the party through dictatorship and removal of all institutional limitations on Fascist power.[199] Farinacci in particular described the party as the only authentic expression of the spirit of Fascism, a reminder of its agrarian, provincial roots and of the dynamics of *squadrismo*.[200] Most members of the old guard were also extremely critical of newcomers to the PNF, whose motives they distrusted, advocating instead their expulsion and the blocking of further 'opportunistic' inflows of new members.[201] Tensions surfaced very early, especially in the field of appointments, where the so-called 'Fascists of the first hour' felt they had been sidelined in favour of sympathetic traditional figures or 'newcomers', members who joined the PNF after the March on Rome.[202] However, the tension reached a critical point during the Matteotti crisis, which lasted for more than six months. The mobilisation of the extremists, their pressure on Mussolini for a 'second wave' of fascistisation during the Matteotti crisis, and the threat from local Fascist organisations not to obey the Duce if he did not assume dictatorial powers and separate the party from the state, contributed to the decision to establish the dictatorship in January 1925.[203]

The appointment of Farinacci as Party Secretary signalled a victory for the intransigents, but it was an ephemeral one. The dictatorship had strengthened the authoritarian, leader-oriented character of the Fascist system without in reality rewarding the party as an institution of the Fascist regime with increased political influence in the decision-making process.[204] Faced with a clash between Farinacci and the Ministry of the Interior Federzoni over the status of the militia in 1926, the Duce did not hesitate to dismiss the former, endorse the etatist approach of the latter, and minimise the role of the *squadri*.[205] In the same vein, the institutionalisation of the Grand Council as the highest organ of the state (by a law of 9 December 1928) highlighted the intention to bring the party under the control of the state.[206] Meaningfully, with the law of 24 December 1925, Mussolini as Head of the government was recognised as the sole repository of the Crown's power.[207] After Farinacci, the position of Party Secretary was offered to less independent members of the PNF (the leader of Fascism in Brescia Augusto Turati (1926–30), and D'Annunzio's former minister in Fiume, Giovanni B. Giurati (1930–1)) who assumed the responsibility to monitor the activities of the party *gerarchi* and *ras*, thus further distancing Mussolini from party structures and opponents.[208]

However, it was during the eight years in which Achille Starace was Party Secretary (1931–9) that the de-politicisation of the PNF reached its peak. Bottai described *staracismo* as a negation of Fascism's interest in the content of politics, as opposed to style and presentation. As he argued in an article published in *Critica Fascista*, the party sacrificed its spiritual intensity for the sake of superficial appearance.[209] For him, under Starace the party accepted its 'expulsion from politics' and its subordination to the necessities of *mussolinismo*.[210] In a similar vein, Grandi attributed the phenomenal unpopularity of the party to Starace's reforms and lack of political substance.[211] With the decree of January 1927, the party was officially subordinated to the state as organ for the indoctrination and organisation of the population.[212] This meant the death warrant of alternative non-etatist conceptions of a Fascist system, Farinacci's idea of a strong party against state control or Rossoni's vision of mass syndicalist organisations.[213] The party secretary was not admitted into the Council of Ministers until 1937, but even this belated participation did not reverse the loss of authority by the PNF. When in 1930 Turati attempted to establish himself as *de facto* deputy of Mussolini, by claiming the position of Under-Secretary to the Interior Ministry (with Mussolini as Minister) as complementary to his role as Party secretary, he was immediately dismissed.[214] As for Farinacci's concept of an elite party organisation, inaccessible to opportunist newcomers through a membership ban, it materialised only temporarily in 1925–6. Then, membership was reopened and in 1932 the idea of compulsory participation to the PNF (in order to include all civil servants of the 'Fascist' state) led to a dramatic increase in the party's membership figures. Further influx of members took place in 1936 and in 1940, transforming the party into a mass organisation of the state's centralised authority over society.[215] With the amendments to the Party Statute of 1932 the Grand Council ceased to be a party organ and was recognised as the highest state organ, while the PNF Secretary became exclusively dependent upon, and accountable to, the Duce, who was responsible for selecting and replacing the holder of the post.

The depoliticisation of the PNF, through its subordination to the political will of the state and the neutralisation of dissident trends within its ranks, reflected Mussolini's ambitions to establish a truly authoritarian model of government. In justifying his policy towards the party, Mussolini stressed in December 1936 that political decision making did not concern the party as an institution; instead, 'the party should always concentrate solely on the political education of the people'.[216] The party was allowed to perform totalitarian functions on a societal level (youth, leisure, press, education) but only once it had been deprived of its collective right to political co-decision.[217] Even after the PNF's crucial role in promoting the racial legislation against Jews, Arabs and Africans, the party remained the semi-effective 'nervous system' of the Duce's political will.[218] Its growing unpopularity with the Italian population hampered the main task of 'militarising' the nation and transforming Fascism into a catholic secular religion for the whole nation.[219] This failure rendered the Duce's authoritarian position even more crucial for the preservation of social unity and gradually reduced his reliance on collective party approval in defining and implementing his radical plans for a 'new state' and a 'new man'. In this sense, *mussolinismo* was reconciled with the totalitarian aspirations of the party, but only once the former had hijacked the political influence of the latter. *Ex post facto* attempts to present the monopolisation of Fascism by Mussolini as predetermined by Fascist political ideology have been taken at face value by exponents of the 'totalitarian power' of the party, like Germino and Emilio Gentile.[220] Such a totalitarianism, however, subjected to authoritarian rule and etatism, was the utter antithesis of the system that syndicalists, *squadristi* and many *gerarchi* had cherished in the early years of the Fascist movement.[221] Many old fighters continued to criticise the alteration of Fascism's character and disapproved of the marginalisation of old members in favour of conservative nationalists, such as Alfredo Rocco and Luigi Federzoni, ex-liberal intellectuals, like Giovanni Gentile, or ambitious younger members, such as Galeazzo Ciano.[222] Bottai kept deploring the pro-German shift in Italian policy, regarding it as a contradiction to the spirit and intellectual traditions of Italian Fascism, although he publicly supported the regime's policy of rapprochement with Nazi Germany (see also Chapter 5).[223] After the war, he castigated Mussolini's efforts to monopolise Fascism in the 1930s, presenting the emergence of *mussolinismo* as a *de facto* negation of the collective, evolving spirit of Fascism.[224] Marinetti accepted his election to the Italian Academy in spite of his aversion to 'intellectual' institutions, but he could not hide his disillusionment with the regime's lack of progress towards a domestic transformation of Italian society. As for Balbo, always the strongest voice of dissent in the Grand Council, he kept criticising Mussolini's distance from the party members and institutions, deploring the change in his *Capo*'s attitude towards the old fighters and underlining the danger that, in his isolation, Mussolini appeared to have lost his political astuteness.[225] In the end, of course, loyalty to the Duce would dictate an acceptance of his political decisions. In all these cases, however, reservations about the regime's developments entailed an implicit criticism of the Duce's personal, authoritarian rule.

The subordination and de-politicisation of the party becomes even more evident in the field of foreign affairs. The Council of Ministers, a body supposed to maintain the collective character of government decision making, gradually came to be dominated by Mussolini's long monologues, losing any real consultative or co-decision function. One of its most prominent Fascist members, Bottai, noted with pessimism in July 1940 that the institution was in a state of 'plain decadence', with its allegedly collective character overshadowed by the authoritarian tendency of *mussolinismo* and the Duce's insistence on monopolising responsibility for every single political issue.[226] Similar feelings were expressed privately even by Ciano, who often found the monopolisation of the meetings by Mussolini and the lack of debate 'deeply humiliating'.[227] The Fascist Grand Council was not consulted in the formulation of the plan to attack Ethiopia, a fact that infuriated both Balbo and Federzoni.[228] Mussolini and Ciano also kept the Council uninformed about preliminary preparations for the invasion of Albania in the first half of 1938.[229] On a number of occasions, Mussolini used the frequent meetings of the Council to legitimise *faits accomplis*. The *Anschluss* was presented as the desired choice of Italian policy by Fascist propaganda, while participation in the Spanish Civil War had already been agreed before the members of the Council applauded Mussolini's determination to promote the alleged interests of international fascism.[230] Individually, however, a number of leading Fascist figures expressed doubts about the advisability of Italy's involvement in Spain. Balbo reacted angrily, criticising Mussolini's awkward handling of sensitive foreign policy issues.[231] At the Council meeting of 21 March 1939, Balbo was even less tactful; he accused Mussolini of 'licking Hitler's boots' and reminded the other participants that there was still the possibility of opting for Britain against Nazi aggression.[232] When the news about the signing of the Pact of Steel reached Rome in late May 1939, not only Bottai but also Federzoni and Grandi could not hide their frustration.[233] Bottai, in particular, offered a more elaborate implicit criticism through the pages of *Critica Fascista*. He accepted the internationalisation of Fascism as a logical extension of its internal vitality and spiritual advantage (compared to the democratic and communist regimes), but warned that such an internationalisation should be promoted very carefully, in order to avoid associating it with opportunistic imitators.[234]

Mussolini allowed discussion and tolerated verbal dissidence (as can be seen by his relatively calm reaction to Balbo's extreme comments of March 1939),[235] but was unmoved by other concepts of foreign policy making, even if these came from prominent Fascist *gerarchi*. He had manifested his determination to control foreign affairs by retaining the portfolio of the Foreign Minister until 1928 and in 1932–6. His two other choices for the post, Grandi and Ciano, were intended to promote the 'fascistisation' of the style of Italian diplomacy but not to enhance the political influence of the party as an institution in the shaping of foreign policy. Grandi, as a moderate and opponent of a strong party, was a *de facto* reluctant agent. Ciano, on the other hand, used the increased role of the *Gabinetto* to promote compliant party colleagues, such as Filippo Anfuso (Head of the *Gabinetto*), who would dutifully support his foreign policy agenda and transform the Foreign Ministry into a docile institution for his personal elevation.[236] As we saw earlier, under both Grandi and especially Ciano, the political power of Fascist elements in the Palazzo Chigi increased rapidly at the expense of the traditional diplomatic groups. Yet, the promotion of selected personnel from the PNF was made on the basis of personal allegiance to the Duce and his appointees as Foreign Ministers. Even the political autonomy of the Foreign Ministers was circumscribed by their detachment from the party's control, by their subordination to the will of the state and by Mussolini's ultimate right to dismiss them at any time. In this sense, the promotion of party members to state positions (Grandi as Foreign Minister (1929–32), Bottai as Minister of Corporations (1929–32) and Education (1936–43), Balbo as Minister of Aviation (1929–33), De Bono to the Ministry of Colonies (1929–35), Ciano to Palazzo Chigi (1936–43)) did entail an increase in their personal political power, but this power was not transferred cumulatively to the party, whose influence upon the leader-oriented decision-making process of the regime waned. In spite of the existence of ideological currents which either contradicted Mussolini's political decisions or aimed to alter them, the party as institution and collective expression of Fascist values conspicuously failed to sponsor a political agenda autonomous from Mussolini's will and thus lost its institutional capacity to effectively influence the decision-making process.[237] In the end, all these leading figures of Fascism found it impossible to push their individual disagreements with Mussolini's political decisions to extremes. The cult of the leader, the notion of loyalty to the *Capo* and the belief that he incarnated Fascist values provided the strongest force of integration within the Fascist regime, overcoming even the strong opposition by the majority of Fascist *gerarchi* to the alliance with Germany and the anti-Semitic legislation. In spite of differences of opinion, they still viewed their allegiance to the Duce as a moral task to serve Fascism. In this sense, the motion of 24/25 July 1943 was consistent with the overall philosophy of the Italian Fascist state in that opposition to the Duce's will could be intelligible only as a vote of no confidence in his overall political position and function as *Capo del Governo*/leader of Fascism and not in individual policies he sponsored.[238]

Germany: Hitler's authoritarianism and the NSDAP's quest for a political role in the Nazi system

In Germany, a similar institutional tension between the totalitarian aspirations of the NSDAP and the authoritarian concept of rule epitomised in Hitler's leadership surfaced long before the *Machtübernahme*. The much longer period of incubation offered the NSDAP significantly wider time margins to crystallise its ideological character and its internal structures of power. By 1930, Hitler had successfully established his position as the indisputable leader of the movement by eliminating the opposition from the more 'left-wing' group of the party.[239] He had also asserted his authoritarian and charismatic concept of rule at the expense of party collective decision making. Plans to establish a party Senate as the highest ideological organ of the NSDAP were tacitly dropped by Hitler. The Führer also thwarted or revoked the systematic reforms of Gregor Strasser in 1928–32, which intended to streamline the whole party organisation; a similar fate awaited Ley's plans from 1933 onwards to centralise and rationalise administrative control over the party organisation.[240] By the time of the acquisition of power, the Führer possessed an ideological and political monopoly over the NSDAP, avoiding any form of collective representation of party interests on the leadership level or any accumulation of permanent power by either individuals or agencies.

At the same time, however, the long duration of the *Kampfzeit* had transformed the NSDAP into an effective institution of mass support for Hitler and a much more sophisticated hierarchical organisation than the PNF. By 1933, the Nazi party had developed a fairly elaborate division of expertise amongst its ranks: Alfred Rosenberg in foreign affairs, Rudolph Hess (Head of the Politische Organisation) and Robert Ley (Head of the DAF) in organisational issues,

Göring in technical and economic issues, and Ernst Röhm as the leader of an alternative military organisation for the armed forces of Nazi Germany (the SA).[241] The strengthening of the political power of certain individuals and groups within the party did not pose an institutional challenge to Hitler's power, as he was seen as the sole originator of policy.[242] It did, however, create an elite within the NSDAP with competences and ambitions which could justify the party's right to co-decide policy issues.

Such hopes were frustrated very quickly, not only because the 'minimum consensus' programme foiled a direct Nazi assault on the state, but also because Hitler was aware of the need to keep up appearances during the difficult period of consolidation. In 1933–4, the SA and Röhm, who aspired to absorb the Reichswehr into their ranks and sponsored the idea of a 'constant revolution', presented Hitler with the last major case of ideological opposition from his party. The purge of June 1934 was, therefore, significant in two different ways. First, it underlined Hitler's determination to safeguard the authoritarian basis of his power against any possible contender, be that from the state or the party. Second, it showed that the Führer was serious about his declarations, on 13 July 1934, that the 'revolution was over', in the sense that the main component of the Nazi system – the Führer's charismatic rule – had been established and would not be institutionally challenged.[243] With the Law for Ensuring the Unity of Party and State (December 1933), the former was recognised as the sole political organisation but was tied to the state and was thus frustrated in its hopes to be the sole 'source of the will of the state'.[244] The party could draw some consolation from the fact that Hess, as head of the Politische Organisation and Hitler's Deputy, was given immediately a position in the cabinet and possessed the privilege of being the only spokesman for Hitler with strong power to control state appointments.[245] However, ironically, the increased powers of Hess led to the strengthening of Hitler's authoritarian rule. The Führer, who had deliberately divided Gregor Strasser's former functions between Ley and Hess, used the Politische Organisation against Ley's effort to accumulate power through the extension of the DAF.[246] He also exploited the SA purge to ban intra-party political debate and to cleanse the party of dissident voices.[247] In contrast to Italy, where the Council of Ministers remained in function until the fall of the regime, in Germany the Cabinet lapsed into oblivion from 1934 onwards, thwarting a more effective fusion between state and party and strengthening the Politische Organisation's reliance upon Hitler's personal will.

The old fighters were disappointed by the slow pace of fascistisation of the state.[248] Wilhelm Frick, the Minister of the Interior, had successfully fought an institutional battle against the NSDAP in 1933, legislating against the mass influx of party members into the civil service.[249] By 1937, none of the department heads of the Ministries had been members of the party before 1933, and only two could claim any connection with the NSDAP.[250] The *alte Kämpfer* opposed the opening of the party membership in 1937, as they were deeply distrustful of the newcomers' motives and feared the loss of the elite status of the party.[251] They also regretted the party's lack of control over powerful institutions and policy areas. Attempts to fascistise the armed forces by establishing commissars in charge of indoctrinating the soldiers did not have much success until the war years (see Chapter 6).[252] As for the party's ambition to 'determine the final form of foreign policy', as the *Völkischer Beobachter* claimed in May 1933, the mere presence of Neurath as Foreign Minister, his relatively good relations with Hitler until 1937 and the very limited fascistisation of the Wilhelmstrasse during the same period underlined the failure of the party's totalitarian ambitions in that field.[253]

Contrary to Italy, the role of leading party members was enhanced as a result of the radicalisation of Nazi policies after 1936. Hermann Göring supervised the Four-Year Plan with enhanced powers over economic planning and rearmament; under the new law of 1937, Hess controlled all appointments to the Civil Service; Ribbentrop gradually established himself as the new supremo of Nazi diplomacy, while Heinrich Himmler was allowed to expand the political and military jurisdiction of the SS.[254] Hitler himself became increasingly reclusive, indifferent to day-to-day internal affairs and concentrating more and more on his foreign policy plans. His gradual retreat from domestic affairs after 1936 allowed a small group of leading party officials significant latitude in implementing Nazi policy and in running the government. Apart from those already mentioned, Goebbels rose to prominence in the last years before the war as Propaganda Minister, while Martin Bormann (Rudolf Hess's Secretary until his flight to Britain in 1941, and then Head of the Chancellery) gained Hitler's confidence and strengthened his position as the main link between the leader and the outside world as Hess's power diminished.[255]

This, however, did not result in the strengthening of party influence as a whole at the expense of Hitler's authoritarianism. In fact, delegation of power took place mainly on the administrative, and not the political, level only after the Politische Organisation in association with Hitler had neutralised the last major enclaves of opposition within the party. The Führer's confidence in the unshakeable basis of his supreme power is manifested by the delegation of the *Führerprinzip* to the Reich ministers at the beginning of 1936.[256] He also believed that differences of opinion could be resolved and settled through time without necessitating his bureaucratic intervention.[257] His authoritarian concept of rule actually presupposed a considerable level of party political autonomy and experimentation with alternative, radical forms of policy making. The party provided a dynamic mechanism for implementing Hitler's policies, deciphering his intentions and ensuring optimal conditions for successful policy making. As state institutions and traditional elites were becoming increasingly incompatible with the Führer's political demands, he relied on party officials and strengthened party influence over the state. Like Mussolini, however, he perceived politics as a matter of personal trust and avoided any permanent institutionalisation of power. The party was important as a reservoir of multiple alternative solutions to policy problems. This explains why he was willing to defy government protocol in favour of a party favourite or to abandon one previous party ally for another. Yet, in the end, the NSDAP as a whole institution lacked any form of collective representation or political power in the Nazi system. Hitler's authoritarian system increasingly made use of the party's totalitarian ambitions against the authority of the state, but also created a sphere of administrative responsibility for party officials which remained separate from, and subordinate to, his exclusive prerogative to generate policy or have the ultimate say as mediator in policy disputes.

This dualism between authoritarianism and totalitarianism becomes evident in the realm of foreign policy, an area which Hitler, like Mussolini, strove to monopolise.[258] Initially, the party played a limited role in either influencing or implementing policy decisions. After the failure of Rosenberg to make an impression with his London visit in 1933, Hitler relied on Neurath and the Wilhelmstrasse for the execution of the regime's official foreign policy. The party's autonomy in dealing with subversive organisations outside the Reich, like the Austrian National Socialists and Henlein's Sudeten German Party, was supported by Hitler as a Trojan horse for future German irredentist claims over these states.[259] However, the failure to control party activities during the Vienna Coup of July 1934 convinced him of the need to curtail party political initiatives and to strengthen Hess's role in co-ordinating and monitoring more effectively the NSDAP.[260] In this sense, the contribution of the party to foreign policy decision making until 1936 was minimal, but the party itself continued to operate as the laboratory of radical solutions for future expansionist projects, like the *Anschluss*, the Sudeten problem and the Polish Corridor. Ribbentrop's special role in dealing with Britain and Göring's responsibility for Danzig and the promotion of German–Italian relations underline Hitler's determination to exploit all possible avenues in search of the best solution for foreign policy making.

The party's role became more influential with the Spanish Civil War. Against the wishes of Neurath, Hitler allowed significant latitude both to the AO members in Spain and to his special envoy Prince Philip of Hessen in dealing directly with Franco's officials in Spain and with the Italian Fascist leadership, respectively.[261] A year later, Hess was authorised to establish the 'Office of the Special Assistant for Foreign Policy Questions'. This was an important development as it highlighted Hitler's decision to enhance the party's involvement in foreign affairs while retaining his grip over decision making through subjecting party activities in this field to the scrutiny of his loyal Deputy. Hess had accumulated powers since 1934 and his office played a pivotal role in the *Anschluss*, alongside Göring. In the aftermath of the crisis, Hess – and not the Reich ministers – acquired the right to control and approve the legislation of the new Austrian government under Seyss-Inquart.[262]

However, Hitler's shift to the party did not entail either a waning of his autonomous basis of power or an institutional boost to the party as a whole. The Führer retained his right to appoint Gauleiters and make them directly accountable to him.[263] He also favoured certain groups and individuals within the NSDAP; Himmler's SS were again linked directly to Hitler, bypassing both the Wehrmacht leadership and the party bureaucracy, while Göring enhanced his power base by assuming control of the Aryanisation programme in the occupied areas.[264] The NSDAP participated in the decision-making process as a conglomerate of individuals and agencies with no institutional cohesion and no permanent political roles. Responsibilities and jurisdictions were allocated on an *ad hoc* basis, lacking any co-ordinated plan for division of labour. If the party played a crucial role in the Austrian crisis of March 1938 (through its direct links with the Austrian National Socialist Party), its contribution to Hitler's policy towards Czechoslovakia in 1938 was confined to continued dealings with the Sudeten party leadership, while with regard to Poland in 1939 the party's role again was limited to co-operation with the local organisations in Danzig. Ribbentrop was by then the indisputable luminary of Nazi diplomacy, overshadowing even Göring, who, after the *Anschluss*, shifted to a less warlike and aggressive policy of German expansion, thus losing favour with Hitler.[265] However, Ribbentrop was never a 'party' man. He had always been regarded by the *alte Kämpfer* as an outsider. Rosenberg, for most the obvious 'party' expert in foreign affairs, did not refrain from criticising the main parameters of Nazi foreign policy in the last years before the war. Using the 1936 Party Rally at Nuremberg as a forum for expressing his alternative ideas, he gave a speech on the 'ideological character' of Nazi foreign policy, repeating his basic motto of eastern expansion and alliance with Britain. Two years later, at the last Party Rally before the war, he emphasised the importance of Germany's 'interests in the east'. He was relatively relieved when Ribbentrop promoted the Anti-Comintern Pact, but was extremely sceptical of what he perceived as its predominantly anti-British implications.[266] However, by entering one of the senior offices of the state Ribbentrop had been placed in the sphere of Hitler's authoritarian power, insulated from criticism and invested with significant powers for the handling of foreign affairs. This underlines the idiosyncratic character of the partification of the state in Germany; Nazi figures eroded the state mechanism but, once in state positions, they fell more firmly under Hitler's political influence and weakened their ties with the party organisation.

The centrality of the leader in the fascist system's decision-making process was predetermined neither by any plans nor by clear fascist theory of state. The way the fascist state evolved until the outbreak of the Second World War does reflect the two leaders' determination to safeguard their authoritarian rule against power sharing with other fascist and non-fascist elite groups. The separation of their sphere of power from the administrative layers of policy making resulted in a chaotic system of government where no clear or permanent division of labour and jurisdiction was ever imposed. In both cases, however, the central authority of the fascist leaders emanated from their exclusive prerogative of defining the framework of policy making and of acting as the ultimate arbiter of political battles. Co-decision making was simply an ephemeral stage in the transition to authoritarian rule which reduced the influence of the traditional elites and of the party as a whole to a functional level of providing solutions for the promotion of the leadership's objectives. This system did not prevent individuals from winning the leaders' trust and influencing their short- and medium-term plans or strategies. These were, however, not institutional limitations on the leaders' power, in the sense that they did not obligate the leaders to treat either state institutions or party agencies as normative features of the decision-making process. At the end of the day, Mussolini and Hitler were institutionally free to choose from the available policy options and then discard policies and individuals without any obligation to accountability or consistency.

4

FASCIST EXPANSIONISM IN PRACTICE

Foreign policy making (1922–39)

Hindsight is a dubious privilege for a historian. On the one hand, knowledge of the evolution of the two regimes' expansionist plans into the Axis alliance and war has helped to relate the radicalisation of fascist expansionism to early ideological elements in the worldviews of the two leaders, thus highlighting a degree of internal consistency in their objectives and policies. On the other hand, accusations of reading history backwards attacked the idea that either the alliance or recourse to war had been pre-determined by any programmatic core in the expansionist policies of the two regimes. The notion of a consistent programme of expansion has been contrasted with the view that the drive to large-scale territorial aggrandisement and war was determined by either opportunism or social imperialism, or both. At the same time, even the originality of fascist foreign policies has been questioned. The debate about the continuities between liberal and fascist expansionist programmes revolves around similar questions: did the fascist take-over mark a break with previous foreign policies, sponsoring a new vision and style of expansion, or did it simply reproduce traditional great-power objectives, albeit couched in a more dynamic fashion?

This is where hindsight becomes a crucial privilege: knowing the ultimate scope of fascist expansionist aspirations (as manifested in the two regimes' war aims), can it be shown that the short-term expansionist policies of the fascist regimes served an integrated long-term and large-scale vision? So far, we have seen that the ideological fusion in the Italian and German Right since the First World War enabled fascist ideology to reproduce traditional 'great power' and revisionist themes in a new, dynamic and activist style of policy making. Fascism's emphasis on the esoteric value of expansion gradually radicalised the tactics for attaining widely shared goals. At the same time, it aimed to eliminate any political distinction between utopian and realisable objectives, a distinction implicit in the *Realpolitik* of the previous liberal and conservative governments in the two countries. In legitimising the notions of spatial expansion and historic irredentism, the fascist regimes introduced territorial expansion as a central element of their worldview. However, in the short-term, foreign policy making displayed a flexibility and even opportunism which allude to lack of an all-encompassing 'programme'. Instead, decision making remained for a long time circumscribed by domestic and international limitations, adhering to traditional arguments and justifications such as revisionism and irredentism, and thus upholding an impression of continuity.

The aim of the ensuing analysis is to discuss the short-term expansionist initiatives of the Italian and German regimes until the summer of 1939, and to analyse their experiments with two basic forms of expansion. The first were traditional arguments for specific territorial readjustments (*border policy*). Revisionist, irredentist and colonial policies will be examined separately in order to highlight the function and importance of each form in the overall fascist expansionist policies. The second form of expansion extended beyond the traditional demands for border modification(s) and was underpinned by the much broader fascist commitment to *living space* (see also Chapter 2). In the context of this analysis, two questions will be addressed. First, how innovative were the foreign policies of the two regimes in comparison with traditional expansionist aspirations? Second, to what extent can we integrate the revisionist, irredentist and colonial goals pursued by the two regimes into a consistent, large-scale expansionist vision which underpinned the foreign policy decisions of the two regimes and was not contradicted in the long term by diplomatic flexibility or opportunism?

Revisionism: the legacy of the Peace Treaties and the juridical argument for territorial expansion

From the outset, it became clear that the Peace Treaties had failed to base the postwar settlement upon a stable compromise between the conflicting claims of the European states. Strong feelings of dissatisfaction were common not only among the defeated, but also in the case of victorious or newly founded states. While the former had anticipated a conciliatory peace with mild territorial terms, the latter's expectations had been so inflated after the victory of the Entente powers and the declaration of Wilson's Fourteen Points, that it was impossible to be satisfied *in toto* under any conceivable peace plan.[1] This concerted attack by winners and losers alike at the Peace Treaties undermined the legitimacy of the postwar settlement and challenged its permanent character. Thus, the notion of *revisionism* was introduced into the political vocabulary of European affairs, becoming a catch-phrase for both territorial losses and unsatisfied promises or claims.

Since the Peace Treaties had intended to provide a definite solution to territorial rivalries in Europe and overseas,[2] revisionism formed the political platform for a synthesis of the European and colonial policies of the discontented states. It managed to adapt the traditional expansionist attitudes to the new circumstances that the end of war and the spirit of the Peace Treaties had established. As an open-ended commitment to future expansion, it succeeded in keeping the whole territorial debate alive and in presenting it as a juridical issue with concrete references to the 'unjust' treaties. The previous tensions between colonial and continental expansion were brushed aside in favour of the right to expansion *per se* which seemed to subside in the face of the postwar exhaustion and craving for security. The discontented states exploited the plurality of their expansionist claims to achieve revision of the Peace Treaties not merely for the sake of specific amendments. Their ultimate goal was to deconstruct the permanent character of the settlement and to create a precedent for future, more concrete expansion. In this sense, revisionism should not be seen as either a form, or an autonomous goal, of expansion. It was rather a political and judicial excuse to re-legitimise the right to expansion in all its diverse forms (colonialism, irredentism, prestige expansionism and so on) in a manner that was politically relevant to, and acceptable in, the postwar circumstances.

The Versailles settlement was regarded as a setback for the expansionist aspirations of Italy and Germany for entirely different reasons.[3] As the main defeated nation of the First World War, Germany saw its territory reduced in two ways. First, as a result of the application of the concept of self-determination, she was forced to concede vast areas of her pre-1914 national territory to the victorious powers and the new states of central Europe (Poland, Czechoslovakia). She lost the province of Alsace-Lorraine to France, nearly the whole of west Prussia to the resurrected Polish state, the Memel area to Lithuania, and small western districts to Belgium.[4] Furthermore, the Rhineland area was demilitarised in order to strengthen the security of France's eastern frontier with Germany.[5] At the same time, Germany had to accept the geographical separation of East Prussia from the rest of Germany due to the establishment of the so-called Polish Corridor, linking mainland Poland with the 'Free City' of Danzig.[6] The treaty also acknowledged the independent character of Austria, thus rejecting the German claim for a union between the two states.[7] Finally, the Saar territory was placed under international control for a period of fifteen years (with the provision for a plebiscite after fifteen years),[8] while other plebiscites in North Schleswig and Upper Silesia[9] determined the extent of the territories that were to be ceded from Germany to Denmark and Poland respectively. Second, in the field of colonies, the Weimar Republic was forced to renounce all her rights over all her colonial possessions. The German colonial argument had been significantly weakened by the German military defeats in Africa during the First World War, defeats that had resulted in a virtual territorial decimation of her colonial empire.[10] On top of that, the Entente powers used as a pretext the accusation that Germany had proved incapable of administering colonies (the 'Colonial Guilt' clause[11]), and distributed the former German colonies to Britain, France, Belgium, Japan, Australia, South Africa and New Zealand in the form of 'mandates' from the League of Nations.[12]

In contrast to Germany, postwar Italy – as a nominal victor – made modest gains in the Peace Conferences. After long and difficult negotiations, she secured the extension of her northern frontier up to the strategic Brenner Pass. This meant that not only the territories of Trento, but also a large part of the South Tyrol region – with a German-speaking majority – were incorporated into the Italian state.[13] Additionally, in 1920 Italy signed the Treaty of Rapallo with

Yugoslavia, under which she secured moderate territorial gains in Istria, Zara and Dalmatia.[14] Furthermore, the Italian government succeeded in securing her position in the Aegean Sea by extending her occupation of the Dodecanese and by acquiring control of the Adalia 'sphere of influence' in Asia Minor under the Treaty of Sèvres (1920).[15] Even after the triumph of nationalist Turkey in 1922 and the consequent overthrow of the 1920 Treaty,[16] Italy successfully defended her rights over the Dodecanese.

At the same time, however, the territorial gains from the Peace Treaties fell significantly short of the expectations which had prompted the Salandra government to enter the war in 1915. The London Treaty of 1915 (see Chapter 1) included provisions for substantial territorial compensations in Europe and Africa which were not fully realised in the postwar negotiations. The Entente powers could not disregard the new reality on the east coast of the Adriatic with the formation of the Yugoslav state.[17] They were also reluctant to give up their predominant position in the Mediterranean by conceding part of their colonial possessions in north Africa to Italy, despite their promises for colonial compensation in 1915. Orlando, on the other hand, went to Paris with a programme of territorial claims that not only took the London Treaty for granted, but also succumbed to the nationalist propaganda by adding Fiume to the long list of Italian demands.[18] In these circumstances, it is easy to understand the Italian resentment at the decision, first, to establish Fiume as a Free State under the Rapallo Treaty of 1920[19] and, second, to exclude the issue of the Italian colonies from the final treaties. The occupation of Fiume by D'Annunzio in September 1919 was the first ominous indication of Italian revisionist aspirations.[20] Such was the annexationist fervour in postwar Italy that the dissatisfaction for the unfulfilled territorial claims totally overshadowed the enthusiasm for victory and the Brenner issue.[21]

A detailed account of Italian and German revisionist activities prior to the advent of the PNF and NSDAP to power does not lie within the limits of this study. In Italy, this period was a short interlude, fraught with social divisions and economic encumbrances which kept the liberal governments occupied with the task of domestic consolidation rather than with any serious effort to advance revisionist plans. In the field of foreign policy, the 1918–22 liberal *interregnum* was marked by endeavours to defend the precarious postwar territorial gains and to stabilise Italy's new international position in Europe and the Mediterranean. It was a period of normalisation in her relations with Yugoslavia, Albania, Greece and the western powers.[22] At the same time, the Fascist movement emerged as the fiercest vocal critic of the foreign policy strategy of the Italian liberal governments and formally introduced the claim for revision of the peace settlement.[23] The occupation of Fiume by D'Annunzio was eventually suppressed by the new Giolittian administration in 1920, but this show of strength did not silence the nationalist and Fascist propaganda, which kept up the pressure for a 'just' regulation of the Dalmatian issue.[24] In Germany, on the other hand, Weimar revisionism covered a significantly longer period (1919–32). However, such was the extent of the country's postwar problems and restrictions under the

Versailles settlement that territorial revisionism presupposed advances in four more basic forms of revision: economic, against reparations; diplomatic, against isolation and exclusion from the international system; legal, against Germany's inequality of rights; and military, against the massive restrictions on the armed forces. The moderate policies of Stresemann made significant advances in all four fields, but peaceful revisionism failed to deliver any tangible gains with regard to the territorial issue.[25] By 1933 the Weimar governments had managed to free the country from most of its previous legal and economic restrictions, yet Germany still remained confined within the humiliating territorial arrangement of 1919.

Italy: revisionist policies

The Fascist episode in European politics started with the March on Rome in October 1922. As Prime Minister and Foreign Minister of a government with high nationalist credentials, Mussolini realised the priority of dealing with the complications of the Peace Treaties in a manner suggestive of the regime's dynamism. He was also conscious, however, of two main limitations on his revisionist aspirations. The first pertained to the necessity to reassure foreign governments and international public opinion about the law-abiding intentions of the new Fascist government.[26] The second was related to the reluctance of the major pro-status quo powers in Europe (namely Britain and France) to discuss any revision of the postwar settlement, especially after such difficult and time-consuming negotiations. These two considerations seemed to prevail in the first year of Fascist rule, and Mussolini hastened to affirm his respect for the Peace Treaties in his first foreign policy speech to the Chamber (and again throughout the first half of 1923). He concluded, however, with an ominous remark about the ephemeral character of treaties in general, and this reflected his long-term unwillingness to accept the postwar settlement as a definite territorial solution to Italy's aspirations.[27]

There were two categories of territorial issues that the new Italian government could include in its revisionist agenda. The conclusion of the Peace Treaties in 1920 had still left a number of territorial questions pending for a future solution. Of particular interest to Italy's expansionist aspirations were the issues pertaining to the final adjustment of the Italo–Yugoslav border,[28] to the Italo–Turkish–Greek dispute over the sovereignty of the Dodecanese,[29] and finally to the colonial compensation which had been promised to Italy under the London Treaty. The postwar liberal governments had dealt with the first two questions, yet the settlements remained inconclusive at the time of Mussolini's appointment. The Santa Margherita Accords, adjusting territorial issues in the area surrounding Fiume, were handed over to the new Fascist government for final ratification. In spite of his earlier opposition to the agreement,[30] Mussolini honoured his promise to respect the concluded treaties and ratified the accords in February 1923, but refused to sanction the secret protocol. This complication laid the foundations for the re-examination of the Italo–Yugoslav frontier in

1923. With regard to the issue of the Dodecanese, there were the Italo–Greek agreements of 1919–20, according to which the islands (except Rhodes) were to be ceded to Greece.[31] This had been cancelled by the Treaty of Sèvres, which reaffirmed the temporary sovereignty of Italy over the Dodecanese. By the time of Mussolini's appointment, however, the resurgence of nationalist Turkey in Asia Minor had completely overthrown all previous adjustments and the whole question of the Aegean Sea was opened again for negotiations. By contrast, the issue of deciding the extent of Italy's colonial compensation in Africa had not received any concrete response up to October 1922, due to the evasive attitude of the British and French governments. Italy's Entente partners had no intention of sharing their joint domination of the Mediterranean with any other state, even less so with a Fascist state. Therefore, between 1922 and 1924 they remained unresponsive to Mussolini's pressure for either a settlement on the issue of the Italian minority in Tunisia, or a prestigious Italian participation in the negotiations for the future status of Tangier.[32] The loss of the Adalia 'sphere of influence' in Asia Minor under the Treaty of Lausanne (1923) was a further blow to the Italian dreams for domination of the eastern Mediterranean. It strengthened, however, the Italian argument for colonial compensation and became the sharp edge of Fascist propaganda against Britain and France for concessions in Africa.

Mussolini's revisionist policies delivered tangible gains on all three fronts. The re-negotiation of the Italo–Yugoslav frontier produced the Rome Protocols of January 1924, according to which Italy acquired control of the city of Fiume by granting the surrounding territories to Yugoslavia. There was no real concession there; these same territories had been initially granted to Yugoslavia under the secret protocol of the Santa Margherita Accords, which Mussolini had refused to ratify.[33] This was the first victory of Italian revisionism, not only against the new state of Yugoslavia but also against the French concept of security in the Balkans and the Adriatic. It was also a symbolic triumph for the Fascist regime on the highly emotive issue of Dalmatia–Istria which had become the cornerstone of Italian irredentism since the beginning of the twentieth century.[34] The Italo–Yugoslav rapprochement was achieved through the co-operation between Mussolini and Salvatore Contarini, Under-Secretary to the Foreign Ministry.

Furthermore, the Treaty of Lausanne sanctioned the continuing occupation of the Dodecanese by Italy, thus annulling the 1919 Tittoni–Venizelos agreement for the return of the islands (except Rhodes) to Greece. The most important victory, however, for the Italian regime was the decision of the new British government to cede an extensive part of the Jubaland district (between Ethiopia, Somalia and Kenya) to Italy in early 1924, and then Jarabub (between Egypt and Libya) in 1925. This was a success not simply in territorial and colonial terms, but primarily as a manifestation of the Fascist regime's diplomatic consolidation in the European system.[35] The origins of this arrangement are to be found in the Milner–Scialoja agreement of 1920, which related the compensation to Italy under Article 13 of the Treaty of London to the cession of Jubaland and Jarabub. Under the conditions of this new agreement, Britain gave up a previous crucial precondition for colonial concessions to Italy: the return of the Dodecanese, or part of them, to Greece.[36] The cession of Jubaland regardless of the fate of the Dodecanese ensured a prestige victory for Italian colonial revisionism not only in east Africa but also in the vital area of the part of the eastern Mediterranean. Finally, the Italo–Albanian Treaty of 1927 re-established Italian influence over the region after the much-criticised decision of the liberal administration to withdraw the troops from Valona in 1920.[37]

In general, Mussolini's revisionist policies added very little to the traditional ambitions of Italian diplomacy for border readjustments in the Balkans and in Africa. The successes in Fiume, the Dodecanese, Jarabub and Jubaland were endorsed by the diplomatic establishment as constructive steps in the direction of strengthening Italy's influence in the Mediterranean and the Balkans. This impression of continuity was reinforced after Mussolini's adherence to the Locarno Pacts of 1925 and the absence of aggressive expansionist ventures during the so-called 'decade of good behaviour' until 1935. At the same time, Mussolini's highly selective and inconsistent invocation of the revisionist principle has been criticised by historians as evidence of the absence of a coherent expansionist strategy.[38] Such a reading, however, overlooks two major factors. First, the Duce showed little interest in the normative value of revisionism as a principle for border readjustment. His endorsement of anti-Versailles rhetoric was circumscribed by his perception of Italy's strategic and security interests. This meant that he was determined not only to pursue the Adriatic claims of the revisionist argument but also to encourage other countries (for example, Hungary) in their revisionist aspirations,[39] and further, to oppose the same principle regarding the sensitive issue of the *Anschluss*, which could jeopardise Italy's security at the Brenner. Second, Mussolini's ambitions in the Adriatic and the wider Mediterranean basin went beyond what the traditional revisionist agenda could justify as legitimate territorial readjustments. The violent occupation of Corfu in August 1923 (see Chapter 3) was not simply 'a colossal error of miscalculation and blind ambition', as Salvernini described it[40] it was decided before the assassination of Tellini, and provided Italy with the ultimate control point to the whole of the Adriatic Sea. Mussolini's subsequent policy of *penetration pacifique* in Albania and his ambition to provoke an internal collapse in Yugoslavia revealed his long-term intention to establish a virtual monopoly of power in the Adriatic and the Balkans. Such an objective implied a radical reorientation of Italian foreign policy towards the Balkan states, which included traditional revisionist claims but was by no means confined to them or underpinned by the pre-1914 commitment to informal imperialism in the region.

Germany: revisionism

In contrast to the Italian case, the revisionist policies of the Nazi regime in Germany after 1933 took place in a completely different diplomatic context. Hitler had to take into account two severe limitations on his anti-Versailles plans. The first limitation concerned the inauspicious diplomatic and military position of post-1918 Germany. With the Locarno Treaty, the Disarmament Conference and the plans for the amendment of the reparations obligations, the policies of the Weimar Republic had improved Germany's standing in the international system.[41] They had failed, however, to achieve either equality of rights or the restoration of the country's military potential. This double reality meant that the new Nazi government had both limited diplomatic margins for peaceful revision and still no chance of success should it choose to resort to forceful changes of the Versailles status quo. The second limitation originated from the unfavourable international attitudes and reactions to the intentions of the new Nazi regime in Germany. If the British and French governments had been sceptical, or even irritated, at Italy's great power aspirations in the Mediterranean and the Red Sea, they were now significantly more alarmed at the rise to power of a politician who had never concealed his determination to shatter the Versailles Treaty and reclaim Germany's lost power. At the same time, the Italian Fascist leadership continued to have mixed feelings about the restoration of the Reich's position in the European system. Although a possible ally in exercising pressure over France, a strong Germany represented a tangible threat to Italy's position in central Europe and the Balkans. As Mussolini was moving to a pro-status quo attitude in 1933–4,[42] Hitler's gambles on the sensitive issue of Austria in July 1934 turned Italy from a possible (and future) partner in revisionism into a temporary opponent (see Chapter 5).

Despite these limitations, Hitler could take advantage of a much more developed revisionist conscience in 1933, not only among the discontented nations but also among the guarantors of the postwar territorial settlement. The careful handling of the revisionist issue by the Weimar Republic, and the progress in all other directions except for the territorial issue,[43] had greatly legitimised Germany's claims for the return of, at least part of, her pre-1914 territories, in Europe and overseas.[44] Moreover, the revisionist experiments of Fascist Italy in the 1920s had exposed the difficulties in defending the postwar settlement as a definite territorial solution for the European system. Consequently, the Versailles status quo had become much less unassailable in 1933 than it was, or had appeared to be in the previous decade. This was something that even Britain and, to a lesser extent, France had come to acknowledge, first on the issue of reparations and then in the question of equality of legal and military rights. Undoubtedly, the transition from legal to territorial revisionism proved significantly more time-consuming for interwar Germany. By 1935, however, re-adjustments in all other aspects of the postwar settlement had resulted in a restoration of Germany's power, so that territorial revision ceased to be a purely juridical matter. Nazi Germany now possessed both the diplomatic status to pursue peaceful revisionism *and* the economic–military potential to expand by force. This was the main consideration behind the shift in British and, later, French foreign policies to tolerance and appeasement from the mid-1930s onwards.

In purely territorial terms, Nazi revisionism adhered to the traditional lines of the policy sponsored by the Wilhelmstrasse and the Reichswehr leadership throughout the Weimar Republic.[45] The April 1933 Declaration of Principles (prepared by the State Secretary to the Foreign Ministry von Bülow and endorsed by von Neurath) described the revision of the Versailles Treaty as Germany's 'most pressing concern'. Priority was given to the 'transformation of the Eastern Frontier' at the expense of more far-reaching changes (such as the *Anschluss*), which presupposed a radical international realignment. At the same time, however, the Memorandum placed primary emphasis on the need to 'recover our [military and economic] power' by pursuing a consistent policy of rearmament and exploiting 'the most favourable moment for the revision of each particular part of the treaty'.[46] After 1933, conscription was regarded as a necessary prerequisite for rebuilding the power of the Reichswehr by the military leadership, given the anticipation of failure at the Disarmament Conference at Geneva.[47] Furthermore, the remilitarisation of the Rhineland, a traditional objective of German revisionism since Locarno, constituted a medium-term priority for both the army and the Wilhelmstrasse in order to strengthen German security vis-à-vis France.[48]

After his appointment as Chancellor in January 1933, Hitler exploited every opportunity to reassure military and diplomatic circles about his cautious revisionism intentions. In the famous speech to the Reichswehr generals in early February 1933, he described rearmament as the 'most important prerequisite for achieving...political power' with a view to conducting a 'battle against Versailles'.[49] The withdrawal from the Disarmament Conference and the League of Nations in October 1933 was the culmination of a consistently obstructive Germany policy throughout 1933 which was master-minded by the Wilhelmstrasse and was endorsed by the military leadership.[50] Neurath had never concealed his dislike of the League, and Blomberg continued to press Hitler for an immediate withdrawal from Geneva. Ironically, the particular timing of the decision to withdraw is the only case in which Hitler postponed, rather than pushed forward, a foreign policy initiative. His reluctance to sanction an earlier withdrawal stemmed not from scepticism about the advisability of this move (he had made his decision clear since May 1933[51]), but from a determination to avoid negative repercussions from the impression that Germany had deliberately sabotaged the disarmament negotiation.[52] As for the next major revisionist move, namely the introduction of conscription, it took place in early 1935 with the complete agreement of Blomberg and with the tacit approval of the Foreign Office (see Chapter 3).

However, the real *pièce de résistance* of Nazi revisionism was the unilateral remilitarisation of the Rhineland in March 1936, in contravention of Article 42 of the Versailles Treaty and of its reaffirmation in the Locarno pact. Given the endorsement of the objective by the military and diplomatic conservative elites (see Chapter 3), the French–Soviet Pact of 1935 provided Hitler with the diplomatic ammunition to announce the termination of Germany's commitment to the Locarno pacts.[53] This implication was not missed by Neurath, who worked consistently throughout 1935 to pave the way for a diplomatic solution to the problem of the Rhineland; a solution which was also favoured by the Reichswehr leadership.[54] Although Hitler eventually decided to overcome the hesitations of Neurath and Blomberg, opting for a speedy military action, Neurath endorsed the move and advocated the completion of the operation. It was a risky undertaking, given that the actual size of the German military forces crossing the Rhine did not exceed 3,000. It was also the most nerve-racking moment in Hitler's career: the Chancellor and his War Minister nearly ordered the withdrawal of the forces, only to be persuaded by Neurath's resolute belief in the eventual success of the operation.[55] In the end, it was an unmitigated personal triumph of the Führer's 'high-risk' strategy, the first in a series of gambles that resulted in victories and nurtured Hitler's belief in the infallibility of his instinct. 'Hitler beams', noted Goebbels in his diary on the day of the remilitarisation. 'We have sovereignty again over our own land'.[56]

The continuity between conservative and Nazi revisionist objectives demonstrated in 1933–6 renders Weinberg's description of early Nazi foreign policy as a 'diplomatic revolution' rather exaggerated.[57] A.J.P. Taylor used this high degree of conservative consensus until 1936 to make the provocative statement that 'Hitler's foreign policy was that of his predecessors, of the professional diplomacy at the Foreign Office and of virtually all Germans'.[58] Even if Taylor overstated the case of continuity, other historians too have questioned the originality of Hitler's revisionist policies, highlighting instead the traditional character of its major objectives.[59] This impression was further strengthened by the fact that, unlike in Italy, the commitment of the traditional diplomatic and military elites to revisionism was temporary and open-ended,[60] disguising wider expansionist schemes in the east. The example of Poland is indicative of such intentions. Since the early 1920s, the Reichswehr leadership regarded the mere existence of the Polish state, in the words of General von Seect, as 'intolerable', urging its total disappearance through an alliance with Russia. In Bülow's 1933 memorandum, there is an explicit reference to the need to reject any solution which 'applies to Danzig alone', favouring instead another 'partition' of Poland. The same intransigent attitude dominated Neurath's briefing of the cabinet in April 1933, which restated Bülow's assertion that any agreement with Poland was 'neither possible nor desirable'.[61] As for the Reichswehr, the scenario of a war against Poland had been one of the favourite hypotheses of the military exercises organised by Blomberg since the late 1920s.[62]

However, from the outset Hitler's eastern policy revealed an interesting divergence. In a speech delivered on 23 March, he appealed to Germany's neighbours for peaceful relations.[63] This message was interpreted by the Polish leader, Piłsudski, as a departure from the traditional anti-Polish line of German diplomacy. For this reason, and at Polish request, negotiations for an agreement carefully by-passed the Wilhelmstrasse[64] and soon extended far beyond what Neurath regarded as an economically beneficial treaty[65] to the possibility of a political pact.[66] In this direction, Hitler instructed the Nazi party in Danzig to avoid any provocation, paving the way for an extensive agreement between the Free City and the Polish government in August 1933.[67] In spite of rising tension in German–Polish relations throughout the spring and summer of 1933 (fuelled by rumours about an impending Polish–Soviet pact against Germany), Hitler continued to offer assurances to Poland about his peaceful intentions and to explore the possibilities of a diplomatic rapprochement. So, when the prospect of a Polish–Soviet alliance subsided in September 1933 and the Polish Foreign Minister Beck came to Berlin for talks, both sides declared their commitment to improving their bilateral relations. The ensuing negotiations in Berlin made significant progress in the last three months of 1933, leading to the signing of the Non-Aggression Pact in January 1934. On its own, the pact with Poland appeared to thwart Germany's revisionist ambitions in the east but did not seriously alarm the Wilhelmstrasse,[68] as most diplomats interpreted Hitler's surprise mainly as the result of Germany's diplomatic isolation after withdrawing from Geneva in October. However, the developments in German–Polish relations should be contrasted with the changing Nazi policy towards the Soviet Union. The importance of maintaining good relations with the USSR – first recognised by von Seeckt in the early 1920s and realised in the Treaty of Rapallo in April 1922 and the Treaty of Berlin in 1926 – was emphatically reiterated in Bülow's memorandum of April 1933. Although Neurath was not the most fervent advocate of Soviet friendship, he did play a crucial role in the ratification of the Berlin Treaty in April 1933.[69] For his part, the new German Ambassador in Moscow, Nadolny, pressed his government in Berlin to consolidate friendly economic and political relations with the Soviet Union.[70] However, by October 1933 Hitler considered an improvement in German–Russian relations as 'impossible' and rejected Nadolny's numerous appeals for a rapprochement.[71] After the pact with Poland in January 1934, Nadolny expressed his opposition to this policy and, when the Soviet proposal for a comprehensive political agreement submitted to the German government in May 1934 was not even considered by Hitler, he resigned in protest.[72] At the same time, the Führer used Göring as a special envoy to Poland in order to explore Piłsudski's attitude to the prospect of a military alliance against the Soviet Union.[73] He also appeared determined to preserve the atmosphere of rapprochement by dealing with problems in such sensitive areas, such as the Corridor and Upper Silesia, in an accommodating spirit.[74]

In this sense, Hitler's commitment to revisionism in 1933–6 displayed a selectivity dominated by the prerequisites of a more far-reaching eastern policy. Although he seemed to share the traditional diplomats' view of revisionism as a short-term formula to disguise more extensive expansionist ambitions, he was also willing to sacrifice emotive revisionist claims (in the Corridor and Upper Silesia) and the colonial argument for the sake of an eastern policy dominated by a distinctly anti-Soviet orientation. The conclusion of the pact with Poland (which in October 1933 had stumbled over Neurath's unwillingness to accept Polish demands regarding the flow of coal from Upper Silesia, but was immediately given a boost by Hitler's orders to make substantial concessions[75]) shows his flexibility with diplomatic opportunities, but his subsequent thoughts about a German–Polish alliance against the USSR highlight his ability to align short-term experiments with long-term plans for eastern expansion. Similarly, he relied on the traditional revisionist agenda of rearmament–conscription–Rhineland, but was also eager to shelve the Wilhelmstrasse's claims for border readjustments in Eupen-Malmedy and North Schleswig.[76] Therefore, the impression of continuity and consensus in German foreign policy was mitigated by these divergences which alluded to a more radical Hitlerite vision for long-term expansion

Irredentism: the distortion of an argument

The second major interwar argument for justifying territorial claims was irredentism. In its original form, irredentism had been a liberal argument, theoretically not linked to territorial expansionism but to certain populations, according to the principle of national self-determination.[77] The emergence of nationalism in the nineteenth century gave rise to the idea of nation-state, a territorial entity which should include the whole of an ethnically and culturally homogeneous population, and only that. In the first chapter we analysed the great difficulties in implementing this principle in the European mosaic of peoples up to 1914. The First World War revived the debate of national frontiers in the European system, and the Wilsonian Fourteen Points offered a new popularity to irredentist claims. The failure, however, of the Peace Treaties to balance the conflicting claims of the different states and the desire of the victors for a punitive arrangement against the vanquished aggravated an already problematic situation. The dissolution of the three great multinational empires (Habsburg, Russian and Ottoman) in 1918 produced a plethora of new states with more or less inflated territorial aspirations. These were satisfied at the expense of the defeated powers. Given, though, the impossibility of drawing clear ethnic frontiers in central and eastern Europe, old *irredenta* were simply replaced – or complemented – by a long list of new ones. The further provision of plebiscites in some disputed areas proved how difficult it was to apply the principle of nationality in areas with limited tradition in etatist culture.

Not surprisingly, the irredentist argument gained greater currency in interwar Germany than in Italy. To the traditional German *irredenta* in vast areas of the erstwhile Habsburg and Russian empires the Peace Treaties added the ethnically German populations of the territories ceded from the Reich to France, Poland, Czechoslovakia and the new Baltic states. At the same time, the collapse of the Habsburg empire stimulated hopes for the long-standing *alldeutsche* claim for a German–Austrian union, which the Treaty of Versailles eventually banned.[78] Finally, the extension of the northern Italian frontier up to the Brenner Pass placed a strong German-speaking minority in South Tyrol under the sovereignty of the Italian state.

What Germany lost in South Tyrol became the major gain of Italian irredentism from the postwar territorial settlement. The other gain was the modest extension of the north-eastern frontier in Istria and Dalmatia by the Treaty of Rapallo in 1920. In this sense, the problem with Italian postwar irredentism was totally different from the German case. Under the Peace Treaties, Italy had succeeded in expanding her territory by capitalising on the international popularity of irredentism. Such was, however, the traditional strength and scope of Italian irredentism that it could not possibly have been satiated by any conceivable postwar settlement. It might have been easy to satisfy its anti-Austrian claim for Alto Adige and the Brenner, but it would be impossible to reward its anti-French (Corsica, Nice) or anti-British (Malta) ambitions, especially under a settlement that was mainly defined and guaranteed by Britain and France.[79] As in the case of colonialism, it was the feeling of limited compensation and injustice that offered a new lease of life to Italian irredentism in the interwar period.

In spite of this fundamental difference, however, there was a common element in the revival of the irredentist debate in postwar Italy and Germany. On the one hand, irredentism was a major form of attack upon the principles of the Peace Treaties. It could exploit the issue of nationality in order to expose the inconsistent, selective application of the maxim of self-determination in redrawing the map of Europe after the First World War. In this way, irredentism could disguise significant territorial claims in the framework of a legal revisionism that appeared more justifiable, yet no less extensive than any conceivable Italian or German plan for continental expansion after the war. On the other hand, irredentism, whether in the context of revisionism or not, was the only available platform for the justification of territorial claims in the continent. This was of particular importance for the future of fascist foreign policies in both Italy and Germany, since 'unredeemed' territories formed a crucial part of the greater expansionist visions held by the two fascist leaderships. Italy needed Fiume as a strategic port in the Adriatic,[80] and needed Malta and Corsica as control points for the centre of the Mediterranean[81] in order to consolidate Italy's geopolitical position in the area. In a similar way, the Polish Corridor stood in Hitler's way towards the unification of the western and eastern German territories and the conquest of *Lebensraum* in Russia. In order to achieve that, he also required the economic and defensive advantages of the neighbouring states in central Europe. In all these cases, irredentist arguments succeeded in covering the middle ground between traditional claims over *irredenta*, continental revisionism and the large-scale expansionist ambitions of the two fascist regimes.

The incorporation of the irredentist principle into the wider geopolitical framework of fascist expansionism was marked by a highly selective and unprincipled application by the two regimes. Instead of being a normative concept referring to populations, fascist irredentism focused on territories and was exploited as part of the justification for wider expansionist plans. This, of course, was not a fascist novelty: a similar radical irredentist tendency had developed between 1890 and 1914 in the two countries. It was this prewar tradition of radical irredentism that initiated the shift in the focus of irredentism from the ethnic character of populations to the geographical and historic dimensions of territorial claims. The fascist regimes, however, were innovative in that they came to value the significance of irredentist issues on an individual and flexible basis, according to their expansionist priorities and their wider political alliances or rivalries. This tendency resulted from the fact that the irredentist argument lost its political autonomy in postwar Italy and Germany. Until the First World War it had more or less managed to retain its normative character within the nationalist discourse. It had also been treated as a semi-utopian concept which kept it away from the tests of political action. This situation changed completely in the interwar period. The gradual absorption of the nationalist movement into fascism in both countries deprived the irredentism argument of those implications that were incompatible with the spirit of radical nationalism. Evidently, there was no room in fascism for the 'liberal' respect for other nationalities that had limited the territorial scope of irredentism in the past and kept it free from aggressive implications. Thus, irredentism was transformed into an aggressive principle serving the irrelevant (that is, territorial and not ethnic) ambitions of a large-scale territorial expansionism.

Furthermore, the Peace Treaties had greatly individualised and politicised the issue of 'unredeemed' territories. Interwar irredentism was not simply about ethnically kin populations that had not as yet been incorporated in the national Italian or German territory. It also involved peoples and geographic areas that had been transferred to other states, old and new, through the legal force of the Peace Treaties. The political conflict between rival nationalisms had conceptualised the issue of *irredenta* in terms of international antagonism and had increased the number of potential territorial conflicts. Before the First World War, Italian irredentism was directed mainly against those territories still under the control of the Habsburg empire in particular, and to some extent those of France and Switzerland also. After 1919 the Yugoslav state was added to the list as the usurper of certain Habsburg territories with an alleged Italian character. Interwar German governments faced a similar, yet more extensive and complicated problem. German 'unredeemed' areas, previously under Russian or Habsburg control, were divided among a plethora of new states in central and eastern Europe. Additionally, Germany lost part of her pre-1914 territory to France, Belgium and Poland. Finally, the issue of Austria and the fate of the German-speaking minority in South Tyrol opened a new front in the south, this time against Italy.

Both Mussolini and Hitler were aware that they needed allies in order to pursue their great power aspirations. In this sense, irredentism in its postwar form was unsuitable as an overall principle of foreign policy strategy. Its full implications would engage Italy and especially Germany in a quixotic battle against every other European state. This realisation prompted the selective political use of the irredentist arguments by the two fascist regimes. Mussolini focused on the Italo–Yugoslav conflict over Fiume, and the defence of Austria's independence as a safeguard against German influence in the Brenner. His main interest lay in upholding the image of Italy as the main arbiter of the European balance of power in the decade between Locarno and the Ethiopian campaign, and this induced him to tone down the anti-French and anti-British goals of Italian irredentism. Of course, he was a politician who resisted definite commitments, and the irredentist objectives in the Mediterranean were important for his plans for transforming the region into an Italian *mare nostrum*, but control of the Adriatic and stability in the northern frontier were more immediate tasks. Therefore, although he never ceased to support irredentist activities in Malta and Corsica, he nevertheless abstained from a hard line on this issue.[82]

The success of Italian irredentism in Fiume in 1924 did not shift Mussolini's attention from the Danubian–Adriatic region. This tendency intensified in the following years as the restoration of German power and the rise of Hitler to power appeared to threaten the balance of power in central Europe (see Chapter 5). As, however, the rapprochement between the two fascist regimes was growing (complemented with a German opt-out on the issue of South Tyrol), the focus of Italian irredentism started to move again towards the Mediterranean. This was reflected in the popularity of the studies on various regions of the Adriatic–Mediterranean area that were published in Italy in the late 1930s.[83] At the same time, as relations with France were steadily deteriorating after 1935, the neglected Italian claims on the south-east coast of France were resuscitated.[84] Quite symbolically, Ciano's speech in front of the Chamber in April 1939 was dramatically interrupted by loud cries for the occupation of 'Corsica, Nice, Savoy'.[85] It is doubtful, however, that Mussolini had firm intentions to pursue his anti-French and anti-British irredentist agenda in an aggressive, unilateral manner. Throughout 1937–9 these territorial issues were repeatedly mentioned in the context of the diplomatic talks with British and French officials, but only as ancillary arguments in favour of a wider territorial settlement between Italy and the west, which would also include colonial and wider strategic gains for the Italian side.

Hitler's irredentism, on the other hand, showed a similar selectivity, but a more stable pattern of political priorities. The Führer's unwavering emphasis on eastward expansion provided the German irredentist claims – traditional or revisionist – against Poland and the Baltic states with the highest political significance. Quite conveniently, the Polish Corridor and the 'unredeemed' territories of East Prussia were also the top priorities of the Reichswehr leadership and the conservative diplomats. In an event organised by the War

Minister von Blomberg only a few weeks after the Nazi *Machtergreifung*, Hitler spoke clearly to an audience of army officials about the need for rearmament in order to achieve the goals of eastward expansion.[86] At the same time, the *alldeutsche* ideological platform of the NSDAP, which had contributed to its electoral appeal up to 1933, brought the issues of Austria and the Sudetenland to the forefront of the political debate about Germany's role in central Europe. Before the war, the irredentist claim for the incorporation of the German territories of the Habsburg empire into the Reich had been the sharp edge of the pan-German propaganda against the Bismarckian notion of a 'satiated' Germany. In the postwar period, the unifying web between the Austrian and the Sudetenland claims (that is, the Habsburg empire) ceased to exist and the fates of the two territories/populations diverged. Austria became a homogeneous German-speaking independent state, while the lands of the Sudeten German minority were incorporated in the new Czechoslovak state which was formally protected by France.[87] Consequently, conservative German diplomacy and the Reichswehr leadership continued to view the Austrian issue as a more feasible and politically justifiable irredentist claim. By contrast, they temporarily relinquished the Sudetenland claim because of its secessionist implications threatening the integrity of Czechoslovakia. This different assessment was also reflected in the Nazi strategic planning for central Europe. Hitler had been prepared to raise the issue of Austria's union with the Reich as one of the top priorities of his foreign policy, and this was manifested in the premature Nazi Putsch in Vienna in July 1934 (see Chapter 3).[88] Towards Czechoslovakia, though, he had initially requested only a defensive plan with no immediate annexationist implications.[89]

This situation changed radically in 1936–7. Austria and Czechoslovakia were linked in Hitler's foreign policy strategy as necessarily complementary steps towards the consolidation of a German sphere of influence in central Europe. The indispensability of this objective was further underlined by its defensive and economic significance for the Nazi plans for large-scale eastward expansion in the near future.[90] As the Nazi regime was embarking on a course of rapid rearmament and on a high-risk foreign policy from 1936 onwards, the question of economic resources and security became of the utmost importance for the attainment of the Nazi long-term expansionist goals. These considerations formed the new unifying link between the Austrian and the Sudeten irredentist issues, in the latter case transforming the defensive planning into offensive.[91]

Hitler's handling of the two issues in 1938–9 revealed the limitations of his irredentist beliefs. The ethnic argument might have been a sufficient political formula for the pursuit of the *Anschluss*, and the western powers – especially Britain – had long ago hinted at their *disinteressement* for a peaceful absorption of Austria by the German Reich. Lord Halifax had repeatedly implied to Hitler that a *peaceful* revision of the Austrian issue would be acceptable to Britain.[92] Mussolini's eventual consent to the union in March 1938 opened the way for a solution which at least kept up irredentist appearances. For their part, the

National Socialist leaderships in Berlin and Vienna did their best to uphold an image of legality, by presenting the German intervention as emanating from the wishes of the Austrian population and government, not of the Nazi side.[93] The Sudeten crisis, however, in the summer and autumn of the same year (see below) was based on quite different issues. Hitler's strategy after 1937 aimed at the occupation of the whole Czechoslovak state, a goal for which the irredentist claim over the Sudetenland provided only a politically insufficient and geographically partial justification.[94] When in September 1938 Hitler raised his price in his negotiations with Chamberlain by demanding the Sudetenland *and* Bohemia, he exploited the card of Slovak, Polish and Hungarian irredentism,[95] but he also indicated his determination to liquidate the Czechoslovak state by force. This was hardly an irredentist objective, and it exposed the Führer's political manipulation of the ethnic argument in order to promote purely expansionist plans. The problem was that the British government took the irredentist alibi of Nazi expansionism quite seriously, eager to make concessions on these lines, without realising that no territorial offer on *ethnic* grounds would ever satisfy the *geographical* prerequisites of the fascist 'new order'. The final, if ephemeral, solution, namely the cession of the Sudetenland to the Reich, was authorised on the grounds of the overwhelmingly German character of the population and the region.[96] This irredentist justification offered a new lease of legitimacy to Nazi expansionism, provided Germany with valuable time for military preparation, and removed a significant geopolitical obstacle to eastward expansion.[97]

The insincerity of the *alldeutsche* pretensions of Hitler's foreign policy, how-ever, was even more clearly manifested in the dropping of the German irredentist claims in Alsace and South Tyrol. The two German-speaking minorities living in these regions had been traditionally seen as integral parts of the dream of a pan-German state at the heart of Europe. It was with regard to these two minorities – and their home territories – that the alleged irredentist principle of Nazi foreign policy was totally overshadowed by the crude geopolitical considerations of Hitler's large-scale expansionist plans. In the first case, the region of Alsace was geographically irrelevant to the Nazi vision of *Lebensraum* expansion in the east. This greatly explains Hitler's cool attitude towards the fate of this minority, at least compared with his active interest in the German populations in central and eastern Europe. Undoubtedly, the Alsatians had developed a fairly idiosyncratic cultural identity, quite distinct from either the French or the German, and had also resisted legislation aiming at political, cultural or religious assimilation by either of the two sides.[98] However, the symbolic significance of the region, if not only in irredentist at least in revisionist (overthrow of Versailles) and historic (memories of the 1870 victory) terms, would have justified a more energetic political exploitation of this issue by the Nazi regime; something that was far from the case.

The second ethnic issue, concerning the minority in South Tyrol, is more enlightening as regards the political manipulation of the irredentist argument by

Hitler. Directly linked to the status of Austria, this question acquired a symbolic importance for the revisionist and *alldeutsche* aspirations of German nationalism after the war.[99] It was, however, its interrelation with the *Anschluss* issue that implicated the fate of the South Tyrolese German-speaking minority in another sensitive aspect of European stability: Italo–German relations.[100] The political and defensive importance of the Brenner for Italy transformed this problem into a bone of contention in her relations with the Nazi regime. This put Hitler in a complex political dilemma: to adhere to the priority of the pan-German argument at the expense of Italian friendship, or to sacrifice a vital irredentist claim in order to achieve an Italo-German alliance.[101] It was a difficult political question, but Hitler's decision to pursue the second option had been an unwavering guideline of his foreign policy strategy since the early 1920s. Since 1922 he had plainly declared that 'for us the question of South Tyrol does not exist, nor will it ever exist'.[102] Both before and after 1933, he reiterated many times his basic thesis that 'the fate of some thousands of erstwhile Austrian citizens should not influence the relations between the two states'.[103] Consequently, German irredentism in the Brenner was dropped in favour of a strategic consideration (alliance with Italy) which was far more important for the Nazi wider expansionist plans in the long term. What is more striking, however, is that the irredentist issues of Austria and South Tyrol were politically separated and treated on a completely different political basis, despite the fact that they were interrelated and referred to the very same principle.

This inconsistency in the application of the irredentist principle by both the Italian and the German fascist regimes leads us to three main conclusions. First, the irredentist argument under fascism was reduced to a propagandistic function in the much wider context of fascist expansionism. For the purposes of such an aggressive territorial policy, irredentism was transformed into an expansionist justification with aggressive political connotations. Second, the irredentist argument gradually lost its normative value. It was subjected to an opportunistic function that assessed the desirability of individual claims over populations according to the political significance of the involved territory for the wider plans of fascist expansion. Third, as the scope of Italian and German great power ambitions gradually increased in the 1930s, the ethnic element of the irredentist justification became a limitation to fascist expansionist aspirations. With large-scale expansion becoming the top priority of the two fascist regimes in the late 1930s, irredentism could no longer sustain its primary emphasis on disputed and territorially limited claims based on the ethnic identity of populations. When the territorial potential of both revisionism and ethnic irredentism had been almost exhausted, the need to justify wider expansion introduced the argument of *living space* as the main idea underpinning further expansionist objectives.

From border to space policy: towards large-scale fascist expansion

The adherence of the two fascist regimes to traditional arguments of territorial expansion, such as anti-Versailles revisionism and irredentism, upheld an impression of continuity between pre-fascist and fascist foreign policy objectives. Until 1935–6, both Mussolini and Hitler exploited the legitimacy of such traditional claims to achieve territorial changes of limited scale, in the form of border readjustments. However, as we saw, the fascist commitment to border policy was mitigated by a selective endorsement of certain goals and a tepid attitude towards others, as well as by specific moves (the Corfu incident, the 1934 German–Polish pact) which were either against or beyond the logic of revisionism. From the fascist point of view, adherence to border policy was an interim step towards the unfolding of a larger-scale *space* policy, dominated by emphasis on constant activism and expressing the right of the two peoples to expand in their historic spheres of influence. In *Mein Kampf*, Hitler had rejected the 'absurdity of the 1914 frontiers', advocating the need to avoid a myopic border policy in favour of a 'soil policy of the future'.[104] This argument was reactivated with renewed vigour at the Hossbach conference, where the Führer stated that 'the aim of German policy is to preserve the national community and to enlarge it. It is therefore a question of space' (see also Chapter 3).[105] For his part, Mussolini's early vague references to the Mediterranean as a *mare nostrum* took a more concrete form after 1935: in his Milan speech of 1936, he alluded to Italy's wide expansionist intentions in order to escape from geopolitical 'imprisonment' in the Mediterranean,[106] while in February 1939 he spoke of the need to 'march to the Oceans' in terms of a 'historic necessity'.[107] In this sense, the radicalisation of the expansionist policies of the two fascist regimes from the mid-1930s onwards reflected a change of focus and pace towards living space policy as an open-ended leitmotif for large-scale expansion. Each of the two regimes made specific strategic choices and followed different tactics in implementing their more 'radical' plans. These raise complex questions about whether the character of these decisions was pre-determined, and about continuities or discontinuities in Italian and German foreign policy. Below, we will examine the colonial and continental expansionist ventures of the two regimes, assessing their relevance to the wider expansionist visions of the two leaders and their function in the overall framework of the Italian and German foreign policies.

Colonialism

Fascist Italy and early colonial policies

As Prime Minister, Mussolini had both the political freedom and the ideological propensity to integrate colonial claims in the framework of his large-scale expansionist vision. Despite the fact that the First World War had re-focused attention on the long-standing claims for continental expansion, this proved only a temporary shift. With the conclusion of the Peace Treaties, the new territorial map of Europe was again presented as unalterable, and the colonies resumed their political function as the field of territorial compensation for the discontented and as the legitimate prize for international antagonism.[108] His aspiration to make Italy the superpower of the Mediterranean required control of a vast area from Gibraltar to the Red Sea.[109] This involved a strong position not only in the European coast, but also on the African side. In this sense, the prestige factor of Fascist colonialism could also serve the ideological and geopolitical ambitions of the Fascist regime in the Mediterranean. Two further developments encouraged Mussolini's focus on colonial policies at the expense of continental expansion. The stabilisation of the European system between the Locarno Pact (1925) and the advent of Hitler to power (1933) rendered any desire to alter the territorial arrangements in the continent inopportune, if not totally inconceivable during the above period. Thus, the greatest part of the Italian efforts for prestige were channelled into the colonial field, in which the western powers were more willing to make promises or even concessions in return for Italy's support for the European status quo. Furthermore, the emergence of Nazi Germany made Mussolini himself more sensitive to the importance of the European balance of power. Thus, in order to preserve his 'determinant' position in the continent and increase his fascist prestige towards Germany, the Duce exploited the colonial card, taking advantage of what he had perceived, from 1932 onwards, as favourable British and French attitudes towards a colonial campaign against Ethiopia.

In territorial terms, Mussolini's colonial policy was undoubtedly the most successful part of his expansionist activities. In 1922 he inherited from his liberal predecessors a meagre colonial 'empire' in north (Libya) and east (Somalia, Eritrea) Africa, where Italian control had almost collapsed due to pressure from indigenous rebels.[110] In spite of his failure to elicit a colonial mandate in 1923, Mussolini showed an unwavering determination to restore Italy's colonial reputation, pursue traditional colonial aspirations and instil some sort of colonial enthusiasm among the population.[111] Having achieved the cession of Jubaland and Jarabub by the British, he initiated comprehensive campaigns in Libya and Somalia in order to restore Italian authority over the rebellious regions.[112] Emphasis on re-establishing Italian control over Libya and Somalia dated back to the beginning of the 1922, when the liberal Minister of Colonies, Amendola, spoke of the need to resurrect Italy's *Impero*.[113] A few months after he had been appointed Prime Minister, in early 1923, Mussolini adopted an intransigent attitude towards the indigenous populations in Somalia and in Cyrenaica (N. Libya). In the former case, the Italian Governor and member of the *quadrumvirate* in 1922, Cesare De Vecchi di Val Cismon, eliminated any trace of resistance by local tribes and established total control in the region by 1928.[114] In Libya, the previous policy of compromise with the indigenous Sanussis was repudiated by the Italian government in 1923, giving way to a long drawn-out military conflict.

123

Lack of tangible progress by 1930, however, prompted Mussolini to grant control of the operations to General Graziani who, in co-operation with Marshal Badoglio (Governor of Libya since 1928), instigated a ruthless policy of eliminating the Sanussis. Through a combination of extensive warfare and genocidal methods, Graziani was able to announce the 'pacification' of Libya by 1932.[115]

The Ethiopian campaign

However, the most impressive part of Mussolini's colonial policy was the successful execution of the Ethiopian campaign in 1935–6.[116] This has undoubtedly been the most hotly debated foreign policy initiative of the Italian Fascist regime in the 1930s, raising all sorts of questions about continuities in Italian foreign policy and about Mussolini's long-term expansionist intentions. Renzo De Felice has described the Ethiopian campaign as 'Mussolini's masterpiece',[117] in the sense that the Duce pursued it with obsessive determination and increased the regime's prestige both domestically and on the international level. Such a view directly challenged the Salveminian orthodoxy of viewing the campaign as the 'prelude to the Second World War', and was disputed by C. Segrè and R.J.B. Bosworth, who underlined the long-term destabilising effects of the campaign for the whole European system.[118] Both authors compared the invasion of Ethiopia with the ill-conceived Libyan campaign of 1912, but they also detected a lack of foresight in Mussolini's strategy which contrasted with Giolitti's more realistic expansionist policy. Others, like L. Pastorelli, analysed the Ethiopian campaign as the beginning of a new, more aggressive phase in the expansionist policies of the Fascist regime, breaking a line of continuity which had been upheld by the allegedly moderate foreign policy of the previous decade.[119] By contrast, an influential interpretation of Mussolini's decision to attack Ethiopia in 1935 pointed to the direction of its utility for domestic purposes. F. Catalano viewed the venture as a diversionary move, aimed to distract attention from the mounting economic crisis which hit Italy later than many other countries.[120] This social imperialistic argument was shared by G. Rochat and G. Baer, who underlined Mussolini's conscious exploitation of foreign policy for primarily domestic purposes, as a means to strengthen the legitimacy of the regime after a period of stagnation and waning public enthusiasm for Fascism.[121] An intriguing middle way is reflected in M. Knox's thesis that the Ethiopian campaign combined a long-term ideological goal of the Duce's expansionist vision with his ambition to use an impressive foreign policy success to promote a revolutionary transformation of the domestic system in a more totalitarian direction.[122]

In terms of continuity with the liberal foreign policy, there was nothing particularly novel in choosing Ethiopia as a goal for territorial expansion. Italian interests in east Africa had been consolidated since the 1880s, when successful expansion in Eritrea and Somalia laid the foundations of an Italian colonial

Impero in the last available region of Africa.[123] Crispi's ill-fated campaign against Ethiopia in the 1890s seemed the obvious policy in order to establish a large colonial network around the southern exit of the Suez Canal. The humiliating defeat of 1896 at Adowa caused a deep national trauma but did not thwart the Italian expansionist ambitions in the region. In 1906 a tripartite agreement between Italy, Britain and France comprised a secret acknowledgement of an Italian sphere of influence in Ethiopia.[124] Strategic plans for an attack on Ethiopia from Eritrea dated back to 1908.[125] Even under Fascist rule, the diplomatic establishment of the Palazzo Chigi nurtured concrete hopes of an expansionist move in Ethiopia. The Italian–British agreement of December 1925 reaffirmed the informal division of the country into spheres of influence, implying a British recognition of Italy's continuing interest in the region. In the ensuing period until 1932, the Italian government followed a policy of 'friendship', culminating in the 1928 agreement with the Ethiopian emperor Menelik, while at the same time encouraging the consolidation of Italian economic interests in Ethiopia.[126] However, by 1932 this policy was officially described as a failure by the Palazzo Chigi. In one of his last initiatives as Foreign Minister, Grandi gave priority to the *politica periferica* in early 1932, requesting a detailed examination of the prospects of an aggressive war in east Africa.[127] In an extensive memorandum published in August 1932, the Director of European Affairs at Palazzo Chigi, Guariglia, expressed the need to strengthen Italy's military presence in Ethiopia *on the basis of British and French consensus*.[128] A year before, the same diplomat had also spoken of Italy's expansionist ambitions at the expense of Ethiopia, alluding to a future course of expansion, 'probably with war'.[129]

However, this continuity between liberal and Fascist foreign policy strategies towards Ethiopia should not overshadow Mussolini's consistent personal interest in the prospect of a war in east Africa. This interest dates back to 1925, at the time of the agreement with Britain over Ethiopia, when the Duce spoke of his desire to pursue an 'integral violent solution' when more auspicious international circumstances prevailed.[130] Such an idea took a more concrete shape by 1932, when Mussolini asked the Ministry of Colonies, headed by Emilio De Bono, to draft an operational plan for an offensive action against Ethiopia.[131] The memorandum envisaged a large-scale invasion in the near future, but at the same time reiterated the same strategic precondition with Guariglia's report: the consent of Britain and France.[132] At the same time, Mussolini asked his supreme commander of the armed forces, Badoglio, to examine the prospects for an offensive action in east Africa. Badoglio's subsequent vehement criticism of De Bono's plan had much to do with his personal antipathy towards the Minister of Colonies and his anger with Mussolini's decision to appoint De Bono as commander in the event of a war in Ethiopia (see Chapter 3). However, Badoglio's hostility to the plan also reflected a fear that the assumption of British and French consensus to the invasion of Ethiopia was dangerously misplaced.[133]

It is in this light that we should examine Mussolini's eventual decision to authorise the campaign against Ethiopia in late 1934. The directive of 30

December 1934 unequivocally stated as its goal the 'whole destruction of the Ethiopian armed forces and the occupation of the whole of Ethiopia'.[134] Security in Europe, however, had been relegated to a secondary condition under the impression of French acquiescence. This optimism dated back to 1931, when, in a conversation between Grandi and his French counterpart Laval, the latter had used the example of Ethiopia as a possible compensation for an Italian compromise on the issue of Tunisia.[135] A few days after the directive, the Mussolini–Laval agreement consolidated the former's impression that Italy had been granted a 'free hand' in Ethiopia.[136] The diplomatic omens became even more favourable in the spring of 1935 with the formation of the Stresa front by Britain, France and Italy in reaction to Germany's unilateral introduction of conscription. The final text of the agreement made a specific reference to the need to uphold stability 'in Europe', a reference which was added by the British delegation but was interpreted by the Italian leadership as a further indication of tacit consensus for expansion in Africa.[137] At the same time, a separate Italian–French military agreement to oppose any German plans in Austria strengthened the impression that German aggression in the Danube region would be effectively contained by the Stresa front.[138] However, the ambiguity of the British position prompted the Italian diplomats to press for a more definite clarification of the British attitude to Italy's claims in east Africa. The visit of the then British representative to the League of Nations, Anthony Eden, to Rome in June 1935 was accompanied by a proposal for a diplomatic compromise, under which Italy would be granted a corridor via Zeila to Somalia, but the plan was explicitly rejected by both Mussolini and Guariglia (who had been appointed in 1935 as Head of the Special Office for the Ethiopian Question).[139] In July 1935, another initiative to refer the issue to international arbitration under the aegis of the League of Nations was dismissed by the Duce as 'humiliating for Italy',[140] while a similar attempt in August–September to place Ethiopia under an international mandate and to recognise a formal Italian interest was rejected by the Fascist Grand Council. Instead, plans for a large-scale mobilisation of the Italian armed forces went forward during the summer of 1935, with over 300,000 soldiers transferred to Eritrea and Somaliland, accompanied by planes and heavy artillery.[141]

Mussolini's determination to pursue a violent occupation of the whole of Ethiopia, in spite of alarming indications that Britain would oppose such an action and that France was against the idea of an aggressive campaign, is further illustrated by his rejection of the objections raised by both the King and Marshal Badoglio. Their fears stemmed from the traditional belief of the conservative establishment in the indispensability of British friendship, and reflected their conviction that such a friendship would be seriously jeopardised by an attack on Ethiopia.[142] It is true that Mussolini and his diplomatic advisers, including Ciano, chose to underestimate the indications of British hostility to the campaign.[143] Until June 1935, he kept the channels of communication with London open in the hope that the issue would not be brought to the League of

Nations and that Britain would not risk the cohesion of the Stresa front by adopting an intransigent line towards Italy. However, the referral of the dispute to the League in July and the British–German Naval Agreement a month earlier caused considerable irritation and alarm to the Italian Fascist leadership.[144] From that point onwards, British acquiescence ceased to be a prerequisite for Italian action in Ethiopia. The self-confidence of the regime was further strengthened by intercepted information by the Servizio Informazione Militari (SIM, the Intelligence Service) about the low level of mobilisation and fighting potential of the British fleet in the Mediterranean.[145] Therefore, Mussolini pushed forward his aggressive plans in the belief that Britain would refrain from counter-measures in the Mediterranean and in Africa, but also in the knowledge of British opposition to the campaign.

In this sense, the decision to launch the invasion in October 1935 combined a long-term significance with a short-term assessment of the international situation. Throughout the 1920s, Mussolini displayed a determination to reconstitute and expand Italy's colonial empire in Africa. After restoring control in Libya and Somaliland, he turned his attention to east Africa and the Arabian peninsula with a two-edged policy of penetration in Ethiopia and Yemen.[146] By the end of 1934, while plans in Yemen foundered, the impression of French and British acquiescence in an Italian expansion in Ethiopia convinced Mussolini that the situation was opportune, an impression which was further strengthened by the Stresa front and Germany's diplomatic isolation. This favourable short-term realignment of international relations, according to J. Petersen, constituted the catalyst for prioritising the invasion plan in the first half of 1935. When this window of opportunity dramatically narrowed in August with the failure of the Tripartite conference in Paris, and in September with the British mobilisation in the Mediterranean,[147] Mussolini appeared determined to pursue his geopolitical ambitions in Ethiopia in spite of the adverse international circumstances. He gave explicit instructions to the Italian delegation in the League of Nations to refuse to negotiate any concessions,[148] and when Guariglia advised him to accept a compromising solution to refer the issue to an international committee,[149] he dismissed the suggestion without further discussion. However, Mussolini had not as yet finalised his strategy, aware of the French intentions to broker a wider agreement and of the British reluctance either to support the imposition of economic sanctions or to block the Suez Canal. The eventual decision of the League of Nations to apply sanctions did cause alarm to the Italian government, and led to a somewhat more accommodating attitude towards the French proposals of ceding extensive Ethiopian territories to Italy while reducing the remaining regions to the status of a virtual Italian protectorate.[150] This willingness to discuss a negotiated settlement regarding Ethiopia seems to endorse R. Quartararo's assertion that Mussolini had not irreversibly decided on the *whole* conquest of Ethiopia and remained interested in a certain diplomatic solution that would enable Italy to consolidate her position in east Africa.[151] However, throughout the autumn of 1935, Mussolini became increasingly disillusioned with British procrastination tactics. By the time of the Hoare–Laval compromise plan in December 1935 (named after the two Foreign Ministers of Britain and France, who secretly discussed it) he had reverted to an intransigent position: after having initially dismissed the offer, he was convinced by Aloisi to consider it but only as a basis for future discussion and with a series of counter-proposals for revisions. Given the negative assessment of the plan by Suvich, Mussolini's delaying tactics until 18 December should hardly be interpreted as a sign of interest in a compromise agreement with the British and the French. Instead, Grandi's reports from 16 December about the massive opposition to the Hoare–Laval plan amongst the British parliament and public opinion should have convinced Mussolini that the compromise offer was about to be dropped in London before any serious discussion. Indeed, on 19 December, Hoare resigned and the Permanent Under-Secretary to the Foreign Office, Vansittart, informed Grandi that no other initiative outside the framework of the League of Nations should have been expected from the British side.[152]

The ensuing period until Badoglio's entry into Addis Ababa in May 1936 was marked by the advance of the Italian armed forces in Ethiopia and growing popular support for the campaign at home. Especially after the imposition of sanctions in November 1935, the popularity of the Fascist regime reached unprecedented heights.[153] Even the initially sceptical King endorsed his Prime Minister's uncompromising attitude towards the League of Nations,[154] while Badoglio, by then commander of the forces in Ethiopia (see Chapter 3), confessed to Giuseppe Bottai his wish to lead the Italian army into the Ethiopian capital.[155] Alfredo Rocco and other ex-Nationalists did not conceal their delight with the prospect of 'avenging Adua'.[156] On their part, prominent members of the PNF welcomed the campaign as a real opportunity for action and a prelude to the spiritual regeneration of Italy.[157] But it was also a wave, albeit ephemeral, of public enthusiasm which greeted the official declaration of the *Impero* by Mussolini on 9 May 1936. Although the occupation of the whole of Ethiopia was far from complete, with the capture of Addis Ababa there was genuine exaltation when Mussolini called the people 'to salute, after fifteen centuries, the re-emergence of the *Impero* on the hills of Rome'.[158]

This implication of the Ethiopian campaign gives considerable credence to the social imperialistic argument that Mussolini's colonialism was chiefly a device of diversionary policies.[159] This is only partly correct, in the sense that any other regime, fascist or not, would have attempted to capitalise on a success against the whole international community such as the victory in Ethiopia. Undoubtedly, success in Ethiopia was not simply a territorial acquisition; it also signified the restoration of Italian imperial tradition and the symbolic inauguration of the 'new' Italy into the pantheon of 'great powers'. However, exclusive or primary emphasis on the diversionary function of the decision to attack Ethiopia in 1935 tends to obscure two crucial long-term implications of the campaign for the whole foreign policy of the Fascist regime. The first pertains to the geopolitical significance of the occupation of Ethiopia and the creation of Italian

East Africa (*Africa Orientale Italiana*). This was the culmination of a consistent colonial policy of expansion in the Mediterranean and the Red Sea which consolidated Italian control over the traditional possessions of Libya, Eritrea and Somalia, extended them with the cession of Jubaland and Jarabub, and attempted to expand the whole colonial empire with the penetration of Yemen and the occupation of Ethiopia. The second long-term implication of the Ethiopian campaign regarded the change in Mussolini's strategic planning for territorial expansion. The second half of 1935 proved a highly formative period for the Duce's future expansionist strategy. From 1929 onwards, Italian foreign policy had attempted to establish the country as the 'determinant weight' and the ultimate international arbiter in a fluid European system.[160] Since 1933 this policy had acquired a more concrete shape with the formation of the Four Power Pact (signed by Italy, Germany, Britain and France) which, in De Felice's opinion, aimed at a policy of 'equidistance' between Paris and Berlin (see also Chapter 5).[161] Despite Mussolini's disillusionment with Nazi foreign policy after the July coup in Vienna and the unilateral introduction of conscription, the timing of the Ethiopian campaign reflected his ambition to achieve a 'speedy victory' and return to his role as arbiter of the European system with enhanced prestige.[162] However, his disappointment with the policy of the western powers in the autumn of 1935 initiated a change in his strategic thinking which would be felt in 1936. His intransigent attitude to the Hoare–Laval plan was followed by the German–Italian agreement over Austria in January 1936 and later by the two countries' cooperation in the Spanish Civil War (see also Chapter 5). By the beginning of 1936, the prospect of a rapprochement with Nazi Germany had ceased to be the *ultima ratio* of Mussolini's strategy;[163] by the autumn of the same year, after the conclusion of the Axis alliance, it constituted the default orientation of Italian foreign policy.

Nazi foreign policy and colonialism: a half-hearted affair

Unlike Mussolini, Hitler did not wish to antagonise the other European powers in the colonial field. For a start, he knew that he did not possess the necessary means (strong navy, economic resources) to sustain a colonial campaign. He was also aware that the Versailles Treaty had placed Germany in a highly underprivileged colonial position, from which it would be time-consuming, if not impossible at all, to recover. He therefore chose to follow the advice of traditional diplomats (such as von Bülow and von Neurath) and restrict himself to the colonial revisionist argument, while antagonising the European powers in the continental field, for which Germany was better equipped.[164] This left colonialism outside the nucleus of German great power aspirations in the 1930s and reduced it to an ancillary function in the wider context of revisionism.[165]

Hitler's inconsistent political handling of the colonial issue underlined its secondary importance in the overall framework of Nazi foreign policy. In

December 1935 he emphasised the link between the recovery of the pre-1914 German colonies and Germany's return to the Disarmament Conference, from which she had withdrawn in the autumn of 1933.[166] Three months later, in the shadow of the widespread alarm at the remilitarisation of the Rhineland, he made a similar offer, now relating colonial revisionism to Germany's return to the League of Nations.[167] At the same time, Hjalmar Schacht, the Reich's Minister of Economics, was authorised to conduct wide-ranging negotiations with British and French officials, offering the same *quid pro quo*: security in Europe, return of Germany to the collective security system and renunciation of war in return for colonial concessions.[168] Hitler, however, had never been a colonial enthusiast. In his *Mein Kampf*, he referred to the reasons why the acquisition of colonies was not the solution to Germany's economic problems.[169] The same argument permeated his passionate monologue at the Hossbach Conference, where he repeated that the recovery of the pre-1914 colonies would not address the agricultural and industrial limitations of German economy.[170] His ephemeral interest in the colonial issue was more of a diplomatic manoeuvre than an actual political U-turn. In the four years before the invasion of Poland, he made numerous references to the alleged importance of reclaiming the German colonies for reasons of prestige and justice.[171] Colonial revisionism was diplomatically useful in 1935–6 in sustaining the legal attack on the concept of Versailles security, and it was even more useful in 1937–9 in keeping open the channels of communication between Berlin and London. As, however, the British government was lowering the price for an agreement with Germany (with the Foreign Secretary Lord Halifax stressing that 'it was not necessarily thought that the status quo must be maintained under all circumstances'[172]), Hitler's confidence after the successes of the post-1936 period made him increasingly disinterested in a colonial agreement *per se*.[173] When Lord Halifax visited Berlin and held talks with Hitler in November 1937, Hitler could hardly disguise his lack of interest towards a comprehensive discussion of the colonial issue; instead, he insisted on focusing the discussion on Germany's continental territorial claims. In the last two years before the outbreak of the war he continued to invoke the colonial argument in order to underline Germany's unjust treatment by the victors of the First World War, but his proposals either lacked any concrete reference to specific goals or were overshadowed by the priority of continental expansion.[174] In two occasions, the first in November 1938 and the second in January 1939, he repeated Germany's vague claim for a return of all pre-war colonies, but noted that this issue would not be solved by the use of force.[175] In front of his own military leadership he was even more explicit: in May 1939 he spoke of the colonies as no solution to the food and space problems of the Reich.[176] Even at the eleventh hour, in his peace offer to the British on 25 August 1939, he did include the return of the colonies to Germany as a condition for the proposed agreement (of lesser importance, though, to the revision of the German–Polish frontier), but he showed no urgency, eager to 'fix the longest possible time limit'; a flexibility he was unwilling to show with regard to the timing of the Polish campaign.[177]

There is no conclusive evidence to suggest (as a number of 'globalist' historians have argued, with A. Hillgruber as the main exponent) that the Führer had a clear plan for world domination which involved the establishment of a vast colonial empire.[178] The continental focus of his exposition at the Hossbach Conference in November 1937 reaffirmed his position that Germany's *Lebensraum* lay in eastern Europe and could not be satisfied outside the continent in the form of colonies.[179] At the same time, however, Hitler was a true social Darwinist and it is difficult to imagine that his drive for expansion had a rigid territorial *terminus*.[180] In the years immediately prior to the attack on Russia he appeared convinced that success in his campaign against the Soviet Union would reduce both Britain and the USA to a state of panic and facilitate the establishment of Germany's domination not only in Europe but in the whole world.[181] Especially in the period 1939–41, he made some references to a vague central African empire and the domination of the Pacific alongside Japan after the eventual defeat of the USA.[182] However, until 1941 his *tour d'horizon* was dominated by the sheer volume and significance of the Soviet Union. This was the goal which had given substance to his *Lebensraum* vision and encapsulated all his opposition to communism and the Jews. Beyond that, his plans were limited to abstract declarations, projecting his ideological belief in constant struggle and in the superiority of the German nation, but falling significantly short of a crystallised strategy for world domination. The reversal of Germany's fortunes on the eastern front from 1942 onwards prevented the widening of Hitler's expansionist horizon and ensured that such plans, even if they existed, would remain confined to Hitler's personal utopian sphere.

Expansion on the continent: beyond traditional justifications of expansion

Italy

On the continental level, the prevailing intention of the victorious powers in 1918 to agree on a stable, long-lasting territorial pattern to the European map manifested their determination to establish a semi-permanent territorial settlement in Europe and to stave off future territorial disputes. Even if the invocation of the revisionist and irredentist principles came to be seen as a legitimate argument for frontier readjustments (as in the case of Fiume, Austria and the Sudetenland), claims for further aggressive territorial revisions were unacceptable by the main guarantors of the Versailles system. The sensitivity of the European Great Powers to territorial revision on the continent was shown on a number of occasions, from the reaction to the occupation of the Corfu in 1923 to the formation of the Stresa front in 1935 and the Munich conference in September 1938.

Nevertheless, ever since the 1920s the Italian Fascist foreign policy had displayed double standards regarding the principle of maintaining European stability. While the participation of Italy at the Lausanne conference and in the Locarno pacts had turned her into one of the pillars of the European status quo, Mussolini's Balkan policy entailed the expansion of Italian interests in the region without ruling out the use of military force to effect territorial changes. Apart from the Corfu incident and the plans for war against Turkey and Yugoslavia in the early 1920s (see Chapter 3), the Duce continued to plot with Croat and Macedonian separatists against the integrity of the Yugoslav state and to entertain hopes of a civil war which would justify Italian intervention. At the same time, his geopolitical designs included a consolidation of Italy's position in Albania, something that was achieved with consensual, rather than military, methods after the two treaties of 1926 and 1927.

The shift of Mussolini's attention to the *politica periferica* from 1932 onwards did provide an ephemeral diversion from aggressive plans in the Balkans. However, with the successful conclusion of the Ethiopian campaign in May 1936, Mussolini felt obliged to return to the issue of the European balance of power, reconsidering his policy options in the light of French hostility and the resurgence of Nazi Germany. Participation in the Spanish Civil War was the first indication that the Duce intended to use aggressive means on the continent to promote his wider geopolitical ambitions in the Mediterranean, in defiance of international agreements and of the need to uphold stability in the continent. This prospect alarmed the traditional diplomats and the King, who feared an irreversible re-orientation of Italian foreign policy towards Nazi Germany.[183] Such fears were strengthened after the official declaration of the Axis alliance in 1936, the signing of the Anti-Comintern Pact and Italy's withdrawal from the League of Nations in 1937. Yet, the pro-German tendency in Italian foreign policy remained short of a definite commitment until 1939. If Mussolini conceived the 1937 pact with Yugoslavia as a means to subvert the cohesion of the Little Entente and limit French influence in the Balkans,[184] he also showed increasing alarm at German expansion southwards with the *Anschluss* and the annexation of the Sudetenland.[185] During 1938, extensive talks with Britain took place on the Italian initiative,[186] leading to the Easter Accords of April 1938 which were meant to discourage German aggressive intentions against Czechoslovakia.[187]

As, however, the European system gradually disintegrated into chaos in 1938–9 as a result of German aggression, Mussolini identified new opportunities for making forceful changes in the Balkan territorial status quo. His major expansionist initiative in the period before the outbreak of the Second World War, namely the invasion of Albania in April 1939, appeared as the logical conclusion of his Adriatic policy ever since the mid-1920s. He considered Albania as instrumental for Italy's Mediterranean aspirations in two ways: first, because of its geographic position at the entrance to the Adriatic Sea, and second, as a bulwark against both Yugoslavia and Greece. In a meeting of the

Council of Ministers in December 1936 he described the establishment of a semi-protectorate in 1927 over Albania as a political anomaly, creating 'an Italian province without a prefect'.[188] He reiterated emphatically the geopolitical argument in his speech to the Grand Council in February 1939, adding that Albania was the only concrete territorial goal of Italian foreign policy in the continent.[189] Furthermore, the geopolitical importance of the country was complemented by its alleged historic ties with Italian culture and civilisation throughout the centuries. A plethora of studies on Albania were published in Italy during the late 1930s, emphasising the 'racial' and 'cultural' affinities between the two peoples, as well as their difference from the predominantly Slav character of Yugoslavia.[190]

The annexation of Albania in April 1939 prompted Mussolini to restate the country's significance as a 'geographic "constant"' in Italy's Mediterranean aspirations and to conclude that this success had transformed the Adriatic into an 'Italian lake'.[191] Although the idea that Albania held the key to the balance of power in the Balkan region was grossly exaggerated, these statements shed light on Mussolini's subsequent tactics towards Yugoslavia and Greece in the spring and summer of 1939. With the fall of the pro-Axis Stoyadinovic government early in 1939, Mussolini abandoned his brief flirtation with Yugoslav friendship, based on the pact of 1937, and reverted to the policy of internal subversion with the co-operation of Croat separatism.[192] In June 1939 Ciano spoke of the need to consolidate the success in Albania by dismembering Yugoslavia, taking the whole of Dalmatia and creating 'a territorial continuity as far as Albania'.[193] At the same time, after the Greek rejection of the Italian proposal for renewing the 1928 Pact of Friendship, Mussolini started thinking in terms of using Albania to put pressure on Greece or even launching a military campaign towards the Aegean Sea. In August, he ordered the drafting of such a plan to be used in the contingency of a large-scale European war.[194]

In general, the shift of Italian foreign policy towards expansion in the Balkans reflected the geopolitical reasoning of a Mediterranean *mare nostrum* but lacked either definitive medium-term expansionist priorities or a crystallised long-term strategy of how to achieve it. The expansionist venture in Albania and the continuous subversion of Yugoslav and Greek interests underlined Mussolini's determination to promote a wide expansionist vision in the Balkans which would complement his peripheral strategy in the Mediterranean and the Red Sea (Ethiopia–Yemen). In this sense, the conjunction of aggressive colonial and continental expansion in 1935–9 advanced a single long-term vision, but the uncertainty about both German and British intentions encouraged Mussolini to experiment with a number of diplomatic and military options. Undoubtedly, his increasing willingness to use military force against his Balkan neighbours marked a departure from the post-1918 liberal policy of peaceful co-existence and acknowledgement of the Balkan status quo. Another departure began during the Ethiopian campaign, which strengthened the pro-German orientation of Italian foreign policy. In the famous Grand Council meeting of 2 February 1939,

Mussolini gave an exposition of his immediate foreign policy plans towards France. What is striking about his long speech lies not so much in the large scale of his ambitions in the Mediterranean basin (demands for settlement regarding Tunis, Corsica and Djibuti) but mainly in the defiant tone of his strategy: either France would agree to negotiate without conditions or 'a recourse to arms was inevitable'.[195] As by the end of 1938 Mussolini and Ciano considered the 1935 accords with Laval as dead, the change of priorities in Fascist foreign policy is conspicuous: Italy would not rule out a diplomatic solution to the antagonisms of the European powers in the Mediterranean but she would no longer be bound by the rationale of peaceful resolution.

Having said that, Salvemini's linear view of the Ethiopian campaign as beginning an irreversible process of aggression culminating in the declaration of war in June 1940[196] disregards the fact that the tactical flexibility of Mussolini's foreign policy during that period mirrored a lack of clear interim strategies and an uncertainty about the opportunities offered by the international system for the advancement of his Mediterranean vision. Other considerations, such as the awareness of Italy's military unpreparedness for a large-scale conflict, the divisions in the British government as to the best policy towards the Axis and the frenetic pace of Nazi expansion, forced Mussolini to oscillate between aggression and peaceful diplomacy in 1938–40. Therefore, the use of geopolitical and historic irredentist arguments to justify the gathering pace of Italian expansionism in the late 1930s may be seen as evidence of long-term intentions but not of a categorical guiding principle which dictated short-term action at that stage.

Germany

In Germany, the focus of the revisionist and irredentist agenda on territorial readjustments in Europe gave a predominantly continental character to the Nazi expansionist policies. Until the summer of 1938, Hitler had adhered to the logic of the 'artichoke theory', extending the Reich's territory in the west (Rhineland) and the south (Austria) while gradually rebuilding Germany's military might and strengthening her strategic position in central Europe. He was aware of the need to present his expansionist ventures as legitimate actions originating from the 'unjust' Versailles settlement and the principle of uniting the whole German population within the territory of the Reich. This was plainly reflected in the wording of the Directive for Operation Otto for Austria, which was drafted on 11 March 1938 as a reaction to Schuschnigg's unilateral decision to call a plebiscite on the issue of Austria's status vis-à-vis Germany. The Directive stressed that the Anschluss should be presented 'in the form of a peaceful entry welcomed by the population',[197] and in the following days Göring did his best to ensure that the Nazi regime would gain the battle of impressions. Through his direct communication with the Viennese lawyer and favourite of the Nazi leadership for the position of Prime Minister, Seyss-Inquart, Göring demanded the drafting of a letter by the new Austrian government which 'invited' the

German forces to intervene and restore order. As the forged document was issued at the same time that the Nazi troops entered Austrian territory and spoke in the name of the Austrian population, it formally removed the stigma of aggression and preserved an artificial impression of legality in accordance with the exercise of the right of self-determination by the Austrian 'people' (see also Chapter 3).

In this sense, there was a major qualitative difference between the annexation of Austria and the preparation for Operation Green against Czechoslovakia later in 1938. Although Hitler had since 1937 expressed his intention to liquidate the whole of Czechoslovakia, his initial plan involved a pre-emptive strike in the context of a future war against France.[198] However, in the aftermath of the Hossbach Conference he spoke of his intention to carry out 'an offensive war against Czechoslovakia' in order to 'solve the German problem of living space'. The same plan envisaged the execution of the operation even 'before the completion of Germany's full preparedness for war' if there were indications that there would be no opposition from the western powers to the plan. This latter assumption did not contradict the views of the traditional military leadership, since General Beck had already been working on the offensive plan against Czechoslovakia on condition that Britain would remain neutral. However, by the end of May 1938 Hitler had again altered his plan for Operation Green; now the crisis was described as unavoidable[199] and the liquidation of the whole Czechoslovak state would take place 'in the near future'. For the first time, the Führer was determined to pursue a large-scale space policy without seeking recourse to the legitimate argument of irredentism and was willing not simply to await, but to 'bring about the suitable moment'.[200]

The escalation of the Czech crisis during the summer and early autumn of 1938 divided not just the army generals but also the Nazi leadership down the middle (see Chapter 3). The views of General Beck, the Secretary of State von Weizsäcker, Goebbels and Göring converged upon a platform of opposing a military showdown as potentially disastrous for Germany. This widespread opposition may have weighed upon Hitler's mind and led him to change his mind on 28 September and accept the proposal for an international conference. Equally influential must have been Mussolini's decision to request a postponement of the military mobilisation and to endorse Chamberlain's proposal for a negotiated compromise solution. If, however, the crisis was temporarily resolved in a peaceful manner with the Munich Agreement and the cession of only the Sudetenland to Germany (on the basis of the *German* character of the population inhabiting the territory), the events of August–September 1938 were indicative of far-reaching changes in Hitler's foreign policy. The Führer now appeared to be working on the assumption that Britain would not oppose German expansion in central Europe, not because of a lack of interest in the region but mainly due to her military unpreparedness which would not allow an effective military action before 1941 or 1942.[201] The opposition of Beck, Göring and Goebbels to 'Operation Green' originated from their rejection of exactly this strategic assumption.[202] For them, it had become obvious that Hitler was thinking in terms of a 'lightning' campaign which assumed British non-involvement but, as von Weizsäcker noted, no longer depended on it.[203]

The shift of Hitler's strategy to a high-risk space policy could not be disguised by the irredentist justification behind the dismemberment of Czechoslovakia at Munich. Less than a month after the agreement, he gave explicit orders for the liquidation of the 'remainder of the Czech state' *at any time*.[204] This obscurity, however, regarding the timing of the operation reflected a much wider uncertainty about his short-term strategies and priorities. During the last months of 1938 Hitler turned his attention back to Poland. As he confessed to his generals in August 1939, his preference was for a compromise solution over Danzig before a war with the West.[205] He therefore ordered Ribbentrop to approach the Polish Ambassador in Berlin, Lipski, with concrete proposals for the incorporation of the Free City to the Reich in return for a guarantee to respect Polish sovereignty and a renewal of the 1934 pact.[206] The proposal, first presented in October and renewed in November 1938,[207] was met with a flat rejection by the Polish government.[208] By the time the Polish leader, Beck, came to Berlin to discuss the issue with Hitler (January 1939) and to propose a division of the Free City between the two countries, the Chancellor had reverted to a puzzlingly intransigent position, ruling out any compromise solution and demanding nothing less than the return of the whole city.[209] In the meantime, he had once again readjusted his strategy; Poland would be dealt with first, after the liquidation of the rump Czech state which was traditionally regarded as a strategic prerequisite for any attack on Poland.[210] Within three weeks from the march into the rest of Czechoslovakia (March 1939), Hitler issued instructions for Operation White against Poland, which envisaged the completion of preparations by 1 September.[211] The new strategic plan prioritised a 'lightning' action (*Blitz*) to 'destroy the Polish state and armed forces', then war with the West and finally 'turning against the east'.[212] His decision to attack was accompanied by a unilateral abandonment of negotiations with Poland at the beginning of April.[213]

German foreign policy after the end of 1937 confirmed the shift from the limited border policy of the previous years to the living space principle which would underpin the large-scale expansionist ventures of the Nazi regime in the following years. The 'expansion in the east' theme dominated the rationale of Hitler's major foreign policy actions and strategic moves, adding an element of historic urgency to his *Lebensraum* vision and relegating colonial goals to a secondary, if not insignificant, level of importance. Although the territorial objectives of Nazi expansion in 1938–9 were shared to a great extent by the conservative military and diplomatic elites, the Führer's decision to force the pace of expansion, disrupt traditional priorities, use the military power of his armed forces and risk a major confrontation were in sharp contrast to the long-term strategic planning of the conservative establishment. Having said that, even by the beginning of 1939 Hitler did not appear to know what kind of war he wanted.

136

His experiments with Poland between autumn 1938 and spring 1939 forced him to adjust his strategic plans, abandoning his initial proposal for turning Poland into an essentially vassal state of Germany and choosing instead to invade the country.[214] He was unsure of the British attitude, and had no tangible indication of Russian intentions towards Poland and Germany. By the time he spoke to the army commanders of 23 May he seemed poised to unleash his military machine but betrayed his uncertainty as to the west's attitude and the most favourable date for the invasion. His strategy regarding the conflict continued to change in the few following months in the face of international developments, and was not crystallised until the last days of August (see Chapter 6).

The radicalisation of Italian and German expansionism in the mid- and late 1930s entailed both a quantitative and a qualitative change. It rested on a shift from *border* to *living space* policy, alluding to more ambitious, large-scale territorial goals both on the continent and, for Italy, in the colonial field as well. Since most of these goals went beyond what the guarantors of the Versailles system perceived as legitimate expansion, their attainment presupposed the increasing use of military means instead of diplomatic procedures. Although a start was made with the Italian aggressive campaign against Ethiopia, it was the Nazi regime which started to gravitate towards war from 1938 onwards at a time when Mussolini strove to keep his options open by experimenting with both diplomatic and military strategies. Having said that, there was a high degree of continuity between the early objectives of Fascist expansion and the more radical goals of the late 1930s. Mussolini's east African and Adriatic ventures were intended to consolidate or extend previous successes, while Hitler's expansion in Austria and Czechoslovakia rested upon the Wehrmacht's restored military capacity through rearmament and, in the case of the *Anschluss*, aimed to succeed where there had been failure in the past (in the Vienna putsch). This continuity underlined the determination of both fascist leaderships to exploit opportunities offered and to produce favourable conditions for the promotion of their long-term designs for acquiring living space in eastern Europe (for Germany) and the Mediterranean region (for Italy).

War had come significantly closer in 1938–9, as the two regimes showed an increasing determination to pursue their more extensive territorial objectives. Yet, the ideological nature of the two leaders' expansionist visions cannot on its own account for the occurrence of the particular military conflict which Germany started in September 1939 and Italy joined in July 1940. The two regimes' strategies and priorities continued to be affected by both domestic and international developments, not only in the remaining period until the beginning of the war but also throughout the duration of the conflict. The next two chapters will examine the conditions which gave the final momentum to the radicalisation of the two regimes' foreign policies and defined the parameters, as well as the fate of, the great fascist war.

5

BETWEEN CO-OPERATION AND RIVALRY

Relations between the two regimes

In one of the concluding remarks of his study on Nazi foreign policy, Klaus Hildebrand emphasises the need to set the evolution of Hitler's foreign policy 'in the historical context of international politics in the 1930s and 1940s'. In this way, he continues, it will become easier 'to establish how far Hitler was able to influence the course of world affairs during the twelve years of his rule, and how far international circumstances enabled him to carry out his plans or forced him to limit or modify them'.[1] This raises the question of the relation between ideological goals and political actions in the realm of fascist foreign policy. The questions he asks about Nazi Germany are relevant to the nature of foreign policy under fascism in both Germany and Italy. If there is a consensus among researchers about the traditional 'revisionism' of fascist foreign policies in the first stages of the two regimes' domestic consolidation, the radicalisation of fascist expansionism in the second half of the 1930s remains an issue of heated historical debate. Hildebrand's conclusion seems to suggest that, notwithstanding the validity of the primacy of domestic politics thesis, the analysis of the Italian and German fascist foreign policies in the 1930s requires a wider European or even international perspective. This would enable us to extend beyond the domestic origins and functions of foreign policy decisions, and beyond the debate about their ideological consistency, in order to relate foreign policy ambitions with the opportunities and limitations arising from the international situation.

The first systematic attempt was made in the 1960s by A.J.P. Taylor, who produced a study of international relations in the 1930s and located the main causes of the Second World War in the escalating tension between the main European powers. Although Taylor's work was supposed to be a general account of the origins of the war from an international perspective, it focused heavily on Nazi Germany and Hitler, making only limited – and often dismissive – references to the responsibility of Italian Fascism.[2] In a similar vein, G. Salvemini played down the responsibility of the Italian Fascist regime for the outbreak and escalation of the war. In his famous arithmetic of blame, he attributed five-tenths of the guilt to Hitler, three-tenths to Stalin and only one-tenth to Mussolini's alleged reckless and irresponsible opportunism.[3] In 1980,

Rosaria Quartararo published an extraordinary account of Italian foreign policy in the 1930s from the viewpoint of Italian-British relations. Building upon Renzo De Felice's and A.F.K. Organski's distinction between Nazi radical expansionism and Fascist more traditionalist foreign policy, she interpreted the radicalisation of Mussolini's expansionist policies as the consequence of his frustration with the unresponsive British attitude to Italian overtures and the alliance with Nazi Germany as the last alternative to diplomatic isolation.[4]

What, however, neither of the above works sufficiently emphasised is the cumulative dynamics of the interaction between the two fascist regimes themselves. The classic study of Elisabeth Wiskemann, *The Rome–Berlin Axis*, covers basically the years after 1935 and is dominated by an emphasis on the importance of Nazi foreign policy for the radicalisation of fascist expansionism after 1937, while J. Petersen's work *Hitler und Mussolini* focuses on the interaction between the two fascist leaders in the pre-1937 period, and does not therefore provide sufficient information on the reasons behind the radicalisation of fascist expansionism after 1937.[5] Through the interaction of their different expansionist visions, Mussolini's Italy and Hitler's Germany gradually established an idiosyncratic bilateral relationship that should be treated as a distinct aspect of the two regimes' expansionist policies. It is, therefore, essential to draw attention to the importance of this exclusive political relation between the two fascist regimes for the radicalisation of Italian and German expansionist policies in the second half of the 1930s. The following analysis traces the origins of the process which led to the diplomatic convergence of Italy and Germany after 1935, and eventually produced a joint programme of expansion to be carried out collectively by the two fascist regimes. This *internationalisation* of the fascist expansionist vision, namely the co-ordination of the two expansionist policies and their incorporation into a wider framework of fascist territorial expansion, unleashed a new sense of dynamism in the conduct of fascist foreign policy which each of the two regimes endeavoured to harness in pursuit of its more 'radical' expansionist plans. Far from being simply the sum of their cumulative energies, the 'political dynamism' of the rapprochement between the two fascist regimes[6] manifested itself both in terms of mutual co-operation and growing rivalry, with both elements contributing equally to the radicalisation of the style, implements and scope of their expansionist policies.

Internationalisation of fascism: the difficult course of Italo–German rapprochement

Mussolini as 'the Duce of Fascism' and the emergence of Nazism

If the internationalisation of fascism has been related to the new diplomatic situation produced by the Ethiopian campaign and the Spanish Civil War, its origins should be located in the period between 1929 and 1935. From the

March on Rome up to Hitler's appointment as Reich Chancellor, the Italian Fascist regime remained the only political expression of the new 'fascist' creed. Despite his dealings, either secret or official, with other European fascist movements and revisionist regimes, for the greatest part of the 1920s Mussolini insisted on the purely *national* character of Italian Fascism. As a reaction to the internationalism of his previous comrades, and now arch-enemies, in the Socialist and Communist parties, he renounced any aspiration to 'export' Fascism. Even his contacts with the German nationalists (and most notably with NSDAP officials[7]) should be seen in the wider framework of his efforts to subvert the European Versailles system by encouraging the activities of various revisionist groups and countries. His principal aim was to promote his country's long-standing revisionist–expansionist aspirations in central Europe and the Mediterranean, regardless of future alliances. In the absence of another discontented country powerful enough to energetically challenge the postwar territorial arrangements, Mussolini played a dubious diplomatic role in the 1920s. On the one hand, especially after his acquiescence in the Locarno Treaties in 1925, he figured prominently among the guarantors of the European order. On the other hand, even during this period of 'good behaviour' in foreign affairs, the Italian Fascist leadership never refrained from conspiring with Croat separatists, Bavarian nationalists, Hungarian revisionists, Maltese nationalists, Corsican separatists and others at the expense of the European stability it was supposed to defend.[8] Clearly, however, these dealings did not reflect any wider scheme for a new fascist order in Europe; they were rather exercises in political activism which originated from the traditional Italian 'great power' ambitions.

The landscape started to change in the autumn of 1930. In the celebrations for the eighth anniversary of the March on Rome, Mussolini for the first time declared that fascism was an 'export product'. Two years later, in his *Doctrine of Fascism*, he went even further and presented fascism as a doctrine of universal applicability:

> If every age has its own characteristic doctrine, there are a thousand signs which point to Fascism as the characteristic doctrine of our time...fascism has henceforth in the world the universality of all these doctrines [socialism, liberalism, democracy] which, in realising themselves, have represented a stage in the history of the human spirit.[9]

In presenting the Italian Fascist prototype as the new 'conquering creed' of the twentieth century, Mussolini was essentially responding to new international challenges. First, he wished to establish fascism as a real political alternative – and not a simple short-term reaction or crisis phenomenon – to the crumbling liberal democratic system, and as a barrier to the spread of the Marxist doctrine. Second, and most important, he intended to establish *Italian* fascism as the ideological model and the political Mecca of right-wing polemic against socialism and liberal democracy in post-1929 Europe. It is not coincidental that the Duce's first pronouncement of the universality of fascism came only weeks after the electoral triumph of the NSDAP in the elections of September 1930. The emergence of a powerful ultranationalist party in a country with the greatest thirst and potential for territorial revisionism against the Versailles settlement created both an opportunity and a challenge for the Italian Fascist regime. On the one hand, it could put Germany on the track of a more ambitious revisionist foreign policy at the expense of the British–French vision of security in the European system, expressed in the Peace Treaties of 1919–20. This was a highly desirable prospect for Italian expansionism in the Mediterranean, since it could induce the British and French governments into making territorial concessions in exchange for Italy's support for order in Europe. On the other hand, the possibility of a nationalist regime in Germany posed certain logistical problems for Mussolini's territorial aspirations. If Germany's revisionist aspirations in the west served Italy's plans to press France into colonial concessions in the Mediterranean, Hitler's irredentist declarations meant that the two countries would clash on the issue of Austria and South Tyrol.[10]

Mussolini's hopes and fears were all confirmed after Hitler's appointment as Chancellor in January 1933. Despite the lack of major foreign policy initiatives during the first fifteen months of the Nazi regime, the emergence of a nationalist Germany revived the debate among the European powers about the need to reassess aspects of the territorial, economic and military postwar arrangement. At the same time, Hitler's Germany appeared as a potential second pole – and revisionist *par excellence* – in the European state system. This could enable Italy to play a crucial diplomatic role by capitalising on her privileged diplomatic position as guarantor of European security under the Locarno pacts, but also ideologically associated with its main challenger. In this vein, Mussolini achieved the signing of the Four Power Pact in July 1933,[11] a treaty which bore the signatures of the main pro-Versailles western powers (Britain and France) alongside that of its – then only supposed – nemesis (Nazi Germany). The fact that it was Fascist Italy that brought about this unique diplomatic alignment emphasised the Fascist regime's new-found diplomatic confidence as the 'determinant weight' of the European balance of power and a pillar of stability between the western powers and the revisionist bloc.[12] By pursuing his famous policy of 'equidistance' towards Britain/France and Germany, Mussolini could play the one side against the other, using the former against the latter in central Europe and doing the reverse in the Rhine region.

However, there were ominous signs from the outset. Germany's withdrawal from the Disarmament Conference was the first indication of the problems involved in the policy of incorporating Nazi Germany into the European security system (see Chapter 3). The German decision caused considerable vexation to the Italian leader, as it was interpreted as a blow to the Four Power Pact.[13] The aggressive intentions of the Nazi regime towards Austria, however, were not just a diplomatic problem for the Italian regime. Since it cast a serious shadow over the security of the Brenner, it impinged upon the issue of Italy's territorial integrity. Understandably, all postwar Italian governments had been extremely sensitive about the symbolic importance of the Brenner as the only reward for Italy's participation in the First World War, and Mussolini was not in the slightest prepared to jeopardise his nationalist credentials by making any concessions on this issue. Furthermore, the reactivation of German revisionism in central Europe posed an even more comprehensive threat to Italy's diplomatic position in the European system. By becoming the champion of the anti-Versailles revisionism the Nazi regime could question Italy's special relations with the revisionist bloc (i.e. Hungary) and remove those countries from the Italian sphere of influence. Such a development could restrict Mussolini's diplomatic flexibility and relegate the international image of Italian Fascism to a secondary position in favour of a potentially powerful and successful German version.

In this sense, from the beginning of 1933 the two fascist regimes were in an ambiguous political relationship. Mussolini saw Hitler's rise to power as a further triumph of the anti-democratic, anti-liberal and anti-socialist struggle that his regime had initiated in 1922. Moreover, the new German Chancellor never concealed his admiration for the Duce and the influence that his political techniques had exerted on the Nazi movement.[14] Mussolini, however, quickly realised that the success of the Hitler experiment in Germany included beneficial elements for the future of European fascism, but was also a potential threat to the co-operation between the two countries. In the framework of the German nationalist ideology, the irredentist claim for the unification of all German-speaking populations in central Europe possessed a similar symbolic significance to postwar Italy's obsession with the Brenner. The 1920 Programme of the NSDAP expressly stated that 'we do not abandon any German in Sudetenland, in South Tyrol, in Poland, in ... Austria'.[15] This was, however, exactly the problem – that the *alldeutsche* aspirations of the Nazi regime involved not only the *Anschluss* question or the Polish Corridor, but also the future of the German-speaking minority in South Tyrol (Alto Adige). Having been incorporated into the Italian national territory in 1919 and undergoing a continuous policy of Italianisation, the German-speaking population of South Tyrol saw in Hitler's rise to power an excellent opportunity for their reunion with the German *Vaterland*. Of course, as we saw earlier (in Chapter 4), Hitler had no intention of risking the fragile equilibrium of the German–Italian relations for the sake of a German minority inhabiting an area that he acknowledged as part of the Italian 'sphere of influence'. There was, however, a crucial discrepancy in the geopolitical perspectives of the two regimes with reference to the Danubian area. For Hitler, the South Tyrol issue could be separated from the fate of Austria. He was, therefore, ready to sacrifice his irredentist credibility by offering a guarantee for the Brenner frontier in exchange for Italy's support on the question of *Anschluss*. In May 1933, he even proposed a plan for the 'fusion' of Austria (which removed the negative implications of the word *Anschluss*) in return for promises of Italian territorial compensation elsewhere.[16] For Mussolini, however, this separation was as yet inconceivable, both for strategic (an independent Austria was the perfect buffer state between Germany and Italy) and prestige reasons. While he offered his diplomatic support to the Dollfuss regime so as to draw Austria closer to the Italian sphere of influence,[17] Hitler never ceased to subvert the country's internal stability, aiming at her future peaceful absorption in the German Reich.

The meeting of the two fascist leaders in June 1934 and the subsequent abortive coup in Vienna (see Chapter 3) exposed the problems of the German–Italian diplomatic relations.[18] This indication of Hitler's expansionist aspirations seriously alarmed Mussolini and cast a shadow on the co-operation between the two regimes that was to last until 1936. Hitler became disillusioned about the prospect of an alliance with Italy, but was determined to continue his efforts to build a basis of understanding between the two regimes, in spite of Neurath's disinclination to a closer diplomatic understanding with Italy.[19] Mussolini, on the other hand, strengthened his support for the independence of the Austrian government, reverted to the policy of equidistance and attempted to re-establish his relations with the West, despite long-standing disagreements on the colonial issue.[20] The events of the summer of 1934, however, produced a positive development for the stability of the European system. Due to their mutual distrust and antagonism, the two fascist regimes became more interested in stabilising their positions rather than engaging in further expansionist plans.[21] Hitler's determination to bring Britain and Italy closer to Germany achieved equal priority with rearmament and economic preparation,[22] and dictated moderation in the conduct of foreign affairs in order not to further alienate his two potential allies. In the aftermath of the July 1934 abortive putsch the German government was forced to postpone or call off any forceful activity regarding the Austria issue.[23] At the same time, Mussolini's plans for a colonial campaign against Ethiopia[24] had to be postponed, since the situation in Europe demanded vigilance and readiness.

This was the first evidence that the incompatibility between the revisionist–expansionist objectives of the two regimes could act as a restraint upon each regime's propensity for aggression. In the period up to the Ethiopian war the antagonism intensified, reaching a climax at the beginning of 1935. The reintroduction of conscription in the Reichswehr, in violation of the disarmament clauses of the Versailles Treaty, prompted Italy to join Britain and France at the Stresa Conference in an effort to isolate Germany and discourage future challenges to the European status quo (see Chapters 3 and 4). The same logic was behind the Italian proposal for an Austro-Hungarian pact, aimed as a deterrent to further German expansion in the Balkans.[25] The anti-German shift of the Italian foreign policy had become manifest in the Mussolini–Laval pact of January 1935 (which was then greeted as a decisive step towards resolving Italian–French differences in the colonial field),[26] but was further consolidated at Stresa by what Mussolini interpreted as a 'free hand' for expansion in east Africa conceded by France and, to a degree, by Britain.[27] However, the visit of the

British Foreign Secretary Sir John Simon in Berlin, and the subsequent talks with Hitler, angered the Duce, who feared a British–German rapprochement over the colonial issue in Africa.[28] Evidently, the Italian Fascist leader intended to use his long-prepared campaign against Ethiopia as a further means of solidifying his diplomatic position towards Germany and of dissuading the Nazi leadership from following an aggressive policy in central Europe. Abandoning the traditional line of Italian foreign policy (security in Europe as prerequisite for colonial expansion), he aimed to use a military victory in Africa as a reminder of Italy's power in the European system. It was a risk, but a risk which seemed worth taking under the impression that it would be tolerated by France and Britain.

Carving up 'international fascism': Ethiopia and Rhineland

The reality was quite different. Mussolini's impression about the 'free hand' was another manifestation of his penchant for misunderstanding situations: it was Britain and France who opposed the campaign, and Germany who gradually developed a positive attitude towards it.[29] With his Ethiopian war, Mussolini dealt a double blow to the stability of the European system. He was the first to violate one of the two principal dogmas on which the postwar settlement rested: he turned his back to peaceful diplomacy and used violence to achieve his colonial aspirations. Also, by alienating Italy from the other guarantors of European security (Britain and France), he enabled Germany to play the role of the ally and supporter against the punitive attitude of the West (for example, against the imposition of sanctions through the League of Nations). Diplomatic isolation and a shared feeling of injustice brought the two fascist regimes for the first time to the same camp. In the meantime, the Nazi leadership, taking advantage of the confusion that the Ethiopian war had caused to the European system, scrapped the last remaining restriction in the Versailles Treaty by re-militarising the Rhineland (see Chapter 4).[30] This was a move designed to provoke the western powers, since Italy was neither against the German aspirations in the Rhine nor in a position to effectively react while engaged in war in Africa.[31] Mussolini not only encouraged Hitler when he was informed of the plans for the campaign, but he also hastened to declare the Stresa front 'dead' in the aftermath of the crisis.[32]

It is tempting to see the period of the Ethiopian war and the operation in the Rhineland as a turning point in the relations between the two fascist regimes and the establishment of fascism as an international force.[33] Undoubtedly, Germany's refusal to join the League of Nations in the imposition of the embargo on Italy was a crucial factor in the subsequent Italian–German diplomatic rapprochement.[34] This was further facilitated by the refusal of the Italian government to impose sanctions on Germany for breaching the Locarno Treaty after the remilitarisation of the Rhineland.[35] Moreover, Hitler's decision to abandon neutrality (contrary to the counsel of his Foreign Minister, von Neurath) and initiate limited exports of military materiel, raw materials and foodstuff to Italy in November 1935 weighed decisively in Mussolini's change of direction on the Austrian issue two months later.[36] His January 1936 declaration in favour of an Austrian–German pact which would render Austria a 'German satellite' was welcomed by the German leadership, despite the tensions that it generated between the Duce and his anti-German Under-Secretary to the Foreign Ministry, Fulvio Suvich, who continued to support an anti-German line, distrustful of the intentions of the Nazi leadership.[37]

There are, however, strong arguments against treating the Ethiopian war as an actual turning point. The extent of Hitler's assistance to Italy during the campaign should not be exaggerated. On the military level, it has now been established that Germany had helped Ethiopia to rearm prior to the outbreak of hostilities, in order to make sure that the country could fight against Italy.[38] Hitler wished to avoid two extreme outcomes: defeat for Italy (which would shatter the prestige of European fascism in general) or a quick victory (which would enable Italy to use her newly-acquired prestige *against* Germany).[39] The prolongation of the campaign enabled him to capitalise on his 'good services' to Italy, and to bring Italy closer to Germany by taking advantage of deteriorating Italo–British relations. Additionally, during the conflict he could promote his immediate rearmament and revisionist plans without significant reaction from the European powers. On the political level, Hitler was willing to help his 'ideological' ally but not to the point of jeopardising his recent achievements in the German-British relations. In spite of his long-standing plans for an alliance between the two fascist countries and Britain, the signing of the Naval Pact with the latter in the summer of 1935 elevated the importance of Britain in his political calculations.[40] Therefore, faced with a possible dilemma to choose Britain *or* Italy (due to the clash between the two countries during the Ethiopian campaign), he would still opt for the former.

The international 'crusade' of fascism: the Spanish Civil War

Undoubtedly, the eventual success of Italy in Ethiopia and of Germany in the Rhine prepared the ground for the change in the European balance of power which was to become evident in 1936–8. Victory brought confidence to the two fascist regimes and introduced a dynamism in the conduct of their foreign affairs. At the same time, the consolidation of the British–French bloc prompted the two fascist regimes to join forces for the first time, even on a limited and opportunistic basis. Evidence of an Italian shift towards an anti-British and anti-French policy may be traced in Mussolini's remark late in 1935, that '*the decrepit powers search to block the young nations in their search for space*'.[41] This was still, however, a reaction to the opposition of the Western powers, lacking the characteristics of a positive fascist alliance. There was scepticism on both sides that the rapprochement might have been a step 'too far'. At the same time, the Italian government hastened to offer reassurances to the French government about the nature of the Italian–German rapprochement, while the German leadership vented its irritation at the British–Italian understanding of 1937.[42]

It was the Spanish civil war which transformed the Italian–German relations and offered fascism the first chance for universality. This development did not become immediately evident, as the two fascist regimes decided to intervene on General Franco's side for quite different reasons and in different ways. After an initial period of hesitation, Mussolini committed a large, if ill-equipped and ill-trained, part of his armed forces to the struggle against the Republican government. The main reason behind this transformation was the widespread belief among the Fascist leadership that the Nationalists would overrun the Republican forces within weeks. Mussolini intended to use his army in a relatively safe and brief operation, in order to further enhance his diplomatic prestige, acquire part of Spain's raw materials and establish Italy as the major power in the Mediterranean. He was also interested in preventing the consolidation of another Popular Front government (after France) in the western Mediterranean, or even a successful revolution of the left in Spain.[43] There was, however, a further long-term geopolitical consideration that dramatically increased the importance of the Spanish Civil War for Mussolini's expansionist aspirations: Gibraltar. The Italian leader had long ago emphasised that the Italian vision of a *mare nostrum* in the Mediterranean presupposed effective control of its two strategic exits (Suez Canal and Gibraltar). Since a direct conflict with Britain was both unfeasible and undesirable, Mussolini decided to aid Franco, hoping that a future nationalist Spain would co-operate with Italy against Britain's domination of the Mediterranean. In the context of this strategy, Mussolini did not conceal his territorial ambitions for the Balearic Islands as a further step in consolidating his position in the western Mediterranean.[44] In this sense, Italy's extensive engagement in the Spanish Civil War originated not so much from the idea of a 'crusade' against Bolshevism (as the regime later claimed), but from the anti-British Mediterranean strategy of the Italian regime and fear of losing control of a vital part of the Mediterranean.

For his part, Hitler did not hesitate much in sending the first German troops in the summer of 1936. In his Second Book he had established Spain as a possible ally in his anti-French strategy,[45] but had seen his plans fail after the rise of left-wing governments in both Spain (1933) and France (1936). Now, Franco's revolt offered an opportunity to reverse the situation. A nationalist government in Spain would put considerable pressure on the Popular Front in Paris, and even facilitate a military campaign against France sometime in the future. Furthermore, Germany's precarious economic situation in the summer of 1936 made the question of raw materials even more important for German rearmament.[46] Göring's plans for the shipment of copper, tungsten and ore from Spain played a significant role in Hitler's decision to intervene (see also Chapter 3).[47] As in the case of Mussolini, however, it was the anticipation of a swift victory by Franco's forces which gave the final impetus to Germany's involvement in Spain. Although Hitler did not wish an extremely quick victory for Franco (the civil war kept Italy busy in the Mediterranean and halted the Italian plans for further expansion in Africa or in Central Europe), he expected a relatively short war in Spain and a clear victory by Franco's forces. The overestimation of the Nationalists' fighting power created the impression to the Nazi leadership that they could obtain raw materials, test their new weapons and achieve a diplomatic victory with minimum risk.

There is nothing to suggest that either of the two fascist leaders initially sought co-ordination in their military involvement, or that the Italo–German rivalry for the title of the fascist Mecca had in any way diminished. Despite the rapprochement during the Ethiopian war, the geopolitical differences of the two countries remained unresolved, and their separate interference in the Spanish Civil War increased mutual suspicion and antagonism. Undoubtedly, Hitler wished to avoid further deterioration in Italo–German relations at any cost, and this explains why he sent the Prince of Hessen and Canaris to Italy in order to reassure the Duce about Germany's limited involvement and objectives in Spain.[48] The plans for military co-operation were deferred, however, not least because Neurath refused to fly to Italy in order to co-ordinate the joint fascist military intervention in Spain.[49]

The situation started to change in the autumn of 1936. The decision of the British and French governments to abstain from involvement in the Spanish crisis ('non-intervention') offered the Republican government the justification to turn to Stalin for the much needed military aid against Franco. The involvement of the Soviet Union in Spain coincided with the first indications that the conflict would not be as brief or pre-determined as Mussolini and Hitler had anticipated. These two elements invested the civil war with an international significance which involved the two major conquering creeds of the twentieth century.[50] As Franco's victory seemed far from certain in 1936–7, the 'export' of Bolshevism in Spain and the prospect of a humiliating defeat of fascism by communism placed the issue of Italo–German co-operation in a totally new light. Despite Neurath's cool attitude towards the overtures of the Italian Fascist leadership throughout the summer of 1936,[51] Ciano's successful visit to Germany in October 1936 paved the way for the first official declaration of fascism's international dimension: the Axis.[52] Ironically, it was Mussolini who announced in Milan that 'this vertical line between Rome and Berlin is not a partition, but rather an axis',[53] and he reiterated his newfound confidence in the Italo–German relations many times thereafter. The anathema of Bolshevism served as a pretext for fascist intervention in Spain, and co-operation between the two fascist regimes was provided with the element of an ideological crusade that it initially lacked.[54] This new element transformed their involvement into a symbolic struggle for the prestige of fascism in general. The first fruits of this new rapprochement were an agreement between von Neurath and Ciano for military co-ordination of the two countries' armed forces in Spain, and the joint decision to recognise the Burgos government.[55] As, however, the prospect of victory was becoming more and more distant in the first half of 1937, the national interests which initially prompted Mussolini and Hitler to intervene were somewhat overshadowed by the common concern for a prestige victory against Bolshevism at any cost.

Antagonism, of course, did not fade away. Both Italy and Germany gradually increased their military commitment to the Civil War, and this enabled General Franco to manipulate the two regimes' antagonism and distrust in order to elicit more aid.[56] At the same time, after the defeat of the Italian troops at Guadalajara and the parallel successes of the German units, Mussolini felt impelled to restore the honour of his armed forces and defend their efficiency against Spanish and German criticisms.[57] The implicit competition between Italy and Germany increasingly became a battle for prestige. Mussolini kept pressing Franco for a commanding role for the Italian forces in the conduct of war, while showing great alarm at the British–German contacts and struggling to obtain more economic concessions from Franco at the expense of his Axis ally.[58] Especially towards the end of the war, when the outcome of the Civil War had been determined in favour of the Nationalists, the military activity of the Italian air force (the fierce raids over Spanish cities) seemed to have little relevance to the needs of the situation. It demonstrated, however, the growing pressure on Mussolini's regime to re-establish its diplomatic and military significance *vis-à-vis* the Nazi challenge. This was the first example of a radicalisation of style and means of policy making which was not the direct outcome of either ideological commitments or diplomatic initiative; the first in a long list of similar developments in the period between the Spanish Civil War and the outbreak of the Second World War in September 1939. The need for prestige, which was the logical product of the 'great power' ideology, committed Mussolini to a dynamic course of action disproportionate to Italy's geopolitical interests, and beyond the capabilities of the country's domestic system.

In this sense, the Spanish Civil War *is* a real turning point in the radicalisation of fascist expansionist policies. The German successes in Spain were seen as the first tangible evidence of the country's dramatic military and diplomatic recovery from the limitations imposed upon her by the Versailles arrangement. The image of a powerful Nazi Germany, technologically advanced and domestically monolithic, contributed crucially to the transformation of the European balance of power in 1937–9. After a long period in which fascism was indisputably an Italian innovation, Germany emerged as the unquestionable heir apparent. The direction of new fascist ideas and techniques was reversed: up to 1936 Italy had been the 'exporter' and Nazi Germany the beneficiary[59]; now the evolution of fascism was becoming a German responsibility. This does not imply that Mussolini was forced by the Nazi dynamism to relinquish his autonomy in the shaping of the Italian expansionist objectives, as Elizabeth Wiskemann and Denis Mack Smith have argued.[60] In the period up to the summer of 1939 he followed a double strategy to offset the disadvantages of Italy's military weakness.

On the one hand, building on the tradition of 'determinant weight', he endeavoured to use diplomacy in order to contain German expansionism without either jeopardising his newly established alliance with Hitler or risking a confrontation with the British–French bloc.[61] On the other hand, he did his best to conceal his inferior position by struggling to keep up with German expansionist policies. With this strategy he intended to restore his country's prestige, to avoid a capitulation to the inflated Nazi expansionist aspirations, and to gain time in preparing for war. The problem was that these three goals proved to be either incompatible with each other or not within the control of the Italian leadership. Since the initiative had been usurped by a Germany determined to expand, and Mussolini's efforts to check German aggression had limited success, the Italian leadership was forced to conduct its foreign policy on a short-term basis, largely defined by German actions. Time was evidently running out, resources were limited, and co-ordination between military, economic and political circles was poor. Prestige evidently dictated a response to equal Nazi Germany in expansion and in 'fascist' dynamism. The revisionist initiative, however, eluded the Italian regime and, even worse for the Duce, this seemed an irreversible process. The Nazi leadership, strengthened from the German successes in Spain and freed from the postwar military restrictions, was now in a position to dictate the terms of the European diplomatic game.

Furthermore, the fascist military involvement in Spain produced a completely different verdict on the two fascist regimes. German weapons and the German air force were utterly successful in military terms, while the performance of the Italian armed forces encouraged scepticism among the country's political and military circles about the degree of their readiness for a European conflict.[62] The difference was that, in Germany's case, success in Spain belied the initial hesitations of the Foreign Office and of the Reichswehr about the level of the armed forces' readiness. The cumulative outcome was that these parallel successes in the domestic and international arena for the Nazi leadership intensified a propensity (ideological and political) for further and more extensive expansion. By contrast, the Italian regime woke to the realisation that its armed forces were not in a position to contest militarily either the British domination in the Mediterranean or the German dynamism in central Europe. This was an uncomfortable admission at a period when the competition for the leadership of international fascism with Germany was escalating.

The German success in the Rhineland and the impressive military showing of her armed forces in Spain had an immense psychological impact upon Mussolini personally. The latent admiration of the Duce for the achievements of his German counterpart was further fostered during his visit to Germany in September 1937.[63] Officially, he could now speak of a 'community not only of ideas, but also of action', of 'many common elements in the [two regimes'] worldviews', and of a 'common destiny'.[64] In private, however, he was becoming fascinated by the power and dynamism that the Nazi regime had achieved in Germany within such a short time. He and his new Foreign

Minister, Ciano, promoted the Axis project after 1935 with an enthusiasm that found little response amongst the most prominent Fascist figures. Only Farinacci and the journalist Giovanni Preziosi had been traditional supporters and admirers of Germany, both as a cultural entity and as Nazi system.[65] By contrast, Curzio Malaparte had been adamant in his rejection of Nazism since the early 1930s. In 1930 he published the *Technique du coup d'état*, in which he described Hitler as a caricature of Mussolini, a man whose brutality betrayed his ideological weakness and whose party lacked the ideals of dignity, liberty and culture which, according to Malaparte, characterised Italian Fascism.[66] Bottai, on the other hand, did endorse the project of universal fascism but underscored the need to be cautious towards the Nazi regime. He saw the alliance with Nazism as a necessity dictated by the two systems' common hostility to the democracies but remained sceptical about the ideological affinities between them. After the war, he described the alliance with Germany as an 'ideological abdication in the hands of Nazism', resulting from Mussolini's obsession with German power and Ciano's limited ability to appreciate the ideological differences between the two systems.[67] Yet, as he always did, Bottai publicly supported the regime's policy of rapprochement with Germany until the Grand Council meeting of July 1943. Balbo, on the other hand, was not as diplomatic as his friend and fellow *quadrumvire* Bottai. According to Ciano, he 'detested the Germans' and regarded the Axis as a big mistake that might repudiate the autonomy and essence of Fascism. From the columns of his newspaper *Corriere Padano*, he launched a bitter anti-German attack in the autumn and winter of 1939, sending an implicit message to his *Capo* which Mussolini did not fail to understand and reject in anger.[68] From 1935 until his death in 1940 Balbo used every opportunity to make his strong objections to the Axis known, using the Grand Council meetings to openly criticise the Duce for his handling of foreign affairs and for his exaggeration of the affinities between the two regimes (see Chapter 3).

Mussolini himself felt uneasy sometimes about certain totalitarian aspects of the German regime (especially the anti-Semitic propaganda[69]), but as a social Darwinist he could not but interpret Germany's political, economic and military power as a sign of superior national qualities. In the same vein, he came to view German expansion as a necessity to be contained rather than opposed. This was a significant transformation in Mussolini's foreign policy ideas, but at the time it was relevant mainly to the issue of Austria. As already indicated, the first signs of change in Italy's position on the *Anschluss* appeared in 1936 and were the outcome of a political gesture on Italy's part in recognition of Germany's aid during the Ethiopian campaign. The first actual concession on the issue was the German–Austrian Agreement, signed between the German and Austrian governments in July 1936, which Mussolini welcomed as a step towards relieving tension in central Europe.[70] The pact with Yugoslavia in March 1937, and the thoughts about its extension to a Balkan–Danubian treaty with Bulgaria and Rumania or Austria and Hungary, did have the intention of forming a barrier to further German expansion in the south.[71] These plans were, however, more of a deterrent than a threat to the plans of an Austrian reunion with Germany. Mussolini tried to postpone what seemed such a 'fatal' event as long as possible, being aware of the negative repercussions of such a capitulation in Italian public opinion.[72] Therefore, he rejected anew the traditional German bargain on the Brenner (guarantee in return for *Anschluss*) during his visit to Germany in 1937; he gave priority to rapprochement with Britain (culminating in the 'Gentlemen's Agreement' of 1937 and the British recognition of the Italian *Impero*), but at the same time alluded to a *disinteresement* with regard to the Austrian issue in a conversation with von Ribbentrop on 6 November 1937, noting that Italy now viewed Austria as 'German state number two'.[73]

The evolution of Italian–German relations and the radicalisation of fascist expansionist policies (1938–9)

The events between the Hossbach conference (November 1937) and the signing of the Pact of Steel (May 1939) proved how significant the transformation in the Italo–German relations was for the radicalisation of fascist expansionism. In his discussion with the heads of the military, diplomatic and political organisations of his regime, Hitler made it clear that his foreign policy objectives were an open-ended commitment to expansion in central and eastern Europe for the acquisition of living space.[74] The revisionist–irredentist facade of German expansionism remained almost intact during the plebiscite crisis which led to the *Anschluss*, but the Hossbach conference (see Chapter 3) had established a wider concept of territorial aggrandisement. There was, however, a mixture of urgency and dynamism in his speech at the conference, which was to be the guiding principle of his foreign policy in the period up to the outbreak of war. If the urgency may have been primarily attributed to his personal obsessions (a pathological fear that he would soon die[75]) and to domestic pressures (inability to finance further rearmament under a peacetime economy, while his enemies were rapidly rearming), the dynamism was chiefly related to external factors. We shall turn now to these factors, and to their impact on the formulation of the Italian and German foreign policies between 1938 and May 1939.

The 'next victim' syndrome and the impact of the Nazi successes upon Mussolini

The first external factor was the cumulative effect of the Nazi foreign policy successes from the beginning of 1938. Tim Mason has referred to the 'next victim' syndrome which dominated German expansionism after the *Anschluss* in March 1938. He thus attributed the 'promiscuity of aggressive intentions' demonstrated by the Nazi regime in 1938 and 1939 to an expansionist momentum that was nurtured by each successful campaign.[76] Every objective attained confirmed the *Führerprinzip*, increased the regime's confidence to its military potential and created a pressure for further expansion. Given Mussolini's diplomatic support and Britain's commitment to appeasement policies, Hitler saw an opportunity to use expansion to fulfil his regime's *Grossdeutschland* pledges and to intimidate his conservative critics in the armed forces and the administration. In 1938 and in the first half of 1939 he achieved an unprecedented extension of the Reich's territory without engaging his country in war with the western powers. This was not a major surprise in the *Anschluss*; after all, the British regarded the development as ineluctable since late 1937 (and the new British Prime Minister, Neville Chamberlain, had not refrained from saying so in his direct talks with Ciano in February 1938).[77] Yet, during the Sudeten crisis, it certainly demonstrated the tolerance of both Britain and Italy towards German expansion.[78] The same happened in the liquidation of the remaining Czech state in March 1939. This was not simply successful expansion with major military and economic benefits, although the incorporation of Czechoslovakia into the Reich provided the Nazi military machine with an excellent source of raw materials and an advanced industrial infrastructure.[79] It also signified the symbolic vindication of Hitler's intuitive leadership, personal vision and political calibre.

For Mussolini, the effect of the German successes was ambiguous. On the one hand, he attempted to exploit the dynamism of Nazi foreign policy in order to put further pressure on Britain and France for concessions. Italy's accession to the Anti-Comintern Pact in November 1937 brought about a co-ordination of international fascism not only against Bolshevism, but also against Britain and her empire, as stated in the text and acknowledged by Ciano.[80] Furthermore, the threat of German expansion in central and eastern Europe enabled Italy to play again a version of the 'determinant weight' policy in European affairs. Mussolini's role in the resolution of the Munich crisis established Italy as an important factor in the stability of the European system, due to her more or less good relations with both Germany and the Western bloc.[81] This newly acquired prestige allowed the Italian Fascist government to negotiate with the British and the French for colonial concessions,[82] while at the same time constantly strengthening its alliance with Germany *against* the 'plutocratic democracies'.[83] On the other hand, Germany's impressive military potential and her territorial aggrandisement in central Europe had a demoralising effect on Mussolini. Increasingly after the Austrian crisis he realised his relegation to a secondary position in the fascist partnership, stating that 'when an event is fated to take place, it is better it takes place with you rather than despite of or against you'.[84] Until the beginning of 1939, he had hoped to utilise his diplomatic advantage in order to offset Italy's weak economic–military position. The Munich conference gave him the impression that he could re-establish his country's prominent position in the European system as a diplomatic arbitrator capable of influencing the German foreign policy. This explains why Mussolini was initially resistant to the idea of a military alliance with Germany, as presented to him in 1938 by the new German Foreign Minister Ribbentrop.[85]

This anticipation, however, was soon to be thwarted by Hitler's determination to pursue his expansionist objectives regardless of the diplomatic good offices of his ally. By that time, Mussolini's efforts to split the British–French front by isolating France had failed.[86] Chamberlain's visit to Rome in January 1939 failed to alleviate the tension in the relations of the Italian regime with the west and cast a fatal shadow on the negotiations with France for a general agreement.[87] Diplomatically, Mussolini's only hope of retaining a role of prominence in European affairs was in a long-term alliance with Germany that would postpone war for the future (1942 or after). This was his strategy behind the apparent Italian capitulation to Nazi foreign policy in the signing of the Pact of Steel in May 1939.[88] Although the idea of a military treaty between the two Axis partners had been suggested by Nazi Germany in 1938, talks had stumbled upon Mussolini's sceptical stance towards the implications of such a pact. Only after the dramatic events of spring 1939 (dissolution of the rump of Czechoslovakia, deadlock in the negotiations between Italy and the western powers, invasion of Albania), did the Duce give his final consent and impetus to the talks, which culminated in the ceremonial signing of the Pact in Berlin. The commitment of the two sides to consultation prior to the assumption of major activities, and the express agreement on a postponement of military plans for at least three years seemed to offer those guarantees which the Italian side desperately needed to safeguard her political autonomy within the Axis camp (see also Chapter 3).

Struggle for initiative: Italo–German antagonism within the Axis

The second external factor in the radicalisation of fascist expansionism was the political interaction between the two fascist regimes. It has been argued that Mussolini was resigned to a secondary position in the fascist alliance, and that he actually succumbed to the German expansionist dynamism after 1937.[89] This is only partly true. Objectively, the internationalisation of fascism after the Spanish Civil War had resulted in an atmosphere of indirect competition between the two regimes. This was a battle that Italy, due to her inferior economic and military potential, was bound to lose. Increasingly from 1937, symptoms of an inferiority complex and a sense of 'jealousy' at the powerful political and military performance of Nazi Germany became evident in Mussolini's behaviour.[90] This explains to a great extent his growing obsession with the 'great power' ideology in the last years before the war. In the logic of this ideology, however, it was impossible for him to abandon the idea of regaining the initiative; and the prestige associated with it. What, of course, Mussolini could not appreciate was that he had been forced to conceptualise his contest with Germany in *military* – rather than *diplomatic* – terms. This in itself was the outcome of the dynamism generated by the Nazi expansionism in 1938 and 1939, as well as a proof that the initiative had completely eluded the Italian regime. After the Munich interlude, when diplomacy fared better than military threat, Mussolini followed an unorthodox diplomatic strategy towards Germany: either he made concessions to German expansionism (acceptance of the German offer of military alliance; denunciation of the 1935 Italian–French agreement) in order to preserve his restraining influence on Hitler;[91] or he too resorted to expansionism to strengthen his bargaining position and restrain Germany in geographical terms. The latter objective underpinned the timing of Italy's decision to invade Albania in the April of 1939, just a few weeks after the liquidation of Czechoslovakia by Germany.[92] As we saw, Albania had traditionally been an area of Italian political influence and economic penetration since the beginning of the century.[93] Its geopolitical importance for the control of the Adriatic and eastern Mediterranean had been emphasised by Mussolini long before the decision for invasion was finalised (see Chapter 4). Until 1937, however, there had been no definitive timetable for aggressive expansion in that direction. The invasion plan was clearly timed by the Italian government to balance the successes of Nazi expansionism in the wider central European area and to block further German intervention in the Balkan sphere.[94] This is attested to by Ciano's earlier comment that the move against Albania was timed in such a way as to irritate Germany and to hinder further German contacts with the Albanian King Zogu.[95] Ironically, the invasion was supported by Germany alone and thus increased suspicion in the West that it was part of a concerted Axis activity in the region. The result was a further radicalisation in the scope of fascist expansionist initiatives, as well as a deepening of the division between the Axis and the western blocs. It also reflected, however, how much the radicalisation of fascist expansionism from 1938 onwards had slipped away from the two regimes' capacity for rational foreign policy making.

Dropping diplomacy: the shift towards aggressive expansion

The transformation of the two regimes' expansionist strategy was also a by-product of the dynamism unleashed by the expansionist ventures of the two fascist regimes in the 1930s. Until 1937, diplomacy constituted the primary technique which the two fascist regimes exploited in order to claim or acquire territorial concessions in Europe and overseas. At the same time, the demonstration of military power was mainly intended to enhance the impact of diplomatic pressure rather than consciously risk a major conflict. From the beginning of 1938, however, the situation started to change. Hitler, confident after his initial successes, decided to utilise his powerful – and now politically neutralised – diplomatic and military mechanisms in order to promote his expansionist plans more aggressively. By 1937, he had lost his patience with the diplomatic bargaining of the Western appeasers and subscribed to Ribbentrop's anti-British strategy, despite his contrary personal inclinations and long-term plans regarding Britain as an ally. The prospect of Britain's opposition to the German expansionist plans obliterated the last major use of diplomacy for Hitler.[96] His foreign policy strategy between the *Anschluss* and the Polish campaign revealed a determination to pursue expansionist plans, by the use of force if necessary, without any intention of keeping up diplomatic appearances. In this way, he seemed increasingly prepared to risk a military confrontation and was determined to use the whole of his military potential as the major instrument for the German expansionist plans. The most striking indication of this shift was the emphasis on naval rearmament, which by definition was directed against Britain. Signs of an anti-British naval policy were evident since the beginning of the 1930s. The funds allocated to naval rearmament increased tenfold between 1932 and 1938, unaffected by the 1935 Naval pact with Britain, reaching record levels in 1939–40.[97] At the same time, the traditional militarist spirit, which had somehow been overshadowed by a more rational co-operation between diplomacy and armed forces during the Weimar period, re-emerged in its most extreme form in 1938–9.[98] The major consequence was that the political recognition of German power by its allies and enemies became now associated with the power of the German armed forces. This also meant that the attainment of the *Grossdeutschland* objectives of the Nazi regime was now expected to result entirely from the country's military performance.

Italian policies were not unaffected by this major change in the European system. Although militarism never had strong roots in the mentality of the Italian nation, the 'export' of fascism from Germany and the antagonism between the two regimes introduced this novelty in the conduct of Italian foreign policy. Mussolini had been traditionally more interested in the technological side of warfare; hence, his obsession with the plans to transform the Regia Aeronautica into the largest air force in Europe.[99] He had also demonstrated his liking for the role of diplomatic mediator in the European system, a traditional tool of Italian fascist foreign policy ever since Locarno, Grandi's policy of *peso determinante* (determinant weight), and Mussolini's own 1933 Four Power Pact. In the negotiations preceding the Munich compromise over the fate of the Sudetenland, he manifested his preference for a diplomatic solution to the demands of Nazi expansionism in central Europe by playing a crucial role in the final compromise of the Munich agreement.[100] His attitude, however, showed signs of progressive change from the moment that the alignment between the two fascist countries became closer and acquired more blatant military implications. The accession of Italy to the Anti-Comintern pact and the signing of the Pact of Steel entailed the acceptance of a mainly offensive foreign policy by Mussolini. Although it is true that the Duce often felt uneasy about the implications of these alliances, he became more accustomed to the idea of using his military potential to promote foreign policy goals and at the same time antagonise Nazi Germany. Faced with the successful aggressive Nazi foreign policy, Mussolini too turned his back on the prospect of a diplomatic solution in European affairs and subscribed to the option of war in the context of an increasingly anti-system foreign policy. This was the logical culmination of his own ideological and political commitments – his own expansionist vision of a vast Mediterranean *Impero* – but also of fixation with prestige and his desire to usurp the initiative from Germany.[101]

Ideology versus short-term developments

The fourth factor of the radicalisation in fascist expansionist policies concerns the relation between ideology and action in fascism. As we have already seen, the programmatic approach to fascist expansionism tends to view ideological commitments and pronouncements as determinant factors in the conduct of German foreign policy, while it is less willing to concede a similar degree of consistency to the Italian expansionist programme (see Introduction). The relation, however, between ideology and foreign policy is a significantly more complicated one. The impact of the political and military alliance between the two fascist regimes, the dynamism that their co-operation and antagonism generated, played a crucial role in the joint expansionist programme of the fascist 'new order'. The expansionist element was inherent in the ideological traditions of the two countries since unification (see Chapters 1–2), and was crucially bolstered and accented by a set of specific 'fascist' ideological values. Irredentist aspirations, colonial compensations and revisionist claims kept that element alive in the period between 1919 and the mid-1930s. There were, however, two restraining factors. First, the stability of the European system did not allow for any serious discussion of territorial changes. Second, neither of the two countries – and especially Italy, which has been described as the 'least of the great powers'[102] – initially possessed the necessary economic and military power to challenge this stability. For these reasons, at least until 1935, the idea of an extensive territorial expansion remained an active, yet essentially utopian characteristic of the Italian and German foreign policies.

The situation changed after the first successful revisionist attempts by both Italy (Ethiopia) and Germany (Rhineland, overthrow of the Versailles economic and military restrictions). A crumbling system of European security and the tolerant attitude of its main guarantors (Britain, France and Italy) towards German revisionism further encouraged the 'next victim' syndrome of the Nazi leadership. Chamberlain's opinion that if Hitler desired to invade and liquidate Czechoslovakia, there was no possible way of actually preventing him from doing it, underlined the loss of confidence in the ability of the pro-Versailles bloc to defend the postwar territorial settlement.[103] At the same time, expansionism became the platform of the two fascist regimes' co-operation and competition, unleashing new opportunities and speeding up the process of radicalisation. This new framework of Italian–German rapprochement facilitated the attainment of previously unfeasible goals of Nazi territorial expansion. Had it not been for

Mussolini's indirect acquiescence in Hitler's plans to re-militarise the Rhineland (an acquiescence that came at a time when Hitler was still wavering and thus strengthened his resolve to proceed with his military plan), and for his 'friendly' passivity and resignation during the *Anschluss* crisis (in sharp contrast to his forceful reaction in July 1934), Hitler could not have afforded to push the situation to extremes. His relief and gratitude were reflected in his exchange with Prince Philip of Hesse on 11 March 1938, where he repeated many times that he 'would never forget him [Mussolini] for this'.[104] Yet, the new spirit of co-operation between the two fascist regimes was even more important for the Italian regime, as it has been disputed whether Mussolini would have embarked on an imprudently ambitious expansionist programme as early as in the late 1930s–early 1940s had it not been for Hitler's influence and the Duce's passion for precedence.[105] Expansionism became the hard currency of fascist foreign policies, and by 1938 Mussolini had given priority to territorial expansion, both to promote Italy's geopolitical interests and to compete against Nazi Germany. The new international climate reactivated a latent extremism in Mussolini's foreign policy programme and strengthened his determination to pursue anti-system goals at the expense of his previous more 'realistic' handling of foreign affairs.[106] The Italian regime was now more willing to pursue wide expansionist plans against the interests of international security in order to strengthen national power and prestige. This suggests that the decision to expand was the product of both an ideological necessity, rooted in the fascist worldview, and a political opportunity for expansion offered by international developments. This newfound political dynamism which facilitated the transition to radical expansionism (both as a positive action prescribed by Fascist ideology and as a reaction to German expansion) found fertile ground in the ideological traditions not only of the Fascist regime *per se*, but also of Italian nationalism in general, of which Fascism claimed the spiritual heritage.[107] What differentiated Fascist expansionism from previous nationalist visions was the Fascist regime's intention not to confine itself to colonial issues or to a cautious border policy on the continent, but to abandon the policy of equidistance and to upset the European territorial system in order to realise these previously utopian visions. At this point, the importance of German influence in the context of the Axis alliance becomes a crucial factor in understanding the changing tone, style and devices of Italian foreign policy after 1935.

Let us finally turn back to Hildebrand's question and apply it both to the German and Italian fascist regimes: to what extent were Mussolini and Hitler constrained or aided by the international circumstances in the pursuit of their most 'radical' expansionist ambitions before the outbreak of the war? The answer is that the radicalisation of fascist expansionism from the mid-1930s onwards owes much to the exclusive political interaction between the two fascist regimes. In political terms, an expansionist foreign policy also required an external political momentum.[108] This was provided within the framework of the

Axis alliance, and was strengthened by both collaboration and rivalry between the two fascist regimes. Expansion was an option prescribed by fascist ideology, but not the inevitable outcome of either ideological beliefs or domestic crisis alone. The internationalisation of fascism, the dynamism unleashed by initial successes, and the complex alliance between Italy and Germany created a further political stimulus to the expansionist visions of the two regimes. This stimulus, strengthened by domestic pressures, transformed an initial limited expansionist opportunity into a radical, aggressive large-scale priority which gradually monopolised the domestic and foreign policy activities of the two fascist regimes. The tension between collaboration and rivalry sealed the history of the Axis alliance and helps to explain why latent ideological extremes were activated in the second half of the 1930s, and why certain expansionist policies of the two regimes were pushed further than was initially desired or justified in rational political terms.

6

FASCIST EXPANSIONISM AND WAR (1939–45)

The military conflict which developed into the Second World War was intended to be, and indeed was, the ultimate test for the two fascist regimes and the future of fascism in the international system. The radicalisation of fascist foreign policies in the second half of the 1930s had created a yawning gap between what the two regimes demanded from territorial expansion and what the western powers were willing to concede in a long-drawn-out process of negotiation. The limited character of British and French appeasement confronted the two fascist leaders with the question of means versus ends: it soon became obvious that the mythical core of fascist expansionism – and its 'radical' long-term objectives – could not be approximated by diplomatic means. At the same time, the establishment of the Axis alliance produced a powerful strategic alternative and a political momentum that were lacking before 1936. Taken together, these two factors transformed war and aggression from a vague ideological *desideratum* into a legitimate political instrument for future action. War was intended to be the ultimate formula for unifying the political with the mythical aspects of the fascist worldview; or, in other words, for uniting reality with utopia and deeds with words.[1]

Having said that, an all-out military showdown remained a far from certain development until 1939. The increasing determination of the two leaders to use the threat of force, or even actual force, in the second half of the 1930s to advance territorial goals did not, as we saw earlier, originate from a fixed decision to launch the Second World War. If Mussolini and Hitler, confident after the signing of the Pact of Steel in May 1939, spoke more openly about preparing for war and the unavoidability of a general conflict,[2] there is no evidence whatever of any definite ideas about the timing and the form of the future conflict. This point has been emphasised by Geyer, who has warned against the tendency either to 'over-determine' war, as the consequence of a fixed fascist ideology, or to 'under-determine' it, as the sole by-product of structural problems or failures.[3] We should also not forget that the war of 1939–45 was both a *decision* (to enter the conflict, to set the targets for expansion) and a *strategy* (how to wage the war, given the various short-term and long-term circumstances). There has been considerable discussion about the actual intentions of the two leaders in 1939–40: did they categorically seek a military confrontation, or was war the *ultima ratio* of their expansionist strategies? This debate will be reviewed later in the chapter separately for each regime. This is, however, only part of the problem surrounding the aims of the two regimes in the Second World War. The conflict took its shape gradually, through a series of decisions and reactions to them which produced new and largely unforeseeable circumstances: Germany's decision to invade Poland in September 1939 and the reaction of the western powers; Italy's path from non-belligerence to the entry into the war in June 1940; the launch of Mussolini's 'parallel war' in the autumn of 1940; and Hitler's decision to invade the Soviet Union in June 1941. The following analysis focuses on these pivotal decisions and assesses to what extent they were determined by ideological considerations or were imposed upon the two leaders by domestic or international pressures. In the context of this analysis, two main questions are addressed. First, did the two leaders intend to wage this particular war, at that particular time and in this particular form or sequence of events? Second, did they use the conflict to promote the mythical core of their expansionist visions or did their policies give way to war making with short-term considerations?

Germany's decision to launch the war

There are various indications that Hitler intended to use Poland as the pretext for launching his first war of aggression. The Munich conference represented for him exactly what should be avoided in the next crisis. He did not vent his irritation openly until little over a week before invading Poland. In his speech to his generals on 22 August, he declared his determination to avoid the interference of any *Schweinehund* and the repetition of the Munich compromise; this time he meant to 'test [Germany's] military machinery'.[4] His vexation, however, was implicit in his secret speech to a group of Wehrmacht officers, where he stated that the war was imminent and would not be avoided this time.[5] This conviction was emphatically restated in his other major speech to his army commanders on 23 May: 'there will be war…a short war [or]…a war of from ten to fifteen years' duration'.[6] Once the failure of the negotiations with the Polish government established Poland as the next victim of German aggression, Hitler took concrete steps to pre-empt any possible 'irredentist' compromise formula. He had already informed the Danzig Nazi party of his decision not to accept any negotiated solution, before giving specific orders to the German minority's organisation in Poland to remain inactive during the period of the crisis.[7] He repeatedly responded to the British proposals for a negotiated solution with promises of talks *after* the Polish campaign.[8] He also kept up appearances by alluding to a compromise proposal to the Polish government, but gave specific orders not to release the plan until 1 September.[9] In his speech to the Reichstag announcing the invasion of Poland, Hitler could hardly hide his enthusiasm that his 'repeated proposals' had been rejected.[10]

At the same time, Hitler appeared to regard the campaign against Poland as a preliminary step in his plans for a showdown with the west. As he stated to the League of Nations' Commissioner for Danzig, Burckhardt, on 11 August, he would have to 'beat the West' first before contemplating war in the east.[11] Such a war contradicted one of the ideological constants in his expansionist vision – alliance with Britain – and entailed a major diversion from his priority to *Lebensraum* expansion in the territory of the Soviet Union. As we saw, however, his change of strategy in the summer of 1938 involved both an acceptance of the possibility that a war against the British Empire might occur, and a decision to give priority to large-scale expansion regardless of the attitude of the Western powers (see Chapter 4). Even before the culmination of the Czech crisis, on 28 May 1938, he had expressed his determination to attack the West *after* settling accounts with 'the east'.[12] The same hope of avoiding a two-front war was expressed in the 22 August speech to the generals, where Hitler repeated his decision to turn against the West after the conclusion of the Polish campaign and the full mobilisation of German resources.

When, however, the uncompromising British and French attitude in the summer of 1939 linked the two projects into one, determined to make Hitler's invasion of Poland a *casus belli* between Germany and the West, the prospect of the much-dreaded two-front war became a distinct possibility, throwing Hitler's strategy once again into disarray.[13] The ratification of the treaty of diplomatic guarantees to Poland by the British government on 25 August caused considerable alarm and anger in the German leadership.[14] On top of that, the Nazi leadership learnt on the same day about Mussolini's refusal to enter the conflict, contrary to Hitler's confident expectations and Ribbentrop's conviction that 'Italy's attitude is determined by the Rome–Berlin Axis'.[15] This was a highly undesirable double *volte-face* which prompted Hitler to cancel the provisional order for invasion – initially arranged for the 26th – setting instead the 2nd of September as the last possible day for the attack.[16] Two days later, he spoke again to the Wehrmacht generals, insisting that the war was inevitable[17] and rejecting anew the prospect of a compromise solution for Danzig alone.[18] On 29 August he also launched a diplomatic initiative, asking for a Polish Plenipotentiary to go to Berlin by the 30th, but the extremely tight deadline set by the German government implied at best a half-hearted commitment to the plan; an implication which was not missed by the British government, who refused even to communicate the proposal to the Poles unless more time was allowed for the negotiations.[19] In the final directive for Operation White, Hitler preferred to start the invasion one day earlier than his latest acceptable date, ordering the attack for 1 September. He also stated clearly that 'if Britain and France open hostilities against Germany, it is the task of the Wehrmacht…to contain their forces…and thus maintain the conditions for a victorious conclusion of the operations against Poland'.[20]

The other major diplomatic development of August 1939 was the signing of the German–Soviet pact of Non-Aggression on the 23rd. The negotiations had started earlier that year, on a parallel level with the talks between the Soviet leadership and Britain.[21] Moscow's tenet behind its policy of rapprochement with other European countries was to avoid a military conflict at a time when the Red Army was unprepared to meet the task, due to limited resources and the widespread purges of 1938.[22] As negotiations with Britain reached a stalemate in early spring, Hitler embarked upon his boldest diplomatic venture; to lure Stalin into a political and military agreement. The replacement of the Soviet Foreign Minister Litvinov – an advocate of collective security and rapprochement with the west – by Molotov in May 1939 was a careful indicator of the changing Soviet attitude towards Germany and the Nazi government responded immediately.[23] While in London there was bewilderment at the rejection by Stalin of a vague proposal for co-operation against Germany, Hitler was anxious to reach agreement regardless of the price. His offer of partitioning Europe was accompanied by an unconditional acquiescence in Molotov's demands for Russian control in the Baltic region and the northern Balkans. He also insisted that the date for the conclusion of the talks be brought forward to the 23rd, anxious to secure a few days' margin before launching Operation White, which at that time had been scheduled for the 26th.[24] The Secret Protocol to the Agreement cast the die: the Vistula river would be the line of partition in Poland, while the northern border of Lithuania would represent the frontier between the two countries' spheres of influence.[25]

Why, then, did Hitler decide to launch a campaign which contradicted so blatantly all his long-term strategic constants (alliance with Britain, *Lebensraum* at the expense of the Soviet Union and avoidance of two-front war)? A.J.P. Taylor believed that he was the victim of 'diplomatic miscalculation' by delaying his proposal for the Polish Plenipotentiary until the 29th, instead of launching it earlier and allowing ample time for negotiations.[26] Although he had repeatedly spoken of his decision to attack Poland regardless of the British and French attitude, Taylor's Hitler was a traditional German *Realpolitiker* who kept bluffing in anticipation of a British compromise proposal which would avert a totally undesirable war with the West. He was essentially an old-fashioned opportunist whose main priority was the revision of the Versailles Treaty and was determined to exploit all circumstances offered by international developments in order to achieve a favourable territorial readjustment. The only programmatic consistency which Taylor conceded to Hitler was the latter's desire to avoid a conflict over Poland, especially with Britain. In this sense, invasion was reluctantly authorised in the very last days of August after the failure of diplomatic initiatives.[27]

The significance of Taylor's interpretation lay in its effort to redirect the historiographical attention from the 'demonic' nature of Hitler's personality to the international factors which contributed to the outbreak of the Second World War. It also introduced an interesting debate about the continuities in post-unification German expansionist policy, thus paving the way for Fischer's controversial work on the subject a few years later. His account, however, of

162

Hitler's strategic thinking at the period prior to the invasion of Poland was blurred by emphasis on long-term continuities and disregarded its deviation in two crucial areas. First, Taylor's insistence on portraying Hitler as averse to the prospect of a military conflict with Poland is incompatible with a substantial body of evidence. On numerous occasions during 1938–9, Hitler provided a retrospective account of his foreign policy as following consistent priorities leading to an inevitable showdown with Poland and the West.[28] Taylor might have been correct in reading the *Führer*'s comments as mere propaganda and *ex post facto* justification,[29] but he did not sufficiently account for the reasons behind the radicalisation of Nazi expansionist policies from 1938 onwards. Signs of this radicalisation may be detected in the Hossbach Conference in November 1937 (whose literal value Taylor summarily dismissed[30]), but it was the Czech crisis which provided the first tangible manifestation of Hitler's willingness to use Germany's military power in an offensive campaign for expansion. The timely intervention of the British Prime Minister Neville Chamberlain and Mussolini in September 1938 did avert a general conflict over Czechoslovakia but, ironically, strengthened Hitler's determination to deal with the rump state of Czechoslovakia and Poland in an uncompromising manner, rejecting diplomatic solutions or 'a repetition of Czechia'[sic].[31] The Polish government had been given a chance to yield to Germany's condition for the return of the Free City of Danzig to the Reich in return for a guarantee of Polish independence. Their adamant refusal to succumb to pressure, and the British guarantee of Polish independence in March 1939,[32] convinced Hitler that Poland should be the first victim of his formidable armed forces. As the Chief of the General Staff of the Wehrmacht, Halder, commented in the summer of 1939, the Führer was determined to have his war in Poland.[33]

Second, Taylor disregarded the impact of Ribbentrop's ideas on Hitler's strategic thinking in 1938–9.[34] His belief in the unavoidable conflict with Britain dated back to 1936, during his term as Ambassador in London, but was reiterated even more emphatically in 1937 and 1938.[35] Hitler's interpretation of the international situation before the Polish campaign incorporated two of Ribbentrop's pivotal strategic convictions: namely, that large-scale war in the east would not be tolerated by Britain, thus rendering a reckoning with the West a *conditio sine qua non* for eastern expansion; and that the unpreparedness of British military forces would impede a large-scale war with the West until 1940–1.[36] Hitler did his best to isolate the campaign against Poland from the project of war against the West. He had engineered the pact with the Soviet Union as the ultimate deterrent to British engagement in Poland, but Chamberlain's reply stressed that the pact would not impede Britain from honouring her guarantee to Poland.[37] The decision to cancel the attack on 25 August revealed the Führer's willingness to allow some more time to the efforts of isolating Poland from Britain. What, however, Taylor failed to take into account was that Hitler's strategy had undergone a far-reaching change, of which his intransigence during the Munich crisis was only the first indication. Apart from having accepted the probability of having to fight the West before turning to the east, he also decided that the attitude of Britain should not determine his expansionist priorities or timetable. By August 1939, his directives for Operation White stated that 'the destruction of Poland is the priority' even if 'war breaks out with the west'.[38] British neutrality would be a welcome development, but not a sufficient reason to call off the operation, a conviction reiterated in the final directive for the attack.[39] This was the impression of the majority of the Wehrmacht generals: Hitler and Ribbentrop meant war this time.[40]

The choice of Poland as the battlefield for the first military campaign of the Nazi regime raises reasonable questions about social imperialist motives behind Hitler's decision to order the invasion. The Munich crisis had exposed the negative feelings of the majority of the German population at the prospect of aggressive expansion, while at the same time confronting Hitler with the reluctance of his generals to risk a general war for the sake of a secondary territorial goal like Czechoslovakia.[41] Poland, on the other hand, had tradition-ally been viewed with hostility by both the Reichswehr and the Wilhelmstrasse officials, not only due to the issue of Danzig but also because the whole state owed its existence to the Versailles *Diktat* (see Chapter 4). Therefore, Hitler's determination to proceed with a united domestic front could have been best served through the manipulation of the emotive issue of the Corridor in order to justify the risk of a military conflict. In this calculation, Hitler proved right. The decision to prioritise Operation White and break off negotiations with Poland in April 1939 was greeted with enthusiasm by an opponent of war against Czechoslovakia in 1938, the State Secretary von Weizsäcker.[42] The prospect of witnessing the re-incorporation of the territories of eastern Prussia to the Reich created an atmosphere of anticipation, both amongst the conservative elites and the German population, that was in complete contrast to the apathy or even alarm during the Czech crisis.[43]

However, this impression of unity was shattered in August 1939 as a result of two separate developments. First, the alarming prospect of a showdown with the West revived the same fears that had dominated the conservative opposition to Hitler's plans for war against Czechoslovakia. Only a few high-ranking officials of the Wehrmacht could still express their unqualified support and optimism.[44] The majority had once again assumed the role of the 'dove', fearing the prospect of a two-front war.[45] During the Salzburg meeting between Ribbentrop and Ciano, the Head of German Counter-Intelligence, Wilhelm von Canaris, had striven to elicit a definite refusal from the Duce, hoping that it would suffice to curb Hitler's reckless aggressive intentions.[46] Now, even Weizsäcker had second thoughts, especially after the reports about Britain's determination to fight alluded to a completely different picture than the one delineated by Hitler and Ribbentrop.[47] At the same time, although there was significantly less alarm amongst the population at the escalating crisis with the West, this was mainly due to the belief (or hope) that Hitler would still manage to repeat the Munich formula, namely to extend the Reich's territory peacefully.[48]

The second development was the conclusion of the German–Soviet Pact of Non-Aggression. This Nazi stratagem to avoid a two-front war convinced the Wehrmacht leadership that a major obstacle for Operation White had been lifted, and restored some optimism amongst the high command.[49] However, the generosity of the agreement with the Soviet Union, allowing her to occupy a large portion of Poland and to extend her supremacy in the Baltic region, mitigated the initial positive impression. Weizsäcker and Göring endorsed the pact only as a major trump card to avoid the impending confrontation with the West, in spite of their opposition to the extensive concessions to the Soviet Union.[50] Others, like Alfred Rosenberg, criticised what seemed to be an alliance with the ideological arch-enemy of the Reich. In the last crucial days of August, Rosenberg deplored the 'moral loss of face' of the Nazi regime and ventured a gloomy metaphysical prediction: 'revenge will fall on National Socialism one day for this ideological repudiation'.[51] When eventually the war broke out in September 1939, the attitude of the public was calm but far from enthusiastic. In spite of the careful propaganda preparation of the population, the vilification of the Polish state and the triumphant rhetoric surrounding the return of Danzig to the Reich, public opinion remained desirous of a quick settlement to avert or, after 1 September, to end the war.[52]

The waning public support for Hitler's political blend of militarisation and mobilisation for war in 1938–9, combined with his hurried preparation to launch the attack on Poland against the counsel of prominent party figures, prompted Tim Mason to formulate a modified version of the social imperialist argument with regard to the decision for war in August 1939.[53] Mason's account was a far more elaborate attempt to restate the 'primacy of domestic politics' thesis, in that he did accept that 'Nazi Germany was always bent *at some time* upon a major war of expansion', originating from the regime's ideological obsession with racial theories and anti-Bolshevism.[54] His emphasis, however, was on the timing of Hitler's project to launch war and his headlong preparation to embark on a campaign which contradicted all his long-term strategic preoccupations. According to Mason, Hitler and Ribbentrop were very well conscious of the British determination to fight for Poland, and launched Operation White in full awareness that it would lead to a general conflict with the West.[55] Mason also interpreted Hitler's wavering strategy towards Poland in 1933–9 as an indication that he intended to use her as an ally against the Soviet Union in a future war of conquest. His sudden change of mind in early 1939 can only be attributed to domestic pressures which necessitated a quick, easy foreign policy triumph to raise public morale.[56] What then were these domestic pressures? Mason listed the regime's failure to produce a coherent overall social policy which caused considerable labour unrest, the 'overheating' of the German economy by 1938–9 which impeded the realisation of the extremely ambitious rearmament targets for 1939, the rapid decline in living standards as a result of the sacrifices needed to approximate these targets, and the crisis of the whole Nazi rearmament policy as a result of erratic, non-programmatic decision making in the previous years.[57] This situation, according to Mason's analysis, amounted to a deep socioeconomic crisis which necessitated expansion, a 'smash and grab' policy and the ruthless exploitation of the resources and the populations of the conquered areas. This necessity underpinned Hitler's *volte-face* in August 1939, when he jettisoned his long-term strategic constant (alliance with Britain), allied Germany with her supposed arch-enemy and rushed headfirst into an unwanted general conflict.[58]

Mason's argument offered an interesting perspective upon Nazi foreign policy and the decision for war from the viewpoint of a 'history from below'. His interpretation of the timing of the invasion of Poland provided an emphasis on the structural factors behind the decision without, however, disregarding Hitler's long-term intentions. He correctly identified Poland as a secondary objective for Hitler's expansionist vision and highlighted the latter's lack of clear short-term strategy in those crucial months of 1939. He also accurately located serious problems in the regime's long-term economic and social policy and gave a rational assessment of the system's capabilities and weaknesses. Here lies, however, the major weakness of Mason's social imperialist argument. Whether the cumulative problems of rearmament and lack of coherent planning amounted to a crisis situation in 1938–9 is a technical matter of definition, as the acrimonious debate between Mason and Richard J. Overy has shown.[59] Yet Mason's emphasis on *perceptions* of crisis, based on a rational reading of the socio-economic conditions, overestimated the capacity for rational assessment and decision making in the Nazi system. There is absolutely no evidence in Hitler's expositions in 1938–9 which alludes to a realisation of any deadlock, nor any indication that his *volte-face* in the first half of 1939 originated from any such awareness.[60] Examples of concern or even alarm from bureaucrats about the future of the German economy abounded in Mason's accounts. Even such high-ranking Nazi officials as Göring and Goebbels expressed doubts about risking a major war in these circumstances, the first because he wanted to see the completion of the 1938–9 rearmament programme, the second fearing the impact on public opinion.[61] Yet, the authoritarian tendencies of the Nazi system had insulated Hitler's predominant position in the decision-making process, especially in the field of foreign affairs, which he regarded as a near-exclusive political privilege (Chapter 3). This might not have been rational, but it shows why a 'history from below', placing primary emphasis on social issues and economic decisions, distorts the significance of the leader-oriented character of the Nazi decision-making process and fails to show that this socioeconomic reality very rarely reached the highest echelons of the Nazi leadership.

Furthermore, Mason overestimated the capacity of the system for rational assessment in the crucial area of international developments. He interpreted Hitler's decision to launch Operation White as bewildering, since the German leader had been repeatedly warned by the British government that 'any attempt by a state to dominate the world...must be resisted' and that 'they are prepared to employ without delay all the forces at their command' even after the conclusion of the pact with the Soviet Union.[62] If experienced diplomats – such as Weizsäcker and the then Ambassador in Moscow, Herbert von Dirksen – or Wiedemann, Hitler's own adjutant, were almost convinced about Britain's determination to fight, there is no reason why Hitler should not have been. His declared belief that the Western powers could not honour their commitments to Poland stemmed from his earlier impression that British defence policy would not achieve a sufficient level of mobilisation before 1941.[63] Yet, his decision to call off the attack on the 25th and his subsequent instructions regarding a possible involvement of the West in Poland reveal his awareness of the high stakes involved in the launching of Operation White.[64] With hindsight, his decision to proceed with the invasion in the face of British opposition might have been a 'miscalculation',[65] but it was far more ideologically conditioned than Mason conceded. Hitler had chosen to play down the seriousness of the British threats, convinced that the British armed forces could not effectively fight a European war. His impression from Munich had fostered his view that the Western leaders were 'small fry' and 'below average', reflecting, in his opinion, the declining 'spiritual power' of the British and French nations. Poland would be overrun with a 'lightning' action within a very short period of time, according to the natural law of 'the stronger man is right', he argued to his generals on 22 August. While he had authorised preparations for the launch of a propagandistic magazine called *Signal* (a project aimed at counteracting his opponents' propaganda in the occupied territories of the Reich), he showed no willingness to speed up the process in August 1939 (something he only did before launching the attack on the Low Countries next spring, by which time he had been convinced of the irreversibility of Western opposition).[66] In spite of British warnings that such swift action would not lessen the West's determination to fight, he ignored Göring's last-minute appeal to abandon the plan and decided to play for all or nothing,[67] still hoping that the danger from a British–French military action was minimal at that stage.

This leads us to the last weakness in Mason's argument, the insufficient attention to Hitler's foreign policy strategy. Mason's emphasis on domestic, exclusively German factors seems less appropriate for interpreting the actions of a leader so alert to international circumstances and opportunities offered by external developments. He therefore disregarded the significance of the Führer's change of strategy just before the Czech crisis. In his speech to the Generals on 22 August 1939, Hitler insisted that his international opponents' alleged political and military weakness offered a window of opportunity that would not last forever. He was determined to seize the initiative and dictate the rules of international relations, rather than being constrained by the slow-moving, over-cautious Western policy of appeasement. As he mentioned several times in August, he would rather fight the West now than in the distant future, alluding once again to his fear that time was running out for Germany and for him personally.[68] Therefore, the invasion of Poland was a *personal* enterprise, a confirmation of Hitler's monopoly of strategic wisdom in foreign-policy decision making, and a prelude to a wider confrontation first with the West and then with the East. Faced with a clash between his ideal vision of expansion and the adverse reality of domestic (not optimum level of preparation) and international circumstances (opposition from the west; Italian 'non-belligerence'), Hitler made a decisive choice to pursue his mythical project regardless, confident that he would be able to shape the political prerequisites of victory in the process. His failure to choose the time of dealing with the Britain and France was regretted, as his sentimental reaction to the British ultimatum on 3 September showed,[69] but again it was not a sufficiently strong factor to detract him from his strategic agenda. At the same time, reservations expressed by prominent party figures (Rosenberg, Göring, Goebbels) had no effect and definitely no political place in a system where the leader's will was paramount. Most of them targeted Ribbentrop, but became unintelligible once the Führer had decided to proceed with his aggressive plans without any further delay.

Italy's decision to enter the war

Mussolini's decision to declare Italy's non-belligerence in September 1939 and to enter the conflict ten months later raises complex questions about his ideological and strategic consistency, as well as his freedom of action. Undoubtedly, the refusal to join the war in September stemmed from an awareness of Italy's military unpreparedness and a lack of strategic interest in a war in eastern Europe.[70] However, references in the Cavallero Memorandum of May 1939 to the need to postpone war for three or four years (Chapter 3) have raised doubts about Mussolini's overall inclination to use war as an instrument for promoting his expansionist vision. Renzo De Felice interpreted these references as an indication of the Duce's peaceful intentions, while Quartararo saw them as an attempt to avoid an irreversible commitment to the Nazi policy of aggression.[71] They both pointed to Mussolini's 'decision' not to fight in August 1939, to his attempts to mediate between Germany and Poland and to his intention to break off the alliance with Germany after the signing of the German–Soviet pact as evidence that he neither meant to wage war nor to succumb to the alliance with Germany.[72] Quartararo also described Italian policy during the period of non-belligerence as a consistent attempt to avoid military commitment, to negotiate with the unresponsive British side and finally to postpone the half-hearted intervention as long as possible.[73] The eventual decision to declare war, according to Renzo De Felice and Giorgio Rochat, entailed a 'modest commitment', underpinned by the belief in a short war and a swift, 'better peace'.[74] A similar conclusion was reached by Denis Mack Smith, who saw Italy's entry into the war as a diplomatic move and not a real military commitment to large-scale expansion and war-making.[75] By contrast, Knox interpreted Mussolini's path to war as the culmination of an increasingly aggressive expansionist strategy since 1938. According to him, the Duce's references in May 1939 to the unavoidable showdown with the West should be taken at face value instead of being dismissed as mere bluff.[76] Similarly, Alatri viewed the same decision as the logical conclusion of Mussolini's overall expansionist strategy since 1935, while Rumi maintained that it stemmed from his vast geopolitical ambitions in the Mediterranean and was not simply dictated by the dynamism of Nazi expansionism.[77]

This historiographical debate highlights two separate but interconnected issues regarding the long-term characteristics of Italian foreign policy. The first pertains to Mussolini's attitude to war as an option in his expansionist strategy. The second regards the Italian regime's commitment to the Axis alliance and the project of a new territorial order in Europe throughout the period of non-belligerence. We saw in the previous two chapters that the Italian Fascist regime displayed a growing determination to employ the threat of aggression or actual force in promoting expansionist goals after 1935, and that the alliance with Nazi Germany provided the impetus for the radicalisation of the Italian foreign policy objectives. Although Mussolini concluded the Pact of Steel under the assumption that war would not erupt at least until 1942, there are indications that he had seriously considered the option of war before 1940. Since December 1937 he had given orders to the Chief of the Regio Esercito, General Pariani, to draft operational plans for an attack on Egypt in the event of a German war against France.[78] This project was accompanied by a major study by the Regia Marina regarding the feasibility of a landing at the Suez Canal and a parallel occupation of Malta.[79] Although the plans were apparently abandoned in the wake of the Czech crisis in September 1938, just before the Munich Conference Mussolini ordered the mobilisation of the Italian army and navy for a possible war in the eastern Mediterranean in case of a conflict between Germany and the West.[80] A few months later, in his famous speech to the Grand Council in February 1939, he expressly stated that Greece and Egypt should be considered as 'enemies of the Italian expansion' in the Mediterranean, impeding Italy's 'march to the Ocean'.[81] In the same frame of mind, Ciano expressed his belief that the Balkans would soon become the battlefield of the struggle between the 'totalitarian and the democratic' fronts, stating that the Axis alliance would enable Italy to extend her control over the Balkans.[82] In this general conflict between the two fronts, as Ciano claimed, Italy would 'crush' France and establish her predominance in the Mediterranean.[83]

The Salzburg meeting between Ciano and Ribbentrop in August 1939, where the – hitherto secret – plans for the German attack on Poland were unveiled, caused indignation to the Italian leadership and prompted a re-examination of the regime's foreign policy.[84] In spite, however, of the Italian proposals for a negotiated solution to the Polish crisis and Ciano's angry comments about the insincerity of Nazi policy,[85] Mussolini's position remained far from certain throughout the rest of August. Until the 19th he still contemplated military action against Greece, and hoped that the long-awaited internal collapse of Yugoslavia would enable him to move into Croatia.[86] Ciano's conversion to a vehemently anti-German line divided the Fascist government and party, with Bottai, Grandi and Balbo in favour of neutrality and Farinacci, Starace and Dino Alfieri (then Ambassador to the Vatican) supporting the Axis alliance. This division mirrored earlier disagreements within the Fascist party about the soundness of allying Fascism with Nazism.[87] Mussolini kept vacillating, one moment acknowledging Italy's military unpreparedness and Germany's disloyal attitude and the other stating his obligation to honour his commitment towards his Axis partner.[88] The King's strong opposition to intervention and the subsequent indignation at the conclusion of the German–Soviet Pact strengthened Mussolini's non-belligerent frame of mind and prompted him to write the letter to Hitler explaining Italy's inability to intervene militarily at that stage.[89] Yet, as Ciano himself admitted on numerous occasions during September 1939, the Duce's conversion was far from secure: 'I do not see him certain yet', he confessed to Bottai as late as on 7 September.[90]

Throughout the following autumn and winter, the split between Ciano's anti-German line and Mussolini's sentimental attachment to the Axis became increasingly evident. The Foreign Minister's support for the idea of a neutral bloc in the Balkans stumbled upon Mussolini's reluctance to commit Italy to a political formation underpinned by the principle of neutrality and was dropped in December.[91] The Duce continued to order military preparations: apart from the revival of the 'Croat Plan' early in 1940, he placed emphasis on the reinforcement of Libya, a long-term project which had started in the aftermath of the Ethiopian crisis.[92] At the Grand Council meeting of 8 December 1939, he gave a gloomy prediction about Italy's prospects in the future; whether the British or the Germans won the war, Italy would lose a great part of her political autonomy. However, he alluded to the necessity to intervene at a later stage, when the two sides would be exhausted, and spoke of the need to prepare for the future conflict, rejecting Ciano's analysis about the benefits of non-intervention.[93] Although the Italian Foreign Minister suggested to the British Ambassador Lorraine on 16 December 1939 that the Pact of Steel had essentially been annulled, Mussolini compiled a memorandum later in December, in which he stated categorically that Italy would honour her commitments towards her Axis partner and that a war against Germany was not an acceptable option for Italian foreign policy.[94]

The ambivalence of Mussolini's position during the period of non-belligerence reached its peak in the first week of January 1940 with the long letter he sent to Hitler.[95] The letter reminded the German leader of the priority of an ideological war against the Soviet Union, predicted that Germany could not win the war against the Western democracies alone and restated the Italian proposal for a compromise peace with the West. On its own, the tone of the letter reveals Mussolini's disillusionment with the closer contact between Germany and the Soviet Union at the expense of Italy and epitomises the growing doubts of the Italian Fascist leadership about the soundness of the Nazi foreign policy after the Salzburg meeting. For De Felice, this amounted to a reaffirmation of the policy of *peso determinante* and a reminder to the German leadership that Italy was determined to pursue a policy of 'open options'. It was, he argued, the culmination of a shift in Italian foreign policy away from Germany and a last-ditch attempt to exploit the channels of communication with Germany to bring the conflict to an end.[96] Quartararo used Ciano's assessment of the letter as a masterpiece of 'wisdom' to interpret it as evidence of Mussolini's non-committal attitude to the European conflict and of the strengthening of Ciano's influence upon the Duce, rejecting the view that the latter had already made a definite choice to intervene on the side of Germany.[97] However, Mussolini's subsequent statements, long before Hitler's reply arrived in March, attest to a diametrically different frame of mind. On 23 January he spoke at the Council of Ministers against neutrality, instead urging the military to mobilise the armed forces for a 'parallel war...against France'.[98] Although the task of military preparation depended on the import of raw materials and on much-needed foreign exchange from exports, in February he rejected an attractive British trade proposal in favour of a much less beneficial barter agreement with Germany.[99] On 1 March he emphatically spoke of the friendship with Germany which prevented Italy from selling weapons to the West.[100] To Ciano's dismay, Mussolini did very little to avert the imposition of British embargo on Italian trade and continued to talk of an offensive against Yugoslavia as part of the joint Axis struggle against 'the democracies'.[101]

In this sense, the die had been cast before Hitler's evasive reply to Mussolini's January letter arrived in Rome on 10 March, followed by the German Foreign Minister Ribbentrop.[102] Mussolini's declaration to Ribbentrop that Italy would join Germany in the war against the West when military preparations permitted it should not be attributed to a mysterious 'conversion' which took place between the first and the second conversation with the German Foreign Minister.[103] Undoubtedly, as Andrè underlined, Ribbentrop's declaration at the first meeting that Germany's decision to fight against 'the plutocratic clique...is irrevocable' must have strengthened Mussolini's impression that his diplomatic freedom of action had already been severely compromised by the Nazi war initiatives.[104] Yet, such a strong statement simply magnified Mussolini's previous sentimental predisposition instead of being the primary cause of it. After the meeting he had no illusions about either the German determination to attack France or the proximity of the showdown.[105] This would inevitably transform the war into a pan-European conflict and, as he had stressed in February, Italy could not 'stay out of this drama which will re-make the continent'.[106] Only a few days after the meeting with Ribbentrop, Mussolini summoned the new Chief of the Army Staff Graziani (who had succeeded Pariani in 1939) and ordered plans for a 'parallel war' in the Mediterranean with defensive preparations in the Alps and an offensive against Yugoslavia.[107] At the Grand Council meeting of 2 April he was even more explicit; if Germany attacked France, Italy could not avoid the war but should join 'as late as possible' in order to allow time for maximum military preparation.[108]

The remaining period until the official declaration of war on 10 June 1940 was dominated by Mussolini's growing impatience for intervention, magnified by the urgency which the March 1940 meetings with Ribbentrop and Hitler had introduced in his strategic thinking. He continued to contemplate a two-front attack on Yugoslavia (from Croatia and Albania), a plan which Ciano himself was not averse to as it offered the opportunity to realise the long-coveted goal of complete domination of the Adriatic.[109] The German attack on Norway at the beginning of April caused the widening of the conflict which the Duce had always considered as the prerequisite for Italy's intervention. Since he now considered the German army 'invincible', he gave orders for the mobilisation of the navy for a parallel war in the Mediterranean against British targets.[110] By the end of April, the pace of German advances had overwhelmed him, deepening the rift between him and his Foreign Minister, who continued to view intervention as evidence of Italy's enslavement to the Nazi regime's ferocious will for expansion.[111] Another source of opposition came from King Victor Emmanuel III, who became alarmed at the changing tone of Mussolini's references to Italy's future foreign policy after the meetings with Ribbentrop in March. The King repeatedly singled out Ciano, either personally or through the Minister of the Royal Household Aquarone, for a concerted move to avert intervention.[112] On one occasion, in mid-March, Aquarone even hinted at a monarchical *coup d'état* with the toleration of Ciano in order to remove Mussolini from power, but Ciano's lack of alternative strategies and his personal loyalty to his father-in-law prevented him from acquiescing to the suggestion.[113] This was the highest point of the anti-interventionist opposition. Ciano continued to give vent to his disappointment with the pro-German orientation of the Italian foreign policy until the end of May, but displayed increasing signs of resignation and fatalism.[114] Grandi (who was moved from London back to Rome as Minister of Justice and President of the Chamber in 1939) never concealed his opposition to a war on Germany's side, and throughout May he kept warning Rome about the possible implications of intervention in the war.[115] Bottai privately remained a strong supporter of neutrality, but by May 1940 he had also resigned to the inevitable and used the *Critica Fascista* to reiterate the official regime justification of Italy's necessary war against plutocratic powers who had imprisoned her in the Mediterranean.[116] Balbo made a last-ditch attempt to convince Mussolini not to proceed with the plan to intervene at a meeting on 31 May 1940, but he was frustrated even in his efforts to elicit a slight postponement. He went back to Libya extremely disappointed, but still prepared to place his loyalty to the Duce first, and did his best to ensure that the armed forces in Libya were sufficiently prepared to wage war against Egypt.[117] As for the King, he reverted to his previous position of passive disagreement, angering Mussolini with his indecision and his initial refusal to delegate control of the armed forces to him, secretly hoping that the West would resist the Nazi attack, but eventually capitulating to Mussolini's demands and succumbing to the latter's warlike drive.[118]

The only ephemeral glimmer of hope for the anti-interventionist camp came in early May with the Duce's declaration that the entry into the war would probably take place after August, since a swift German attack on France was less likely after success in Scandinavia.[119] In a letter sent to Hitler at the end of April, he alluded to a similar date, invoking reasons of military unpreparedness. Voices of concern about Italy's military preparedness were abundant; Badoglio repeatedly declared his preference for postponement until 1942, while the Chief of the Regia Marina Cavagnari expressed his scepticism about a premature intervention.[120] Events, however, were beyond Mussolini's control and wishful thinking. The Nazi attack on the Low Countries started on 10 May, catching the Italian leadership completely unawares as the news were communicated to Rome only half an hour before the invasion was scheduled to begin.[121] With the impressive advance of the Wehrmacht forces, all voices of opposition vanished.[122] While Mussolini ordered preparations for a war against France and Yugoslavia, Ciano seized the opportunity to suggest an attack on northern Greece, territorial enlargement of Albania at the expense of Serbia and expansion in north Africa.[123] Also, ironically, the same man who on 7 May had welcomed modest French proposals for a territorial settlement between the two countries now dismissed the French last ditch concessions in north Africa as a step taken 'too late'.[124] A few days later, Mussolini convoked the Military High Command and asked Badoglio to complete mobilisation by 5 June.[125] Both Badoglio and the Chief of the Regia Marina Cavagnari did not question the political soundness of Mussolini's decision but invoked the slow pace of preparation and suggested a postponement until the end of the month, but the Duce did not budge from his earlier position. Only Hitler's letter, asking for a slight postponement due to strategic reasons, prompted a reluctant re-scheduling for the 10th. The only effect of Badoglio's concerns was a readjustment of the operational plan, ruling out an initial offensive action against France as infeasible due to logistical problems of preparation and limited resources.[126]

In the light of this evidence, it is indeed difficult to uphold Quartararo's – and to a certain extent also De Felice's – thesis that Mussolini remained uncertain about his allegiances until May 1940.[127] It is true that the Salzburg surprise and the German–Soviet pact of August 1939 angered the Duce, who did not take kindly to Italy's relegation to the status of a second reserve of Nazi Germany.[128] His bitterness with this 'ideological revision' permeated his January letter to Hitler, which has correctly been interpreted as the highest point in Mussolini's disillusionment with his Axis ally.[129] The policy of non-belligerence was intended to restore Italy's freedom of action in the face of the Nazi inclination to treat Italy, as Ciano put it, 'like the Romans treated Messinissa'.[130] However, even at periods of crisis, the Duce never refrained from declaring his adherence to the Axis, arguing like a frustrated ally rather than an undecided neutral or a potential defector. Both Quartararo and De Felice confused Ciano's opposition to the Axis with Mussolini's desire to delay his *set* decision to intervene, as he stressed on 10 April 1940, on the side of Germany 'when we are...absolutely certain about the victory'.[131] It was Ciano who alluded to the invalidation of the Pact of Steel at the same time that Mussolini added references in favour of the Axis to his Foreign Minister's speeches;[132] it was Ciano who kept the 'secret channel' of communication with the West open until May 1940[133] in the face of the Duce's blanket refusal to discuss any conciliatory proposal from either France or Britain in the winter and spring of 1941. Furthermore, Mussolini's determination to postpone intervention as far as possible and his subsequent vacillation about the most suitable date reveal uncertainty about the practicalities of the joint Axis war and not about the orientation of Italian foreign policy.[134] As even De Felice conceded, the decision to enter the war was Mussolini's *personal* responsibility, a reaffirmation of his unassailable authoritarian position in a leader-oriented system, taken in the face of opposition from the monarchy, his Foreign Minister, the leadership of the armed forces, and a number of prominent party *gerarchi* who saw it as a step too far in the misguided alliance of Fascism with Nazism;[135] it was not, as Quartararo described it, 'a decision on the ninety-ninth hour'.[136]

This said, Italy's entry into the war was far from the *guerra fascista* which Mussolini had envisaged since 1937 and strove to postpone until 1943 or 1944. His consistent references to 'necessity' and 'inevitability' of intervention, his urgency to bring the date forward after the invasion of Norway and, especially, after the attack on the West originated from a growing determination to abandon the embarrassing state of neutrality and participate in the reshaping of Europe.[137] The necessity to avoid being relegated to the status of 'Switzerland' had been acknowledged by no less a figure of opposition to the Axis than Ciano since 1 September, and was reiterated by Mussolini in March and Badoglio later in the spring.[138] In this sense, intervention was more dictated by the Nazi drive for expansion than chosen by Mussolini as the vehicle for launching the real *guerra fascista*.[139] His uncertainty regarding the time of the Italian entry into the war and his decision to move the date from 1942 to 1941 and finally to June 1940 reflected how little freedom of choice the frenetic pace of German expansion had left him. In the spring of 1940, especially after the meetings with Ribbentrop and Hitler in March, he realised that this was primarily Germany's war. In April he noted to the press that 'our non-belligerence is the result of the fact that this great nation [Germany] has not yet needed us'.[140] A few days earlier he also spoke to the Council of Ministers about 'a war…(of) six months, because a longer duration could cause grave financial problems; insurmountable'.[141] Awareness of structural limitations and acquiescence in the Nazi military initiative convinced Mussolini that a *guerra fascista* in these inauspicious circumstances would be impossible. He therefore entered the conflict with a short-term, mainly defensive agenda and in the hope that the main confrontation could be postponed at least until 1942, when Italian military preparation would justify a more ambitious expansionist policy.[142] Unlike Hitler, Mussolini decided to give precedence to political considerations and postpone the realisation of his mythical *mare nostrum* plans for the not so distant future.

Towards the *guerra fascista*: Mussolini's parallel war in the Mediterranean and the collapse of Italian Fascism

Italy's entry into the European conflict took place under conditions that Mussolini had tried to avoid and failed to avert since August 1939. When Badoglio spoke to the other commanders of the armed forces in April 1940, he described Italy's intervention as 'on the side of Germany' as opposed to 'for Germany'.[143] Mussolini's numerous references to the *guerra parallela* after January 1940 underscored his determination to reassert his country's political autonomy in a war that would complement Germany's campaigns in Europe, but would also promote Italy's own strategic and geopolitical aims. Therefore, when he was forced to readjust the date of intervention according to Hitler's military *faits accomplis* in the west and to remain on the defensive until France surrendered on 17 June, he could hardly disguise his dejection.[144] He had hoped at least for an Italian advance to Marseilles, but lack of resources and military unpreparedness thwarted his ambition.[145] Mussolini's territorial demands against France were accepted by Hitler, in spite of the extremely modest military contribution of the Italian armed forces: free hand in the French African colonies, occupation of French territory up to the Rhône and in the southern coast.[146] Yet, only a few hours later, he alone decided to launch a limited offensive in the Alps in order to achieve a military success which would raise Italy's prestige. The attack did not achieve much, falling short of attaining the minimum target of occupying Nice, but by 22 June the French had already signed the armistice with the Germans. One of the French generals commented to the German delegation that, although 'Italy had declared war but not waged it', she would claim more than the Germans for territorial compensation.[147] He was proved wrong; although the Germans had accepted Italy's territorial goals in Europe and Africa, on 22 June Mussolini suddenly informed Hitler that Italy would abandon her substantial claims 'in the Rhône, Corsica, Tunisia and Djibouti', asking instead for a modest demilitarised zone adjacent to the Italian–French border.[148] The armistice signed on 24 June was extremely modest in its claims, surprising even the French delegation.[149] When Ciano visited Berlin on 7 July, he tried to resuscitate the Italian claims over Nice, Corsica, Tunisia and east Africa, but this time Hitler was adamant in rejecting any new territorial settlement or a separate French–Italian peace before the defeat of Britain.[150]

Although the German attack on the British Isles was far from certain at that point, Mussolini hastened to offer his assistance, fearing that the Germans might exclude Italy from a major reorganisation of the European system either by negotiating a separate peace with Britain or by defeating Britain alone.[151] His fears were partly confirmed, as Hitler rejected the offer of substantial Italian assistance against Britain. Instead, he urged Mussolini to concentrate on the Mediterranean and Africa, stressing that any strike in Egypt or Suez 'is an enormous gain'.[152] Furthermore, informed about Ciano's plans for action against Yugoslavia and Greece, Hitler advised caution in the Danubian–Balkan area, pointing to the danger of a Soviet involvement in Rumania and Turkey.[153] This diversion from Europe to Africa amounted to a polite but plain indication that Germany viewed Mussolini's parallel war as a secondary device of the main Nazi war in Europe. The Duce dutifully replied that he would order attacks in east and north Africa so that they would coincide with Germany's launching of Operation Sea Lion.[154] The invasion of Britain was for him the definite deadline for any action, as he regarded British defeat inevitable and a prelude to peace.[155] At least, the prospect of a swift peace with Britain dissolved after Hitler's belligerent speech on 19 July and his conversation with Ciano on the following day.[156]

Yet, the Italian successes in Sudan and British Somaliland in the end of July[157] were only a slight consolation for Italy's exclusion from Europe and for lack of progress in Libya. Mussolini's orders for an attack on Egypt in mid-July had been thwarted by the procrastination tactics of the new Italian Commander in Libya, Graziani, who took up Balbo's position after the latter's sudden death in June 1940. As indications that the German attack on Britain was imminent at the beginning of August multiplied (fuelled by reports from the Italian Ambassador in Berlin, Alfieri[158]), the Duce decided to step up the pace. He ordered Graziani to proceed immediately with the attack on Egypt and at the same time showed an increasing interest in Ciano's project for an invasion of Greece from Albania.[159] This last plan gradually became a higher priority than the offensive action against Yugoslavia, which had been prepared since July, as it was now essential to ensure control over the lines of communication between north Africa and southern Europe. However, German opposition to any intervention in the Balkans remained a constant of Nazi strategy, as Ribbentrop made clear to the new Italian Ambassador in Germany, Dino Alfieri (who had succeeded the less enthusiastic supporter of the Alliance, Bernardo Attolico, at Germany's demand in the spring of 1940), on a series of conversations throughout August.[160] Consequently, the plan had to be postponed in favour of action in Libya, remaining an open option for future action in more favourable circumstances.

Towards the end of August, however, a sequence of dramatic events started to unfold, transforming the shape of the Axis war and enhancing Italy's importance. On 27 August, Mussolini declared that he was happy with the prospect of facing a longer war, possibly lasting beyond the coming winter![161] By that time, he had been informed of the problems which impeded the German attack on Britain and which Hitler and von Brauchitsch had used as justification for the delay in launching Operation Sea Lion.[162] At the same time, he realised the growing tension between Germany and the Soviet Union over the control of Rumania, which he interpreted as an opportunity to intervene in the Balkans and restore the balance of power in favour of the Axis.[163] While there were indications that the persistent bombardments of the Luftwaffe would exasperate the British and might force them to contemplate a peace deal, there was no talk of imminent collapse. Neither the Führer's reassurances that the attack would go on as planned, nor Ribbentrop's customary optimism in his meeting with the Italian leadership on 19–20 September, succeeded in allaying the impression of insurmountable problems.[164] Although Hitler officially announced the postponement of Operation Sea Lion on 4 October, the Italian leadership considered the plan dead by 30 September.[165] By that time, Italy at last had achieved a first modest but encouraging success at an important sector of the war against Britain; Graziani had bowed to pressure from Rome and advanced to Sidi el Barrani in Egypt.[166] This advance had a tremendous psychological effect on Mussolini, offering him the first glimpse of the opportunity to use the German failure in Britain in order to transform this war into an Italian war, a true *guerra fascista*. He therefore gave explicit orders to Graziani to continue his advance in Egypt towards Alexandria.[167] He was still willing to heed the German advice to avoid disturbances in Yugoslavia due to rising tension in the north Balkans, but he continued to consider an attack on Greece as part of his campaign against Britain in the Mediterranean.[168] He was in very good humour, as Ciano noted, and kept rejoicing at the possibility of facing a long war, in which Italy would lead the Axis effort against the west.[169] He took every step necessary to ensure that this would be an unmitigated Italian triumph. He and Badoglio rejected the offer of German military assistance for the campaign in north Africa.[170] He also expressed his doubts about German plans for the occupation of Gibraltar (Operation Felix; see below) and tried to ensure that Spain's possible accession to the Axis would not limit Italy's territorial claims or jeopardise her privileged position in the Axis hierarchy.[171] Freed from the deadline of the Sea Lion, aware that he had gained the military initiative from Germany for the first time since 1936, he was poised to succeed.[172]

Until 12 October, Mussolini's main priority was to set Graziani's forces in Egypt in motion again, overcoming his general's tergiversations and unwillingness to proceed any further. Ciano continued to work on the Greek project but not as an immediate task. This situation changed dramatically, however, after the 12th. The German move into Rumania, without any prior consultation with Italy or invitation for a joint operation, alarmed and angered the Duce, who had always been suspicious of German designs in the Balkans.[173] On 15 October he summoned his army commanders and declared his determination to occupy 'the whole of Greece', a plan he had contemplated for a long time as an integral part of his anti-British strategy.[174] To an ecstatic Ciano, who always considered the Greek plan as his own personal project linked to the previous occupation of Albania, he spoke of his decision to confront Hitler with a *fait accompli* in the Balkans and escalate his two-front attack on Britain, in Egypt and the Aegean.[175] As Graziani once more rejected demands from Mussolini to proceed and asked for a three-month postponement, Greece acquired the highest priority.[176] In his letter to Hitler on 19 October, the Duce described Greece as 'one of the main points of English [sic] maritime strategy', the key to holding the Mediterranean.[177] With the parallel advancement of Graziani towards Alexandria in the near future, Mussolini continued, Britain would be brought to her knees without the need to lure either France or Spain into the peripheral war. No German assistance was needed until the final confrontation in Cairo; Greece would be overrun within a few weeks, as Ciano had confidently predicted in October.[178]

The radicalisation of Mussolini's attitude to the conflict could not have been more striking. This was not the man who spoke of a short war for a few months, the man who awaited a German triumph as a prelude to negotiations and a compromise with Britain, the man who did not intend to wage a large-scale war. This was a man who would lead the assault against Britain, who would dictate terms to Nazi Germany and eliminate every trace of British presence in the Mediterranean, the man who deplored his generals' aversion to war.[179] The Mussolini of September–October 1940 was overpowered by hubris, poised to promote his mythical vision of *mare nostrum*, eager to confer upon Italy 'the glory she has sought in vain for three centuries'.[180] If the decision for non-belligerence in 1939 and for a defensive attitude in June 1940 were dictated by what Quartararo termed 'realism',[181] his two-front offensive action in the autumn of 1940 was decided in total defiance of the advice of his military experts. Apart from Graziani, who refused to move prior to the completion of a 'convenient military preparation', the three heads of the General Staff and Badoglio backtracked from their acquiescence in the plan in their meeting with Mussolini on the 15th and expressed fears about both the state of the military forces and the feasibility of the operational plan.[182] However, the Duce's determination to proceed with his *guerra fascista* was much stronger than any awareness or reminder of military limitations. Badoglio, who at the beginning of the month considered the Greek plan indefinitely postponed, bowed to the inevitable on 18 October without resorting to any of his strategic or logistical arguments.[183] The attack would go on as planned, with a slight postponement until 28 October. Unlike Ciano's earlier thoughts about a limited operation to seize strategic positions in the north and east of the country, this plan entailed total occupation. The ultimatum which would be given to the Greek government would allow neither the time nor the political basis for any negotiations; there was simply 'no way out for the Greeks', as Ciano commented on 22 October and the Italian Ambassador in Athens Grazzi confirmed to the Greek dictator Metaxas in the early hours of the 28th.[184] As Mussolini himself stated to Hitler in a meeting that took place on the morning of the Italian attack on Greece, emphasis should now be placed on guaranteeing the ultimate victory against Britain.[185]

Politically, the attack on Greece was a *tour de force*, in the sense that it caught the German leadership unawares and raised the stakes of Italy's war. Hitler remained calm during the meeting with Mussolini in Florence on 28 October 1940, but the news of the Italian attack on Greece caused him irritation and anger.[186] His fears were soon confirmed; in military terms, the attack proved to be an utter disaster. The Albanian front became the first battleground in which Axis forces were forced into a humiliating retreat.[187] The negative consequences, however, of the reversal of Italian fortunes in Greece were not confined to this particular theatre of operations. Priority in the allocation of military resources to the rescue of the Balkan front resulted in serious limitations on the assistance dispatched to Graziani in Libya, in spite of the latter's repeated warnings that the north Africa forces were not sufficiently equipped to face the British troops.[188]

The details of the fate of the Italian 'parallel war' need not be recounted here.[189] On the morning of 12 November British forces attacked the Italian fleet at the southern port of Taranto, inflicting extensive damage on the new Italian battleships which were supposed to lead the campaign of the Regia Marina against the British fleet in the Mediterranean.[190] While the situation in Greece showed no signs of improvement, at the beginning of December the British troops in north Africa assumed the offensive and forced Graziani's forces into a steady retreat, first out of Egypt and, by the end of January, also out of Cyrenaica.[191] Mussolini's misplaced hopes for a reversal of the situation in all fronts were quickly frustrated. By the early spring of 1941, the Italian armed forces had been defeated in north-western Greece and were retreating steadily in both Libya and Sudan. The remaining prestige of the Italian fascist regime was shattered after Germany took over the first two operations and succeeded where Italy had so dramatically failed. It took the German armed forces a little more than a month to occupy Yugoslavia and Greece, while the joint German–Italian forces in north Africa resumed the offensive under the command of General Rommel.[192]

Mussolini imposed his wishful thinking on his military and diplomatic advisors, in spite of their opposition to his reckless, uncoordinated strategy. Yet, as Balbo had predicted in 1936, he fell prey to his own image of the 'infallible' leader (*Mussolini ha sempre ragione*).[193] Mussolini's assumption of total authority in both the political and military decision-making process during the war produced a decision-making mechanism which gravitated dangerously towards his personal 'charismatic' authority. Despite the military soundness of appointing a Supreme Commander to co-ordinate the three arms of the armed forces, he refused to promote Badoglio to this position, fearing such a concentration of power and mistrusting his Marshal's intentions.[194] He believed that political will was a sufficient guarantee for the successful execution of military plans, and perceived the military leadership as disposable.[195] He refrained from drafting an overall plan for the army's strategic goals to allow for a more rational distribution of resources between the African, the Balkan and the Mediterranean fronts. Instead, he resorted to an unnecessary and imprudent promiscuity of objectives, constantly shifting priorities and targets. In the summer and autumn of 1940 he kept oscillating between the plans for an attack against Yugoslavia and for a campaign against the northern part of Greece, while avoiding fixing the date of the operations in north Africa and the Balkans.[196] Lack of strategic planning proved fatal, both in Greece and in Libya, but the failures were interpreted by Mussolini as an indication of his generals' inability to comprehend the spirit of Fascism.[197] At the most crucial stage in Italy's *guerra parallela*, in December 1940, he decided to force Badoglio to resign and replaced him with the much more servile and apolitical figure of Cavallero. Cavallero was the right choice in the sense that he could still nurture his leader's ambitions with his unjustified optimism about the prospects of the campaign against Greece. He was also willing to execute Mussolini's hysterical orders for attack in December and again March, in spite of objective logistical problems.[198] Yet, as Bottai wrote in his diary in December 1940, after the situation in all fronts had deteriorated to a critical point, this was a deep 'crisis', not just in military terms but primarily on a political level, a crisis of the whole system.[199]

The realisation of defeat did not prompt necessary changes in the attitude of the regime. Hopes were nurtured that a victory of the Axis forces in north Africa and the Balkans would offer Italy extensive territorial gains in the region. Such hopes were partly realised; in accordance with the logic of 'spheres of influence', Germany conceded full control of Greece to the Italian government.[200] At the same time, the fascist regime decided to assist Operation Barbarossa by sending troops to the eastern front. Undoubtedly, the secretive way in which the whole operation was prepared by the Nazi leadership caused considerable irritation on the Italian side. In his instructions to the Wehrmacht in early March 1941, Hitler explicitly stated that both the Italians and the Japanese should be kept in the dark about Operation Barbarossa.[201] The Italians' agonised requests for participation in the operation reflected Mussolini's desperate attempt to salvage what was left of the damaged prestige of Italian Fascism.[202] He was ecstatic when in late September 1941 he was informed of the Italian contribution to the Axis victories against the Red Army.[203] He desperately desired an impressive showing by the Italian armed forces in order to re-establish Italy as Germany's major partner in the Axis alliance. So, when in October the Rumanian troops were making significant progress in the southern front of Ukraine, he confessed his sadness to Ciano for 'having taken second place to the Rumanians'.[204] The situation continued to deteriorate, however, and by the end of 1942 the Axis forces were fighting a losing war against the advancing Allied forces in north Africa. This meant that soon Italy would be exposed to an attack from the south. Furthermore, as Germany's military position grew weaker on the continent, the northern parts of Italy suffered from increasing air attacks which disrupted industrial production and demoralised the population.[205] Collapse became imminent when, in June 1943, the Allied forces invaded Sicily and steadily stepped up the pressure on Rome.[206] Within a few weeks, the Fascist Grand Council decided to curtail the powers of Mussolini and then, in co-operation with the King, to dismiss him from office. Under the new Badoglio regime, Italy negotiated an armistice and put a hasty end to her participation in the Axis war.[207] Mussolini was rescued from his prison by German commandos and was re-established as the leader of a puppet state in the north of the peninsula, but this did not save Fascism from a humiliating collapse. The Italian Social Republic (Repubblica Sociale Italiana), as the state was called, remained under the political control of Germany and reflected long-term Nazi plans for a future Italian state under German tutelage.[208]

Mussolini's war, as an alternative, autonomous enterprise, was dead, and the Italian failure was irreversible, after the heavy human and material losses drastically reduced the fighting capacity of the Italian armed forces. From that point, Germany conducted her own war and enjoyed the whole prestige of Axis victories in Europe and Africa. This was reflected in the military planning of the Axis from 1941, where Italy ceased to be referred to separately as a military force, and was placed as second in the 'German–Italian war'.[209] Mussolini deeply resented the relegation of Italy's role in the Axis alliance and continued to be jealous of the successes of his German allies. In private, he even expressed hopes that Germany's victory in Europe would be difficult and painful.[210] He was, however, aware that in his alliance with Germany there was no way back or out, and resigned to the fact that the window of opportunity for Italy's great power aspirations had been shut in the early months of 1941. When Ciano was replaced as Foreign Minister in early February 1943, Mussolini thanked him for his services, agreeing with his son-in-law that the impending defeat was the result of Germany's unilateral hasty initiatives and her refusal to consult the Italian leadership in the formulation of the Axis war strategy.[211] However, neither the collapse of the war in Russia in 1943 nor the invasion of Sicily would make him consider alternative policies to his alliance with Germany.

Launching the Nazi 'ideological' war: Operation Barbarossa and defeat

In spite of his initial frustration with the British declaration of war in early September 1939, Hitler soon regained his self-confidence and the political initiative, especially after the tremendous success of his 'lightning' campaign against Poland.[212] By the end of the month, he could not hide his impatience for turning against the West immediately and destroying Britain's capacity to resist.[213] On 9 October he issued Directive no. 6, in which he stated his decision to launch an offensive war against the Western powers without any further delay.[214] His urgency stemmed from what he perceived as an extremely narrow window of opportunity, a favourable international situation, given Italy's support, Russia's inactivity and America's fragile neutrality.[215] He also warned his generals that an unnecessary prolongation of the war would stretch Germany's limited resources and project an image of weakness to prospective allies and potential enemies. Faced, however, with the opposition of his own Wehrmacht generals, who invoked logistical problems regarding the transfer of forces from the eastern to the western front, Hitler was forced to delay the operation until the middle of November and finally to postpone it indefinitely on the 15th due to adverse weather conditions.[216]

During the winter of 1939–40 the differences in the strategic perceptions of Hitler, the army generals and the navy leadership became evident. The Führer continued to refer to the necessity of bringing Britain 'to her knees' and destroying her power completely.[217] This prospect alarmed many officials of the

Wehrmacht, who were desperate to avoid a headlong confrontation with the western powers. With the exception of the servile Commander-in-Chief of the Army, Brauchitsch, most of the other generals feared a repetition of the First World War scenario or expressed doubts about the ability of the German army to beat the Western defences.[218] The navy leadership, on the other hand, did share Hitler's strategic principle that the real enemy in the west was in fact Britain, but were extremely sceptical of the capacity of the German battleships or U-boats to wage an effective war before the completion of the rearmament programme (scheduled for 1944).[219] Yet, Hitler continued to view a swift victory in the west and the ejection of the British forces from the continent as the pivotal *sine qua non* before contemplating his next major move. Operation 'Weser Exercise' against Norway in March 1940 was merely a pre-emptive strike to secure supply of vital raw materials from Scandinavia and to stave off a British threat from the Baltic Sea.[220] From February 1940 priority had been given to the preparation for Operation Yellow, which would 'bring about the decision on land', remove the threat of a two-front war once and for all and consolidate Germany's monopoly of power on the continent 'after 300 years of British and French domination'.[221] Early successes in Poland and Scandinavia had strengthened his authority in foreign affairs and overcome the initial doubts of party figures about the advisability of his strategy. Even Rosenberg, a strong advocate of an alliance with Britain until September 1939 and one of the most vehement critics of Ribbentrop's anti-British arguments, had by early 1940 been converted to the official line of crushing the Western powers at any cost.[222] The operation against France was hugely successful, with the German troops occupying Paris by 14 June and chasing the British forces out of the continent, although the failure of the German air force to avert the evacuation of a large portion of the British troops at Dunkirk mitigated the enthusiasm of the Nazi leadership.

The signing of the armistice with France on 22 June signified the end of the first part of the war against the West and the fulfilment of the strategic preconditions for the attack on the British Isles, as Hitler had emphasised in November 1939. Now, the Führer had three options for dealing with Britain. First, he could use the triumph of the German forces and the consequent isolation of Britain in order to force the British government to acknowledge the German monopoly in the continent and come to a comprehensive peace agreement which would put an end to a war he never desired. This was the basis of his peace offer to Britain which he delivered in front of the Reichstag on 19 July.[223] Second, he could continue his military pressure on Britain by ordering air raids, intending to cause the collapse of the economic capacity of British industry, demoralise the government and the population, and thus force Churchill to capitulate. Third, he could use his air force to prepare the ground for the invasion of the British Isles and the total destruction of the British Empire.

The first option was ruled out after the official British reply to Hitler's peace offer of the 19 July. Just like in the first peace sounding after the occupation of Poland, when the British government rejected any conceivable compromise proposal by the Nazi regime, Lord Halifax repeated his government's determination to fight against Germany.[224] However, Hitler himself appeared not to expect much from his vague, rhetorical appeals to Britain, as three days before the peace offer he had already issued Directive no. 16 for a landing operation against Britain.[225] The directive explicitly stated his determination to proceed with the preparation of the invasion and, 'if necessary to carry it out', but only as a last resort and after the failure of political and military pressure to induce Britain to accept compromise. On 22 July Hitler reiterated to his army leadership the dangers implicit in the invasion of the British Isles and ten days later, in another meeting with the whole leadership of his armed forces, he did not refrain from expressing 'scepticism regarding the technical feasibility [of the invasion plan]'.[226] In the meantime he had encouraged his Axis ally, Italy, to concentrate on a peripheral campaign against British targets in north Africa, especially Egypt and the Suez Canal. He appeared to have expected that Britain would yield to diplomatic and military pressure and accept defeat, and did not conceal his bewilderment with the British government's determination to continue fighting.[227]

However, towards the end of July, two new options started to crystallise in Hitler's mind. In the expositions he gave to army officials on 22 and 31 July, he attributed the perplexing British refusal to give in to 'hopes pinned on Russia and the United States'.[228] According to his new analysis, if Germany succeeded in defeating Russia, then both Britain and the USA would abandon hopes for a German defeat and grant a free hand in the continent to the Reich. He, therefore, ordered preparations for a campaign against the Soviet Union to be carried out if the invasion of the British Isles did not take place, preferably in the spring of 1941. Although Hitler's rationale behind this new order pointed to a strategic war against the Soviet Union as a secondary precondition for the successful outcome of the campaign against Britain, the Führer also described this operation's aim as the destruction of the whole state of Russia with one blow. The second option, which would be an extension of Italy's parallel war in the Mediterranean, involved attacking the British Empire in Gibraltar, Suez, north Africa and the Persian Gulf and 'delivering the decisive blow' in the periphery. This plan was initially formulated by the OKM (Navy High Command) and revealed the disagreement of the navy leadership with the preparations for crossing the Channel. The main advantage of the plan was that it could be implemented parallel to the preparations for the invasion of the British Isles and could be given priority if Operation Sea Lion had to be cancelled.[229]

Undoubtedly, Hitler preferred to establish a permanent settlement with the Western powers before turning towards the east, thus avoiding the possibility of a two-front war. Conscious of the importance of establishing air control before any landing was contemplated, he issued Directive no. 17 on 1 August, in which he ordered the Luftwaffe to carry out intensive bombing operations and thus destroy both the military defences and the morale of the population.[230] However, the failure to attain these prerequisites had become evident to Hitler by the beginning of September, when the losses of the Luftwaffe continued to be high and the British government showed no signs of contemplating surrender.[231] His speech on 4 September included bitter verbal attacks against the British government but refrained from making any concrete references to the outcome of the German operations and the future of the Sea Lion.[232] Long before he announced his decision to his Italian ally, the Führer had come to the painful decision to postpone Operation Sea Lion due to weather problems and the failure to establish superiority in the air.[233] The Chief of Navy Staff, Admiral Raeder, had realised this failure even earlier and had approached Hitler on 9 September with an emphatic reminder of the Mediterranean option as the only effective means of continuing the war against Britain.[234] On 26 September, and encouraged by the postponement of Operation Sea Lion, Raeder gave a more detailed exposition of his Mediterranean project to Hitler. The Admiral stressed the importance of seizing *both* Suez and Gibraltar, while at the same time reinforcing the Italian front in north Africa. He did not conceal his pessimism about Italy's chances of defeating the British alone but expressed his confidence that, with adequate transfers of German troops, the Mediterranean could be 'cleared up during the winter months' of 1941.[235]

Hitler's foreign policy in the ensuing period until the end of 1940 has given rise to a historiographical debate about his actual intentions and priorities before the final decision to invade the Soviet Union. This debate has revolved around two separate but interrelated questions: first, did Hitler seriously pursue the Mediterranean project as an alternative to the campaign against the Soviet Union; and, second, when and why did he decide to launch the war of annihilation against his former ally in the east? A group of intentionalist historians, including Weinberg, Hillgruber and Hildebrand, interpreted Hitler's flirtation with the Mediterranean plan as an interim and half-hearted move aimed to elicit the long-coveted compromise agreement with Britain or, at least, to stabilise the front against the British forces.[236] According to this interpretation, the Führer's interest in the Mediterranean was circumscribed by his unwavering priority to his *Lebensraum* war in the east, the decision for which had crystallised in his mind before the deterioration of the German–Soviet relations in the autumn and winter of 1940–1. However, this thesis has been challenged in two different ways. First, Hitler's efforts to bring about a 'continental bloc' during the second half of 1940 have been regarded by some historians as wholehearted and insistent, amounting to a real strategic priority to the plan advocated by his Foreign Minister Ribbentrop for the formation of a large anti-British alliance, even with the inclusion of the Soviet Union.[237] Second, Hitler's plan to attack the Soviet Union remained an open option until his meeting with Molotov in November 1940, or even until Franco's eventual refusal to join the war in December, and was only given priority after November 1940, that is after the mounting tension between Germany and Russia over the control of the Balkans had rendered their mutual alliance strategically unattainable.[238]

The evidence shows that Hitler did his best to convince the Spanish and French regimes to accede to the anti-British bloc in the second half of 1940. In mid-September he sent a letter to Franco stating the reasons in favour of Spain's entry into the war, but the Caudillo rejected the German request for the occupation of Spanish ports.[239] At the beginning of October Hitler discussed the plan with Mussolini, and on 20 October he travelled to Spain and Vichy France to elicit the consent of the Spanish dictator General Franco and of the leader of Vichy France, Marshall Petain, but again he stumbled on the two leaders' evasive attitude.[240] In spite of these adverse results, he issued Directive no. 18 on 12 November 1940, in which he reiterated the strategic importance of Spain's participation in the Axis war effort and of the seizure of Gibraltar. He had already given orders for the preparation of this operation, code-named Felix, and he expressed his optimism to the Spanish Foreign Minister Serrano Suner that it could be carried out during the following winter if Spain decided in favour of entering the war.[241] However, Suner again objected to the German demands for Spanish ports and invoked economic and military problems as the main reason behind Spain's neutrality. Still, lack of a definite negative reply from Franco nurtured hopes in the Nazi leadership that the Mediterranean project was not dead yet. On 5 December Hitler issued new orders for the projected war in the Mediterranean, including Operation Felix with a provisional date for February 1941 and an expected duration of four weeks.[242] However, Franco's negative reply on 7 December caused considerable consternation to the Nazi leadership and prompted the halting of the preparations for Operation Felix.[243] In the following two months, Hitler continued to press the Spanish government for a reconsideration of its position, but Franco's continuing resistance forced him to abandon his efforts completely on 22 February 1941.[244] Yet, since the end of December the Mediterranean project had already been regarded as stillborn, in the sense that it had failed to achieve its main objective, namely the decisive German victory against British forces and targets in the Mediterranean. Not coincidentally, on 18 December Hitler had also issued Directive no. 21 for Operation Barbarossa, which stated that the Wehrmacht's main priority would be the defeat of the Soviet Union 'even before the conclusion of the war against England [sic]'.[245]

Even before Franco's negative reply in December 1940, there were indications that Hitler's commitment to the Mediterranean project had specific limits and conditions. First of all, one of the basic tenets of the Axis alliance was the clear delineation of the two partners' spheres of influence and the alleged compatibility of their expansionist objectives. According to this tacit agreement, the Mediterranean and Balkan regions constituted Italy's exclusive zone of influence.[246] Although Mussolini had initially agreed to Hitler's plan for a 'continental bloc' with the inclusion of Spain and Vichy France, his general attitude was determined by his desire to stave off any external interference in his own sphere of influence, especially during the conduct of the *guerra parallela* in north Africa. This was the point behind his doubts about France's and Spain's entry into the war that he expressed to Hitler in his letter on 18 October 1940 and again in his conversation with the German Ambassador in Rome, von Mackensen, in December.[247] As we also saw, he refused the offer of German military assistance in the operation against Egypt in September. Only when the Italian attack on Greece had seriously floundered in the Albanian front and Graziani's troops were on the defensive against advancing British forces in Egypt by early January 1941 did Mussolini allow the German troops to enter the Mediterranean theatre of war and assist in the conduct of the military operations.[248] Yet by that time, Hitler had given up any illusions about the chances of defeating the British forces in the Mediterranean. His orders underlined the danger of a collapse in the African front and intended to stabilise the Axis positions in the face of the Italian armed forces' incapacity to hold against the British.[249]

This leads us to the second limit in Hitler's endorsement of the Mediterranean project: his lack of confidence in Italy's ability to defeat the British in north Africa on her own resources. The limited capacity of the Italian forces in Egypt was known to Hitler since July, when he stressed that the Italian contribution to the Mediterranean project would be of limited importance.[250] This impression was reconfirmed in September by Raeder, who predicted that the seizure of Suez by Italian troops only would not be feasible, and in November by General Thoma, who inspected the Italian positions in Egypt and conveyed his strong scepticism about the viability of the Italian front in north Africa.[251] By the time Hitler issued Directive no. 18 on 12 November 1940, he had given up hopes for seizing Suez during the winter, limiting his maximum goals to the seizure of Gibraltar, although the one target without the other cancelled the whole effect of encircling the British forces in the Mediterranean.[252]

The failure of the Italian *guerra parallela* against Greece and Egypt complicated the situation even further for the German strategic planning and practically annulled the prospects of a decisive Axis victory in the Mediterranean during the winter of 1940–1. However, Hitler appeared much more inclined to rescue the Balkan front from collapse than to intervene in favour of Italy in north Africa. In Directive no. 18 he prioritised the operation in the Balkans but stated that any help in Egypt *could* be authorised only after the Italians had achieved a (highly unlikely) further advance towards Alexandria. On 13 December he hastened to issue the directive for Operation Marita, intending to occupy Greece by the end of April 1941. It took him another month, during which the British advances in north Africa had obliterated the Italian gains of the last months, to order the dispatch of additional forces to Egypt.[253] But this was as far as he would go in order to save the wounded prestige of his Axis partner. He showed no inclination to salvage Italy's east African *Impero* which fell to the British by late May 1941, despite the fact that Ethiopia was supposed to be the base for Axis operations against both the Suez and Sudan–Egypt.[254] Germany's intervention in Italy's Mediterranean–Balkan sphere of influence followed clear priorities which were meaningful only in the framework of strategic preparation for Operation Barbarossa. The strengthening of Germany's military presence in Rumania in October, the plans to bring Bulgaria into the Tripartite Pact in spite of fierce Soviet opposition, and the invasion of Greece in the spring of 1941 were strategic prerequisites for covering the southern German flank against the Soviet Union.[255] Stabilisation of the situation in north Africa was also significant for the security of southern Europe, especially after the defeats of the Italian armed forces. Ethiopia and Somaliland, on the other hand, were of limited importance only for the moribund Mediterranean project, which had already been demoted in Hitler's priorities by the end of 1940.

There is another strong indication that Hitler's Mediterranean strategy in 1940–1 was subordinated to the prerequisites of Barbarossa, namely the time factor. His decision in July to postpone the attack on the Soviet Union until May 1941, with eight weeks of prior preparation, left him with a window of opportunity to tackle the Mediterranean theatre until the beginning of spring 1941. This deadline explains to a great extent Hitler's abandonment of the efforts to lure Spain into the Axis war in late February and the concurrent cancellation of Operation Felix. In his conversation with Suñer in November 1940, he had spoken of late winter as the latest possible time for the operation in Gibraltar, envisaging completion by the end of March. During the winter, he kept contemplating the possibility of an action in Spain, but the pacification of the Balkan front after the Italian failure in Greece acquired a higher priority.[256] The execution of Operation Marita in early spring 1941 necessitated a further slight postponement of Barbarossa, possibly until June, but this would be the latest conceivable deadline. As he had envisaged in July 1940, the complete defeat of the Soviet forces could be completed within three-to-five months; therefore, launching the operation by early summer would leave sufficient time to destroy the Soviet Union before the winter season.[257]

How important, then, was the attitude of the Soviet Union towards Germany in Hitler's decision to launch Operation Barbarossa in June 1941? Koch has stressed that preparation against Russia had been initiated by the OKW (Wehrmacht High Command) before Hitler made his first reference to the need to 'crush' the Soviet Union in July 1940.[258] The Wehrmacht's plan was conceived as a reaction to fears of Russian mobilisation on the borders with Germany and entailed a pre-emptive action in case Russian expansion in the Balkans threatened Germany, either directly or by obstructing her position in central Europe.[259] However, Hitler was adamant in his belief that Russia would not take offensive action against the Reich due to her alleged military and economic weakness, a view he reiterated to his generals in January 1941; that is, *after* the definite decision to launch Barbarossa in June.[260] Unlike the mainly pre-emptive plan of the OKW, his project was a large-scale offensive action, intended to destroy Russia and force Britain and the USA to acknowledge the

German domination of the continent. Interestingly, there was no sense of alarm in this speech at Russia's grandiose ambitions in the Balkans and the Baltic states, which Molotov had alluded to in his conversations with Hitler and Ribbentrop in November 1940.[261] This evidence seems to contradict Koch's analysis of the developments in German–Russian relations during November 1940, which identified Stalin's increasing demands for Finland and the Balkans as the primary reason behind Hitler's decision to proceed with Operation Barbarossa.[262] Undoubtedly, after Molotov's visit to Berlin Hitler could not conceal his disillusionment with the prospects of a constructive relationship with the Soviet Union. This impression was strengthened by Molotov's reply to the German invitation to enter the Tripartite agreement on 13 November. In his response, Molotov asked for the complete withdrawal of the German troops from the Finnish territory and for an agreement with Bulgaria regarding Russia's access to the Dardanelles.[263] Although the price asked by the Soviet leadership was high, it stemmed from the generous German concessions which accompanied the Non-Aggression pact of 1939 but which the Nazi leadership had decided not to abide by in the critical situation of 1940–1. Koch regarded this particular document as the catalyst in Hitler's decision to proceed with the preparation for Operation Barbarossa and the real turning point in the re-orientation of Nazi foreign policy towards the east. It seems, however, that Hitler had had few doubts about the viability of the German–Soviet alliance before Molotov arrived in Berlin. Two days before the Russian Foreign Minister's arrival he ordered the preparations for Operation Barbarossa to continue 'regardless of what results the talks will have'.[264] Then, addressing his generals on 5 December, he emphasised his decision to prioritise the operation against the Soviet Union and reconfirmed his initial schedule for an early summer campaign. He did not even have to wait until Franco's negative reply on 7 December to shelve the Mediterranean project.

Undoubtedly, the Soviet leadership bore some responsibility for the deterioration in the German–Russian relations from the summer of 1940 onwards. It was the Red Army who occupied the whole of Lithuania, thus violating the conditions of the Secret Protocol to the 1939 pact with Germany, although a compromise solution was eventually negotiated between the two countries in December 1940. It was also the increasing Russian interference in the Balkans, with the occupation of Bessarabia and the claims over Bulgaria, that placed the bilateral relations of the two countries under considerable strain.[265] It was the mobilisation of Russian troops on the border with Germany that first alarmed the OKW leadership and resulted in preparations for a preventive strike.[266] There is evidence that since the early summer of 1940, the Russian operational plans were based on the assumption that Nazi Germany would be the main enemy and envisaged a German attack in the near future, although it was known to the Wehrmacht leadership and to the German Ambassador in Moscow von Dirksen that the nature of this planning was purely defensive.[267] However, the real deterioration in German–Russian relations after Molotov's visit to Berlin resulted primarily from German obstinacy or lack of interest in maintaining a minimum of co-operation. In spite of Russian complaints about the German military occupation of Rumania in October 1940, it was known to Hitler that Stalin did not contemplate any move to obstruct the German action.[268] At the same time, negotiations for an economic agreement between the two countries came to a fruitful conclusion in January 1941 with extremely beneficial arrangements for the German side.[269] As the German Ambassador in Russia noted to Ribbentrop, the Soviet leadership was prepared to pay a high price to restore good diplomatic and economic relations with the Reich.[270] Yet, none of these indications and arguments proved sufficiently strong to effect alterations in Hitler's strategic planning for Barbarossa. This was not a preventive, pre-emptive war, nor a strategic campaign of limited scope and goals. As he stressed to his generals in March, this was going to be a war of total extermination.[271] His directives for Barbarossa underscored the necessity of mobilising 'all available units and resources', including the reversal of a previous order for partial demobilisation, in order to ensure total success against both the Red Army and the whole Soviet state.[272]

The launching of Operation Barbarossa on 22 June 1941 constituted the most emphatic affirmation of Hitler's monopoly of power in foreign policy decision making. His decision to abandon the war against Britain and concentrate instead on a new target was criticised by prominent figures in both the military and the diplomatic hierarchy of the Nazi regime. The traditional, conservative line of criticism, epitomised by the objections of Raeder, Weizsäcker and the German Ambassador in Rome, Ulrich von Hassell, underlined the danger of a two-front war and questioned the soundness of the decision to attack a non-enemy country with which Germany still had advantageous economic and trade relations.[273] Others in the army, like Halder, did not express political objections to the project but criticised the lack of a clear strategic plan behind the preparations for Barbarossa.[274] Ribbentrop, on the other hand, initially voiced his reservations about the timing of the operation, pending the formation of the 'continental bloc' against Britain and the struggle against the British Empire,[275] but he was eventually persuaded that the war against the Soviet Union would be short and have an extremely positive effect on the campaign against Britain. His personal anti-British strategy, however, had by then been irreversibly shelved, signifying the beginning of his declining influence upon Hitler in the remaining years until 1945.[276] As for Göring, his reservations again stemmed from logistical considerations, since both war production and rearmament had not yet reached the projected optimal level. Instead, he emphasised the need to concentrate all available resources against Britain and then refrain from further large-scale expansion in order to 'digest' the vast resources of the occupied areas.[277] However, as had happened in all the other cases of his disagreement with Hitler, he placed his loyalty to the Führer first and participated in the preparations. Only Alfred Rosenberg and the SS leadership understood from the first moment the ideological implications of the war and endorsed the effort wholeheartedly.[278] Rosenberg was ecstatic about Operation Barbarossa, regarding it as a return to the ideological core of Nazism and a historic opportunity to defeat Bolshevism and the Jews.[279] Himmler was equally jubilant, not only for the ideological significance of the undertaking but also for the opportunities it offered to his SS for wider responsibilities and jurisdictions. On 13 March 1941, Hitler personally granted extensive powers to SS units in the Nazi empire, allowing them 'to act independently and under [Himmler's] responsibility'.[280] Himmler himself could not conceal what was at stake in this operation. In a speech to SS units on the day that Operation Barbarossa was launched he stressed that this war was the beginning of a fundamental reorganisation of Europe and the whole world.[281]

As Hitler stated in his letter to Mussolini on the day of the invasion, this war was a return to his ideological origins and concepts, which at last had set him 'spiritually free'.[282] In taking his decision he had contradicted his two pivotal long-term strategic principles: agreement with Britain, avoidance of a war on two fronts (or three, in this case, with the inclusion of north Africa). However, here lay the essence of the ideological nature of this war; namely, that it was launched in total defiance of material, structural and strategic considerations, with an unjustified confidence in swift victory which stemmed from an ideologically-driven underestimation of Russian power, and against the counsel of his most senior military and diplomatic advisors. At exactly this point in the history of the Nazi war, Hitler abandoned his previous tactical flexibility, gave up his efforts to produce optimal preconditions for the attainment of his *Lebensraum* vision, and retreated irreversibly into the mythical sphere of his worldview.

The spectre of defeat after 1942 prompted a decisive strengthening of the authority of the party at the expense of state institutions and bureaucracies. According to Hitler, the NSDAP was a guarantee of 'victory-minded mentality', a quality which was in short supply amongst the bureaucrats and the generals of the armed forces.[283] This shift towards the party entailed the transfer of a vast range of responsibilities from the state to party organisations or individuals. The Gauleiters continued to report directly to Hitler about the situation in their provinces, and there was no co-ordinated policy at national level. Ribbentrop's Foreign Ministry had to wage an enormous – and losing – battle against both the Ministry of Propaganda and the SS for the control of the occupied areas.[284] The pace of Nazification of the armed forces was significantly accelerated after 1943 with the introduction of the institution of Commissioners.[285] At the same time, the Führer continued to concentrate even more authority in his hands, both in the shaping of the policies and in the conduct of the war effort. He even blamed the failure of the German offensive in Russia on the military leadership and assumed supreme command of the armed forces in December 1941[286] after dismissing his Commander-in-Chief of the Army Brauchitsch. Distrust of the abilities of his subordinates (and, in particular, the Wehrmacht generals, whom he repeatedly blamed for the reverses in the eastern front[287]) and excessive confidence in his own capacity to regulate such an immense system, prevented him from considering the advice of his party colleagues, his military specialists and the diplomats. Undoubtedly, his failure to effectively supervise the war effort alone made him increasingly dependent on a distorted, limited view of the events. Yet he refused to admit failure in his own strategy, despite warnings from those immediately involved in the conduct of the war.[288] This tendency became most clear in the eastern front after 1941. He brushed aside the advice of the Wehrmacht leadership in August 1941 to proceed to the occupation of Moscow, ordering instead advances in the north sector of the front.[289] He also rejected the appeals of the generals for a strategic retreat in the winter of 1941–2, issuing directives to all army groups in the eastern front to defend the occupied territory because 'withdrawal would produce a crisis of confidence in the leadership'.[290] A similar inability to contemplate tactical withdrawal in the face of adversity led him to overrule Rommel's defensive strategy in north Africa and order his troops to stand firm in their positions. The result was that, by May 1943, the last German forces in Tunisia had surrendered after having suffered tremendous human and material losses.[291]

A glimmer of hope was offered to the Germans with the success of the second major summer offensive of 1942, but the Russian counter-offensives reduced the German campaign to a desperate exercise in hopeless defence and self-sacrifice, as the Nazi leadership continued to dismiss calls from the Wehrmacht generals for a tactical retreat. Hitler preferred to condemn his forces to defeat and decimation in Stalingrad than to accept capitulation or withdrawal.[292] Attempts to seize the strategic initiative in the east continued in 1943 with the launching of Operation Citadel, but this was a limited offensive action which bore little relevance to the initial large-scale objectives of Barbarossa and it nevertheless failed to reverse the inauspicious situation in the east.[293] From mid-1943 onwards the German forces were forced into a steady retreat with minimum co-ordination and extremely heavy casualties. Despite Hitler's orders for an all-out defence and the 'scorched earth' directive,[294] the Nazi military machine had been brought to its knees. It is questionable whether Hitler was aware that the war had been lost by 1943, as Speer maintained,[295] and in any case he was determined to maintain the fight until the very end. Yet by that time, the domestic system had reached a critical point of paralysis. After such a long time of 'Hitler myth' propaganda, the Nazi system was unable to consider alternatives to Hitler's personal strategy, to react to the self-destructive policies of the leadership, or to actively seek an alternative to the impending destruction.[296] The plot of 20 July 1944 was the ultimate proof that it was impossible to change the course of Nazi policy with Hitler still in charge. In contrast to what happened in Fascist Italy, however, when defeat became apparent, allegiance to the Führer remained a powerful factor of the Nazi regime until the very end. Most Nazi officials remained loyal to their leader, while those who, like Göring and Himmler, sought to replace him in the last months before collapse were effectively thwarted in their plans by Hitler and his faithful entourage.[297]

The fascist war practically ceased to be a war of expansion during 1941–2. First, the defeat of the Italian armed forces on all fronts (Egypt, Greece, Ethiopia) put a swift end to Mussolini's aspirations for a real *guerra fascista*. Second, the failure of the German *Blitzkrieg* against the Soviet Union by the end of 1941 and the ineffectiveness of the Wehrmacht offensives in 1942 thwarted Hitler's ideological goal of annihilating the Soviet army and leadership. From that point onwards the foreign policies of the two fascist regimes were reduced to war making which gradually assumed a desperate defensive character and led to the fall of Mussolini in 1943 and the eventual collapse of the Nazi regime in 1945. In 1940–1 the two fascist leaders embarked upon the realisation of their ultimate expansionist visions, transforming the war into a fundamental campaign for the triumph or collapse of fascism as a whole. By the time domestic and international factors had annulled the hopes of a fascist victory, the two regimes had long before crossed the Rubicon of normality to be able to contemplate any form of compromise. Any alternative policy or course of action was meaningful only *after* the removal of the leader from power, constitutionally if that was possible (the Grand Council motion of 24–5 July 1943 in Italy) or in a conspiratorial manner (for example, the 20 July plot in Germany; and Victor Emmanuel III's schemes in March 1940). In the same way that the war had become the personal project of Mussolini's and Hitler's ideological obsessions, fascism itself completed its total identification with the decisions and the fate of its two charismatic leaders.

CONCLUSIONS

The study of fascist expansionism: ideology and other factors

In concluding his *Fascism: A History* (1996), Roger Eatwell notes that 'fascism emerged as a significant force...as a result of a complex inter-relationship between national traditions, the actions of key leaders...and socio-economic developments, especially crisis'.[1] It is vital to stress that the study of fascism and of its political choices – not least of all, territorial expansion – cannot be properly comprehended from a single viewpoint. The widening of the scope of research, encompassing ideology, structural factors and international relations, has contributed to the elaboration of our understanding of fascism, and of its expansionist policies in particular. Furthermore, the debate about fascism's relations with the national past has introduced a fruitful interest in studying fascism not simply as *sui generis* case, but in relation to a plethora of long-term and short-term dimensions: intellectual traditions, institutional developments, the crisis of the *anciens régimes*.

Why study ideology, then, in order to analyse fascist expansionism? The first reason for this is to gain a general insight into the most extreme fascist policies, of which expansionism (with all its consequences) was a striking example. The extension of the intentionalist-structuralist debate to the issue of the Holocaust, the bitterness of the *Historikerstreit*,[2] and the immense interest in the Goldhagen controversy, to mention only recent historiographical developments, have shown that the discussion on the significance of ideology in fascism is not over. If large-scale expansionism and war were responses to domestic deadlock or the outcome of cumulative radicalisation, then why should we assume that expansion was the obvious and logical choice for diversion from domestic problems? Why was radicalisation expressed in these terms? Even if we dismiss the ideological pronouncements of Mussolini and Hitler as propaganda, even if we interpret expansion as a reaction to domestic crisis, there is always a process which formulates intentions and prioritises options. This process is not

193

ahistorical: it takes place within a framework of long-term intellectual and political developments, and it reflects what a given individual or group perceives as legitimate and/or desirable in a certain historical context. As S.C. Azzi has noted, traffic accidents do not happen 'solely because of the existence of automobiles'.[3] Expansionism was neither the only nor the most obvious or predetermined policy option at the disposal of the two fascist leaderships.

This justifies the focus of research on fascist *Weltanschauung* as a means to interpreting fascist practice. However, the capacity of ideological predispositions to determine foreign policy should not be exaggerated. The endeavours of the fascist regimes to translate ideas into action belonged to the realm of *intentions*. The reality was radically different. Neither of the two leaderships possessed any concrete idea as to how they could achieve their long-term objectives, what it entailed to promote them, and what the measure of success was *in the short term*. In fact, their obsession with long-term visions made them opportunistic *par excellence*. Fascist 'new territorial order' was such a long-term goal, opening up vast new opportunities and fuelling their ambitions. It was associated with certain prerequisites: domestic unity, authoritarian state, rearmament, a new 'fascist' mentality for the masses, a more radical handling of foreign affairs. Yet, what was conspicuously lacking was a concrete idea about how to manage the process of change. This is true not only of Italian Fascism, where the lack of programmatic pronouncements by Mussolini has been widely discussed, but also of Nazism, where Hitler's alleged clarity of intention (as expressed in *Mein Kampf* and in the *Second Book*) should not be exaggerated. Both regimes provided the necessary short-term impetus by advocating an uncompromising activism, they could rally support by invoking the emotional power of their utopias, but the rest was left to experiment, risk and the alleged intuition of their leaders.

In this sense, the study of ideology is a necessary, but not a sufficient factor in explaining the specific choice and sequence of expansionist initiatives undertaken by the Italian and German fascist regimes. Domestic structural conditions and long-term features of the two systems affected decision making and often limited the freedom of the two leaderships to conduct foreign affairs according to their wishes and preferred style. Renzo De Felice attributed the relative lack of radical expansionist moves by the Fascist regime during the 'decade of good behaviour' to the priority given to domestic consolidation and re-organisation.[4] Cassels also underlined the restraining influence of traditional bureaucrats, especially of the Foreign Office, on the Duce's diplomacy.[5] In the late 1930s, the low level of preparation and the limited capacity of the system for economic and military mobilisation delayed Italy's entry into the war until June 1940, in spite of Mussolini's ascertained desire to join Nazi Germany in the major territorial reorganisation of the 'new order'. In Germany, the economic and military limitations of the Versailles Treaty convinced Hitler of the vulnerability of the country's defensive position and dictated a relatively more cautious and limited foreign policy until 1936. At the same time, the strength of the traditional elite groups and institutions – a feature that was much less pronounced in the Italian state – created a more pluralistic framework of foreign policy making, in which the intentions of the Nazi leadership had to be negotiated with the expert advice and procedures of powerful state institutions, such as the armed forces and the Wilhelmstrasse. A further potential problem pertained to the NSDAP's more elaborate structure and more pronounced ambitions to replace the state and play a central role in the reshaping of the domestic system in a totalitarian direction. Only gradually did the establishment of an authoritarian, leader-oriented system result in the subordination of elite groups and party ambitions to the rule of the two leaders, depriving the former of their right to co-decision making and relegating the latter to a functional status of interpreting and executing the leaders' charismatic will.

Another important factor for understanding the interaction between ideological intentions and structures was the framework of international relations. According to De Felice, the absence of radical initiatives in Italian foreign policy after the Corfu incident had to be linked with a general lack of external opportunities for expansion in a European system still geared to defending the stability of the postwar status quo at all costs. In the second half of the 1930s, the Nazi expansionist momentum forced the pace and radicalised the style of Fascist expansionist policies, both through the opportunities offered by the Axis alliance and as a reaction to German unilateral actions. While the illusion of opportunity speeded up plans for the conquest of Ethiopia in 1935, the impact of Nazi successes in early 1940 forced the Duce to reconsider Italy's 'non-belligerence' and to order participation in a war he could only partly control and even less shape. In Germany, the July 1934 coup in Vienna served as an eloquent reminder to Hitler that the attainment of anti-system goals presupposed a more favourable international constellation and a more developed revisionist culture amongst the other European powers which was wanting at that point. Munich was another lesson, this time regarding the aversion of the Western powers to aggressive solutions and use of force for territorial changes. Much though A.J.P. Taylor exaggerated the importance of international developments in the ensuing period until September 1939 for the outbreak of war, he was right in one respect – the invasion of Poland took place in circumstances which had been neither anticipated nor desired by the Nazi leadership. In this sense, Nazi foreign policy until the launching of Operation Barbarossa reflected the necessity to cope with the inauspicious strategic consequences of September 1939 and the abject failure of Italy's 'parallel' war. Failure to rectify the situation in late 1940–early 1941 (namely, by forcing Britain to accept defeat) compromised the planning and execution of the invasion of the Soviet Union in June 1941.

The significance of these factors in the shaping of foreign policy underscores the need to rethink our definition of *programme*. Much of the confusion and acidity surrounding interpretations of fascist foreign policies has emanated from a flawed distinction between programme as 'general ideas' and programme as a rigid 'stage by stage' guide for action. This has led to an equally inflexible contrast between opportunism and 'blind' expansion, on the one hand, and programmatic consistency, on the other.[6] Just like ideology, 'programmes' allude to long-term goals and priorities but not to the day-to-day conduct of foreign affairs. No political elite has ever come to power with a definite agenda for action *and* has managed to abide by it without diversions, reassessments and setbacks. In this respect, the only meaningful distinction should be between *primary*, that is persistent, and *secondary*, flexible and alterable goals of foreign policy making, as well as between choice of objectives and decision about timing, strategies and means. The crucial test for the 'programmatic' character of a regime's foreign policy is whether these primary objectives were consistently reflected in pronouncements and underpinned the long-term rationale of foreign policy making; whether they were pursued with determination; and whether secondary goals were designed to aid – or, at least, not to contradict – the attainment of those primary objectives. Rather than dismissing opportunism and tactical flexibility as lack of ideological commitment, we should perhaps analyse the logic of such pliability and how it related to long-term priorities or declared goals. However, this is precisely what is lacking even in the most sophisticated social imperialist approaches. They correctly emphasise how the timing of certain initiatives reflected attempts to boost the popularity of the fascist regimes and how success was exploited by the regimes' propaganda industry to strengthen their legitimacy. They do, however, concentrate heavily on the short-term reasoning of foreign policy making and thus lose sight of the wider priorities and aspirations which underpinned the long-term conduct of foreign affairs by the two leaderships.

This long-term dimension in the foreign policy of the two fascist regimes was informed by a complex notion of *living space*. The visions of a Mediterranean *mare nostrum* in Fascism and of a vast eastern empire in Nazism encompassed concrete geographical areas of expansion and were prescribed by general ideological beliefs shared by the two regimes. The foci of expansion were defined through a combination of historic, geopolitical and ideological elements which linked each country's glorious past with the right to reclaim its historic position of greatness in the future. However, the acquisition of living space was also presented as a 'natural' necessity, justified by the belief in history as the domain of the 'fittest', by the alleged 'elite' character of the two nations, and by the symbolic significance of territory for great-power status. In this sense, the notions of *spazio vitale* and *Lebensraum* became figurative and composite expressions both of a general propensity for expansion – as an open-ended, permanent state of affairs – and of concrete aspirations, reinforced by historical, geopolitical and ideological factors specific to each country and regime. Particular goals were prioritised (Adriatic, north Africa, Suez and southern Balkans for Italy; *Mitteleuropa* and Soviet Union for Germany), but timing and planning were greatly determined by external opportunities and limitations. Because of the vague character of their long-term expansionist visions, each regime could constantly reassess its short-term strategy and choose from a plethora of options and methods of policy-making. Opportunity arose from the lack of clearcut strategies, and this was both a curse and a blessing for the two fascist regimes. It was a curse because it could not generate clear standards, against which the achievements of the regimes could be assessed. This deprived the two regimes of a clear idea about the suitability of their means, the soundness of their strategies and the feasibility of their goals. It was, however, a blessing because it enhanced the tactical flexibility of the two leaders. In practice, many of the political ventures of the two regimes failed to produce desirable developments or conditions conducive to the advancement of the fascist visions. However, the extent of these failures was not as apparent to the leaderships then as it seemed with the benefit of hindsight. The far-reaching character of fascist visions rendered only one failure intelligible: total defeat. Anything short of that presented new opportunities and hopes.

'National' traditions and 'fascist' innovations: the continuity debate

The second major question pertinent to the nature of fascist expansionism is whether it was informed by idiosyncratic 'fascist' values and aspirations or was simply an expression of pre-existing national traditions and practices. If fascist ideology was indeed a 'scavenger', amalgamating different nationalist and revolutionary traits into a new ideological edifice and re-launching past utopias as realisable goals of foreign policy,[7] then how truly unique was the fascist commitment to territorial expansion in style and scope? With regard to style, fascism clearly followed a more active and uncompromising approach to the handling of foreign affairs. O'Sullivan has spoken of the 'activist style of fascist politics' as a feature which distinguishes fascism from previous liberal and conservative regimes in Italy and Germany.[8] Emphasis on action, violence and war was dictated by pivotal beliefs at the heart of the fascist ideological minimum: social Darwinism, revolutionary dynamism, the ideal of a 'citizen-soldier', the glorification of military values in national history, as epitomised in the Roman Empire and the Teutons. At the same time, the leader-oriented, authoritarian style of rule signified an efflux of authority from traditional state institutions and bureaucracies to the fascist leaderships, whose approach to foreign policy making was characterised by a distinct lack of attention to procedures and protocol. Charisma and routine proved extremely difficult to reconcile, thus resulting in a much more unpredictable and dynamic attitude to foreign policy, unbound by the usual prerequisites and subtleties of *Realpolitik*. Aggression became a legitimate weapon of fascist policy for attaining 'just' goals, regardless of its destructive implications for others.

It is, however, with regard to the nature and scope of fascist expansionism that the debate on continuity has raised a series of objections to the putative 'fascist' character of the two regimes' expansionist policies. Renzo De Felice spoke of the 'years of consensus' with reference to the period between 1929 and the Ethiopian campaign. His belief in the genuine, deep character of such a consensus might have been exaggerated, failing to take into account the superficiality of 'fascistisation' at a societal level.[9] There was, however, undoubtedly wide popular support for the regime's foreign policy until the mid-1930s, even for such 'radical' initiatives as the occupation of Corfu and the invasion of Ethiopia.[10] In Germany, a similar sense of consensus surrounded the successful pursuit of revisionist and irredentist goals by the Nazi regime until 1938. As Kershaw has shown, the cult of the Führer reached its peak in the second half of the 1930s, when the territory of the Reich was extended dramatically and dextrously without necessitating a military engagement.[11] Even when disagreements between the Nazi leadership and conservative officials in the armed forces and the Wilhelmstrasse arose in 1938–9, these pertained mainly to the timing and the potentially disastrous international repercussions of the use of aggression.

The debate on continuities between fascist and pre-fascist foreign policies has hit raw nerves in both countries, often offending the moral desire to castigate fascism by presenting it as an aberration of national history, alien to its long-term legacies and characteristics. However, much that fascism comprised a coherent, autonomous system of thought, it was also to a great extent the product of interwar crisis, derived from a different reading of the same historic data. Its place within the tradition of radical nationalism, as well as its ideological debts to previous currents, movements and mentors, have all been well established and documented. In this sense, continuity was the result of fascism's own process of production and systematisation, as well as an important factor in its popular appeal. As a 'nationalism plus' phenomenon, fascism fused its own intrinsic ideological and political traits with conventional national beliefs, suppressed or frustrated aspirations, and more extreme, latent pre-existing tendencies.

It was, however, the nature and parameters of this fusion that determined the limits of continuity. Each fascist regime displayed a selectivity towards traditional goals and forms of border policy, prioritising some and playing down or even relinquishing others. Even before the radicalisation of fascist expansion-ist policies in the second half of the 1930s, the regimes often showed a desire to go beyond these widely shared objectives (for example, intervention in the Spanish Civil War) in pursuit of wider goals and to the dismay of traditional diplomatic and military elite figures. From the extensive reservoir of what was perceived as legitimate territorial aggrandisement (revisionism, colonialism, continental living space, irredentism), each regime made choices and established priorities which were informed by a long-term vision of acquiring living space in areas identified through historic, geopolitical and ideological factors. The shift from border to living space policy might have been consistent with previous radical nationalist calls for world power status, but was popularised, radicalised and pursued by the fascist regimes with a dynamism and historic urgency which emanated from a specifically 'fascist' commitment to unite utopia with reality. In this respect, the unconventional fascist approach to foreign affairs cancelled the

Realpolitik distinction between feasible and unattainable goals, dictating instead an attitude that took utopia at face value and pursued it to its extremes. This tendency became more conspicuous in the context of war from 1940 onwards, when both regimes turned their back to rational assessments of domestic capabilities and international factors in pursuit of their more far-reaching expansionist goals. The legitimisation of violence and war and the elitist basis of the fascist worldview opened up opportunities and offered solutions which previous liberal and conservative regimes were less inclined to subscribe to. If we remove these elements from our interpretation of fascist foreign policies, then fascist expansionism is deprived of an overall explanation for its specific choices and methods.

Therefore, while the long-term objectives of fascist expansionism were by no means the exclusive domain of fascist ideology, their systematisation, prioritisation and dynamic pursuit were underpinned by specific 'fascist' values and prescriptions. This dualism between the *national* and the *fascist* underscores the need to abandon the rigidity of the 'continuity versus discontinuity' debate, opting instead for an understanding of fascist expansionism as a special form of ideological commitment to living space expansion, whose individual goals and justifications were derived from nationalist utopias and myth-making but synthesised and pursued according to 'fascist' priorities and views. This idiosyncratic variety of territorial expansionism brings Fascist Italy and Nazi Germany to the focus of a double comparative approach, both as radical articulations of generic *fascist* values and as culminations of analogous historical trajectories and intellectual traditions *à la longue durée*. What draws them even closer to each other was also the fact that, of all those interwar movements in Europe that displayed a commitment to abstract 'fascist' values, only in Italy and in Germany did the 'fascist' component seize and exercise power autonomously for a considerable length of time. As a result of the consolidation of fascist power in the two countries and of the gradual radicalisation of the two regimes' policies, expansionism evolved from the status of a vague intellectual commitment to territorial aggrandisement to concrete policy making and, eventually, to a defining political choice of fascism in Italy and Germany.

Leaders, 'fascist' values and 'national' interest

In the transition from movement to regime, the two leaders (Mussolini and Hitler) occupied a special position in the collective mythology of fascism as the historic guiding forces at the time of oppositional struggle, as the persons who led fascism to power, codified disparate beliefs and systematised the fascist doctrine. In the hostile environment of the first coalition governments in 1922 in Italy and in 1933 in Germany, their symbolic importance increased; they now bore the responsibility of safeguarding fascism against 'normalisation' and of ensuring its final dominance in the domestic system. Mussolini and Hitler used the powers derived from their position as heads of leader-oriented regimes to identify themselves with two loyalties, to fascism and to the nation as a whole. This difficult task depended upon, first, their ability to express collective fascist values accurately and effectively in the name of their movements; and, second, upon their success in convincing public opinion that these fascist values and aspirations would represent national interests in the best possible way. With regard to foreign policy, this task presupposed that they could fuse the spirit of fascism into foreign policy making, combining expansionist goals with the fascist demand for a radical social-economic and spiritual transformation. It also rested upon their ability to show in a tangible way that fascism could interpret, formulate and promote national interests better than previous political ideologies, thus enabling their nations to fulfil their destiny.

In performing this fusion, however, each leader reached different levels of success and persuasion. Mussolini's decision to align Italy with Nazi Germany remained a phenomenally unpopular choice until the very end, both amongst most Fascist *gerarchi* and in public opinion. After the war, Bottai described the Axis and the war fought in 1940–3 as a 'Mussolinian', as opposed to a 'Fascist' project.[12] This was probably an exaggerated statement, since all Fascist leaders eventually endorsed the regime's policy, reaffirming the symbolic capacity of their *Capo* to represent Fascist interest and values. It serves, however, to indicate that Mussolini did not convince even his closest colleagues in the regime and party that *that* particular policy of expansion would promote general Fascist goals, both inside Italy and in the whole of Europe. As domestic transformation was an integral (and, for many Fascists, central) part of the Fascist worldview, Mussolini failed to relate the specific objectives of expansion in the context of Axis to such domestic goals. As Bottai commented, war and aggression halted civilian and cultural development when they were supposed to accelerate and deepen it.[13] Such doubts damaged the 'infallible' image of the Duce and enhanced the gap between *mussolinismo* and Fascism, bringing prominent Fascists face to face with an uneasy clash of loyalties. At the same time, public apathy after the Ethiopian campaign and general hostility to Nazi Germany raised doubts amongst the population as to Mussolini's ability to represent the country's national interests in the framework of such a policy. Again, loyalty to the Duce remained for a long time a strong element of public perseverance to disasters, but it gradually became insufficient to overcome the impression that Fascism would not save the country and that defeat was impending. After 1941, when shortages of food and destruction by Allied bombardments dislocated domestic life, the Italian population did not exempt Mussolini from their bitter attacks on Fascism: he, Ciano, the other Fascist leaders, the detested party, the whole of Fascism had to go.[14]

Hitler faced a similar challenge to his charismatic authority with his major 'ideological revision' of August 1939 (the Ribbentrop–Molotov Pact), when he struck a deal with Nazism's arch-enemy in the east. A public opinion indoctrinated according to the tenet of Bolshevik–Jewish conspiracy was startled, while many Nazi figures were shocked by the change of attitude that this decision involved. The Führer also remained unmoved by the exhortations of even his closest aides (Göring, Goebbels) to reconsider his decision to launch the campaign against Poland at that particular time. Success, however, proved the strongest integrative factor for the 'Hitler cult' – an element that Mussolini did not enjoy after the Ethiopian campaign. Furthermore, with the prioritisation and launching of Operation Barbarossa in June 1941 Hitler reunited his personal strategy with the most crucial common Nazi values of anti-Bolshevism and anti-Semitism. The attack on the Soviet Union might have been the ultimate stage in his personal obsession with Germany's 'historic' *Lebensraum* in the east, but it also offered opportunities for promoting other radical values and visions cherished by individual Nazi figures in the regime and party. The occupation of vast lands in the east in 1941–3 gave the alibi for radical experiments in the new lands, created personal spheres of jurisdiction for many Nazis and provided a vast *tabula rasa* which could be reorganised along the lines of Nazi ideology's most extreme prescriptions. At the same time, the significantly more tangible threat of Bolshevism in Germany (due to her geographical proximity to the Soviet Union) provided a stronger factor for public loyalty (or lack of opposition) to the regime, even when defeat and collapse became a certainty. For the majority of the population, Hitler had led Germany into an unavoidable war with Communism and the Jews which would decide the fate of the whole German nation. Compromise with, or capitulation to, such an enemy was unacceptable, if not totally unintelligible. With 'Barbarossa' Hitler had managed to combine his personal fate with that of Nazism and Germany as a whole, in a way that Mussolini failed to do after the Ethiopian campaign.[15]

In the end, the allegation that through the evolution of fascism from movement to regime the two leaders usurped the meaning of the word 'fascism' and distorted its initial ideological content might be true in rigid terms. However, personal charisma remained the most powerful unifying force of the regime-type of fascism. Apart from the intellectual dimension of expansionism, apart from its relevance to commonly shared *fascist* values, its particular practice that marked the history of interwar fascism remained in the exclusive domain of the *regimes*, not of the movements. Alternative concepts of foreign policy making were neither eliminated nor totally absorbed by the two leaders; they were, however, effectively neutralised in the framework of a leader-oriented system, where the personal charisma of Mussolini and Hitler appropriated the privilege to represent fascism on the level of politics. Whether the consolidation of the fascist systems after the acquisition of power bore any relevance to early fascist views is a matter of intellectual history. For the study of fascist expansionism in its practical manifestations, emphasis on the evolution of the two leaders' ideas and on their exercise of power is a *sine qua non*, predicated on the basis of the specific nature of the regime model of fascism.

Dealing with differences: the limits of a generic definition of fascist expansionism

The limitations of a generic definition of fascist expansionism should be very carefully recorded and accounted for. While an obsessive emphasis on the specificity of each regime's views and policies obfuscates clear similarities between them, no plausible definition of generic fascism can be couched in terms of uniformity. As a 'nationalism plus' phenomenon, rooted in auto-chthonous radical nationalist traditions, fascism itself retained distinctly *national* features and operated within long-term national structures. Apart from similarities in their ideological commitment to large-scale expansion, each regime recast particular national aspirations which inhered in the general cognitive model of the indigenous society. Furthermore, the realisation of their prescriptions depended on factors which were essentially impervious to, and uncontrolled by, their intentions. Economic resources, military preparedness and potential, international status, effectiveness of state structures, public loyalty to the state, were all fundamental components of foreign policy making but could only partly be influenced during the short lifespan of the two regimes. They remained essentially different in each country and affected the intensity and effectiveness of each regime's policies.[16]

Any conventional typology of generic fascism has treated Nazism, with its greater fighting and destructive power, vast expansionist ambitions and fanaticism, as the most extreme or accomplished variant of fascism.[17] Others have interpreted the unspectacular use of force and aggression by the Italian Fascist regime as evidence of its half-hearted commitment to the goal of large-scale expansion. Especially amongst Italian historians, attempts to overstate the ideological and political differences of the two regimes have for a long time commanded the majority view. The contrast between Nazi atrocities in the Second World War and the notably less aggressive behaviour of the Italian troops in the Balkans;[18] the more circumscribed expansionist plans of the Fascist regime compared to the millenarian racial aphorisms of the Nazi 'new order'; the failure of totalitarianism in Italy as opposed to a projected image of a ruthless Nazi dictatorship based on extreme use of terror,[19] have served both as empirical observations about the nature of the two regimes' policies and as indications of their ideological divergence.[20] De Felice projected the argument even further, in the slippery territory of the leader's personality and of the people's 'national character', stating that Mussolini was not 'cruel', at least not in the way that Hitler was.[21] Denis Mack Smith developed the argument in a totally different direction, portraying Mussolini as a caricature in an 'unserious comedy world' of his own, with little relevance to, or influence upon, the cataclysmic events of the interwar period.[22]

Of course, the potential of Italian Fascism for cruelty and terror was plainly manifested in a series of occasions, from the ruthless policies of 'pacification' in Libya in the late 1920s to the racial policies in the *Impero* and the concentration camp at Ferramonti in southern Italy,[23] although still paling into insignificance compared to the extent of Nazi acts of horror in occupied Europe and the Soviet Union. Similarly, even if the fixations of Mussolini and Hitler might have been of extraordinary importance in such leader-oriented systems, the crude 'either-or' rigidity of the Führer's obsessions was significantly less pronounced or resolute in the Duce's worldview. The establishment of a 'totalitarian' system in Italy was hampered by the fragmentation of public loyalty between state, Crown and Church. Mechanisms of political opposition were largely suppressed by the regime, but bodies like the Fascist Grand Council retained a quasi-pluralistic function which initiated the process for the dismissal of Mussolini from power in 24–5 July 1943. A similar potential for institutional opposition was not possible in Nazi Germany, where allegiance to the state traditionally overshadowed any other forms of loyalty and was further reinforced through the charismatic basis of the Führer's rule. As for foreign policy in particular, Nazi expansionism was more fanatically pursued, to the point of risking and eventually causing a major military confrontation which would decide the fundamental issue of world supremacy. Its effects were significantly more far-reaching than the unsuccessful Italian Fascist bid for Mediterranean mastery in 1940–1, not only in geographical scope but also in effectiveness.

All these statements, however, underscore the importance of studying fascist expansionism both as an ideological commitment and as a process of translating it into reality. Notwithstanding the responsibility of the two leaders for the way their regimes were shaped, operated and acted, long-term economic, military and social structures of their countries were beyond their ephemeral reach. Discarding Italian Fascism as a farce or dismissing the ideological substance of its expansionist aspirations simply because effective foreign policy making was hampered by limited economic capacity, absence of a militarist culture and failure of Fascist efforts to instil genuine loyalty to the state in the population, is to confuse the 'fascist' with the 'national', the ideological with the political, the intention with the result. The challenge for any generic definition of fascist expansionism is to take note of these long-term differences and features in answering why such different societies converged upon a similar radical notion of territorial aggrandisement, why they chose to go to extremes in order to pursue it, and why they became allies in a horrifying undertaking. Concentrating exclusively on 'what actually *happened*', as De Felice and Vivarelli urged,[24] thwarts what Griffin has described as 'a healthy dialectic between theory and empiricism',[25] which is indispensable for the understanding of fascism's long-term national roots, epochal nature and ephemeral success. In this sense, fascist expansionism remained both generic and specific to each country, recasting radical national aspirations with a distinctive 'fascist' urgency, informing the general orientation of foreign policy making, but also shaped into action under the confluence of national and international factors which remained largely impervious to fascist intentions.

The value of the comparative approach to fascist expansionism lies in its capacity to raise intriguing questions about both the similarities and the differences between Italian Fascism and German Nazism, as well as between the course of Italian and German nationalism.[26] Interpreting the expansionist ideologies and policies of the two regimes involves an understanding of a set of common 'fascist' values and prescriptions (the 'ideological minimum'), which explain the prioritisation of territorial expansion by the two fascist leaders. However, it also entails an awareness of national traditions, features of the two systems in the *longue durée*. A generic notion of *fascist expansionist ideology*, shared by the two regimes examined in this study, is validated by referring to the common values of the fascist 'ideological minimum'. Yet, it is also challenged by idiosyncratic autochthonous factors in each country. This study has shown that fascist expansionism has to be examined as *ideology*, *action* and *process* (translating ideology into action and reality). The end result (the actual policies and their effects) was different for each regime in style, dynamism, implications and effectiveness. The influence of internal and international factors, of competing domestic institutions and figures, of each leader's personal interpretations and intuitions, has been noted and compared. If such differences and contradictions are carefully accounted for, then the notion of a *generic* fascist expansionism can be a valuable tool for analysis, providing crucial insight into the ideological visions and political practices of fascism in a way that no singular account for each regime is able to do.

NOTES

INTRODUCTION

1 Griffin, R., *The Nature of Fascism* (London and New York, 1994), 1ff.
2 See, amongst others, Collingwood, R. G., 'Fascism and Nazism', *Philosophy*, 15 (1940), 170ff; Croce, B., *Per la nuova vita dell'Italia. Scritti e discorsi 1943–44* (Naples, 1944), 13ff. For a general assessment of this analysis of fascism see Vincent, A., *Modern Political Ideologies* (Oxford, 1992), 148; De Felice, R., *Interpretations of Fascism* (Cambridge, MA and London, 1977), 14–23.
3 Perfetti, P., *Il dibattito sul fascismo* (Rome, 1984), 10ff; Organski, A.F.K., *The Forms of Political Development* (New York, 1965); Payne, S., *Fascism: Comparison and Definition* (Madison, 1980), 101ff.
4 See, for example, Burleigh, M. and Wippermann, W., *The Racial State: Germany, 1933–1945* (Cambridge, 1991); Epstein, K., 'A New Study of Fascism', in Turner, H.A., Jr. (ed.), *Reappraisals of Fascism* (New York, 1975), 2–25.
5 Salvemini, G., *Dal Patto di Londra alla Pace di Roma* (Turin, 1925); Salvemini, G., *Mussolini Diplomatico* (Bari, 1952); Salvemini, G., *Preludio alla seconda guerra mondiale* (Milan, 1967), also translated in English as *Prelude to the Second World War* (London, 1953); Taylor, A. J. P., *The Origins of the Second World War* (London, 1961); Kirkpatrick, I. S., *Mussolini: Study of a Demagogue* (London, 1964); Mack Smith, D., *Italy: A Modern History* (Ann Arbor, 1969); Mack Smith, D., *Mussolini* (London, 1981); Mack Smith, D., *Mussolini's Roman Empire* (London, 1982).
6 Mason, T., 'Whatever Happened to Fascism', in Childers, T. and Caplan, J. (eds), *Reevaluating the Third Reich* (New York and London, 1993), 254–60.
7 Nolte, E., 'Between Myth and Revisionism? The Third Reich in the Perspective of the 1980s', in Koch, H.W. (ed.), *Aspects of the Third Reich* (Houndmills and London, 1985), 17–38, and Nolte, E., *Das Europäische Bürgerkrieg, 1917–1945. Nationalsozialismus und Bolschevismus* (Berlin, 1987).
8 For a criticism of the methodological and analytical validity of Nolte's recent work, see Evans, R.J., *In Hitler's Shadow: West German Historians and the Attempt to Escape from the Nazi Past* (London, 1989), 24–46. Note also Nolte's role in the *Historikerstreit*, as recorded in Knowlton, J. and Cates, T. (eds), *Forever in the Shadow of Hitler? Original Documents of the Historikerstreit, the Controversy concerning the Singularity of the Holocaust* (New Jersey, 1993), 1–15, 149–54; and in Kühnl, R. (ed.), *Vergangenheit, die nicht vergeht* (Cologne, 1987).
9 Mason, 'Whatever Happened to Fascism', 255ff. See also Payne, S.G., *A History of Fascism, 1914–45* (London, 1997).

10 Mason, 'Whatever Happened to Fascism', 260; Evans, R.J., *In Hitler's Shadow*, 25–46, 86–7.
11 Payne, S., *Fascism: Comparison and Definition* (Madison, 1980); Payne, S., *A History of Fascism, 1914–1945* (London, 1997).
12 Robinson, R.A.H., *Fascism in Europe, 1919–1945* (London, 1981), and Robinson, R.A.H., *Fascism: The International Phenomenon* (London 1995).
13 De Grand, A.J., *Fascist Italy and Nazi Germany: The 'Fascist' Style of Rule* (London and New York, 1995); Eatwell, R., *Fascism: A History* (London, 1995); Bessel, R. (ed.), *Fascist Italy and Nazi Germany: Comparisons and Contrasts* (Cambridge, 1996).
14 Griffin, *Nature of Fascism*, 26–55.
15 Wiskemann, *Rome-Berlin Axis* (London 1966, 2nd edn), and *Fascism in Italy* (London and Basingstoke 1970, 2nd edn).
16 Petersen, J., *Hitler und Mussolini. Die Entstehung der Achse Berlin-Rom 1933–1936* (Tübingen, 1973); Deakin, F.W., *The Brutal Friendship: Mussolini, Hitler and the Fall of Italian Fascism* (London, 1962).
17 Knox, M., 'Conquest, Domestic and Foreign, in Fascist Italy and Nazi Germany', *Journal of Modern History*, 56 (1984), 1–57; Knox, M., 'Expansionist Zeal, Fighting Power, and Staying Power in the Italian and German Dictatorships', in Bessel, *Fascist Italy and Nazi Germany*, 113–33.
18 Thompson, J.B., *Studies in the Theory of Ideology* (Oxford, 1984), 173–204.
19 The best overall discussion of the different interpretations of Nazi foreign policy is to be found in Kershaw, I., *The Nazi Dictatorship: Problems and Perspectives of Interpretation* (London, 1989, 2nd edn), ch. 6. See also Williamson, D.G., *The Third Reich* (Harlow 1995, 2nd edn), 49–77.
20 Trevor-Roper, H.R. (ed.), *The Table Talk of Adolf Hitler, 1941–1944* (London, 1953).
21 Hildebrand, K., *Vom Reich zum Weltreich. Hitler, NSDAP und die koloniale Frage 1919–1945* (Munich, 1969); and 'Hitlers "Programm" und seine Realisierung, 1939–1942', in Funke, M. (ed.), *Hitler, Deutschland, und die Mächte. Materialien zur Aussenpolitik des Dritten Reiches* (Düsseldorf, 1977), 63–93; Hillgruber, A., *Hitlers Strategie. Politik und Kriegführung, 1940–1941* (Frankfurt, 1965).
22 Schubert, G., *Anfänge Nationalsozialistischer Aussenpolitik* (Cologne, 1961); Stoakes, G., 'The Evolution of Hitler's Ideas on Foreign Policy, 1919–1925', in Stachura, P.D. (ed.), *The Shaping of the Nazi State* (London, 1978), 22–47.
23 Bullock, A., 'Hitler and the Origins of the Second World War', in Robertson, E.M. (ed.), *The Origins of the Second World War* (London, 1971), 189–224.
24 Taylor, *Origins* passim. For a discussion of his views, see Wippermann, W., *Wessen Schuld? Vom Historikerstreit zur Goldhagen-Kontroverse* (Berlin, 1997), 61ff.
25 Rauschning, H., *The Revolution of Nihilism* (New York, 1939); 'Ausnahmezustand als Herrschaftstechnik des Nationalsozialistischen-Regimes', in Funke, M. (ed.), *Hitler, Deutschland und die Mächte. Materialien zur Aussenpolitik des Dritten Reiches* (Düsseldorf, 1977), 30–45, and Rauschning, H., 'National Socialism: Continuity and Change', in Laqueur, W. (ed.), *Fascism: A Reader's Guide. Analyses, Interpretations, Bibliography* (London, 1979), 151–92.
26 Mason, T., 'The Legacy of 1918', in Nicholls, A. and Matthias, E. (eds), *German Democracy and the Triumph of Hitler: Essays in Recent German History* (London, 1971), 215–40; Mason, T., 'Innere Krise und Angriffskrieg 1938–9', in Forstmeier, F. and Volkmann, H. E. (eds), *Wirtschaft und Rüstung am Vorabend des Zweiten Weltkrieges* (Düsseldorf, 1975), 158–88.
27 Petersen, J., 'La politica estera del fascismo come problema storiografico', in De Felice, R. (ed.), *L'Italia fra tedeschi e alleati. La politica estera fascista e la seconda guerra mondiale* (Bologna, 1973), 11–56; Vigezzi, B., *Politica estera e opinione pubblica in Italia dall'unità ai giorni nostri. Orientamenti degli studi e prospettiva della ricerca* (Milan, 1991),

98ff; Azzi, S.C., 'The Historiography of Fascist Foreign Policy', *The Historical Journal*, 1 (1993), 187–203.

28 Especially Salvemini, G., *Prelude to the Second World War* (London, 1953).

29 Mack Smith, *Roman Empire*. For an assessment see Finney, P. (ed.), *The Origins of the Second World War* (London, 1997), 7–8.

30 Di Nolfo, E., *Mussolini e la politica estera italiana 1919–1933* (Padova, 1960).

31 Rochat, G., 'Il ruolo delle forze armate nel regime fascista: conclusioni provvisorie e ipotesi di lavoro', *Rivista di Storia Contemporanea*, 1 (1972), 188–99, esp. 101; *Militari e politici nella preparazione della campagna d'Etiopia* (Milan 1971).

32 Catalano, F., *L'economia italiana di guerra. La politica economico-finanziaria del fascismo dalla guerra d'Etiopia alla caduta del regime, 1935–1943* (Milan, 1969). For a criticism of Catalano's economic arguments see Petersen, 'La politica estera del fascismo come problema storiografico', 47–8.

33 Rumi, G., ' "Revisionismo" fascista ed espansione coloniale (1925–1935)', in Aquarone, A. and Vernassa, M. (eds), *Il regime fascista* (Bologna, 1974), 435–64; Knox, M., 'Conquest', 1–57, and 'The Fascist Regime, its Foreign Policy and its Wars: an "Anti-Anti-Fascist" Orthodoxy?', in Finney, *Origins of the Second World War*, 148–68; Alatri, P., *Le origini del fascismo* (Rome, 1963).

34 Pastorelli, L., 'La storiografia italiana del dopoguerra sulla politica estera', *Storia e Politica*, 10 (1971), 603–49.

35 Procacci, G., 'Appunti in tema di crisi dello stato liberale e di origini del fascismo', *Studi Storici*, 6 (1965), 221–37; Vivarelli, R., *Il dopoguerra in Italia e l'avvento del fascismo (1918–1922)*, vol. 1: *Dalla fine della guerra all'impresa di Fiume* (Naples, 1967); Hiden, J., *Germany and Europe 1919–1939* (London, 1977), 24–44 and 158–63.

36 Smith, W.D., *The Ideological Origins of Nazi Imperialism* (Oxford, 1986), esp. chaps 4, 5, 9, 10; Hillgruber, A., *Kontinuität und Diskontinuität in der deutschen Aussenpolitik von Bismarck bis Hitler* (Düsseldorf, 1969); Nipperdey, T., '1933 and Continuity of German History', in Koch, H.W. (ed.), *Aspects of the Third Reich* (Houndmills and London, 1985), 489–508; Jarausch, K., 'From Second to Third Reich: The Problem of Continuity in German Foreign Policy', *Central European History*, 12 (1979), 68–82.

37 Fischer, F., *War of Illusions: German Policies from 1911 to 1914* (London, 1975); Fischer, F., *Germany's Aims in the First World War* (New York, 1967); Fischer, F., *Weltmacht oder Niedergang. Deutschland im Ersten Weltkrieg* (Frankfurt, 1965); and Fischer, F., *From Kaiserreich to Third Reich* (London, 1979). For a discussion see Moses, J.A., *The Politics of Illusion: The Fischer Controversy in German Historiography* (London, 1975); Eley, G., *From Unification to Nazism: Reinterpreting the German Past* (Boston, London and Sydney, 1986), 2–8; Mommsen, W.J., 'The Debate on German War Aims', *Journal of Contemporary History*, 1 (1966), 47–72.

38 Bosworth, R.J.B, 'Italian foreign policy and its historiography', in Bosworth, R.J.B. and Rizzo, G. (eds), *Altro Polo: Intellectuals and their Ideas in Contemporary Italy* (Sydney, 1983), 52–96; *The Italian Dictatorship: Problems and Perspectives in the Interpretation of Mussolini and Fascism* (London and New York, 1998). On the anti-fascist tradition in Italian historiography, see Zapponi, N., 'Fascism in Italian Historiography, 1986–93: a Fading National Identity', *Journal of Contemporary History*, 29 (1994), 547–68.

39 Vivarelli, R., *Il fallimento del liberalismo. Studi sulle origini del fascismo* (Bologna, 1981).

40 Lyttelton, A., 'Italian Fascism', in Laqueur, W. (ed.), *Fascism: A Reader's Guide: Analyses, Interpretations, Bibliography* (Harmondsworth, 1979), 81–114.

41 Taylor, *Origins*, passim; see also Mack Smith, *Italy* and *Mussolini's Roman Empire*, passim.

42 Chabod, F., *Italian Foreign Policy: The Statecraft of the Founders* (Princeton, New Jersey, 1996).

43 See the discussion in Bosworth, *The Italian Dictatorship*, 100–5.

1 ITALIAN AND GERMAN EXPANSIONISM IN THE
LONGUE DURÉE

1 This chapter is largely based on the article 'Expansionism in Post-Unification Italy and Germany until the First World War: On the Ideological and Political Origins of Fascist Expansionism', published in *European History Quarterly*, 28 (1998), 435–62.

2 Griffin, R.D., *The Nature of Fascism* (London and New York, 1994), 221–5.

3 Hiden, J. and Farquharson, J., *Explaining Hitler's Germany* (Totowa, New Jersey, 1983), 158ff; and, generally, Kershaw, I., *Weimar: Why Did German Democracy Fail?* (London, 1990); Baglieri, J., 'Italian Fascism and the Crisis of Liberal Hegemony', in Larsen, S.U., Hagtvet, B. and Myklebust, J.P. (eds), *Who Were the Fascists? Social Roots of European Fascism* (Bergen, 1980), 318–36.

4 Organski, A.F.K., 'Fascism and Modernization', in Woolf, S.J. (ed.), *The Nature of Fascism* (London 1968), 19–41.

5 Mack Smith, D., *Mazzini* (London, 1994), chaps 7–8; Griffith, G.O., *Mazzini: Prophet of Modern Europe* (New York, 1970). See also Chapter 2.

6 Breuilly, J., *The Formation of the First German Nation-State, 1800–1871* (Basingstoke and London, 1996), 49–57; Gall, L., *Bismarck: The White Revolutionary* (London, 1986), vol. 1; Riall, L., *The Italian Risorgimento. State, Society, and National Unification* (London and New York, 1994), 63–75.

7 Reichman, S. and Golan, A., 'Irredentism and Boundary Adjustments in Post-World War I Europe', in Chazan, N. (ed.), *Irredentism and International Politics* (Boulder and London, 1991), 66.

8 On the inability of the Italian and German states to increase trade with their colonies see, amongst others, Stoecker, H., 'The German Empire in Africa before 1914: General Questions', in Stoecker, H. (ed.), *German Imperialism in Africa* (London, 1986), 188ff; Henderson, W.O., *The German Colonial Empire, 1884–1919* (London, 1993), 149–51, Tables 2, 4; Segrè, C.G., *Fourth Shore* (Chicago and London, 1974), 184ff; Anderson, M. S., *The Ascendancy of Europe. Aspects of European History, 1815–1914* (London, 1972), 215ff.

9 Fischer, F., *Germany's Aims in the First World War* (New York 1967), 14ff; Smith, W. D., *The Ideological Origins of Nazi Imperialism* (Oxford, 1986), 32–40, 52ff; Webster, R.A., *Industrial Imperialism in Italy, 1908–1915* (Berkeley and Los Angeles, 1975), passim.

10 Roseman, M., 'National Socialism and Modernisation', in Bessel, R. (ed.), *Fascist Italy and Nazi Germany: Comparisons and Contrasts* (Cambridge, 1996), 220–1.

11 Hughes, M., *Nationalism and Society. Germany: 1800–1945* (London, 1988), 142ff; Chickering, R., *We Men Who Feel Most German: A Cultural Study of the Pan-German League, 1886–1914* (Boston, 1984), 76–7; Frymann, D. (pseudonym for H. Class), *Wenn ich Kaiser wäre. Politische Wahrheiten und Notwendigkeiten* (Leipzig, 1912); Fischer, F. *War of Illusions: German Policies from 1911 to 1914* (London 1975), 245ff.

12 Del Boca, A., *Gli italiani in Africa orientale* (Rome and Bari, 1976), 579–750.

13 Adamson, W., 'Avant-Garde Political Rhetorics: Pre-War Culture in Florence as a Source of Post-War Fascism', *Journal of European Ideas*, 16 (1993), 753–7, and Adamson, W., 'The Language of Opposition in Early Twentieth-Century Italy: Rhetorical Continuities between Pre-war Florentine Avant-garde and Mussolini's Fascism', *Journal of Modern History*, 64 (1992), 22–51; De Grand, A.J., *The Italian Nationalist Association and the Rise of Fascism in Italy* (Lincoln and London, 1978), 23ff; Gaeta, F., 'L'Associazione Nazionalista Italiana', in Gentile, E. (ed.), *L'Italia giolittiana. La storia e la critica* (Rome & Bari, 1977), 253–68.

14 Eley, G., *Reshaping the German Right: Radical Nationalism and Political Change after Bismarck* (New Haven and London, 1980), 41–206; Hughes, 130–40.

15 Chickering, 1–14 (for different views). See also Kruck, A., *Geschichte des alldeutschen Verbandes, 1890–1939* (Wiesbaden, 1954).

16 Chickering, 74–101; Smith, 94–111; Fricke, D. et al., *Bürgerliche Parteien in Deutschland. Handbuch der Geschichte der bürgerlichen Parteien und anderen bürgerlichen Interessenorganisationen vom Vormärz bis zum Jahr 1945*, vol. I (Berlin, 1968), 1–26; Eley, *Reshaping the German Right*, 48–58.

17 Bosworth, R.J.B., *Italy, the Least of the Great Powers: Italian Foreign Policy Before the First World War* (Cambridge, 1979), 45–57; Mack Smith, *Italy*, 141ff.

18 Sandonà, A., *L'irredentismo nelle lotte politiche e nelle contese diplomatiche italo-austriache* (Bologna 1932–1938), II, 151–4.

19 Thayer, J.A., *Italy and the Great War: Politics and Culture, 1870–1915* (Madison and Milwaukee, 1964), 145; Sandonà, I, 124ff.

20 Lowe, C.J. and Marzari, F., *Italian Foreign Policy 1870–1940* (London and Boston, 1975), 50–4, 96ff, 112; Thayer, 125ff, 171; Sandonà, II, 163ff; Seton-Watson, C., *Italy from Liberalism to Fascism, 1870–1925* (London, 1967), 407–8.

21 Segrè, 'Il colonialismo'; Sandonà, II, 151ff.

22 Seton-Watson, 397ff; Alatri, P., *Le origini del fascismo* (Rome, 1963), 13–14. Note that, even in August 1914, the ANI initially supported negotiations with the Triple Alliance (De Grand, *Nationalist Association*, 60ff.).

23 Lowe and Marzari, *Italian Foreign Policy 1870–1940* (London and Boston, 1975), 112.

24 See, for example, Max Weber's preference for a 'complete unification' or for no unification at all, in Mommsen, W.J., *Max Weber and German Politics 1890–1920* (Chicago and London, 1984), 68–9.

25 Lowe and Marzari, 96ff; Bosworth, R.J.B., *Italy and the Approach of the First World War* (New York, 1983), 119.

26 Pastorelli, P., 'Il principio di nazionalità nella politica estera italiana', in Spadolini, G. (ed.), *Nazione e nazionalità in Italia* (Rome and Bari, 1994), 190–1.

27 Adamson, 'Avant-Garde', 753–7; Lotti, L., 'L'età giolittiana', in Spadolini, 56ff. See, in general, Nöther, E.P., 'The Intellectual Dimension of Italian Nationalism: An Overview', *History of European Ideas*, 16 (1993), 779–84.

28 Initially, the Italian Nationalists had criticised the concept of irredentism. See De Grand, *Nationalist Association*, 13ff.; Corradini, E., 'Nazionalismo e sindicalismo', in Perfetti, F. (ed.), *Il nazionalismo italiano dalle origini alle fusione col fascismo* (Bologna, 1977), 91ff; and Corradini, E., 'Classi proletarie: socialismo; nazioni proletarie: nazionalismo', in Castellini, G. (ed.), *Atti del Congresso di Firenze* (Florence, 1911), 21ff. The Congress of Florence (1910) did succeed in temporarily disguising the ideological rifts between the Irredentists and the imperialist wing of the emerging ANI (De Grand, *Nationalist Association*, 23–7).

29 De Grand, *Nationalist Association*, 34ff.

30 Sandonà, III, 151–4.

31 Pastorelli, P., 'Il principio di nazionalità', 189–92; Webster, 334ff; Mack Smith, *Italy*, 142ff.

32 Chickering, 76; Fischer, *War of Illusions*, 263–4.

33 Smith, 109–11.

34 Chickering, 289–90.

35 Chickering, 76; Sheehan, J.J., 'What is German History? Reflections on the Role of the Nation in German History and Historiography', *Journal of Modern History*, 53 (1981), 1–23.

36 Plehn, H., *Deutsche Weltpolitik und kein Krieg* (Berlin, 1913).

37 Fischer, *War of Illusions*, 259ff.

38 For a discussion of the two arguments, see Wehler, H.-U., 'Bismarck's Imperialism, 1862–1890', in Sheehan, J.J. (ed.), *Imperial Germany* (New York and London, 1976), 185–9.

39 Kitchen, M., *Nazi Germany at War* (London and New York, 1995), 180–99; Segrè, *Fourth Shore*, 8ff.

40 See 'Triplice Alleanza', in Levi, F., Levra, U. and Tranfaglia, N. (eds), *Storia d'Italia* (Florence, 1978), vol. 3, 1318–32.

41 Craig, G., *Germany 1866–1945* (Oxford, 1978), 328ff.

42 Stoecker, H., 'The Quest for "German Central Africa" ', in Stoecker (ed.), *German Imperialism in Africa*, 249–61; Henderson, 93ff; Smith, W.D., 68ff.

43 Lichtheim, G., *Imperialism* (London, 1971), 81ff.

44 Craig, *Germany*, 287ff, 294ff; Fischer, F., *From Kaiserreich to Third Reich* (London 1979), 48ff. On the importance of the War Council of 1912 for army expenditure, see Mommsen, 'Debate on German War Aims', 47ff; Fischer, *War of Illusions*, 161ff.

45 Chickering, 267–8; Fischer, *From Kaiserreich*, 48ff; Craig, *Germany*, 318ff; Eley, 'Conservatives and Radical Nationalists', 100–1.

46 Webster, 244–332; Stoecker, 195ff.

47 Webster, 203 and 246–7; Segrè, *Fourth Shore*, 20–32; Thayer, 254ff.

48 See the various contributions in Evans, R.J.W. and von Strandmann, H.P. (eds), *The Coming of the First World War* (Oxford 1988), especially Howard, M., 'Europe on the Eve of the First World War'; von Strandmann, 'Germany and the Coming of War'; and Evans, R.J.W., 'The Habsburg Monarchy and the Coming of War'. Also see Bosworth, *Italy and the Approach of the First World War*, 51–120.

49 Thayer, 253ff, 278ff; Griffin, *Nature of Fascism*, 61–3; Clark, M., *Italy 1860–1995* (London 1996, 2nd edn), 181–5.

50 Gregor, A.J., *Young Mussolini and the Intellectual Origins of Fascism* (Berkeley, Los Angeles and London, 1979), 156–79; De Begnac, Y., *Taccuini mussoliniani*, ed. Perfetti, F. (Bologna, 1990), 30ff.

51 Bosworth, *Italy and the Approach of the First World War*, 121–42; Melograni, P., *Storia politica della Grande Guerra* (Bari 1971).

52 The text of the Treaty of London has been translated and reprinted in Clough, S.B. and Saladino, S. (eds), *A History of Modern Italy: Documents, Readings and Commentary* (New York and London, 1968), 308–17; Saladino, S., 'Italy', in Rogger, H. and Weber, E. (eds), *The European Right: A Historical Profile* (London, 1965), 249–53.

53 Gregor, *Young Mussolini*, 180–202; Ledeen, M.A., *The First Duce: D'Annunzio at Fiume* (Baltimore, 1977).

54 De Begnac, 40; Mack Smith, D., *Italy: A Modern History* (Ann Arbor, 1969), 271ff; Bosworth, R.J.B., *Italy and the Wider World, 1860–1960* (London and New York, 1996), ch. 3; Whittam, J., *The Politics of the Italian Army, 1861–1918* (London, 1977).

55 Clark, *Modern Italy*, 185–90; Mack Smith, *Italy*, 276ff; Saladino, 'Italy', 257ff.

56 In particular, Fischer, *Germany's Aims in the First World War*, 50ff.

57 Craig, *Germany*, 368ff.

58 Kershaw, I., *Hitler: 1889–1936: Hubris* (London 1998), ch. 3; Eley, G., *From Unification to Nazism* (London 1986), 231–53; and Eley, G., 'Conservatives and Radical Nationalists in Germany: The Production of Fascist Potentials, 1912–1928', in Blinkhorn, M. (ed.), *Fascists and Conservatives: The Radical Right and the Establishment in Twentieth-Century Europe* (London 1990), 50–70; Griffin, *Nature of Fascism*, 89ff.

59 Fischer, *Germany's Aims in the First World War*, 475–509; Stoakes, G., 'The Evolution of Hitler's Ideas on Foreign Policy, 1919–1925', in Stachura, P.D. (ed.), *The Shaping of the Nazi State* (London, 1978), 32f, 41ff; Craig, *Germany*, 386–95.

60 Craig, *Germany*, 395ff; Bessel, R., *Germany After the First World War* (Oxford, 1993).

61 Kershaw, *Hitler: Hubris*, 93ff.

2 FASCIST IDEOLOGY AND TERRITORIAL EXPANSION

1 Mason, T., 'Whatever Happened to "Fascism"', in Childers, T. and Caplan, J. (eds), *Reevaluating the Third Reich* (New York and London, 1993), 253–62; Allardyce, G., 'What Fascism is Not: Thoughts on the Deflation of a Concept', *American Historical Review*, 84 (1979), 367–88; Wilford, R., 'Fascism', in Eccleshall, R., Geoghegan, V., Jay, R., Kenny, M., MacKenzie, I. and Wilford, R. (eds), *Political Ideologies: An Introduction* (London and New York 1994, 2nd edn), 185–217. See also Introduction in this study.

2 Griffin, R., *The Nature of Fascism* (London and New York, 1994); Payne, S.G., *A History of Fascism, 1914–45* (London, 1997); Eatwell, R., 'Towards a New Model of Generic Fascism', *Journal of Theoretical Politics*, 4 (1992), 161–94; Mosse, G.L., 'Towards a General Theory of Fascism', in Mosse, G.L. (ed.), *International Fascism: New Thoughts and New Approaches* (London and Beverly Hills, 1979), 1–41. For a summary of individual theories of generic fascism see the selection in Griffin, R. (ed.), *Fascism* (Oxford and New York, 1995).

3 Griffin, *Nature of Fascism*, 48–9.

4 Griffin, *Nature of Fascism*, 29–32; Eatwell, 'Towards a New Model of Generic Fascism', 161–94; Bosworth, R.J.B., *The Italian Dictatorship. Problems and Perspectives in the Interpretation of Mussolini and Fascism* (London and New York, 1998), 99ff.

5 See, for example, Trevor-Roper, H., *The Testament of Adolf Hitler: The Hitler–Bormann Documents, February–April 1945* (London, 1961); Hildebrand, K., *The Foreign Policy of the Third Reich* (London, 1972); Hildebrand, K., 'Hitlers "Programm" und seine Realisierung', in Funke, M. (ed.), *Hitler, Deutschland, und die Mächte. Materialien zur Aussenpolitik des Dritten Reiches* (Düsseldorf, 1977), 63–93.

6 Salvemini, *Preludio alla seconda guerra mondiale* (Milan, 1967); Wiskemann, E., *The Rome-Berlin Axis* (London, 1966). This problem is discussed in this study, Chapter 5.

7 See, for example, Mack Smith, D., *Mussolini* (London, 1981); Hibbert, C., *Benito Mussolini* (London, 1975).

8 Linz, J.J., 'Some Notes Towards a Comparative Study of Fascism in Sociological Historical Perspective', in Laqueur, W. (ed.), *Fascism: A Reader's Guide. Analyses, Interpretations, Bibliography* (Harmondsworth, 1979); Griffin, *Nature of Fascism*, 4–8; Malaparte, C., 'Mussolini and National Syndicalism', in Lyttelton, A. (ed.), *Italian Fascisms from Pareto to Gentile* (London, 1973), 225–41 (esp. 229–31). For a treatment of fascist ideology as a 'positive' phenomenon, see Gregor, A.J., *The Ideology of Fascism: The Rationale of Totalitarianism* (New York, 1969); Mosse, 'General Theory', 1–41.

9 Linz, J.J., 'Political Space and Fascism as Late-Comer', in Larsen, S.U., Hagtvet, B. and Myklebust, J.P. (eds), *Who Were the Fascists? Social Roots of European Fascism* (Bergen, Oslo and Tromso, 1980), 153–89.

10 Linz, 'Some Notes', 29ff.

11 On the interrelation between the descriptive and the normative aspects of ideology, see Thompson, J.B., *Studies in the Theory of Ideology* (Cambridge, 1984), 73–90.

12 Mussolini, B., *Scritti e Discorsi* (Firenze 1934–1939, henceforward cited as *Scritti*), II, 47–9 ('Speculazioni e responsabilità', *Popolo d'Italia*, 25 November 1919).

13 Gentile, E., *Le origini dell'ideologia fascista, 1918–1925* (Rome and Bari, 1975), 74ff; Casucci, C., 'Fascismo e storia', *Il Mulino*, 9 (1960), 225ff.

14 Susmel, E. and Susmel, D. (eds), *Opera Omnia di Benito Mussolini* (Florence and Rome 1951–78, henceforward cited as *OO*), VII, 197, 394, 418. See also Gentile, E., *Il mito dello stato nuovo* (Bari, 1982), ch. 6; De Grand, A.J., 'Curzio Malaparte: The Illusion of Fascist Revolution', *Journal of Contemporary History*, 7 (1972), 73–90.

15 Marinetti, F.T., 'The War as the Catharsis of Italian Society', translated and cited in Griffin, R., *Fascism* (Oxford and New York, 1995), 25–6; Guerri, J.B., 'Bottai: da intelettuale futurista a leader fascista', in De Felice, R. (ed.), *Futurismo, cultura e politica* (Turin, 1986), 223–4.

16 Gentile, E., *Il culto del littorio. La sacralizzazione della politica nell'Italia fascista* (Rome and Bari, 1993), 108ff.

17 Malaparte, C., *Europa Vivente. Teoria storica del sindicalismo nazionale* (Florence, 1961), 93ff; Papini, G., 'The War as a Source of National Renewal', in Griffin (ed.), *Fascism*, 23–4.

18 Ciccardini, B., 'Il fascismo come esame di coscienza delle generazioni', *Terza Generazione*, 3 (1954), 39–44, reprinted in Casucci, C. (ed.), *Il fascismo: Antologia di scritti critici* (Bologna, 1982), 489–502.

19 *OO*, X, 140ff ('Trincerocrazia' in *Popolo d'Italia*, 15 December, 1917); an excerpt is translated in Griffin (ed.), *Fascism*, 28–9.

20 Mosse, G.L., 'Two World Wars and the Myth of the War Experience', *Journal of Contemporary History*, 21 (1986), 491–514; Isnenghi, M., 'Il mito di potenza', in Del Boca, A., Legnani, M. and Rossi, M. C. (eds), *Il regime fascista. Storia e storiografia* (Rome and Bari, 1995), 144ff.

21 *Scritti*, I, 320–1 ('La vittoria fatale', speech in Bologna, 24 May 1918); II, 11ff ('Discorso da ascoltare', *Popolo d'Italia*, 1 May 1919).

22 *OO*, XXI, 359 ('Intransigenza assoluta', speech to the Fascist Congress in Rome, 21 June 1925).

23 *OO*, XVII, 218 ('Programma fascista', 8 November 1921). See also XXIV, 9ff (speech to the Assembly of the Regime, 10 March 1929).

24 *Scritti*, II, 16–7 ('Annessione', *Popolo d'Italia*, 24 April 1919), 52 ('Navigare Necesse' in *Popolo d'Italia*, 1 January 1920).

25 *Scritti*, II, 111 ('Ciò che rimane e ciò che verra', *Popolo d'Italia*, 13 November 1920); Copolla, F., *La crisi italiana* (Rome, 1916), 77–91.

26 Agnelli, A., 'L'idea di nazione all'inizio e nei momenti di crisi del secolo XX', and Gentile, E., 'La nazione del fascismo. Alle origini del declino dello Stato nazionale', both in Spadolini, G. (ed.), *Nazione e Nazionalità in Italia* (Rome and Bari, 1994), 15–32 and 65–124 respectively.

27 Bottai, G., *Pagine di critica fascista*, edited by Pacces, F.M. (Florence, 1941), 9.

28 *Scritti*, II, 28–9 ('Dopo il voto', *Popolo d'Italia*, 2 June 1919); 31–7 (speech in Florence, 9 October 1919); 55–7 ('Rinunciatori', *Popolo d'Italia*, February 1920); 101 (speech in Trieste, 20 September 1920).

29 *OO*, XI, 92 (May 1918); Scritti, II, 31–7 (speech in Florence, 9 October 1919).

30 Mosse, G.L., 'Towards a General Theory of Fascism'; Bobbio, N., 'L'ideologia del fascismo', reprinted in Casucci (ed.), *Antologia*, 621–4.

31 Moeller van den Bruck, A., *Germany's Third Empire* (New York, 1971), 122ff.

32 Merkl, P.H., *Political Violence under the Swastika: 581 Early Nazis* (Princeton, New Jersey, 1975), 382ff, 549ff.

33 Childers, T., *The Nazi Voter: The Social Foundations of Fascism in Germany, 1919–1939* (Chapel Hill and London, 1983), 129–38; Merkl, 322ff.

34 Baynes, N.H. (ed.), *The Speeches of Adolf Hitler: April 1922–August 1939* (London, New York and Toronto, 1942), vol. I, 584–92 (speech in the opening of the House of German Art, 18 July 1937); Hitler, A., *Mein Kampf*, translated by R. Mannheim (London, 1972), 211ff.

35 Struve, W., *Elites Against Democracy: Leadership Ideals in Bourgeois Political Thought in Germany, 1890–1933* (Princeton, 1973), 378; Herf, G., *Reactionary Modernism: Technology, Culture and Politics in Weimar and the Third Reich* (Cambridge, 1984), chaps 2–6.

36 Juenger, E., *Der Kampf als inneres Erlebnis* (Berlin, 1922).

37 Baynes, II, 1218–47 (speech to the *Reichstag*, 21 May 1935).

38 Spengler, O., *The Decline of the West* (London, 1926), 40ff; Moeller van den Bruck, *Germany's Third Empire*.

39 Mosse, 'General Theory', 36.

40 See Hitler's 1921 speech, quoted in Boepple, E. (ed.), *Adolf Hitlers Reden* (Munich, 1933), 6–21.

41 *Scritti*, II, 75 ('Nefasto', *Popolo d'Italia*, 9 May 1920), 77–81 ('Restare a Valona', *Popolo d'Italia*, 13 June 1920).

42 *Scritti*, II, 95 ('Discorso di Trieste', 20 September 1920).

43 *Scritti*, IV, 13–5 ('Francesco Crispi', speech in Rome, 12 January 1924); II, 199–201 (address to the Fascist Congress of Rome, 9 November 1921). See Bottai, G., 'Politica coloniale ardita', *Popolo d'Italia*, 10 May 1919.

44 *Scritti*, IV, 151 (speech in the Chamber of Deputies, 7 June 1924). On Mussolini's demographic ideas see *OO*, XXIII, 215ff ('Regresso delle nascite, morte dei popoli', speech in Bologna, 1 September 1928).

45 Gentile, G., *I Profeti del Risorgimento* (Florence 1944, 3rd edn), and 'Origini e dottrina del fascismo', in Casucci (ed.), *Antologia*, 37–8. For the significance of the 'myth of Rome' see below.

46 Gentile, E., *Ideologia fascista*, 396.

47 *OO*, XVI, 128.

48 Boccioni, U., *Opere complete* (Foligno, 1927), 8ff; Volpe, G., *L'Italia in cammino* (Milan 1931, 3rd edn), preface.

49 For an analysis of the ideology of revolutionary syndicalism in Italy see Sternhell, Z., *The Birth of Fascist Ideology: From Cultural Rebellion to Political Revolution* (Princeton, 1994), 131–59.

50 On the political significance of the Futurist Movement see Zapponi, N., 'Futurismo e fascismo', and Gentile, E., 'Il Futurismo e la politica dal nazionalismo modernista al fascismo (1909–1920)', both in De Felice (ed.), *Futurismo*, 161–76 and 105–60 respectively.

51 Ledeen, M.A., *The First Duce: D'Annunzio at Fiume* (Baltimore, 1977); Mosse, G.L., 'The Poet and the Exercise of Political Power: Gabriele D'Annunzio', in Mosse, G.L. (ed.), *Masses and Man* (New York, 1980), 35–61; Griffin, *Nature of Fascism*, 64–5. On Mussolini's debts to D'Annunzio see De Begnac, Y., *Taccuini mussoliniani*, ed. F. Perfetti, (Bologna, 1990), 577–84.

52 Gentile, *Ideologia fascista*, 218ff; Missiroli, M., *Una Battaglia Perduta* (Milan, 1924), 301ff. For a criticism of the *Fasci* by the ANI, see Pedrazzi, O., 'I Fasci di combattimento. Un errore', *Idea Nazionale*, 25 March 1919.

53 Gentile, E., *Ideologia fascista*, 221ff, 385–6; De Grand, A.J., *The Italian Nationalist Association and the Rise of Fascism in Italy* (Lincoln and London, 1978), 149ff.

54 See, for example, Ercole, F., 'Contro un affretata fusione', *Idea Nazionale*, 20 December 1921; D'Andrea, U., 'Due nature, due compiti', *Idea Nazionale*, 25 November 1921 (also reprinted in Perfetti, F., *Il nazionalismo italiano dalle origini alla fusione col fascismo* (Bologna, 1977), 267–82).

55 Alatri, P., *Le origini del fascismo* (Rome, 1963), 5–31; Gentile, E., *Ideologia fascista*, 385ff; Sternhell, 'Fascist Ideology', 332–8.

56 Rocco, A., 'Genesi storica del fascismo', in his *Scritti e discorsi politici*, vol. III (Milan, 1938), 1118ff; 'Il valore dell'atto', *Idea Nazionale*, 28 February 1923, reprinted in Perfetti, *Il nazionalismo*, 282–4.

57 Domarus, M., *Hitler: Reden und Proklamationen, 1932–1945*, vol. I: *Triumph (1932–1938)* (Würzburg, 1962), 977 (speech to the German Press, Munich, 10 November 1938). See also 609 (speech in Hamburg, March 1936), 743 (speech in Berlin, November 1937).

58 Eley, G., *From Unification to Nazism: Reinterpreting the German Past* (Boston, London and Sydney, 1986), 226ff, and Eley, G., *Reshaping the German Right: Radical Nationalism and*

Political Change after Bismarck (New Haven and London, 1980), 19ff, 356ff; Retallack, J.N., *Notables of the Right: The Conservative Party and Political Mobilization in Germany* (Boston and London, 1988).

59 Andrews, H.D, 'Hitler and Bismarck: A History', *German Studies Review*, 14 (1991), 511–32; Birken, L., *Hitler as Philosophe: Remnants of the Enlightenment in National Socialism* (Westport and London, 1995), 50–1.

60 Baynes, II, 1493 (speech for the *Parteitag* at Nuremberg , 12 September 1938).

61 *Völkischer Beobachter*, 3 April 1939.

62 Hitler, *Mein Kampf*, 215ff.

63 Eley, *Reshaping*, 41–98; Griffin, *Nature of Fascism*, 85–94. For the Weimar period see the analysis of Struve, 232–414; Mohler, 35ff.

64 See, for example, Rosenberg, A., *Krise und Neubau Europas* (Berlin, 1934).

65 Griffin, *Nature of Fascism*, ch. 4; Sontheimer, K., *Antidemokratisches Denken in der Weimarer Republic* (Munich, 1968); Smith, W.D., *The Ideological Origins of Nazi Imperialism* (Oxford, 1986), 196–230.

66 Tyrell, A., *Vom 'Trommler' zum 'Führer'. Der Wandel von Hitlers Selbstverständnis zwischen 1919 und 1924 und die Entwicklung der NSDAP* (Munich, 1975); Carr, W., *Hitler: A Study in Personality and Politics* (London, 1978), 14ff.

67 Baynes, I, 11–3 (speech in the conference of Genoa, 12 April 1922).

68 Speech in front of party audience, 28 July 1922, quoted in Boepple, 19–21.

69 Rich, N., *Hitler's War Aims*, vol. 1: *Ideology, the Nazi State and the Course of Expansion* (London, 1973), xxx–xlii.

70 For an analysis of this term see Griffin, *Nature of Fascism*, especially 32ff, 74ff, 217.

71 Stephenson, J., *The Nazi Organisation of Women* (London, 1981), Introduction.

72 Salvatorelli, L., *Nazionalfascismo* (Turin, 1923); De Felice, R., *Interpretations of Fascism* (Cambridge, MA and London, 1977), 181.

73 Blackbourn, D. and Eley, G. (eds), *The Peculiarities of German History* (Oxford, 1984); Weisbrod, B., 'The Crisis of Bourgeois Society in Interwar Germany'; and Lyttelton, A., 'The "Crisis of Bourgeois Society" and the Origins of Fascism', both in Bessel R. (ed.), *Fascist Italy and Nazi Germany: Comparisons and Contrasts* (Cambridge, 1996), 23–39 and 12–22 respectively.

74 *Scritti*, III, 77 (published in *Gerarchia*, March, 1923); *OO*, XXVI, 44 ('Fra due civiltà', speech in Rome, 22 August 1933); Mussolini, B., 'Political and Social Doctrine of Fascism', in Oakeshott, M. (ed.), *The Social and Political Doctrines of Contemporary Europe* (New York, 1949), 164–79.

75 Gentile, G., *Profeti del Risorgimento*; Simonini, A., *Il linguaggio di Mussolini* (Milan, 1978), 96–9; 'Il monito di Oriani', *Popolo d'Italia*, 14 March 1915, reprinted in Santarelli, E. (ed.), *Scritti politici di Benito Mussolini* (Milan, 1979), 157–60; and *OO*, XX, 244–5 ('Oriani', speech in Cardello, 27 April 1924).

76 Gentile, G., *Guerra e Fede* (Rome 1927, 2nd edn), 55ff.

77 Salomone, A.W., 'The Risorgimento and the Political Myth of the "Revolution that Failed"', *American Historical Review*, 68 (1964), 38–53.

78 *Scritti*, IV, 63–84 ('Cinque anni dopo San Sepolcro', commemorative speech, 24 March 1923); 327–8 (speech in Dalmine, 27 October 1924); 323–5 (speech in Bergamo, 27 October 1924).

79 Mack Smith, D., 'The Prehistory of Fascism', reprinted in Salomone, A.W. (ed.), *Italy from Risorgimento to Fascism: An Inquiry into the Origins of the Totalitarian State* (Newton Abbot, 1971), 103–23.

80 Baynes, II, 1376ff (Hitler's speech of 20 February 1938 to the *Reichstag*). See also Kershaw, I., *Hitler, 1889–1936: Hubris* (London, 1998), 486.

81 Birken, 50–1.

82 Andrews, 511ff.

83 Speech reported in the *Frankfurter Zeitung* (henceforward *FZ*), 15 February 1939.

214

84 Baynes, II, 1012ff (speech to the Reichstag, 21 March 1933).
85 *Völkischer Beobachter*, 21 February 1938, 27 March 1938. See also Hitler, *Mein Kampf*, 351–98, 599ff; Weinberg, G.L. (ed.), *Hitlers zweites Buch. Ein Dokument aus dem Jahr 1928* (Stuttgart, 1961), 115–16.
86 Baynes, II, 1377 (speech to the Reichstag, 20 February 1938).
87 Baynes, I, 989ff (interview with Otto Strasser, 21 May 1930); and II, 1041–2 (speech to the Reichstag, 17 May 1933), 1260–3 (interview in *Paris Soir*, 27 January 1936); *Scritti*, II, 114 ('Ciò che rimane e ciò che verra', 13 November 1920).
88 Domarus, I, 748ff (Hossbach Conference, 5 November 1937); II, 1052 (speech to party members, 30 January 1939); Baynes, II, 1262 (interview in *Paris Soir*, 27 January 1936).
89 *Scritti*, I, 321 ('La vittoria fatale', speech in Bologna, 24 May 1918); Baynes, II, 1547 (speech in Weimar, 6 November 1938).
90 Hartmut, L., 'The Germans as a Chosen People: Old Testament Themes in German Nationalism', *German Studies Review*, 14 (1991), 261–73.
91 Baynes, II, 1520–1 (speech in Sportpalast Berlin, 26 September 1938).
92 Neocleous, M., *Fascism* (London, 1997), 1–18.
93 Mussolini, B., 'Political and Social Doctrine of Fascism' (1932), 164–79, (also in *OO*, XXXIV, 124ff).
94 *Scritti*, III, 60 ('La nuova politica estera', speech to the Chamber of Deputies, 16 February 1923).
95 *Scritti*, I, 320–1 ('Vittoria fatale', 19 May 1918).
96 *OO*, XVIII, 413ff/*Scritti*, II, 307–22 (speech in Udine, 20 September 1922).
97 *Scritti*, V, 109–18 (speech to the Fascist Congress at Rome, 22 June 1925); see also V, 179–81 ('Elementi di Storia', *Gerarchia*, October 1925).
98 *Scritti*, V, 173–81 ('Elementi di Storia', October 1925).
99 *Scritti*, IV, 381–90 (speech to the Chamber of Deputies, 15 November 1924).
100 *Scritti*, V, 179 ('Elementi di Storia', October 1925). See also the analysis in Zapponi, N., 'Fascism in Italian Historiography, 1986–93: A Fading National Identity', *Journal of Contemporary History*, 29 (1994), 559ff.
101 Knox, M., 'Expansionist Zeal, Fighting Power, and Staying Power in the Italian and German Dictatorships', in Bessel, 115–23.
102 Theweleit, K., *Male Fantasies*, vol. II: *Male Bodies: Psychoanalyzing the White Terror* (Cambridge, 1989), xii–xviii, 345–407.
103 Merkl, 540ff.
104 See Juenger, E., *Der Arbeiter. Herrschaft und Gestalt* (Hamburg 1932, 2nd edn), 90, 161f. See also Ernst Juenger's 'Die Totale Mobilmachung', in Juenger, E. (ed.), *Krieg und Krieger* (Berlin, 1930), 14; Herf, ch. 4.
105 Merkl, 616–17.
106 *OO*, XXI, 193f/*Scritti*, IV, 391–402 ('La politica interna al Senato', 5 December 1924).
107 *Scritti*, II, 53/*OO*, XVI, 445 ('Navigare necesse', 1 January 1920); IV, 334ff (speech in Cremona, 29 October 1924).
108 *OO*, XXI, 193 ('Politica interna', 5 December 1924).
109 Mussolini, B., 'Political and Social Doctrine of Fascism', 167ff.
110 *OO*, XXVI, 259ff (speech at Turin, 4 May 1934). See also Mussolini, 'Political and Social Doctrine of Fascism', 168ff. See also Simonini, 138–40.
111 *OO*, XXVI, 308ff ('Dopo le grande manovre' speech, 24 August 1934).
112 Rich, 3–10.
113 Struve, 418ff; Schoenbaum, D., *Hitler's Social Revolution: Class and Status in Nazi Germany, 1933–1939* (New York and London, 1980), ch. 8. See also Rossoni, E., 'Sindicalismo fascista', *La Stirpe*, 6 (1928), 705–7, reprinted in Casucci, *Antologia*, 113–17; Hitler, *Mein Kampf*, 351–98.

114 Struve, 415, n. 1.

115 Pareto, V., *I aiatemi socialisti* (Turin, 1954); Finer, S.E., *Vilfredo Pareto: Sociological Writings* (London, 1966), 51–71. For an assessment of Pareto's influence on Mussolini's thought, see Simonini, 99–104; Borkenau, F., *Pareto* (London, 1936), 18ff, 185ff.

116 O'Sullivan, N., *Fascism* (London and Melbourne, 1983), 149–60; Gentile, E., *Ideologia fascista*, 401ff; Glaser, H., *The Cultural Roots of National Socialism* (London, 1978), 130–5.

117 Birken, 81–7.

118 Gentile, E., *Ideologia fascista*, 197ff; Struve, 344–52, 384ff.

119 OO, XI, 87/*Scritti*, II, 253 (speech to the Chamber, 17 February 1922); Baynes, I, 623 (speech in the Nuremberg Party Rally, 12 September 1938); Domarus, I, 716 (Proclamation, 7 September 1937).

120 Griffin, *Nature of Fascism*, 37; Hitler, *Mein Kampf*, 258–99.

121 *Völkischer Beobachter*, 14 September 1938; and Mussolini's speech on 2 September 1937, published in *Popolo d'Italia*, 29 September 1937, translated in Delzell, C.F. (ed.), *Mediterranean Fascism, 1919–1945* (New York, Evanston and London, 1970), 202–5.

122 *Scritti*, II, 214 (speech to the Chamber of Deputies, 26 November 1921); and Hitler's speech to students in Berlin, published in *FZ*, 8 February 1934, quoted in Speer, A., *Inside the Third Reich* (London, 1970), 14–6.

123 OO, XIII, 147ff.

124 Baynes, II, 1498 (speech in *Parteitag*, Nuremberg, 12 September 1938).

125 De Grazia, V., *The Culture of Consent: Mass Organisation of Leisure in Fascist Italy* (Cambridge, 1981), 220ff; Simonini, 118–20.

126 Mussolini, B., 'Il numero come forza', *Gerarchia*, 9 September 1928, reprinted in Santarelli (ed.), *Scritti di Mussolini*, 248–51; 'Ai combettenti della Battaglia del grano', in *Scritti*, V, 143–4 (speech delivered at Rome, 11 October 1925). For the failure of these policies to result in a demographic boom see Ipsen, C., *Dictating Demography: The Problem of Population in Fascist Italy* (Cambridge, 1996); Caldwell, L., 'Reproducers of the Nation: Women and the Family in Fascist Policy', in Forgacs, D. (ed.), *Rethinking Italian Fascism: Capitalism, Populism and Culture* (London, 1986), 110–41; Willson, P.R., 'Women in Fascist Italy', in Bessel, 84ff. For the comments regarding France, see OO, XVIII, 396ff (June 1923).

127 Domarus, I, 759–60 (speech in Augsburg, 21 November 1937); Baynes, II, 1220 (speech to the Reichstag, 21 May 1935). Again, however, the demographic boom remained a myth. See Stephenson, J., 'Reichsbund der Kinderreichen: The League of Large Families in the Population Policy of Nazi Germany', *European Studies Review*, 9 (1979), 351–75; Knodel, J.E., *The Decline of Fertility in Germany, 1871–1939* (Princeton, 1974).

128 Hitler, *Mein Kampf*, 437–61; Göring, H., *Aufbau einer Nation* (Berlin, 1934), passim; and Schiavi, A., *Esilio e morte di Filippo Turati* (Rome, 1956), 122ff. See also various analyses of this issue in Nolte, E., *Three Faces of Fascism: Action Française, Italian Fascism, National Socialism* (London, 1965), 360ff, 384ff, 404ff; Neocleous, M., *Fascism* (London, 1997), 38–58; Del Noce, A., 'Appunti per una definizione storica del fascismo', in Pavetto, R. (ed.), *Il problema storico del fascismo* (Florence, 1970), 133ff.

129 Baynes, II, 1234–5 (speech to the Reichstag, 21 May 1935), 1252ff (speech in the *Parteitag*, Nuremberg, 11 September 1935), 1331 (speech in the Harvest Thanksgiving Festival, 4 October 1936); *Scritti*, II, 7–14 ('Posizioni e obiettivi' and 'Discorso da Ascoltare', in *Popolo d'Italia*, March 1919 and May 1919 respectively).

130 Baynes, II, 1115 (speech in Berlin, 24 October 1933), 1352 (speech to representatives of the Italian Balilla, 16 June 1937); OO, XXVIII, 248–53 ('Discorso di Tor-

ino', *Popolo d'Italia*, 15 May 1939); see for the report and repercussions of the speech DDI, 8th, V, 29/83.

131 'Irredentismo', in Levi, Levra, Tranfaglia (eds), *Storia d'Italia*, (Florence, 1978), vol. II, 573–83.

132 Vincent, A., *Modern Political Ideologies* (Oxford, 1992), 158ff; Mussolini, B., 'The Political and Social Doctrine of Fascism', in Oakeshott, 164–79.

133 Gentile, G., *Guerra e Fede*, 55f; Gentile, E., *Ideologia fascista*, 350ff.

134 De Felice, R., *Storia degli ebrei sotto il fascismo* (Turin, 1972), 64–78.

135 Segrè, C.G., *Italo Balbo: A Fascist Life* (Berkeley, Los Angeles and London, 1987), 48–9.

136 Hitler, *Mein Kampf*, 258–99; *Zweites Buch*, 32ff. See also Maser, W., *Hitler's Mein Kampf: An Analysis* (London, 1970), 176–8; Ley, R., *Neuadel als Blut und Boden* (Munich, 1930), passim.

137 Baynes, II, 1144–7 (conversation with Lipski, 15 November 1933); Hitler, *Mein Kampf*, 353ff; *Zweites Buch*, 111ff.

138 Schechtman, J., *European Population Transfers, 1939–1945* (New York, 1946), 255–363.

139 Neocleous, M., *Fascism* (London, 1997), ch. 2.

140 *Scritti*, II, 96 (speech in Trieste, 20 September 1920).

141 *Scritti*, IV, 350 (speech to the Chamber of Deputies, 12 September 1924); Missiroli, M., 'Razza e cultura', *Circoli*, 7 August 1939, 981ff; Mack Smith, *Guerre di Duce*, 59ff; Michaelis, M., *Mussolini and the Jews: German-Italian Relations and the Jewish Question in Italy 1922–1945* (Oxford, 1978), 59ff, 83ff.

142 Mussolini, 'Doctrine of Fascism', 169ff.

143 For the Manifesto of the Race see De Felice, *Storia degli ebrei*, 541–2; Gregor, *Ideology of Fascism*, 381–9 (for the text), 265–82 (for an assessment); Michaelis, *Mussolini and the Jews*, 152ff. For a general background of Mussolini's turn to anti-Semitism see Preti, L., *Impero fascista, africani ed ebrei* (Milan, 1968), 87–113, an excerpt of which is translated and cited in Sarti, R., *The Ax Within: Italian Fascism in Action* (London, 1974), 197ff; the following references come from the translated part. See also Michaelis, *Mussolini and the Jews*, 183f, 411ff; Bernardini, G., 'The Origins and Development of Racial Anti-Semitism in Fascist Italy', *Journal of Modern History*, 49 (1977), 431–53.

144 De Grand, *Italian Nationalist Association*, 34–6. For Balbo's arguments see Michaelis, M., 'Il Maresciallo dell'aria. Italo Balbo e la politica mussoliniana', *Storia Contemporanea*, 14 (1983), 351ff.

145 De Grand, A.J., *Bottai e la cultura fascista* (Rome and Bari, 1978), 260–85; Preti, in Sarti, *Ax Within*, 201ff; Gregor, 241–82.

146 Segrè, *Balbo*, 345–53.

147 Zuccotti, S., *The Italians and the Holocaust: Persecution, Rescue, Survival* (New York, 1987); Steinberg, J., *All or Nothing. The Axis and the Holocaust, 1941–43* (London, 1990), passim, esp. 220–41; Michaelis, *Mussolini and the Jews*, 183ff.

148 De Felice, R., *Storia degli ebrei sotto il fascismo* (Turin, 1972), 263ff; Segrè, *Balbo*, 349ff.

149 Goglia, L., 'Note sul razzismo coloniale fascista', *Storia Contemporanea*, 19 (1988), 1223–66.

150 Robertson, E.M., 'Race as a Factor in Mussolini's Policy in Africa and Europe', *Journal of Contemporary History*, 23 (1988), 31–58.

151 Preti, in Sarti, 195ff.

152 *OO*, XVI, 158ff; XIX, 266; Robertson, 'Race as Factor', 31–58.

153 Hitler, A., *Sämtliche Aufzeichnungen*, edited by Jäckel, E. and Kuhn, A. (Stuttgart, 1980), 620ff; Hitler, *Führung und Gefolgschaft* (Berlin, 1934); Domarus, I, 74–6 (speech to the Industry Club at Düsseldorf, 27 January 1932). For the idea that the German

Kultur (as anything Germanic) is superior to other equivalent notions of other nations and races, see Herf, ch. 8.

154 On this issue, see Glaser, 151–3.
155 De Begnac, *Taccuini*, 564–5, 630–1.
156 Baynes, II, 988–9 (interview with O. Strasser, 21 May 1930).
157 Hitler, *Zweites Buch*, 153–4, 219ff; *Mein Kampf*, Ch. 14; Baynes, I, 733 (interview with the United Press, 27 November 1935); II, 1380 (speech to the Reichstag, 20 February 1938), 1471 (Proclamation at the *Parteitag*, Nuremberg, 6 September 1938).
158 Cecil, R., *The Myth of the Master Race: Alfred Rosenberg and Nazi Ideology* (London, 1972), 162–86; Manvell, R. and Fraenkel, H., *Heinrich Himmler* (London, 1965); Ackermann, J., *Himmler als Ideologe* (Göttingen, 1970); Ackermann, J., 'Heinrich Himmler: Reichsführer – SS', in Smelser, R. and Zitelmann R. (eds), *The Nazi Elite* (Houndmills and London, 1993), 100ff.
159 Glaser, 220–30; Pulzer, P.G.J., *Jews and the German State: The Political History of a Minority* (Oxford, 1992); Goldhagen, W., *Hitler's Willing Executioners: Ordinary Germans and the Holocaust* (London, 1996), 27–79; Mosse, G.L., *The Crisis of German Ideology* (London, 1966).
160 Mosse, G.L., *Towards the Final Solution* (London, 1978); Lyttelton, A., 'The "Crisis of Bourgeois Society" and the Origins of Fascism', 12–13.
161 Griffin, *Nature of Fascism*, 226–8.
162 Merkl, 169, 487ff, 522.
163 In sequence: Baynes, II, 1338–9 (speech to the Reichstag, 30 January 1937), 1601 (speech in the Wilhelmshafen Townhall, 1 April 1939); Domarus, II, 2005 (talks with Horthy, 10 April 1943), 2083 (radio address, 30 January 1944); Hitler, *Sämtliche Aufzeichnungen*, 88–90.
164 Baynes, I, 668 (interview with the United Press, 27 November 1935); 707 (speech in 1937 Nuremberg Party Rally, 10 September 1937). See also, for an analysis of these ideas, Goldhagen, 80–128; Kershaw, *Hitler: Hubris*, 559ff.
165 Weindling, P., 'Understanding Nazi Racism: Precursors and Perpetrators', in Burleigh, M. (ed.), *Confronting the Nazi Past: New Debates on Modern German History* (London, 1996), 66–83.
166 Mosse, G.L., 'Towards a General Theory of Fascism', in Mosse (ed.), *International Fascism: New Thoughts and New Approaches* (London and Beverly Hills, 1979), 1–41.
167 Wilford, 'Fascism', 185ff; Eatwell, R., 'Fascism', in Eatwell, R. and Wright, A. (eds), *Contemporary Political Ideologies* (London, 1993), 169–91.
168 Adamson, W., 'Avant-Garde Political Rhetorics: Pre-War Culture in Florence as a Source of Post-War Fascism', *Journal of European Ideas*, 16 (1993), 753–7; Bosworth, R.J.B., *Italy, the Least of the Great Powers: Italian Foreign Policy Before the First World War* (Cambridge, 1979), 95–126; Cunsolo, R.S., 'Italian Nationalism in Historical Perspective', *History of European Ideas*, 16 (1993), 759–66.
169 'The Nationalist Blueprint for a New Italy', programmatic declaration of the Italian Nationalist Association, translated and reprinted in Griffin, *Fascism*, 37–8; 'Nationalism and the Syndicates', in Lyttelton, *Italian Fascisms*, 159–63; Visser, R., 'Fascist Doctrine and the Cult of *Romanità*', *Journal of Contemporary History*, 27 (1992).
170 De Grand, *Italian Nationalist Association*, chaps 1–3; Gaeta, F., 'L'Associazione Nazionalista Italiana', in Gentile, E. (ed.), *L'Italia giolittiana. La storia e la critica* (Rome and Bari, 1977), 253–68.
171 De Grand, *Italian Nationalist Association*, ch. 3; Adamson, 'Avant-Garde', 755–7.
172 Malaparte, C., 'Fascism's European Mission', in Griffin, *Fascism*, 48–9; 'Mussolini and National Syndicalism', in Lyttelton, *Italian Fascisms*, 225–41 (especially 235ff). For an analysis of this internal antithesis see Sternhell, *The Birth of Fascist Ideology*, especially 163–75.

173 *OO*, XII, 311–4 (Second Declaration of San Sepolcro, 23 March 1919); excerpts are translated in Baron Bernardo Quaranta di San Severino (ed.), *Mussolini as Revealed in his Political Speeches (November 1914–August 1923)* (London and Toronto, 1923), 78ff.

174 *Scritti*, II, 95–109 (Discorso di Trieste, 20 September 1920).

175 *OO*, XVIII, 396ff/ *Scritti*, VI, 37–77 ('Discorso dell'Ascensione', Chamber of Deputies, 26 May 1927); and 'Discorso di Roma', reprinted in Santarelli (ed.), 254–64. For Mussolini's demographic policy see Knox, 'Conquest', 18–20; Mussolini, B., 'Political and Social Doctrine of Fascism', 164–79.

176 *OO*, XXIII, 216ff, also in Griffin, *Fascism*, 58–60. See also *OO*, XXII, 364ff (speech in Rome, 26 May 1927).

177 *Scritti*, II, 7–10 ('Posizioni e obbietivi', *Popolo d'Italia*, 28 March 1919).

178 *OO*, XII, 313–4 (San Sepolcro, 23 March 1919).

179 For ANI's ideas on this matter see De Grand, *Italian National Association*, 10ff. For Mussolini's relevant arguments, see the analysis in Knox, 'Conquest', 17–18.

180 *OO*, XVI, 106ff ('Per essere liberi', *Popolo d'Italia*, 8 January 1921); *Scritti*, II, 133–5 ('Legionari di Ronchi', *Popolo d'Italia*, 5 January 1921).

181 *OO*, XXIV, 5ff (speech to the Assembly of the Fascist regime, 10 March 1929).

182 Reprinted in Delzell (ed.), 12–13; De Felice, R., *Mussolini il rivoluzionario* (Turin, 1965), 744ff.

183 *OO*, XIII, 143 (speech in Milan, 22 May 1919).

184 Published in *Popolo d'Italia*, 6 June 1919.

185 *OO*, XV, 217 (speech in Trieste, 9 September 1920); *Scritti*, V, 183–91 (speech in Rome for the anniversary of the Italian victory in the First World War, 4 November 1925). For the 'cult of Rome' in the Fascist regime see Gentile, *Culto del littorio*, 146–54; Visser, 'Cult of romanità', passim.

186 Bernardo Quaranta di San Severino, 107ff (speech in Florence, 9 October 1919).

187 Domarus, M., *Mussolini und Hitler. Zwei Wege – Gleiches Ende* (Würzburg, 1977), 65 (speech in Milan, 5 May 1921).

188 *OO*, XVIII, 453–8/ *Scritti*, II, 339–48 ('Discorso di Napoli', 24 October 1922).

189 Domarus, *Mussolini und Hitler*, 115ff (5 September 1923).

190 *OO*, XVI, 300ff (speech in Milan, 3 May 1921).

191 *Scritti*, II, 55–7 ('Alle Alpi Giulie', *Popolo d'Italia*, 22 February 1920); II, 113 ('Ciò che rimane e ciò che verrà', *Popolo d'Italia*, 13 November 1920).

192 Bernardo Quaranta di San Severino, 328ff (speech in Florence, 19 June 1923).

193 Reprinted in Santarelli, 297–301. See also *Scritti*, III, 98 ('The problem of emigration', speech in Milan, 2 April 1923).

194 *OO*, XVI, 106 ('Per essere liberi', *Popolo d'Italia*, 8 January 1921).

195 Simonini, 96–9.

196 *Scritti*, II, 101ff (Discorso di Trieste, 20 September 1920); Bernardo Quaranta di San Severino, 108ff.

197 *OO*, XVI, 159ff (Discorso di Torino, 6 February 1921); XVIII, 161ff ('Past and Future', *Popolo d'Italia*, 21 April 1922).

198 Ludwig, E., *Colloqui con Mussolini* (Milan, 1950), 58–64.

199 Mussolini, 'Political and Social Doctrine of Fascism', 164ff. See also *Scritti*, II, 149–50 ('Dopo il natale di sangue', second speech in Trieste, 6 February 1921); *OO*, XXVIII, 30 (speech in Lucania, 27 August 1936).

200 *Scritti*, II, 95–100 (Discorso di Trieste, 20 September 1920).

201 *Scritti*, VI, 43ff (Discorso dell'Ascensione, 26 May 1927). See his speech in Trieste (6 February 1932), in Bernardo Quaranta di San Severino, 121ff.

202 *OO*, XXIX, 185–95 (speech to the PNF General Council, 15 September 1938).

203 Weinberg, G.L., *Germany, Hitler, and World War II: Essays in Modern German and World History* (Cambridge, 1995), 30–53; Rich, *Hitler's War Aims*, I, ch. 1; Aigner, D.,

'Hitler's Ultimate Aims – A Programme of World Dominion?', in Koch, H.W. (ed.), *Aspects of the Third Reich* (Basingstoke and London, 1985), 251–66.

204 Hitler, *Mein Kampf*; Weinberg, *Hitlers Zweites Buch*, 102ff.

205 Jäckel, E. and Kuhn, A. (eds), *Hitler: Sämtliche Aufzeichnungen, 1905–1924* (Stuttgart, 1980), 421–7; Weinberg, *Zweites Buch*, 53ff.

206 Hitler, *Mein Kampf*, 598ff.

207 Glaser, 154–62; Smith, 212–3; Mosse, *Crisis of German Ideology*, 246ff; Hamilton, A., *The Appeal of Fascism: A Study of Intellectuals and Fascism 1919–1945* (London, 1971), 91–168.

208 Smith, chaps 5, 7.

209 Smith, 146ff.

210 Mayer, J.P., *Max Weber and German Politics* (London, 1943), 81ff; Smith, 155–60.

211 Stoakes, G., 'The Evolution of Hitler's Ideas on Foreign Policy, 1919–1925', in Stachura, P.D. (ed.), *The Shaping of the Nazi State* (London, 1978), 22–47; Schubert, G., *Anfänge nationalsozialistischer Aussenpolitik* (Cologne, 1963).

212 Feder, G., *Das Program der NSDAP und seine weltanschaulichen Grundlagen* (Munich, 1932), translated and reprinted in Baynes, I, 102–5.

213 Phelps, R., 'Hitler als Parteiredner im Jahre 1920', *Vierteljahrshefte für Zeitgeschichte*, 11 (1963), 289–92 (speech to Munich party group, 10 December 1919). See also, in general, Kuhn, A., *Hitlers Aussenpolitisches Programm* (Stuttgart, 1970).

214 Stoakes, 30–5; Knox, M., 'Conquest', 20ff.

215 Jäckel and Kuhn, *Sämtliche Aufzeichnungen*, 207ff (October, 1920).

216 Baynes, I, 21ff (speech to party organisation in Munich, 27 July 1920).

217 Phelps, 308 (speech to party organisation in Munich, 27 July 1920), 328–9 (speech in Munich, 19 November 1920). See also Stokes, 25ff; Kershaw, *Hitler: Hubris*, ch. 5.

218 Baynes, I, 31–42 (speech in Munich, 'Free State or Slavery', 28 July 1922).

219 Baynes, I, 665ff (Proclamation to the German People, 1 February 1933); Domarus, I, 730–2 (13 September 1937 at the Nuremberg Party Rally); I, 672ff (January 1937 to the Reichstag).

220 Hitler, A., *Die Rede Adolf Hitlers in der ersten grossen Massenversammlung (Münchener Bürgerbräu-Keller vom 27. Februar 1925) bei Wiederaufrichtung der National-Sozialistischen Deutschen Arbeiter-Partei* (Munich 1925), 7–8.

221 Hitler, *Mein Kampf*, 586–609.

222 Hitler, *Mein Kampf*, 587ff. See also the ideas of Rosenberg, whose influence upon Hitler in this respect has been widely acknowledged, in *Pest in Russland* (Munich, 1922).

223 Domarus, I, 728–32 (13 September 1937 at the Party Rally). See also I, 673ff (September 1936 at the Party Rally).

224 In sequence: Baynes, I, 665–8 (Proclamation to the German People, 1 February 1933); I, 791 (January 1932 to Industry Club at Düsseldorf); Domarus, I, 642ff (12 September 1936 at the Party Rally). See also *Mein Kampf*, 598–607; *Zweites Buch*, 102ff.

225 Domarus, I, 732ff (13 September 1937 at the Party Rally); 903ff (September 1938, speech to Wehrmacht soldiers). See also Rich, I, 6–8.

226 Hitler, *Mein Kampf*, 586–9.

227 Nolte, E., *Das Europäische Bürgerkrieg, 1917–1945. Nationalsozialismus und Bolschevismus* (Berlin, 1987); Birken, ch. 5.

228 Knox, 'Conquest', 22–3, 57; Knox, M., *Mussolini Unleashed, 1939–1941: Politics and Strategy in Fascist Italy's Last War* (Cambridge, 1982), 289ff; Aigner, 261–6. See also Bosworth, R.J.B., 'Italian Foreign Policy and its Historiography', in Bosworth, R.J.B. and Rizzo, G. (eds), *Altro Polo: Intellectuals and Their Ideas in Contemporary Italy* (Sydney, 1983), 52–96.

229 Quoted in Rhodes, J.M., *The Hitler Movement* (Stanford, 1980), 43ff.

230 Kershaw, *Hitler: Hubris*, 542; O'Sullivan, 113–30; Gentile, E., *Ideologia fascista*, 229–30.
231 De Felice, R., *Interpretations of Fascism* (Cambridge, MA and London, 1977), 11ff; Perfetti, F., *Il dibattito sul fascismo*, 10ff.
232 *Scritti*, II, 111 ('Ciò che rimane e ciò che verra', *Popolo d'Italia*, 13 November 1920).
233 *Scritti*, II, 159 (speech in Bologna, 3 April 1921); 307–22 ('Discorso di Udine', 20 September 1922), translated in Bernardo Quaranta di San Severino, 143ff.
234 *Scritti*, II, 315 (Discorso di Udine, 20 September 1922). See also Gentile, G., *Origini e dottrina del fascismo* (Rome, 1929), translated as 'The Origins and Doctrine of Fascism', in Lyttelton, *Italian Fascisms*, 303–4.
235 *OO*, XXI, 426 (speech in La Scala, Milan, 28 October 1925); XXII, 128 (speech in Genoa, 23 May 1926); XXVI, 134 ('Il 1934', 2 February 1934). See also Simonini, 108–9.
236 *OO*, XXI, 426 (speech in La Scala, Milan, 28 October 1925); XXVI, 134, ('Il 1934', 2 January 1934).
237 Mussolini, 'Doctrine of Fascism', 165ff.
238 *Scritti*, V, 67–70 ('Contro la massoneria', speech to the Chamber of Deputies, 16 May 1925).
239 Rossi, C., 'La critica alle critiche del fascismo', *Gerarchia*, April 1922; Lyttelton, *Italian Fascisms*, 330–42.
240 Gentile, E., *Ideologia fascista*, 335–42.
241 Pelizzi, C., 'Idealismo e fascismo', *Gerarchia*, October 1922. See also Gentile, G., *Origini e dottrina del fascismo*; Mussolini, 'Political and Social Doctrine', 170ff.
242 *Scritti*, II, 152 ('Dopo due anni', *Popolo d'Italia*, 23 March 1921).
243 *Scritti*, II, 53 ('Navigare Necesse', *Popolo d'Italia*, 1 January 1920).
244 *OO*, XXI ('Intransigenza assoluta', 22 June 1928). See also Gentile, G., 'The Philosophical Basis of Fascism', *Foreign Affairs*, 6 (1928), 300–1.
245 *Scritti*, I, 326ff ('Ossare!', in *Popolo d'Italia*, 13 June 1918).
246 Hitler's speech on 10 February 1939, quoted in Michalka, W. (ed.), *Das Dritte Reich*, vol. I: *Volksgemeinschaft und Grossmachtpolitik* (Munich, 1985), 224ff.
247 Hitler, *Mein Kampf*, 554–85; Maser, 141–51.
248 Domarus, vol. II: *Untergang, 1939–1945* (Würzburg, 1963), 1337ff (speech to party members, 8 November 1942).
249 Baynes, II, 1136 (speech in Kiel, 6 November 1933).
250 Speer, *Inside the Third Reich*, ch. 17; Noakes, J. and Pridham, G. (eds), *Nazism: A Documentary Reader*, vol. III: *Foreign Policy, War and Racial Extermination* (Exeter, 1988), 842.

3 FOREIGN POLICY DECISION-MAKING PROCESSES UNDER FASCIST RULE

1 Eley, G., 'Conservatives and Radical Nationalists in Germany: The Production of Fascist Potentials, 1912–1928', in Blinkhorn, M. (ed.), *Fascists and Conservatives. The Radical Right and the Establishment in Twentieth Century Europe* (London, 1990), 50–70.
2 Lyttelton, A., *The Seizure of Power: Fascism in Italy 1919–1929* (London 1987, 2nd edn); Bracher, K.D., *The German Dictatorship* (London, 1970); Allen, W.S., 'The Nazi Rise to Power: A Comprehensive Catastrophe', in Maier, C.S., Hoffmann, S. and Gould, A. (ed.), *The Rise of the Nazi Regime: Historical Reassessments* (Boulder and London, 1986), 9–18.
3 Koch, H.W., '1933: The Legality of Hitler's Assumption of Power', in Koch, H.W. (ed.), *Aspects of the Third Reich* (Houndmills and London, 1985), 53–4.
4 Kettenacker, L., 'Social and Psychological Aspects of the Führer's Role', in Koch, 98–132.

5 Ungari, P., 'Ideologie giuridiche e strategie istituzionali del fascismo', in Aquarone, A. and Vernassa, M. (eds), *Il regime fascista* (Bologna, 1974), 45–56; Neumann, F., *Behemoth: The Structure and Practice of National Socialism* (New York, 1963), 467ff; Caplan, J., 'National Socialism and the Theory of the State', in Childers, T. and Caplan, J. (eds), *Reevaluating the Third Reich* (New York and London, 1993), 98–102.

6 Mommsen, H., 'National Socialism: Continuity and Change', in Laqueur, W. (ed.), *Fascism: A Reader's Guide. Analyses, Interpretations, Bibliography* (Harmondsworth, 1979), 166ff; Lyttelton, *The Seizure of Power*, 15–41.

7 Knox, M., 'Conquest, Foreign and Domestic, in Fascist Italy and Nazi Germany', *Journal of Modern History*, 56 (1984), 1–57; Germino, D., *The Italian Fascist Party in Power: A Study of Totalitarian Rule* (Minneapolis, 1959), 10ff; Aquarone, A., *L'organizzazione dello Stato Totalitario* (Turin, 1965), 291ff; Gentile, G., 'The Problem of the Party in Italian Fascism', *Journal of Contemporary History*, 19 (1984), 251–74.

8 Boldt, H., 'Article 48 of the Weimar Constitution: Its Historical and Political Implications', in Nicholls, A. and Matthias, E. (eds), *German Democracy and the Triumph of Hitler* (London, 1971), 79–98.

9 Heineman, J.L., *Hitler's First Foreign Minister. Constantin Freiherr von Neurath, Diplomat and Statesman* (Berkeley and Los Angeles, 1979), 44ff; Wheeler-Bennett, J.W., *Hindenburg: The Wooden Titan* (New York, 1967).

10 Orlow, D., *The History of the Nazi Party 1933–1945* (Newton Abbot 1969–1973), 2 vols; Unger, A.L., *The Totalitarian Party: Party and People in Nazi Germany and Soviet Russia* (London, 1974). On the issue of party–state relations, see Noakes, J. and Pridham, G., *Nazism 1919–1945*, vol. II: *State, Economy, and Society 1933–1939* (Exeter, 1984), 233–58; Broszat, M., *The Hitler State: The Foundation and Development of the Internal Structure of the Third Reich* (London and New York, 1981), 199ff.

11 Andreski, S., 'Fascists as Moderates', in Larsen, S.U., Hagtvet, B. and Myklebust, J.P. (eds), *Who Were the Fascists? Social Roots of European Fascism* (Bergen, Oslo NS Tromso, 1980), 52–5; Faye, J.P., *Langages totalitaires. Critique de la raison/l'économie narrative* (Paris, 1972), 407ff.

12 Sonnino, S., *Diario, 1866–1912* (Bari, 1972), vol. 1, 356; Sarti, R., 'Italian Fascism: Radical Politics and Conservative Goals', in Blinkhorn, *Fascists and Conservatives*, 19ff. For Neurath's aversion to the parliamentary system, see Rauschning, H., *Men of Chaos* (New York, 1942), 172.

13 Weisbrod, B., 'The crisis of Bourgeois Society in Interwar Germany', in Bessel, R. (ed.), *Fascist Italy and Nazi Germany: Comparisons and Contrasts* (Cambridge, 1996), 27ff; Geyer, M., 'Traditional Elites and National Socialism Leadership', in Maier, Hoffmann and Gould, *The Rise of the Nazi Regime*, 61. For Italy see Aquarone, *Stato Totalitario*, 106; Clough, S.B., *The Economic History of Modern Italy* (New York and London, 1964), 216.

14 Orsini, F.G., 'La diplomazia', in Del Boca, A., Legnani, M. and Rossi, M.C. (eds), *Il regime fascista. Storia e storiografia* (Rome and Bari, 1995), 278–9; Serra, E., 'La burocrazia della politica estera italiana', in Bosworth, R.J.B. and Romano, S. (eds), *La politica estera italiana (1860–1985)* (Bologna, 1991), 68–72.

15 Bosworth, R.J.B., *Italy and the Wider World, 1860–1960* (London and New York, 1996), 29ff; Orsini, 282–5.

16 Serra, 'Burocrazia', 78–81.

17 Rochat, G., *L'esercito italiano da Vittorio Veneto a Mussolini (1919–1925)* (Bari, 1967), 67–119.

18 Whittam, J., *The Politics of the Italian Army, 1861–1918* (London, 1977); Bosworth, *Italy and the Wider World*, ch. 3.

19 Rochat, G., 'L'esercito e fascismo', in Quazza, G. (ed.), *Fascismo e società italiana* (Turin, 1973), 89–123.

20 Bosworth, R.J.B., *Italy and the Approach of the First World War* (London, 1983), 42ff.

21 Rochat, G., 'Mussolini e le forze armate', in Aquarone, A., Vernassa, M. (eds), *Il regime fascista* (Bologna, 1974), 113–7; and *Esercito italiano da Vittorio Veneto a Mussolini*, 67–119, 397–408.

22 Serra, E., *La diplomazia in Italia* (Milan, 1984), 28–40.

23 Saladino, S., 'Italy', in Rogger, H. and Weber, E. (eds), *The European Right: A Historical Profile* (London, 1965), 209–58.

24 Orsini, 284; Serra, *Diplomazia in Italia*, 39–41.

25 Hamilton, A., *The Appeal of Fascism: A Study of Intellectuals and Fascism 1919–1945* (London, 1971), 11/32.

26 Serra, 'Burocrazia', 81–2.

27 Sarti, R., 'Italian Fascism: Radical Politics and Conservative Goals', in Blinkhorn, *Fascists and Conservatives*, 14–30; Pombeni, P., 'La forma partito del fascismo e del nazismo', in Bracher, K.D. and Valiani, L. (eds), *Fascismo e nazionalsocialismo* (Bologna, 1986), 245–6.

28 Aquarone, *Stato Totalitario*, 75ff; De Felice, R., *Mussolini il fascista*, vol. II: *L'organizzazione dello Stato Fascista, 1925–1929* (Turin, 1968), 166ff; Thompson, D., *State Control in Fascist Italy: Culture and Conformity, 1925–43* (Manchester and New York, 1991), 62–70; Morgan, P., *Italian Fascism, 1919–1945* (Basingstoke and London, 1995), ch. 3.

29 Griffin, R., *The Nature of Fascism* (London and New York, 1994), 74–6; Lyttelton, *Seizure of Power*, 121ff.

30 Santoro, C.M., *La politica estera di una media potenza. L'Italia dall'Unità ad oggi* (Bologna, 1991), 157–60; Knox, M., 'Il fascismo e la politica estera italiana', in Bosworth and Romano, *La politica estera italiana (1860–1985)*, 287ff.

31 Di Nolfo, 45–6; DDI, 7th, I, 2–4/14 (29 October–1 November 1922, reports about the resignations of Sforza, Frassati and the decision of the other diplomats to stay in their positions).

32 Rochat, G., 'Il fascismo e la preparazione militare al conflitto mondiale', in Del Boca, A., Legnani, M. and Rossi, M.G. (eds), *Il regime fascista. Storia e storiografia* (Rome and Bari, 1995), 156–7.

33 Rochat, G. and Massobrio, C., *Breve storia del'esercito italiano dal 1861 al 1945* (Turin, 1978), 196ff, 208ff; Rochat, *Esercito italiano da Vittorio Veneto a Mussolini*, 408ff; Whittam, J., 'The Italian General Staff and the Coming of the Second World War', in Preston, A. (ed.), *General Staffs and Diplomacy Before the Second World War* (Totowa, 1978), 85ff.

34 Barros, J., *The Corfu Incident of 1923* (Princeton, 1966).

35 Di Nolfo, 90ff; Bosworth, *Italy and the Wider World*, 41–2.

36 Cassels, A., *Mussolini's Early Diplomacy* (Princeton, 1970), 91ff; Di Nolfo, 79ff; Salandra, A., *Memorie politiche, 1916–1926* (Milan, 1951), 101–6.

37 Cassels, 112–23. See the anxiety of the diplomats in Rome in case Mussolini again changed his mind and rejected the compromise solution (DDI, 7th, II, 380).

38 Di Nolfo, 85–6.

39 Bernardi, G., *Il disarmo navale fra le due guerre mondiali (1919–1939)* (Rome, 1975), 215ff.

40 The so-called 'decade of good behaviour' thesis is supported by Pastorelli, L., 'La storiografia italiana del dopoguerra sulla politica estera', *Storia e Politica*, 10 (1971), 603ff; Halperin, S.W., *Mussolini and Italian Fascism* (Princeton, 1964). De Felice locates the change in Mussolinian foreign policy between 1929 and 1930 ('Alcune osservazioni sulla politica estera mussoliniana', in De Felice, *L'Italia fra tedeschi e alleati. La politica estera fascista e la seconda guerra mondiale* (Bologna, 1973), 60).

41 Guariglia, R., *Ricordi* (Naples, 1950), 27; Lowe, C.J. and Marzari, F., *Italian Foreign Policy 1870–1940* (London and Boston, 1975), 186–9. See Guariglia's objections to Mussolini's idea in DDI, 7th, I, 523.

42 Di Nolfo, 99–138; DDI, 7th, IV, 126/129.
43 *OO*, XXII, 385 ('Discorse dell'Ascensione', Chamber of Deputies, 26 May 1927).
44 Cassels, 226–30.
45 DDI, 7th, III, 604; IV, 298.
46 Knox, 'Il fascismo e la politica estera italiana', 301ff; DDI, 7th, V, 123/333; Mack Smith, D., *Mussolini's Roman Empire* (London, 1982), 18–19.
47 Mussolini, B., *Scritti e Discorsi*, (Milan 1934–39), II, 55–7 ('Alle Alpi Giulie', *Popolo d'Italia*, 22 February 1920); II, 121–2 ('Fiume', in *Popolo d'Italia*, 2 December 1920).
48 Di Nolfo, ch. 4.
49 Lessona, A., *Memorie* (Florence, 1958), 108ff.
50 Cassels, 315–52; Lowe, Marzari, 208–9, 216–7, 227; Knox, 'Fascismo e la politica estera italiana', 302–5.
51 Cassels, 283–7; De Felice, *Mussolini il fascista*, vol. I: *La conquista del potere, 1922–1925* (Turin, 1966), 559–63.
52 Orsini, 290–2.
53 Guariglia, 53–4.
54 Aquarone, *Stato Totalitario*, 70ff; Melis, G., 'La burocrazia', in Del Boca, Legnani and Rossi, *Il regime fascista. Storia e storiografia*, 244–76.
55 Aquarone, *Stato Totalitario*, 101ff; Hughes, S., 'The Early Diplomacy of Italian Fascism: 1922–1932', in Craig, G. and Gilbert, F.A. (eds), *The Diplomats 1919–1939* (Princeton, 1953), 210–33.
56 Nello, P. (ed.), *Un fedele disubbidiente. Dino Grandi dal palazzo Chigi al 25 luglio* (Bologna, 1993); Knox, M., 'The Fascist Regime, its Foreign Policy and its Wars: An "Anti-Anti-Fascist" Orthodoxy?', in Finney, P. (ed.), *The Origins of the Second World War* (London and New York, 1997), 148–68.
57 Nello (ed.), *Dino Grandi*, 300ff (speech to the Grand Council, 2 October 1930). For an assessment see De Felice, 'Alcune osservazioni sulla politica estera mussoliniana', 57–74.
58 Knox, M., 'The Fascist Regime, its Foreign Policy and its Wars', 160–1; De Felice R., *Mussolini il duce*, vol. 1: *Gli anni del consenso, 1929–1936* (Turin, 1974), 411–13.
59 Nello, P. (ed.), *Dino Grandi: la politica estera dell'Italia dal 1929 al 1932* (Rome, 1985), 451–71 (speech to the Chamber, 14 March 1931). See also Guariglia, 176–8.
60 Nello, *Dino Grandi*, 513–19 (speech at the London Conference, 20 July 1931). For Mussolini's reactions and Grandi's dismissal see Aloisi, P., *Journal 25 Juin–14 Juillet 1936* (Paris, 1957), 5ff; Guariglia, 176ff.
61 Cantalupo, R., *Fu la Spagna. Ambasciata presso Franco, febbraio-aprile 1937* (Milan, 1948), 42ff.
62 Lessona, 108ff; Di Nolfo, 183–5.
63 Schieder, W., 'Fascismo e nazionalsocialismo nei primi anni Trenta' in Del Boca, Legnani and Rossi, *Il regime fascista. Storia e storiografia*, 45–56; Schubert, G., *Anfänge Nationalsozialistischer Aussenpolitik* (Cologne, 1961), 150–67.
64 Cassels, 153–9.
65 De Felice, *Mussolini il duce*, I, 392–402; Di Nolfo, chaps 5, 7.
66 Sadkovich, J.J., *Italian Support for Croat Separatism, 1927–1937* (New York, 1987); Robertson, E.M., *Mussolini as Empire-Builder* (London, 1977), 23–7, 35; DDI, 7th, VI, 131/ 514/ 518–9.
67 Mack Smith, *Mussolini's Roman Empire*, 22ff.
68 *OO*, XXIV, 235ff (speech in Florence, 17 August 1930).
69 Orsini, 311–2; Serra, 'La burocrazia', 82–3.
70 Whittam, J., 'The Italian General Staff and the Coming of the Second World War', 86–7; Lyttelton, A., 'Fascism in Italy: The Second Wave', in Mosse, G.L. (ed.), *International Fascism* (London, 1979), 52ff.
71 Knox, 'Fascismo e politica estera', 302–3.

72 Rochat, 'Mussolini e le forze armate', in Aquarone, A. and Vernassa, A. (eds), *Il regime fascista* (Bologna, 1974), 113–26; Thompson, 87–9.

73 Rochat, 'Preparazione militare al conflitto mondiale', 158ff.

74 Suvich, F., *Memorie 1932–1936* (Milan, 1984), 4ff.

75 DDI, 8th, III, 194 (memorandum 7.2.1936)/533 (memorandum 26.3.1936), respectively.

76 Segrè, C.G., *Italo Balbo: A Fascist Life* (Berkeley and Los Angeles, 1987), 353–9; Robertson, *Mussolini as Empire-Builder*, 56ff; Overy, R.J., *Goering: The 'Iron Man'* (London, 1984), 32–3.

77 Weinberg, G.L., *Hitler's Foreign Policy*, vol. II: *Starting World War II* (Chicago and London, 1980), 268ff.

78 Orsini, 313f; Serra, 'Burocrazia', 83–4.

79 Quartararo, R., *Roma tra Londra e Berlino. La politica estera fascista dal 1930 al 1940* (Rome, 1980), 117ff. See also, in this study, Chapters 4–5.

80 DDI, 7th, X, 423.

81 Knox, 'Fascismo e la politica estera italiana', 317ff; Pelagalli, S., 'Il generale Pietro Gàzzera al ministero della guerra (1928–1933)', *Storia Contemporanea*, 20 (1989), 1040–50.

82 Robertson, *Empire-Builder*, 93–113.

83 Mack Smith, D., *Italy and its Monarchy* (New Haven and London, 1989), 271; Rochat and Massobrio, 247ff.

84 Guariglia, 220ff; De Felice, *Mussolini il duce*, I, 526ff.

85 Suvich, *Memorie*, 275ff. For the diplomatic background to the decision to impose sanctions on Italy, see Lowe and Marzari, 283–90.

86 Orsini, 317ff.

87 Rochat, G., *Militari e politici nella preparazione della campagna d'Etiopia* (Milan, 1971), 110ff.

88 Rochat, *Militari*, 324ff; Robertson, *Empire-Builder*, 98ff; Rochat, G., *Il colonialismo italiano* (Turin, 1973), 137ff; Petersen, J., 'La politica estera del fascismo come problema storiografico', in De Felice, *L'Italia fra tedeschi e alleati*, 42ff.

89 Lowe and Marzari, 242–50; Guerri, G.B. (ed.), *Giuseppe Bottai: Diario, 1935–1944* (Milan 1996, 3rd edn), 17 November 1935.

90 Rochat, *Colonialismo*, 139–45; Bottai, *Diario*, 19 December 1935.

91 Mack Smith, *Monarchy*, 270ff; Binchy, D.A., *Church and State in Fascist Italy* (Oxford 1970, 2nd edn), 637–51.

92 De Felice, *Mussolini il duce*, vol. II: *Lo Stato Totalitario, 1936–1940* (Turin, 1981), 6–7.

93 Tranfaglia, N., 'La modernizzazione contradittoria negli anni della stabilizzazione del regime (1926–1936)', in Del Boca, Legnani and Rossi, *Il regime fascista. Storia e storiografia*, 132ff.

94 Ciano's comments in Bottai, *Diario*, 7 January and 9 March 1936; Guariglia, 328–9. For Ciano's general attitude towards the diplomats, see Orsini, 319–28.

95 Serra, *Diplomazia*, 43–4.

96 Serra, 'Burocrazia', 83–6; Gilbert, 517ff; Guerri, G.B., *Galeazzo Ciano. Una vita, 1903/1944* (Milan, 1979), 163ff.

97 Vigezzi, B., 'Mussolini, Ciano, la diplomazia italiana e la percezione della "politica dei potenza" al' inizio della seconda guerra mondiale', in di Nolfo, E., Rainero, R.H. and Vigezzi, B. (eds), *L'Italia e la politica di potenza in Europa (1938–1940)* (Milan, 1986), 3–18.

98 Guerri, *Galeazzo Ciano*, ch. 6. See also Ciano's nostalgic comments about his relationship with the *Duce* in Muggeridge, M. (ed.), *Ciano's Diaries, 1939–1943* (London and Toronto, 1947).

99 Orsini, 324–5. For the Grand Council meeting see Segrè, *Balbo*, 367–8.

100 Morewood, S., 'Anglo-Italian Rivalry in the Mediterranean and Middle East 1935–1940', in Boyce, R. and Robertson, E.M. (eds), *Paths to War: New Essays on the Origins of the Second World War* (London, 1989), 185–6.

101 Knox, M., *Mussolini Unleashed, 1939–1941: Politics and Strategy in Fascist Italy's Last War* (Cambridge, 1982), ch. 1; Mack Smith, *Mussolini's Roman Empire*, 99ff.

102 Cantalupo, 65ff; Guerri, *Galeazzo Ciano*, 225–74; Rochat, Massobrio, 256–9; Muggeridge, M. (ed.), *Ciano's Diaries, 1937–1938* (London, 1952).

103 Mack Smith, *Mussolini's Roman Empire*, 101–2; Rochat and Massobrio, 256–7.

104 Weinberg, G.L., *The Foreign Policy of Hitler's Germany: Diplomatic Revolution in Europe, 1933–1936* (Chicago, 1970), 294ff; Ciano, *Diplomatic Papers*, 52ff.

105 Guerri, *Galeazzo Ciano*, 234–8.

106 Guerri, *Galeazzo Ciano*, ch. 8; Santarelli, C., *Storia del movimento e del regime fascista* (Rome, 1967), II, 248–65.

107 Toscano, M., *Le origini diplomatiche del patto d'acciaio* (Florence, 1956), 308ff; Quartararo, *Roma tra Londra e Berlino*, 460ff; Santoro, *Politica estera di una media potenza*, 170–1.

108 Mack Smith, *Monarchy*, 279–80.

109 DDI, 8th, XXII, 49–51 (text); Quartararo, 468ff; Candeloro, G., *Storia dell'Italia moderna*, vol. 9: *Il fascismo e le sue guerre* (Milan 1998, 8th edn), 482–3. For the unpopularity of the Axis see the analysis in Colarizi, S., 'L'opinione pubblica italiana di fronte all' intervento in guerra', in Di Nolfo, Rainero and Vigezzi, *L'Italia e la politica di potenza in Europa (1938–1940)* (Milan, 1986), 296ff.

110 Mack Smith, *Mussolini's Roman Empire*, 129–30; Quartararo, 468, 489. For prominent Fascists' attitudes to the alliance with Germany see, in this study, Chapter 5.

111 Bottai, *Diario*, 31 May 1939.

112 Bessel, R., 'The Formation and Dissolution of a German National Electorate: From Kaiserreich to Third Reich', in Jones, L.E. and Retallack, J. (eds), *Elections, Mass Politics, and Social Change in Modern Germany* (Cambridge, 1992), 410ff; and Matthias, E., 'The Influence of the Versailles Treaty on the Internal Development of the Weimar Republic', in Nicholls, A. and Matthias, E. (eds), *German Democracy and the Triumph of Hitler* (London, 1971), 13–28.

113 Griffin, *Nature of Fascism*, 225–35.

114 Müller, K.-J., 'The Structure and Nature of the National Conservative Opposition in Germany up to 1940', in Koch, H.W. (ed.), *Aspects of the Third Reich* (London, 1985), 139–42.

115 Geyer, M., *Aufrüstung oder Sicherheit? Die Reichswehr und die Krise der Machtpolitik 1924–1936* (Wiesbaden, 1980), 80ff, 200ff; Deist, W., Messerschmidt, M., Volkmann, H.-E. and Wette, W., 'Causes and Preconditions of German Aggression', in Deist, W. (ed.), *The German Military in the Age of Total War* (Leamington Spa, 1985), 339–40.

116 Geyer, M., 'The Dynamics of Military Revisionism in the Interwar Years: Military Policy between Rearmament and Diplomacy', in Deist, *The German Military in the Age of Total War*, 111–13.

117 Von Strandmann, H. P., 'Imperialism and Revisionism in Interwar Germany', in Mommsen, W.J. and Osterhammel, J. (eds), *Imperialism and After: Continuities and Discontinuities* (London, Boston and Sydney, 1986), 93ff; Geyer, 'Dynamics of Military Revisionism', 107–13.

118 Carsten, F.L., *The Reichswehr and Politics, 1918–1933* (Oxford, 1966), 338ff, 364ff; Hayes, P., 'Kurt von Schleicher and Weimar Politics', *Journal of Modern History*, 52 (1980), 35–65; Koch, 'Legality', 48ff.

119 Seabury, P., *The Wilhelmstrasse: A Study of German Diplomats under the Nazi Regime* (Berkeley, 1954), 18–21.

120 Laffan, M., 'Weimar and Versailles: German Foreign Policy, 1919–33', in Laffan, M. (ed.), *The Burden of German History, 1919–45: Essays for the Goethe Institute* (London, 1989), 81–102; Eley, 'Conservatives and Radical Nationalists in Germany', in Blinkhorn, *Fascists and Conservatives*, 50–70.

121 Heineman, 59ff; Noakes, J., 'German Conservatives and the Third Reich: an Ambiguous Relationship', in Blinkhorn, *Fascists and Conservatives*, 71–97; Seabury, 21–4.

122 Geary, D., 'The Industrial Elite and the Nazis in the Weimar Republic', in Stachura, P.D. (ed.), *The Nazi Machtergreifung* (London, 1983), 88ff; Stegmann, D., 'Zum Verhältnis von Grossindustrie and Nationalsozialismus, 1930–33', *Archiv für Sozialgeschichte*, 13 (1972), 399–482.

123 Caplan, J., *Government without Administration: State and Civil Service in Weimar and Nazi Germany* (Oxford, 1988); Diehl-Thiele, P., *Partei und Staat im Dritten Reich. Untersuchung zum Verhältnis von NSDAP und allgemeiner innerer Staatsverwaltung, 1933–1945* (Munich, 1971), 21–4.

124 Bracher, K.D., *Nationalsozialistische Machtergreifung und Reichskonkordat: zum Frage des geschichtlichen Zusammenhangs und der politischen Verknüpfung von Reichskonkordat und Nationalsozialistischer Revolution* (Wiesbaden, 1956), 910ff; Kershaw, I., *Hitler, 1889–1936: Hubris* (London, 1998), 532ff.

125 Hitler, A., *Mein Kampf* (London, 1972), 402–10; Kershaw, *Hitler: Hubris*, 539f; Diehl-Thiele, ch. 1.

126 Kershaw, I., *The Nazi Dictatorship: Problems and Perspectives of Interpretation* (London 1989, 2nd edn), ch. 4; Bracher, K.D., 'The Role of Hitler: Perspectives of Interpretation', in Laqueur, *Fascism: A Reader's Guide*, 193–212.

127 Hauner, M., 'The Professionals and the Amateurs in National Socialist Foreign Policy: Revolution and Subversion in the Islamic and Indian World', in Hirschfeld, G. and Kettenacker, L. (eds), *Der 'Führerstaat'. Mythos und Realität* (Stuttgart, 1981), 316ff; Jacobsen, H.-A., *Nationalsozialistische Aussenpolitik 1933–1945* (Frankfurt, 1968), 90–160.

128 Michalka, W., 'Joachim von Ribbentrop: From Wine Merchant to Foreign Minister', in Smelser, R. and Zitelmann, R. (eds), *The Nazi Elite* (Houndmills and London, 1993), 165–72; Jacobsen, *Nationalsozialistische Aussenpolitik*, 120ff.

129 Seabury, 67ff.

130 Craig, G.A., 'The German Foreign Office from Neurath to Ribbentrop', in Gilbert, F. and Craig, G.A. (eds), *The Diplomats* (Princeton, 1953), 427ff; Broszat, *Hitler State*, 278ff; Heinemann, 102–3, 119–20. For Goering's missions to Italy see Weinberg, *Diplomatic Revolution*, 90ff, 130ff; for his relations with Franco's regime see Leitz, C., *Economic Relations between Nazi Germany and Franco's Spain, 1936–1945* (Oxford, 1996), 59ff; and for von Papen, ibid., 195ff, 236–7, 266–71.

131 Seabury, 35ff.

132 Michalka, W., *Ribbentrop und die deutsche Weltpolitik 1933–1940. Aussenpolitische Konzeptionen und Entscheidungsprozesse im Dritten Reich* (Munich, 1980), 249ff.

133 Kordt, E., *Nicht aus den Akten* (Stuttgart, 1956), 230ff.

134 Bracher, K.D., 'Stufen totalitärer Machtergreifung', *Vierteljahrshefte für Zeitgeschichte*, 4 (1956), 30–42.

135 Geyer, 'Dynamics of Military Revisionism', 127ff; Deist, W., *The Wehrmacht and German Rearmament* (London and Basingstoke, 1981), 49–51. See Röhm's criticism of the regime's tendency towards 'normalisation' in Broszat, *Hitler State*, 205–6; Fischer, C., 'Ernst Julius Röhm: Chief of Staff of the SA and Indispensible [sic] Outsider', in Smelser, R. and Zitelmann, R. (eds), *The Nazi Elite* (Houndmills and London, 1993), 173–82. For the purge see Messerschmidt, M., 'Reichswehr und Röhm-Affäre', *Militärgeschichtliche Mitteilungen*, 3 (1986), 107–44; Orlow, *Nazi Party*, II, 111ff; Kershaw, *Hitler: Hubris*, 499ff.

136 Wegner, B., 'My Honour is Loyalty: the SS as a Military Factor in Hitler's Germany', in Deist (ed.), *The German Military in the Age of Total War*, 220–39.

137 Deist, *Wehrmacht and German Rearmament*, 38ff.

138 Kershaw, *Hitler: Hubris*, 548–9.

139 Müller, K.-J., *Das Heer und Hitler. Armee und nationalsozialistisches Regime, 1933–1944* (Stuttgart, 1956), 206ff.

140 Michalka, W., (ed.), *Das Dritte Reich*, vol. I: *Volksgemeinschaft und Grossmachtpolitik* (Munich, 1985), 224ff.

141 Seabury, 30–1. See also Goering's comments in ibid., 25–6; and Rosenberg's similar statement in Seraphin, H.G., *Das Politische Tagebuch Alfred Rosenbergs 1934/5 und 1939/40* (Göttingen, Berlin and Frankfurt, 1956), 20.

142 Craig, 'German Foreign Office', 409ff; Heinemann, chaps 3–4.

143 Wollstein, G., *Von Weimarer Revisionismus zu Hitler. Das deutsche Reich und die Grossmächte in der Anfangsphäse der nationalsozialistische Herrschaft in Deutschland* (Bonn and Bad Godesberg, 1973), 96ff.

144 DGFP, C, 4, 574 (Memorandum by von Neurath, 22 February, 1936).

145 Heinemann, 103f; Weinberg, *Diplomatic Revolution*, 194–6. That the Foreign Office was aware of subversive actions organised by the Austrian Nazi Party is evident in DGFP, C, 1, 207 (Köpke report, 23 March 1933).

146 Kershaw, *Hitler: Hubris*, 522–4.

147 Seabury, 46ff; Craig, 'German Foreign Office', 422ff.

148 Weinberg, G.L., 'Hitler and England, 1933–1945: Pretense and Reality', *German Studies Review*, 8 (1995), 299–309.

149 Carr, W., *Arms, Autarky and Aggression: A Study in German Foreign Policy 1933–1939* (London, 1972), 27–9; Orlow, II, 178ff; Heinemann, 138–42.

150 Kettenacker, L., 'The German View', in Douglas, R. (ed.), *1939: A Retrospect Forty Years After* (London, 1983), 28; Parker, R.A.C., 'The First Capitulation: France and the Rhineland Crisis of 1936', *World Politics*, 4 (1951), 355–73.

151 Reynolds, N., *Treason Was No Crime: Ludwig Beck, Chief of the German General Staff* (London, 1976), 106ff.

152 DGFP, C, 5, 33. For an analysis see Schuker, S.A., 'France and the Remilitarisation of the Rhineland, 1936', *French Historical Studies* (1986), 299–337; Kershaw, *Hitler: Hubris*, 584ff.

153 Heinemann, 142ff; Seabury, 53–4, 60ff.

154 Abendroth, H.-H., 'Deutschlands Rolle im Spanischen Bürgerkrieg', in Funke, M. (ed.), *Hitler, Deutschland und die Mächte. Materialien zur Aussenpolitik des Dritten Reiches* (Düsseldorf, 1977), 472–7; Weinberg, *Diplomatic Revolution*, 287ff.

155 Leitz, 92ff; Schieder, W., 'Spanischer Bürgerkrieg und Vierjahresplan. Zur Struktur der nationalsozialistischen Aussenpolitik', in Michalka, W. (ed.), *Nationalsozialistische Aussenpolitik* (Darmstadt, 1978), 325–59; Overy, *The 'Iron Man'*, 44–5.

156 Weinberg, *Diplomatic Revolution*, 285ff; Heinemann, 149ff. For the Wilhelmstrasse's opposition, see Carr, *Arms, Autarky and Aggression*, 66ff.

157 Craig, 'German Foreign Office', 428f; DGFP, D, 3, 1–2.

158 DGFP, D, 3, 267.

159 Deist, *Wehrmacht and German Rearmament*, 40ff; O'Neill, R.J., *The German Army and the Nazi Party, 1933–1939* (London, 1966), 101ff.

160 Deist *et al.*, 'Causes and Preconditions', 348ff; Mason, T., 'The Primacy of Politics – Politics and Economics in National Socialist Germany', in Woolf, S.J. (ed.), *The Nature of Fascism* (London, 1968), 179ff.

161 Müller, K.-J., *General Ludwig Beck. Studien und Dokumente zur politisch-militärischen Vorstellungswelt und Tätigkeit des Generalstabchefs des deutschen Heers 1933–1938* (Boppard, 1980), 351ff, 447ff, 469ff; Deist, *Wehrmacht and German Rearmament*, 86ff.

162 Heinemann, 153ff.

163 DGFP, D, 1, 19.
164 Müller, 'Structure and Nature of the National Conservative Opposition', 151ff; and Müller, 'The German Military Opposition before the Second World War', in Mommsen, W.J. and Kettenacker, L. (eds), *The Fascist Challenge and the Policy of Appeasement* (London, 1983), 65–75.
165 Hossbach, F., *Zwischen Wehrmacht und Hitler, 1934–1938* (Wolfenbüttel and Hannover, 1949), 68ff; Deutsch, K., *Hitler and his Generals. The Hidden Crisis, January– June 1938* (Minneapolis, 1974), 71–5.
166 Deutsch, *Hitler and his Generals*, 78–215; Deutsch, H.C., *Das Komplott oder die Entmachung der Generale. Blomberg- und Fritsch-Krise. Hitlers Weg zum Krieg* (Zurich, 1974).
167 Müller, *Heer und Hitler*, 263–4.
168 DGFP, D, 1, 294.
169 Schwarz, P., *This Man Ribbentrop: His Life and Times* (New York, 1943), 234–5; Michalka, W., 'Joachim von Ribbentrop: From Wine Merchant to Foreign Minister', in Smelser, R. and Zitelmann, R (eds), *The Nazi Elite* (Houndmills and London, 1993), 168ff.
170 Weinberg, G.L., *The Foreign Policy of Hitler's Germany: Starting World War II, 1937– 1939* (Chicago, 1980), 170ff. Göring's role is documented in DGFP, D, 1, 352 (Hitler's letter to Mussolini, 11 March 1938).
171 DGFP, D, 2, Enclosure to Doc. 221 (Directive for 'Operation Green').
172 Müller, *Beck*, 555f; *Heer und Hitler*, 301–331, 650ff; Weinberg, G.L., *Germany, Hitler, and World War II: Essays in Modern German and World History* (Cambridge, 1995), 136– 43.
173 Geyer, 'Dynamics of Military Revisionism', 141ff; Müller, *Heer und Hitler*, 302–5, 309–13; Noakes, 'German Conservatives and the Third Reich', 87ff.
174 Wiedemann, F., *Der Mann der Feldherrwerden wollte* (Kettwig, 1964), 127ff.
175 Deist, *German Rearmament*, 66–8.
176 Weinberg, *Starting World War II*, 387–8.
177 Weinberg, *Hitler*, 142–3.
178 Weinberg, *Hitler*, 114–5, 139–42.
179 Müller, *Heer und Hitler*, 302ff.
180 Müller, *Beck*, 555ff.
181 Müller, *Heer und Hitler*, 317–33; 'Structure and Nature of the National Conservative Opposition', 169–78; Hoffmann, P., *Widerstand, Staatsstreich, Attentat. Der Kampf der Opposition gegen Hitler* (Munich, 1979), ch. 4.
182 Seabury, 93–4.
183 Michalka (ed.), *Das Dritte Reich*, I, 246; *Ribbentrop*, 249ff. For his subsequent policy initiatives towards Britain, see Michalka, 'From Anti-Comintern Pact to the Euro-Asiatic Bloc: Ribbentrop's Alternative Concept to Hitler's Foreign Policy Programme', in Koch, H.W. (ed.), *Aspects of the Third Reich* (Houndmills and London, 1985), 267–84.
184 For von Weizsäcker's opposition see DGFP, D, 1, 86 (Memorandum, 20 December 1937); Hill, L. (ed.), *Die Weizsäcker-Papiere, 1933–1950* (Frankfurt, 1974), 130ff.
185 Seabury, 58ff.
186 Seabury, 60–1, 71–7.
187 Broszat, *Hitler State*, 297–9.
188 DGFP, D, 4, 202 (Report of a conversation between Hitler and Tiso, 13 March 1939).
189 Müller, *Heer und Hitler*, 263ff; Berghahn, V.R., 'NSDAP und "Geistige Führung" der Wehrmacht, 1939–1943', *Vierteljahrshefte für Zeitgeschichte*, 17 (1969), 17–71.
190 Murray, W., *The Change in the European Balance of Power, 1938–1939: The Path to Ruin* (Princeton, 1984), 24–5; Hancock, E., *The National Socialist Leadership and Total War, 1941–5* (New York, 1991), 16ff.

191 Deist, *Wehrmacht and German Rearmament*, 60ff; Dülffer, J., *Weimar, Hitler und die Marine. Reichspolitik und Flottenbau, 1920 bis 1939* (Düsseldorf, 1973), 501ff.

192 Pombeni, 'La forma partito', 219–64; Friedrich, C.J., 'The Unique Character of Totalitarian Society', in Friedrich, C.J. (ed.), *Totalitarianism* (Cambridge, MA, 1954), 47–60.

193 Gentile, E., *Storia del Partito Fascista, 1919–1922: Movimento e milizia* (Rome and Bari, 1989), 247ff; Giurati, G., *La parabola di Mussolini nelle memorie di un gerarca*, ed. by E. Gentile (Rome and Bari, 1981), 92ff.

194 Mommsen, H., 'National Socialism: Continuity and Change', in Laqueur, W. (ed.), *Fascism: A Reader's Guide. Analyses, Interpretations, Bibliography* (London, 1979), 158f; Plewinid, M., *Hitler. Der völkische Publizist Dietrich Eckart* (Bremen, 1970), 85ff.

195 Strasser, O., *Hitler and I* (London, 1940), 108ff; Kershaw, *Hitler: Hubris*, 325ff.

196 Germino, D.L., *The Italian Fascist Party in Power: A Study in Totalitarian Rule* (New York, 1971), 133–9; Sarti, 'Italian Fascism', 14–30.

197 Gentile, E., *Le origini dell'ideologia fascista, 1918–1925* (Rome and Bari, 1975), ch. 5; Germino, 19ff; Payne, S., *A History of Fascism, 1914–1945* (Madison, 1995), 111–12.

198 Gentile, *Ideologia fascista*, 76–90; Sternhell, Z., 'Fascist Ideology', in Laqueur, 345ff; Sternhell, Z., *The Birth of Fascist Ideology. From Cultural Rebellion to Political Revolution* (Princeton, 1994), chaps 3–4.

199 Payne, *History of Fascism*, 110–3; Germino, 83–104; Gentile, *Ideologia fascista*, passim.

200 Farinacci, R., *Un periodo aureo del Partito Nazionale Fascista* (Foligno, 1927), 155–60. For an analysis of Farinacci's views see Gentile, *Ideologia fascista*, 263–76; Hamilton, 54–6.

201 De Felice, R., *Mussolini il fascista*, vol. I: *La conquista del potere, 1921–1925* (Turin, 1966), 55ff.

202 Gentile, E., 'Partito, Stato e Duce nella mitologia e nella organizzazione del fascismo', in Bracher, K.D. and Valiani, L. (eds), *Fascismo e nazionalsocialismo* (Bologna, 1986), 265–94.

203 Lyttelton, 'The Second Wave', 50ff; *The Seizure of Power*, 237–268; Segrè, *Balbo*, 118–38; Rocco, M., *Come il fascismo divenne una dittatura* (Milan, 1956), 124ff.

204 Aquarone, *Stato Totalitario*, 67–8.

205 De Felice, R., *Mussolini il fascista*, II, 62ff.

206 Aquarone, *Stato Totalitario*, 73–92; Gentile, 'The Problem of the Party', 261–70. The text of the law is in Clough, S.B. and Saladino, S. (eds), *A History of Modern Italy: Documents, Readings and Commentary* (New York and London, 1968), 444–5.

207 Aquarone, *Stato Totalitario*, 395–6.

208 De Grand, A.J., *Fascist Italy and Nazi Germany: The 'Fascist' Style of Rule* (London and New York, 1995), 33–7.

209 Bottai, G., 'Bilancio di cinque anni', *Critica Fascista*, 1 October 1930.

210 Bottai, G., *Vent'anni e un giorno (24 luglio 1943)* (Milan, 1977), 42–4.

211 Grandi, D., *Il mio paese. Ricordi autobiografici*, ed. R. De Felice (Bologna, 1985), 201ff.

212 Fried, R.C., *The Italian Prefect* (New Haven, 1963), 181ff; Brooker, P., *The Faces of Fraternalism: Nazi Germany, Fascist Italy and Imperial Japan* (Oxford, 1991), 153–68.

213 Sarti, 'Italian fascism', 25ff.

214 De Grand, *Fascist Italy and Nazi Germany*, 33–4.

215 Lyttelton, *Seizure of Power*, 271–95; Gentile, 'The Problem of the Party', 263ff. For general membership trends see the figures and analysis in Germino, 50–6.

216 Bottai, *Diario*, 9 December 1936. See also Bottai, *Vent'anni*, 37–44.

217 De Grazia, V., *The Culture of Consent: Mass Organisation of Leisure in Fascist Italy* (Cambridge, 1981), 226ff; Germino, 41–5, 62–82.

218 Gentile, 'Partito, Stato e Duce', 285–6; Michaelis, M., *Mussolini and the Jews: German-Italian Relations and the Jewish Question in Italy 1922–1945* (Oxford, 1978), 109ff; De Felice, R., *Storia degli ebrei sotto il fascismo* (Turin, 1972), 271–301.

NOTES

219 Thompson, 79–81; Gentile, E., *Il culto del littorio. La sacralizzazione della politica nell'Italia fascista* (Rome and Bari, 1993), 107–54.

220 Germino, 144 and ch. 8; Gentile, *Storia del Partito Fascista*, viii, 17ff. See also the discussion of the existing historiography in Bosworth, R.J.B., *Italy and the Wider World, 1860–1960* (London and New York, 1996), 36–8.

221 Sarti, 'Italian fascism', 27ff; Brooker, 157–8.

222 Aquarone, *Stato Totalitario*, 269ff; Gentile, *Ideologia fascista*, 218–28. See also Fanelli, G.A., *Contra Gentiles mistificazioni dell'idealismo attuale nella Rivoluzione fascista* (Rome, 1933).

223 Bottai, G., *Vent'anni*, 72; and Bottai, *Diario*, 30 August 1938.

224 Bottai, *Vent'anni*, 25ff; De Grand, A.J., *Bottai e la cultura fascista* (Rome and Bari, 1978), chaps 4, 6.

225 Segrè, *Balbo,*, 271–5, 372–3; Michaelis, M., 'Il Maresciallo dell'aria. Italo Balbo e la politica mussoliniana', *Storia Contemporanea*, 14 (1983), 350ff.

226 Bottai, *Diario*, 6 July 1940.

227 Quoted in De Felice, *Mussolini il duce*, II, 254–5.

228 Michaelis, 'Il Maresciallo dell'aria', 351–2; Casmirri, S., 'Luigi Federzoni', in Cordova, F. (ed.), *Uomini e volti del fascismo* (Rome, 1980), 294ff.

229 Mack Smith, *Mussolini's Roman Empire*, 70, 150ff.

230 DGFP, D, 1, 399 (Plessen to Foreign Ministry, 25 March 1938).

231 Michaelis, 'Il Maresciallo dell'aria', 334–5.

232 Bottai, *Diario*, 14 February 1939; Muggeridge, *Ciano's Diaries*, 21 March 1939; Segrè, *Balbo*, 357–8.

233 Segrè, *Balbo*, 358–62; Grandi, *Il mio paese*, ch. 41; Quartararo, *Roma tra Londra e Berlino*, 468ff.

234 Bottai, *Vent'anni*, 55–62; De Grand, *Bottai*, Ch. VII.

235 Muggeridge, *Ciano's Diaries*, 21 March 1939.

236 Donosti, *Mussolini e l'Europa*, 12ff.

237 Gentile, E., *Il culto del littorio*, 269ff.

238 Clough *et al.* (eds), *History of Modern Italy*, 514–15. For an analysis, see Schröder, J., 'La caduta di Mussolini e la contromisure tedesche nell' Italia centrale fino alla formazione della Repubblica Sociale Italiana', in De Felice, R. (ed.), *L'Italia fra tedeschi e alleati*, 138ff.

239 Stachura, P.D., *Gregor Strasser and the Rise of the Nazi Party* (Newton Abbot, 1969), 22–66; Tyrell, A., 'Gottfried Feder and the NSDAP', in Stachura, P.D. (ed.), *The Shaping of the Nazi State* (London, 1978), 48–87.

240 Struve, 436–8; Mommsen, H., 'National Socialism: Continuity and Change', 154–5. Hitler declared his desire to establish a Senate in August 1933 (Domarus, M. (ed.), *Hitler: Reden und Proklamationen 1932–1945*, vol. I: *1933–1939: Triumph* (Würzburg 1962–3), I, 292, speech to Reichs- and Gauleiters, 6 August 1933) but nothing came out of these declarations. For Strasser's efforts see Stachura, P.D., 'Der "Fall Strasser": Gregor Strasser, Hitler and National Socialism', in Stachura (ed.), *The Shaping of the Nazi State* (London, 1978), 90ff; and, for Ley's plans, Orlow, *Nazi Party*, II, 85ff, 152f, 183ff.

241 Orlow, *Nazi Party*, II, 56–60, 94ff.

242 Nyomarkay, J., *Charisma and Factionalism in the Nazi Party* (Minneapolis, 1967), chaps 3–5.

243 Domarus, I, 411–28 (speech to the Reichstag, 13 July 1934), 447–8 (Proclamation, 5 September 1934).

244 Diehl-Thiele, 135ff; Mommsen, H., 'Ausnahmezustand als Herrschaftstechnik des Nationalsozialistischen-Regimes', in Funke, M. (ed.), *Hitler, Deutschland und die Mächte. Materialien zur Aussenpolitik des Dritten Reiches* (Düsseldorf, 1977), 35ff.

231

245 Schoenbaum, D., *Hitler's Social Revolution: Class and Status in Nazi Germany, 1933–1939* (New York and London, 1980), 22ff.
246 Diehl-Thiele, 210f; Orlow, *Nazi Party*, II, 131ff.
247 Domarus, I, 401–2 (1 July 1934).
248 Orlow, *Nazi Party*, II, 138ff.
249 Caplan, *Government without Administration*, chaps 5–6; Mommsen, H., *Beamtentum im Dritten Reich. Mit ausgewählten Quellen zur nationalsozialistischen Beamtenpolitik* (Stuttgart, 1966), 45ff. For the role of the Ministry of the Interior under Frick see Peterson, E.N., *The Limits of Hitler's Power* (Princeton, 1969), 77–148, who however exaggerates the importance of these institutional limits to the actual power of the Nazi leader.
250 Orlow, *Nazi Party*, II, 226–7.
251 Orlow, *Nazi Party*, II, 202–7; Brooker, 88–104. On the NSDAP's membership trends, see Kater, M., *The Nazi Party: A Social Profile of Members and Leaders, 1919–1945* (Oxford, 1983), 263–7, figs. 1–5.
252 Berghahn, 'NSDAP und "Geistige Führung"', 19ff.
253 Quote from Jacobsen, *Nationalsozialistische Aussenpolitik*, 45ff.
254 Overy, *Goering*, chaps 3–5; Orlow, *Nazi Party*, II, 178ff; Kershaw, *Hitler: Hubris*, 538ff; Michalka, 'Joachim von Ribbentrop', 168ff; Lösener, B., 'Als Rassereferent im Reichsministerium des Innern', *Vierteljahrshefte für Zeitgeschichte*, 9 (1961), 135–61; Hausser, P., *Soldaten wie andere auch. Der Weg der Waffen-SS* (Osnabrück, 1966), 152ff.
255 Speer, A., *Inside the Third Reich* (London, 1970), chaps 7, 9; Kube, A., 'Hermann Goering: The Second Man in the Reich', and Froehlich, E., 'Joseph Goebbels: The Propagandist', both in Smelser and Zitelmann (ed.), *Nazi Elite*, 62–73 and 48–61 respectively.
256 Orlow, *Nazi Party*, II, 172–3.
257 Von Kotze, H., Krausnick, H. (eds), *Es spricht der Führer* (Gütersloh, 1966), 132–57.
258 Mommsen, H., 'Ausnahmezustand', 43.
259 Weinberg, *Diplomatic Revolution*, 225–6, 312ff; *Starting World War II*, 288ff, 327ff.
260 Ross, D., *Hitler und Dollfuss. Die deutsche Österreichpolitik. 1933–1934* (Hamburg, 1966), passim.
261 Schieder, 'Spanischer Bürgerkrieg', 325–59.
262 Orlow, *Nazi Party*, II, 231–40.
263 Diehl-Thiele, 216ff; Hüttenberg, P., *Die Gauleiter* (Stuttgart, 1969).
264 Krausnick, H., Buchheim, H., Broszat, M. and Jacobsen, H.-A. (eds), *Anatomy of the SS State* (London, 1968). For the Aryanisation Programme, see Orlow, *Nazi Party*, II, 250–1.
265 Overy, *Goering*, 80–1, 88–94; Mommsen, H., 'Reflections on the position of Hitler and Göring in the Third Reich', in Childers, T. and Caplan, J. (eds), *Reevaluating the Third Reich* (New York and London, 1993), 94–5.
266 Cecil, R., *The Myth of the Master Race: Alfred Rosenberg and Nazi Ideology* (London, 1972), 77ff, 141ff.

4 FASCIST EXPANSIONISM IN PRACTICE

1 For the text of Wilson's Fourteen Points see Snyder, L.L., *Historic Documents of World War I* (New York, 1958), 164; and for his 'vision' of a future Europe, Walworth, A., *Wilson and his Peacemakers: American Diplomacy at the Paris Peace Conference, 1919* (New York and London, 1986), 40–63.
2 Foster, A.J., 'Britain and East Central Europe, 1918–1948', in Stirk, P. (ed.), *Mitteleuropa: History and Prospects* (Edinburgh, 1994), 112–15.

3 Matthias, E., 'The Influence of the Versailles Treaty on the Internal Development of the Weimar Republic', in Nicholls, A. and Matthias, E. (eds), *German Democracy and the Triumph of Hitler* (London, 1971), 11–28.

4 Sharp, A., *The Versailles Settlement: Peacemaking in Paris, 1919* (London, 1991), 104–6.

5 McCrum, R., 'French Rhineland Policy at the Paris Peace Conference, 1919', *Historical Journal*, 21 (1978), 623–48.

6 Lundgreen-Nielsen, K., *The Polish Issue at the Paris Peace Conference: A Study of the Policies of the Great Powers and the Poles, 1918–1919* (Odensee, 1979).

7 Stadler, K.S., *The Birth of the Austrian Republic, 1918–1921* (Leyden, 1968); Low, A.P., *The Anschluss Movement 1918–1919 and the Paris Peace Conference* (Philadelphia, 1974).

8 Nelson, H.I., *Land and Power: British and Allied Policy on Germany's Frontiers, 1916–1919* (London, 1963), 272–81.

9 Campbell, F.G., 'The Struggle for Upper Silesia, 1919–1922', *Journal of Modern History*, 42 (1970), 361–85.

10 Henderson, W. O., *The German Colonial Empire, 1884–1919* (London, 1993), 117–33; Stoecker, H. (ed.), *German Imperialism in Africa: From the Beginnings until the Second World War* (London, 1986), 270–96.

11 Schmokel, W.W., *Dream of Empire: German Colonialism, 1919–1945* (New Haven and London, 1964), 64ff.

12 Sharp, 163–5.

13 Anderson, M., *Frontiers: Territory and State in the Modern World* (Cambridge, 1996), 45–8; Temperley, H.W.V. (ed.), *A History of the Peace Conference of Paris* (London 1920–4), vol. 4, 278–95.

14 Albrecht-Carrié, R., *Italy at the Paris Peace Conference* (New York, 1966), 114ff. For the inconclusive Italo–Yugoslav negotiations at Paris see Temperley, 4, 296–326, and 327–37 for Rapallo.

15 Smith, M.L., *The Ionian Vision: Greece in Asia Minor* (London, 1973), 68–82, 129; Helmreich, P.C., *From Paris to Sevres: The Partition of the Ottoman Empire at the Peace Conferences of 1919–1920* (Columbus, 1974), 314–37.

16 Cassels, A., *Mussolini's Early Diplomacy* (Princeton, 1970), 21–45; Smith, *Ionian Vision*, 266–336.

17 Lederer, I.J., *Yugoslavia at the Paris Peace Conference: A Study in Frontiermaking* (Yale, 1963).

18 De Grand, A.J., *The Italian Nationalist Association and the Rise of Fascism in Italy* (Lincoln and London, 1978), 102–5.

19 Federzoni, L., *Il trattato di Rapallo. Con un' appendice di documenti* (Bologna, 1921).

20 Ledeen, M.A., *The First Duce* (Baltimore and London, 1977).

21 Howard, M., 'The Legacy of the First World War', in Boyce, R. and Robertson, E.M. (eds), *Paths to War: New Essays on the Origins of the Second World War* (Houndmills and London, 1989), 50–1; Albrecht-Carrié, *Diplomatic History*, 100–3, 141–9.

22 Hughes, S., 'The Early Diplomacy of Italian Fascism: 1922–1932', in Craig, G. and Gilbert, F.A. (eds), *The Diplomats 1919–1939* (Princeton, 1953), 210–4; Knox, M., 'Il fascismo e la politica estera italiana', in Bosworth, R.J.B. and Romano, S. (eds), *La politica estera italiana (1860–1985)* (Bologna, 1991), 290ff.

23 Di Nolfo, E., *Mussolini e la politica estera italiana 1919–1933* (Padova, 1960), 12ff.

24 Di Nolfo, *Politica estera*, 17–21.

25 Hiden, J.W., *The Weimar Republic* (London, 1974), 25–31. See also Jacobson, J., *Locarno Diplomacy* (Princeton, 1972); Lee, M.M. and Michalka, W., *German Foreign Policy 1917–1933* (Leamington Spa, Hamburg and New York, 1987), 112–48. For the role of Stresemann in German revisionism see Bretton, H.L., *Stresemann and the Revision of Versailles* (Stanford, 1953); Zimmermann, L., *Deutsche Aussenpolitik in der Ära der Weimarer Republik* (Berlin and Frankfurt, 1958).

26 The reactions of the foreign governments to the appointment of Mussolini were mixed. See Cassels, 3–18; DDI, 7th, I, 38/50/84/127/130; Di Nolfo, A., 'L'opinione pubblica europea e l'ascesa di Mussolini', *Il Mulino*, 10 (1954), 635–47.

27 Mussolini, B., *Scritti e discorsi di Benito Mussolini* (Milan 1934–1939), III, 59–73; translated in Delzell, C.F. (ed.), *Mediterranean Fascism, 1919–1945* (New York, Evanston and London, 1970), 45–51.

28 Reichman, S. and Golan, A., 'Irredentism and Boundary Adjustments in Post-World War I Europe', in Chazan, N. (ed.), *Irredentism and International Politics* (London, 1991), 57–61; Lowe, C. J. and Marzari, F., *Italian Foreign Policy 1870–1940* (London and Boston, 1975), chaps 7–8.

29 Cassels, chaps 1, 4, 10.

30 De Grand, *Nationalist Association*, 117f; Salvatorelli, L. and Mira, G., *Storia dell'Italia nel periodo fascista* (Turin, 1957), 153ff.

31 Di Nolfo, *Politica estera*, 54–5; De Grand, *Nationalist Association*, ch. 7

32 DDI, 7th, I, 141/159; Cassels, 201–15; Mack Smith, D., *Le guerre di Mussolini* (Rome and Bari, 1976), 43–58.

33 Cassels, 127–45; Di Nolfo, *Politica estera*, 170ff.

34 For the importance of Adriatic irredentism in Italian nationalism see Vivante, A., *Irredentismo Adriatico* (Florence, 1954); De Grand, *Nationalist Association*, ch. 6; Webster, R.A., *Industrial Imperialism in Italy 1908–1915* (Berkeley and Los Angeles, 1975), especially 333ff.

35 Cassels, 216–18; Di Nolfo, *Politica estera*, 147ff.

36 DDI, 7th, III, 388.

37 Veneruso, D., *L'Italia fascista, 1922–1945* (Bologna, 1981), 137–45; Di Nolfo, *Politica estera*, 173–95.

38 Salvemini, G., *Prelude to the Second World War* (London, 1953), 353ff; Hughes, 223–5.

39 Hughes, 224ff; Lowe and Marzari, ch. 11.

40 Salvemini, G., *Mussolini Diplomatico* (Bari, 1952), 382–3.

41 Zimmermann, ch. 7. For Germany's position in the Disarmament Conference see Craig, G., 'The German Foreign Office from Neurath to Ribbentrop', in Craig and Gilbert, 409–14; Heineman, J.L, *Hitler's Foreign Minister. Constantin Freiherr von Neurath, Diplomat and Statesman* (London, 1979), 51–8.

42 Lowe and Marzari, 223ff.

43 Zimmermann, chaps 6, 9–12.

44 Townsend, M.E. 'The Contemporary Colonial Movement in Germany', *Political Science Quarterly*, 43 (1928), 64–75; Dix, A., *Weltkrise und Kolonialpolitik* (Berlin, 1932).

45 Hillgruber, A., 'Kontinuität und Diskontinuität in der deutschen Aussenpolitik von Bismarck bis Hitler', in Hillgruber (ed.), *Grossmachtpolitik und Militarismus im 20. Jahrhundert* (Düsseldorf, 1974), 22ff; Nipperdey, T., '1933 and the Continuity of German History', in Koch, H.W. (ed.), *Aspects of the Third Reich* (London, 1985), 489–508.

46 Wollstein, G., 'Eine Denkschrift des Staatssekretärs Bernhard von Bülow vom März 1933. Wilhelminische Konzeption der Aussenpolitik zu Beginn der Nationalsozialistischen Herrschaft', *Militärgeschichtliche Mitteilungen*, 1 (1973), 77ff; Krüger, P., Hahn, E. J.C., 'Der Loyalitätskonflikt des Staatssekretärs von Bülow im Frühjahr 1933', *Vierteljahrshefte für Zeitgeschichte*, 20 (1972), 376–410. A translation of its important points is in Noakes, J. and Pridham, G. (eds), *Nazism: A Documentary Reader*, vol. III: *Foreign Policy, War and Racial Extermination* (Exeter, 1988), 653–7.

47 Noakes, Pridham (eds), *Nazism*, III, 632–3; Deist, W., Messerschmidt, M., Volkmann, H.-E. and Wette, W., 'Causes and Preconditions of German Aggression', in Deist, W. (ed.), *The German Military in the Age of Total War* (Leamington Spa, 1985), 343ff.

48 Laffan, M., 'Weimar and Versailles: German Foreign Policy, 1919–33', in Laffan, M. (ed.), *The Burden of German History, 1919–1945* (London, 1989), 81–102.

49 Vogelsang, T., 'Neue Dokumente zur Geschichte der Reichswehr 1930–1933', *Vierteljahrshefte für Zeitgeschichte*, 2 (1954), 435 (and Noakes and Pridham, *Nazism*, III, 628–9, for a translation).

50 Weinberg, G.L., *The Foreign Policy of Hitler's Germany: Diplomatic Revolution in Europe, 1933–1936* (Chicago, 1970), 159–67; Craig, 'The German Foreign Office', 409–18.

51 Domarus, M., *Hitler: Reden und Proklamationen*, vol. I: *Triumph (1932–1938)* (Würzburg, 1962), 278–9 and 305–14.

52 Craig, 'German Foreign Office', 413ff; Wheeler-Bennett, J.W., *The Disarmament Deadlock* (London, 1934), 113ff.

53 DBFP, 2nd, VI, 803ff; and, for French fears about the fate of Locarno and German intentions, DDF, 2nd, I, 36.

54 DGFP, C, 4, Enclosure 529 (Ribbentrop's report, 20 January, 1936); C, 4, 71–2; Funke, M., '7 März 1936. Fallstudie zur aussenpolitischen Führungsstil Hitlers', in Michalka, W. (ed.), *Nazionalsozialistische Aussenpolitik* (Darmstadt, 1978), 277–324.

55 Emmerson, J.T., *The Rhineland Crisis, 7 March 1936: A Study in Multilateral Diplomacy* (London, 1977); Funke, M., *Sanktionen und Kanonen. Hitler, Mussolini und der nationale Abessinienkonflikt 1935–1936* (Düsseldorf, 1970), 135ff; Kershaw, I., *Hitler, 1889–1936: Hubris* (London, 1998), 581ff; Schmidt, P., *Statist auf diplomatischer Bühne* (Bonn, 1949), 319ff.

56 Quoted in Kershaw, *Hitler: Hubris*, 589.

57 Weinberg, *Diplomatic Revolution*, 357–64.

58 Taylor, A.J.P., *The Origins of the Second World War* (London, 1961), 67–8.

59 Kettenacker, L., 'The German View', in Douglas, R. (ed.), *1939: A Retrospect Forty Years After* (London, 1983), 26–8; Craig, G.A., *Germany 1866–1945* (Oxford, 1978), 678ff.

60 von Strandmann, H.P., 'Imperialism and Revisionism in Interwar Germany', in Mommsen, W.J. and Osterhammel, J. (eds), *Imperialism and After: Continuities and Discontinuities* (London, Boston and Sydney, 1986), 90ff.

61 DGFP, C, 1, 142 (Conference of Ministers, 7 April 1933).

62 Geyer, M., *Aufrüstung oder Sicherheit? Die Reichswehr und die Krise der Machtpolitik 1924–1936* (Wiesbaden, 1980), 188ff.

63 Domarus, I, 229–38 and, for a repetition of the same appeal in May 1933, 270–9; Roberts, H.L., 'The Diplomacy of Colonel Beck', in Craig and Gilbert, 579–614.

64 DGFP, C, 1, 168 (Wysocki to Foreign Ministry, 20 April 1933).

65 DBFP, 2nd, 6, 59.

66 DGFP, C, 2, 79/81/82.

67 DGFP, C, 1, 273. See also Weinberg, *Diplomatic Revolution*, 65ff.

68 Seabury, P., *The Wilhelmstrasse: A Study of German Diplomats under the Nazi Regime* (Berkeley, 1954), 38ff.

69 DGFP, C, 1, 136/140/147.

70 Kershaw, *Hitler: Hubris*, 544ff; Craig, 'German Foreign Office', 417–18.

71 DGFP, C, 1, 457; C, 2, 118–9/122.

72 Weinberg, *Diplomatic Revolution*, 182–3; Craig, 'German Foreign Office', 417–18.

73 DGFP, C, 3, 474.

74 Weinberg, *Diplomatic Revolution*, 186–7.

75 DGFP, C, 3, 25.

76 Heinemann, 93ff; Weinberg, *Diplomatic Revolution*, 282ff.

77 Chazan, N., 'Irredentism, Separatism and Nationalism', in Chazan, 139–51.

78 Meyer, H.C., *Mitteleuropa in German Thought and Action, 1815–1945* (The Hague, 1955), 291–7; Temperley, 4, 465–9. For a contemporary presentation of the pro-

union argument see Renner, K., *Deutschland, Österreich und die Völker des Ostens* (Berlin, 1922).

79 'Irredentismo', in Levi, F., Levra, U. and Tranfaglia, N. (eds), *Storia d'Italia* (Florence, 1978), II, 573–82.

80 Webster, 106–7, 336.

81 Knox, 'Fascismo e politica estera italiana', 296.

82 The fascist involvement in irredentist movements in Corsica and Malta is documented in Cassels, 86ff. See also, in this study, Chapter 3.

83 Bianchini, S., 'L'idea fascista dell' impero nell' area danubiano-balcanica', in Di Nolfo, A., Rainero, R.H. and Vigezzi, B. (eds), *L'Italia e la politica di potenza in Europa (1938–1940)* (Milan, 1986), 174ff; Casella, F. 'L'immagine fascista dell'impero: quale ruolo all'Adriatico', in ibid., 187–203.

84 Morewood, S., 'Anglo-Italian Rivalry in the Mediterranean and Middle East 1935–1940', in Boyce and Robertson, 181ff.

85 DGFP, D, 4, 412.

86 Vogelsang, 'Neue Dokumente', n. 7, 434ff; and Noakes and Pridham, *Nazism*, III, 628–9, for translated excerpts.

87 Perman, D., *The Shaping of the Czechoslovak State* (Leiden, 1962); Stadler, K.S., *The Birth of the Austrian Republic 1918–1932* (Leyden, 1968).

88 Pauley, B.F., *Hitler and the Forgotten Nazis: A History of Austrian National Socialism* (London and Basingstoke, 1981), 122–37; Gholdner, F., *Dollfuss: Im Spiegel der US-Akten* (St Pölten 1979), 132–41.

89 Irving, D., *The War Path: Hitler's Germany, 1933–1939* (London, 1978), 61; Meyer, 315–25.

90 Müller, K.-J., *General Ludwig Beck. Studien und Dokumente zur politisch-militärischen Vorstellungswelt und Tätigkeit des Generalstabchefs des deutschen Heers 1933–1938* (Boppard, 1980), 512ff; Wright, J. and Stafford, P., 'Hitler, Britain and the Hossbach Memorandum', *Militärgeschichtliche Mitteilungen*, 42 (1987), 77–123.

91 DGFP, D, 7, Appendix III, Doc. K; Noakes, J. and Pridham, G. (eds), *Documents on Nazism, 1919–1945* (London, 1974), 529–30.

92 DGFP, D, 1, 145/147/151; Weinberg, G.L., *The Foreign Policy of Hitler's Germany: Starting World War II, 1937–1939* (Chicago, 1980), 122ff.

93 Weinberg, G.L., *Germany, Hitler, and World War II: Essays in Modern German and World History* (Cambridge, 1995), 106ff, and *Starting World War II*, 297–8.

94 Wheeler-Bennett, J.W., *Munich: Prologue to Tragedy* (London, 1962); Murray, W., *The Change in the European Balance of Power, 1938–1939: The Path to Ruin* (Princeton, 1984), 195–263.

95 Kirkpatrick, I.S., *The Inner Circle* (London, 1959), 114ff. On Hitler's abortive attempt to implicate Hungary in his campaign against Czechoslovakia, by urging the Hungarians to raise irredentist claims, see DGFP, D, 4, 202. For Slovakia, see Hönsch, J.K., *Die Slowakei und Hitlers Ostpolitik* (Cologne, 1965).

96 The text of the Treaty (DGFP, D, 2, 675) repeatedly emphasises the 'German' character of the ceded territories. For the irredentist justification behind Chamberlain's appeasement efforts in September 1938, see Douglas, R., 'Chamberlain and Appeasement', in Mommsen, W.J. and Kettenacker, L. (eds), *The Fascist Challenge and the Policy of Appeasement* (London, 1983), 83ff.

97 Michalka, *Das Dritte Reich* (Munich, 1985), vol. I: *Volksgemeinschaft und Grossmachtpolitik*, 224–5.

98 Gutmann, E., 'Concealed or Conjured Irredentism: The Case of Alsace', in Chazan, 44ff.

99 Toscano, M., *Alto Adige – South Tyrol: Italy's Frontier with the German World* (Baltimore, 1975), 1–15; Alcock, A.E., *The History of the South Tyrol Question* (Geneva, 1970), 19–

45; De Felice, R., *Il problema dell'Alto Adige nei rapporti italo-tedeschi dall'Anschluss alla fine della seconda guerra mondiale* (Bologna, 1973), Ch. 1.

100 Schubert, G., *Anfänge Nationalsozialistischer Aussenpolitik* (Cologne, 1961), 76ff; De Felice, *I rapporti tra fascismo e nazionalsocialismo fino all'andata al potere di Hitler 1922–1933. Appunti e documenti* (Naples, 1971), 206ff. For the importance of the German-Italian relations for the radicalisation of fascism in the late 1930s see below, Chapter 5.

101 Hitler, A., *Mein Kampf*, translated by Ralph Mannheim (London, 1972), 571–5.

102 DDI, 7th, I, 131; Schubert, G., *Anfänge Nationalsozialistischer Aussenpolitik* (Cologne, 1961), 76–81.

103 Hitler, A., *Sämtliche Aufzeichnungen*, edited by E. Jäckel, and A. Kuhn (Stuttgart, 1980), 727–8 (speech to party members in Munich, 14 November 1922). In general see Petersen, J., *Hitler und Mussolini. Die Entstehung der Achse Berlin-Rom 1933–1936* (Tübingen, 1973), 65–8; and, in this study, Chapter 4.

104 Hitler, *Mein Kampf*, 597–8.

105 DGFP, D, 1, 19 (Hossbach Conference report); and, for a translation, Noakes and Pridham, *Nazism*, III, 681.

106 Quartararo, R., *Roma tra Londra e Berlino. La politica estera fascista dal 1930 al 1940* (Rome, 1980), 307ff.

107 Quoted in Deakin, F.W., *The Brutal Friendship: Mussolini, Hitler and the Fall of Italian Fascism* (New York and London, 1962), 5–6. See also Quartararo, 424ff.

108 Segrè, C.G., 'Il colonialismo e la politica estera: variazioni liberali e fasciste', in Bosworth and Romano, *La politica estera italiana*, 132; Rumi, G., '"Revisionismo" fascista ed espansione coloniale (1925–1935)', in Aquarone, A. and Vernassa, A. (eds), *Il regime fascista* (Bologna, 1974), 448–9, 460, 463.

109 Knox, 'Politica estera italiana', 296, 298–9; Segrè, 'Il colonialismo', 140–1.

110 Segrè, *The Fourth Shore: The Italian Colonization of Libya* (Chicago and London, 1974), 47ff. For Somalia, see Rochat, G., *Il colonialismo italiano* (Turin, 1973), 136; Del Boca, A., *Gli italiani in Africa orientale* (Rome and Bari, 1976), 861–72.

111 De Felice, R., *Mussolini il fascista*, vol. I: *La conquista del potere, 1921–1925* (Turin, 1966), 375; vol. II: *L'organizzazione dello Stato Fascista, 1925–1929* (Turin, 1968), 652ff.

112 Rochat, *Colonialismo*, 96–105, 136. Especially for the case of Libya see Evans-Pritchard, E.E., *The Sanusi of Cyrenaica* (Oxford, 1949); Segrè, *Fourth Shore*, 41, 46–8.

113 Rochat, *Colonialismo*, 98ff; Bosworth, R.J.B., *Italy and the Wider World, 1860–1960* (London, 1996), 104–5.

114 Rochat, *Colonialismo*, 136–7.

115 Rochat, *Colonialismo*, 103–5.

116 Amongst a plethora of works, see Rochat, G., *Militari e politici nella preparazione della campagna d'Etiopia. Studio e documenti, 1932–1936* (Milan, 1971); Rochat, *Colonialismo*, 136–45; Badoglio, P., *La guerra d'Etiopia* (Milan, 1936); Graziani, R., *Il fronte sud* (Milan, 1938); Robertson, E. M., *Mussolini as Empire-Builder: Europe and Africa 1932–36* (London and Basingstoke, 1977), chaps 14–15.

117 De Felice, R., *Mussolini il duce*, vol. 1: *Gli anni del consenso, 1919–1936* (Turin, 1968), 758ff.

118 Bosworth, *Italy and the Wider World*, 48ff; Segrè, C.G., 'Il colonialismo e la politica estera', 121–46.

119 Pastorelli, L., 'La storiografia italiana del dopoguerra sulla politica estera', *Storia e Politica*, 10 (1971), 603ff.

120 Catalano, F., *L'economia italiana di guerra. La politica economico-finanziaria del fascismo dalla guerra d'Etiopia alla caduta del regime, 1935–1943* (Milan, 1969), 7ff. See also Lyttelton, A., 'Italian Fascism', in Laqueur, W. (ed.), *Fascism: A Reader's Guide. Analyses, Interpretations, Bibliography* (Harmondsworth, 1979), 107–8.

121 Rochat, G., 'Il ruolo delle forze armate nel regime fascista: conclusioni provvisorie e ipotesi di lavoro', *Rivista di Storia Contemporanea*, 1 (1972), 188–99; Baer, G.W., *The Coming of the Italo-Ethiopian War* (Cambridge, MA, 1967).

122 Knox, M., 'Conquest, Domestic and Foreign, in Fascist Italy and Nazi Germany', *Journal of Modern History*, 56 (1984), 43–9; and 'Fascismo e politica estera', 329–30.

123 Bosworth, *Italy and the Wider World*, 98–9, 106.

124 Bosworth, R.J.B., *Italy, the Least of the Great Powers: Italian Foreign Policy Before the First World War* (Cambridge, 1979), 329ff.

125 Rochat, *Militari e politici*, 21ff.

126 Vedovato, G., *Gli accordi Italo-Etiopici dell'agosto 1928* (Florence, 1956), 101–5; Candeloro, G., *Storia dell'Italia moderna*, vol. 9: *Il fascismo e le sue guerre* (Milan 1998, 8th edn), 336ff.

127 Knox, 'Fascismo e politica estera', 320–1.

128 Guariglia, R., *Ricordi* (Naples, 1950), 763–73; Rochat, *Militari*, 276–93; Candeloro, 337ff.

129 De Felice, R., *Mussolini il duce*, I, 399ff.

130 *OO*, XXIX, 465.

131 Rochat, *Colonialismo*, 137ff; Lowe and Marzari, 246ff.

132 Del Boca, *Gli italiani in Africa*, 177ff; Rochat, *Militari*, 276ff.

133 Rochat, *Militari*, 225ff, 324–7; Candeloro, 381ff.

134 Rochat, *Militari*, 376–9; *Colonialismo*, 138ff; Knox, 'Fascismo e politica estera', 322ff.

135 DDI, 7th, X, 413.

136 De Felice, R., *Mussolini il duce*, I, 526ff; Quartararo, 97ff.

137 DBFP, 2nd, 12, 722. See also Baer, 159ff; Kirkpatrick, S.I., *Mussolini: Study of a Demagogue* (London, 1964), 275ff; Robertson, *Empire-Builder*, ch. 10.

138 Quartararo, 100ff.

139 Eden, A., *The Memoirs of the Rt. Hon. Sir Anthony Eden, KG, PC, MC*, vol. 2: *Facing the Dictators* (London, 1962), 221ff. For Guariglia's negative attitude, see Guariglia, 245–6.

140 Candeloro, 377.

141 Rochat, *Colonialismo*, 138–40.

142 Candeloro, 383ff; Mack Smith, *Italy and its Monarchy* (New Haven and London, 1989), 270–1.

143 Guerri, G.B. (ed.), *Giuseppe Bottai: Diario, 1935–1944* (Milan 1996, 3rd edn), 19 November–24 November 1935.

144 Candeloro, 374ff; Lowe and Marzari, 270ff.

145 Robertson, *Empire-Builder*, 155–83.

146 Quartararo, R., 'L'Italia e lo Yemen. Uno studio sulla politica di espensione italiana nel Mar Rosso', *Storia Contemporanea*, 190 (1979), 811–67.

147 Aloisi, P., *Journal 25 Juin–14 Juillet 1936* (Paris, 1957), 17 August 1935.

148 Aloisi, 9–10 August 1936.

149 Guariglia, 265ff.

150 For the plan see DDI, 8th, II, 354/360; and, for the Italian reply, II, 366.

151 Quartararo, ch. 2. See aksi De Felice, R., *Mussolini il duce*, I, 389–411.

152 DDI, 8th, II, 860/856/865/870 respectively.

153 Colarizi, S., 'L'opinione pubblica italiana di fronte all'intervento in guerra', in Di Nolfo, Rainero and Vigezzi, 287–301; Colarizi, S., *L'opinione degli italiani sotto il regime, 1929–1943* (Rome and Bari, 1991), 193–7.

154 Mack Smith, *Italy and its Monarchy*, 270–1; Bottai, *Diario*, 6 November 1935.

155 Bottai, *Diario*, 3 May 1936.

156 De Felice, R., *Mussolini il duce*, I, 633ff.

157 Bottai, *Diario*, 10–25 December 1935; and 35–50. See also the Grand Council resolution of 16 November 1935 in *OO*, XXVII, 183.

158 *OO*, XXVII, 268f (speech in Rome, 9 May 1936), and Delzell, 201–2, for a translation.
159 Rochat, *Colonialismo*, 137, 219ff; Baer, passim; Segrè, 'Il colonialismo', 137.
160 De Felice, R., 'Alcune osservazioni sulla politica estera mussoliniana', in De Felice, R. (ed.), *L'Italia fra tedeschi e alleati. La politica estera fascista e la seconda guerra mondiale* (Bologna, 1973), 57–74; *Mussolini il duce*, I, 378–9. See also Knox, M., 'The Fascist Regime, its Foreign Policy and its Wars: An "Anti-Anti-Fascist" Orthodoxy?', in Finney, P. (ed.), *The Origins of the Second World War* (London and New York, 1997), 153–4.
161 For 'determinant weight', see De Felice, *Mussolini il duce*, I, 415ff. For the Four Power Pact see ibid., 464ff.
162 Rochat, *Militari*, 376–9; Lowe and Marzari, ch. 12.
163 De Felice, *Mussolini il duce*, II, 333ff. See Knox's criticism of this view in 'The Fascist Regime', 153–5.
164 DGFP, C, 1, 256–60 (Neurath's views); and Michalka, W. (ed.), *Das Dritte Reich*, vol. 1: *Volksgemeinschaft und Grossmachtpolitik* (Munich, 1985), 216ff (von Bülow's 1933 memorandum).
165 Weinberg, 'German Colonial Plans and Policies 1938–1942', in Besson, W. and von Gärtringer, F. Freiherr (eds), *Geschichte und Gegenwartsbewusstsein. Historische Betrachtungen und Untersuchungen. Festschrift für Hans Rothfels* (Göttingen, 1963), 473ff.
166 DGFP, C, 3, 555. See also Townsend, M.E., 'The German Colonies and the Third Reich', *Political Science Quarterly*, 53 (1938), 197.
167 Weinberg, *Diplomatic Revolution in Europe 1933–36*, 250ff.
168 Schmokel, 95–101; Carr, W., *Hitler: A Study in Personality and Politics* (London, 1978), 48ff.
169 Hitler, *Mein Kampf*, 120–43, 588ff.
170 See above, n. 103.
171 Baynes, N.H. (ed.), *The Speeches of Adolf Hitler, April 1922–August 1939* (New York, London and Toronto, 1942), II, 927 (*Parteitag* speech at Nuremberg, 12 September 1936); II, 1370–2 (speech in Augsburg, 21 November 1937); II, 1574–5 (speech to the Reichstag, 30 January 1939).
172 DGFP, D, 1, enclosure to Doc. 31. See also Schmokel, 110–26.
173 Gilbert, M. and Gott, R., *The Appeasers* (London, 1963), 95ff.
174 Baynes, II, 1359ff (conversation with journalists, 12 September 1937), 1389–90 (speech to the Reichstag, 30 January 1939).
175 Baynes, II, 1574–5 (speech to the Reichstag, 30 January 1939).
176 DGFP, D, 6, 433.
177 Baynes, II, 1686–9 (conversation with Sir Nevile Henderson, 25 August 1939), and Domarus, M. (ed.), *Hitler: Reden und Proklamationen 1932–1945*, vol. II: *Untergang (1939–1945)* (Würzburg, 1963), 1255–9 (conversation with Henderson, 25 August 1939); DGFP, D, 7, 265.
178 Hillgruber, A., *Hitlers Strategie. Politik und Kriegführung 1940–1* (Frankfurt am Main, 1965); 'Der Faktor Amerika in Hitlers Strategie 1938–1941', in Hillgruber A. (ed.), *Deutschlands Grossmacht- und Weltpolitik im 19. und 20. Jahrhundert*, (Düsseldorf, 1977), 197–222; 'Kontinuität und Diskontinuität in der deutschen Aussenpolitik von Bismarck bis Hitler', in Hillgruber, A. (ed.), *Grossmachtpolitik und Militarismus im 20. Jahrhundert. 3 Beiträge zum Kontinuitätsproblem* (Düsseldorf, 1974), 11–36; Aigner, D., 'Hitler's Ultimate Aims – A Programme of World Dominion?', in Koch, H.W. (ed.), *Aspects of the Third Reich* (London, 1985), 251–66.
179 DGFP, D, 1, 19 (Hossbach Conference report).
180 Michaelis, M., 'World Power Status or World Domination?', *Historical Journal*, 15 (1972), 331–60; Koch, H.W., 'Die Rolle des Sozialdarwinismus als Faktor im

Zeitalter des neuen Imperialismus um die Jahrhundertwende', *Zeitschrift für Politik*, 17 (1970), 51–70.

181 Jacobsen, H.-A. (ed.), *Generaloberst Halder: Kriegstagebuch* (Stuttgart, 1962), II, 46ff. For an analysis, see Jäckel, E., *Hitler in History* (Hannover and London, 1987), ch. 4.

182 For references to *Mittelafrika*, see Hitler's exposition to Molotov (November 1940), in DGFP, D, 11, 325/326; Noakes and Pridham, *Nazism*, III, 801–8. See also Hildebrand, 'Deutsche-Mittelafrika – Ein Kriegsziel Hitlers in der Jahren 1940–1942?', in Funke, M. (ed.), *Hitler, Deutschland, und die Mächte. Materialien zur Aussenpolitik des Dritten Reiches* (Düsseldorf, 1977), 383–406. See an interesting discussion and assessment of the various arguments in Kershaw, I., *The Nazi Dictatorship: Problems and Perspectives of Interpretation* (London 1989, 2nd edn), 125–30.

183 Mack Smith, *Italy and its Monarchy*, 272–4.

184 Lowe and Marzari, 294–6.

185 Bottai, *Diario*, 24 November 1938.

186 Muggeridge, M. (ed.), *Ciano's Diaries, 1937–1938* (London, 1952), 18.2.1938; DGFP, D, 1, 119.

187 Quartararo, *Roma tra Londra e Berlino*, 376ff; 'Appendice a Inghilterra e Italia. Dal Patto di Pasqua a Monaco', *Storia Contemporanea*, 7 (1976), passim.

188 Bottai, *Diario*, 5 December 1936.

189 Deakin, 5–6; Casella, 'L'immagine fascista dell'Impero', 189–95.

190 Casella, 193–5; Bianchini, 173–82.

191 Bottai, *Diario*, 13 April 1939; Lowe and Marzari, 326–30.

192 Lowe and Marzari, 323–9; Jankovic, B.M., *The Balkans in International Relations* (Basingstoke and London, 1988), 160–1.

193 Bottai, *Diario*, 9 June 1939.

194 DDI, 8th, XIII, 162.

195 Candeloro, 325ff.

196 See the discussion in Petersen, J., 'La politica estera del fascismo come problema storiografico', in De Felice, R. (ed.), *L'Italia fra tedeschi e alleati. La politica estera fascista e la seconda guerra mondiale* (Bologna, 1973), 45ff.

197 The relevant excerpt is translated in Noakes and Pridham, *Nazism*, III, 703.

198 Noakes and Pridham, *Nazism*, III, 690–1; Deist, W., *The Wehrmacht and German Rearmament* (London and Basingstoke, 1981), 86ff.

199 Müller, *Beck*, 511ff.

200 DGFP, D, 2, 358. The Czech crisis is discussed in full detail in Weinberg, *Starting World War II*, chaps 10–11.

201 Müller, *Beck*, 512ff.

202 Müller, K.-J., *Das Heer und Hitler. Armee und nationalsozialistisches Regime, 1933–1944* (Stuttgart, 1956), 309–33; Müller, *Beck*, 651ff; Weinberg, *Hitler*, 140ff; Weinberg, *Starting World War II*, 384–6.

203 Hill, L. (ed.), *Die Weizsäcker-Papiere, 1933–1950* (Frankfurt, 1974), 136–7.

204 DGFP, D, 4, 81 (Directive, 21 October 1938).

205 Domarus, II, 1234–40 (speech to Generals, 22 August 1939).

206 DGFP, D, 5, 86; Weinberg, *Hitler*, 121–8.

207 DGFP, D, 5, 112.

208 Weinberg, *Starting World War II*, 497ff.

209 DGFP, D, 5, 120–121 (Ribbentrop's and Weizsäcker's reports, January 1939). For Hitler's reply see Noakes and Pridham, *Nazism*, III, 733–4; Weinberg, *Hitler*, 123–8.

210 DGFP, D, 5, 139.

211 DGFP, D, 6, 149/185; Robertson, E.M., 'German Mobilisation Preparations and the Treaties between Germany and the Soviet Union of August and September 1939', in Boyce and Robertson, 330–6.

212 Domarus, II, 1234ff (Hitler's speech, 22 August 1939).

213 DGFP, D, 6, 159/169.
214 Bullock, A., *Hitler: A Study in Tyranny* (Harmondsworth, 1962), 325–6.

5 BETWEEN CO-OPERATION AND RIVALRY

1 Hildebrand, K., *The Third Reich* (London, 1984), 151.
2 Taylor, A.J.P., *The Origins of the Second World War* (London, 1961); Carr, W., 'National Socialism: Foreign Policy and Wehrmacht', in Laqueur, W. (ed.), *Fascism: A Reader's Guide. Analyses, Interpretations, Bibliography* (Harmondsworth, 1979), 119.
3 Salvemini, G., *Prelude to the Second World War* (London, 1953), 515ff.
4 Quartararo, R., *Roma tra Londra e Berlino. La politica estera fascista dal 1930 al 1940* (Rome, 1980); De Felice, R., *Intervista sul fascismo* (Bari, 1975).
5 Wiskemann, E., *The Rome-Berlin Axis: The History of the Relations between Hitler and Mussolini* (London, 1966); Petersen, J., *Hitler und Mussolini. Die Entstehung der Achse Berlin-Rom 1933–1936* (Tübingen, 1973).
6 Funke, M., *Sanktionen und Kanonen. Hitler, Mussolini und der nationale Abessinienkonflikt 1935–1936* (Düsseldorf, 1970), 102ff; 'Die deutsche-italienische Beziehungen: Antibolschevismus und aussenpolitische Interessenkonkurrenz als Strukturprinzip der "Achse"', in Funke M. (ed.), *Hitler, Deutschland und die Mächte. Materialien zur Aussenpolitik des Dritten Reiches* (Düsseldorf, 1977), 828–30.
7 Cassels, A., *Mussolini's Early Diplomacy* (Princeton, 1970), 135–174; Pese, W.W., 'Hitler und Italien, 1920–1928', *Vierteljahrshefte für Zeitgeschichte*, 3 (1955), 113–26; Ludecke, K.G.W.L., *I Knew Hitler* (New York, 1937).
8 Robertson, E.M., *Mussolini as Empire-Builder: Italy and Africa 1932–1936* (London and Basingstoke, 1977), 18ff (Malta), 24ff (Croatia); Knox, M., 'Il fascismo e la politica estera italiana', in Bosworth, R.J.B. and Romano, S. (eds), *La politica estera italiana (1860–1985)* (Bologna, 1991), 308, 316–8. See also, in this study, Chapter 3.
9 Mussolini, B., *Fascism: Doctrine and Institutions* (Rome, 1935), reprinted in Oakeshott, M. (ed.), *The Social and Political Doctrines of Contemporary Europe* (New York, 1949), 178–9.
10 Aloisi, P., *Journal 25 Juin–14 Juillet 1936* (Paris, 1957), 14–1–1933; Weinberg, G.L., *Germany, Hitler, and World War II: Essays in Modern German and World History* (Cambridge, 1995), 45–6.
11 Robertson, *Empire-Builder*, 49–51; Petersen, *Hitler und Mussolini*, 137–185; 'Italia e Germania: due immagini incrociate', in Tosi, F.F., Grassi, G. and Legnani, M. (eds), *L'Italia nella seconda guerra mondiale e nella resistenza* (Milan, 1988), 45–63.
12 De Felice, R., 'Alcune osservazioni sulla politica estera mussoliniana', in De Felice, R. (ed.), *L'Italia fra tedeschi e alleati. La politica estera fascista e la seconda guerra mondiale* (Bologna, 1973), 57–74. See also, in this study, Chapter 4, n. 159.
13 Lowe, C.J. and Marzari, F., *Italian Foreign Policy 1870–1940* (London and Boston, 1975), 227ff; Robertson, *Empire-Builder*, 59. For Mussolini's vexation at the German decision to withdraw from the Conference, see DGFP, C, 2, 4 and 18.
14 Knox, M., 'Conquest, Domestic and Foreign, in Fascist Italy and Nazi Germany', *Journal of Modern History*, 56 (1984), 23–5; Pese, 113–26.
15 Feder, G., *Das Program der NSDAP und seine weltanschaulichen Grundlagen* (Munich, 1932), 19–22. See also Ritschel, K.H., *Diplomatie um Südtirol. Politische Hintergründe eines europäischen Vorsagens* (Stuttgart, 1966), 133ff.
16 DGFP, C, 1, 262; C, 1, 191. See also Weinberg, G.L. (ed.), *Hitlers zweites Buch: Ein Dokument aus dem Jahr 1928* (Stuttgart, 1961), 208ff.
17 Heineman, J.L., *Hitler's First Foreign Minister: Constantin Freiherr von Neurath, Diplomat and Statesman* (Berkeley, Los Angeles and London, 1979), 103–9; Quartararo, R., *Roma tra Londra e Berlino. La politica estera fascista dal 1930 al 1940* (Rome, 1980), 68–79.

18 Petersen, *Hitler und Mussolini*, 344ff; Weinberg, G.L., *The Foreign Policy of Hitler's Germany: Diplomatic Revolution in Europe, 1933–1936* (Chicago, 1970), 87–107.

19 DGFP, C, 3, 566, fn. 7; C, 2, 28/67; C, 4, 61.

20 Petersen, *Hitler und Mussolini*, ch. 5.

21 DGFP, C, 1, 485; C, 3, 152/266/303/376; C, 4, 61.

22 For the concept of a 'German–British–Italian' alliance in Hitler's thought, see Petersen, *Hitler und Mussolini*, 60–1; Hitler, A., *Mein Kampf* (London 1972, trans. R. Mannheim), 554–85; Weinberg, *Hitlers Zweites Buch*, 217ff.

23 DGFP, C, 3, 125/135/161/173/179/424/435.

24 Robertson, *Empire-Builder*, chaps 1–4.

25 DGFP, C, 3, 320.

26 Laurens, F.D., *France and the Italo-Ethiopian Crisis 1935–1936* (The Hague, 1967); Braddick, H., 'The Hoare–Laval Plan: A Study in International Politics', *Review of Politics*, 24 (1962), 69–78; Robertson, *Empire-Builder*, 114ff.

27 Robertson, *Empire-Builder*, Ch. 10

28 Aloisi, 27 March 1935.

29 DGFP, C, 3, 557.

30 Emmerson, J.T., *The Rhineland Crisis, 7 March 1936: A Study in Multilateral Diplomacy* (London, 1977), 77ff.

31 Craig, G.A., *Germany 1866–1945* (Oxford, 1978), 688–91; and Michalka (ed.), *Das Dritte Reich*, vol. I, 224–5.

32 DGFP, C, 4, 579; and DGFP, C, 4, 414/525/579, DDI, 8th, III, 241 respectively.

33 Wiskemann, *Rome-Berlin Axis*, 70; De Felice, R., *Mussolini il duce*, vol. II: *Lo Stato Totalitario 1936–1939* (Turin, 1981), ch. 3.

34 Grandi, D., *Il mio paese. Ricordi autobiografici*, ed. R. De Felice (Bologna, 1985), 401–2.

35 Robertson, E.M., 'Hitler and Sanctions: Mussolini and the Rhineland', *European Studies Review*, 7 (1977), 409–35; and Domarus, M. (ed.), *Hitler: Reden und Proklamationen 1932–1945*, vol. I: *Triumph (1932–1938)* (Würzburg, 1962), I, 812. On Italy's refusal to impose sanctions see DGFP, C, 4, 579; DDI, 8th, III, 434/445.

36 For Neurath's views, see DGFP, C, 4, 167. On exports of raw materials to Italy see DGFP, C, 4, 372 and 485.

37 For Mussolini's declaration, see DGFP, C, 4, 485. For Suvich's disagreements with this pro-German shift in the Italian foreign policy, see De Felice, R., *Mussolini il duce*, vol. I: *Gli anni del consenso, 1929–1936* (Turin, 1974), 732–4.

38 Robertson, *Empire-Builder*, 111, 127, 152–3; DGFP, C, 4, 83/212; C, 3, 557/558.

39 Funke, *Sanktionen und Kanonen*, 84ff, 181ff; DGFP, C, 4, 360.

40 Ingrim, R., *Hitlers glücklichster Tag – London am 18. Juni 1935* (Stuttgart, 1962); and Watt, D.C., 'The Anglo-German Naval Agreement of 1935: An Interim Judgment', *Journal of Modern History*, 28 (1956), 155–75. A different interpretation, dismissing that Hitler really intended an alliance with Britain, is offered in Weinberg, *Germany, Hitler and World War II*, 85–6.

41 DGFP, C, 4, 322 (emphasis added). See also Petersen, *Hitler und Mussolini*, 483–6; Simonini, A., *Il linguaggio di Mussolini* (Milan, 1978), 146–7.

42 DGFP, C, 5, 89; C, 6, 312; DDI, 8th, IV, 186; DDI, 8th, IV, 109, 205; DGFP, D, 1, 784, respectively.

43 Coverdale, J.F., *Italian Intervention in the Spanish Civil War* (Princeton, 1975), 7–15, 388ff.

44 Pastorelli, P. 'La politica estera fascista dalla fine del conflitto etiopico alla seconda guerra mondiale', in de Felice, R. (ed.), *L'Italia fra tedeschi e alleati. La politica estera fascista e la seconda guerra mondiale* (Bologna, 1973), 105. See DDI, 8th, V, 152.

45 Weinberg, *Hitlers Zweites Buch*, 140, 167, 217.

46 Hiden, J. and Farquharson, J., *Explaining Hitler's Germany* (Totowa, 1983), 143ff; Mason, T., 'The Primacy of Politics – Politics and Economics in National Socialist Germany', in Woolf, S.J. (ed.), *The Nature of Fascism* (London, 1968), 178ff.

47 DGFP, D, 3, 603/702; Over, R.J., *Göring: The 'Iron Man'* (London, Boston, Melbourne and Henley, 1984), 44–5.

48 Ciano, G., *Europa verso il catastrofe* (Milan, 1948), 87–99; DGFP, D, 3, 495.

49 Heineman, 150, n. 5.

50 DDI, 8th, IV, 627; V, 264/273.

51 DGFP, C, 5, 554.

52 Ciano, G., *Diplomatic Papers* (London, 1948), 52–61; DGFP, C, 5, 618/622/624 (conversations with Neurath, Göring and Hitler respectively, 21–4 October 1936).

53 Mussolini, B., *Scritti e discorsi* (Milan 1934–39), X, 201ff. For the repercussions of the speech see DDI, 8th, V, 329–333/339/342/346.

54 Craig, *Germany*, 693–6. See also Mussolini's relevant references in his interview to the *Völkischer Beobachter* (18 January 1937), reprinted in Italian in *Scritti*, XI, 43–5.

55 DDI, 8th, V, 256 (military agreement); DGFP, D, 3, 110/121/123; DDI, 8th, V, 133/180/280/375/476 (recognition of the Burgos regime).

56 See, for example, DGFP, D, 3, 363.

57 DGFP, D, 3, 230/236; Muggeridge, M. (ed.), *Ciano's Diaries, 1937–1938* (London, 1952), 20 December 1937. See also Coverdale, J.F., 'The Battle of Guadalajara, 8–22 March 1937', *Journal of Contemporary History*, 9 (1974), 53–76.

58 DGFP, D, 3, 654; 318/328/403; 786, respectively.

59 Carr, W., *Hitler: A Study in Personality and Politics* (London, 1978), 23ff.

60 Mack Smith, D., *Italy: A Modern History* (Ann Arbor, 1969), especially 454ff; Wiskemann, *Fascism in Italy*, ch. 5. For a criticism of this interpretation see Alatri, P., *Le origini del fascismo* (Rome, 1963), 27ff; Petersen, J., 'La politica estera del fascismo come problema storiografico', in De Felice, R. (ed.), *L'Italia fra tedeschi e alleati. La politica estera fascista e la seconda guerra mondiale* (Bologna, 1973), 45–6.

61 DGFP, D, 1, 224/755/769/784. For this interpretation see De Felice, R., *Mussolini il duce*, I, 466ff.

62 Minniti, F., 'Aspetti della politica fascista degli armamenti dal 1935 al 1943', in De Felice, R. (ed.), *L'Italia fra tedeschi e alleati*, 127–36, and 'Il problema degli armamenti nella preparazione militare italiana dal 1935 al 1943', *Storia Contemporanea*, 2 (1978), 1–56.

63 DGFP, C, 6, 568.

64 See Mussolini's speech in Berlin, reprinted in *Popolo d'Italia*, 29 September 1937, excerpts of which can be found in Domarus, M. (ed.), *Hitler: Reden und Proklamationen 1932–1945*, vol. II: *Untergang (1939–1945)* (Würzburg, 1963), 737–8 (and Delzell, C.F. (ed.), *Mediterranean Fascism, 1919–1945* (New York, Evanston and London, 1970), 202–5, for a translation).

65 Hamilton, A., *The Appeal of Fascism: A Study of Intellectuals and Fascism 1919–1945* (London, 1971), 77–8.

66 Malaparte, C., *Technique du coup d'état* (Paris, 1948), 161–72.

67 Bottai, G., *Vent'anni e un giorno (24 luglio 1943)* (Milan, 1977), 63ff.

68 For Mussolini's anger with Balbo, see Muggeridge, M. (ed.), *Ciano's Diaries*, 8 December 1939; and 3 June 1937 for Balbo's initial anti-German comments. See also Segrè, C.G., *Italo Balbo: A Fascist Life* (Berkeley, Los Angeles and London, 1987), 375ff.

69 Michaelis, M., *Mussolini and the Jews: German–Italian Relations and the Jewish Question in Italy 1922–1945* (Oxford, 1978), 138; Mack Smith, D., *Mussolini's Roman Empire* (London, 1976), 44ff.

70 For the agreement see DGFP, D, 1, 152; and for the Italian positive reaction to the agreement, C, 5, 755; D, 1, 155.

71 Lowe and Marzari, 292–7; and DGFP, C, 6, 502. On Italy's imperialist ambitions in the Balkan area see Bianchini, F., 'L'idea fascista dell'impero nell'area danubiano-balcanica', in Di Nolfo, E., Rainero, R.H. and Vigezzi B. (eds), *L'Italia e la politica di potenza in Europa 1938–1940* (Milan, 1986), 173–86.

72 Colarizi, S., *L'opinione degli italiani sotto il regime, 1929–1943* (Rome and Bari, 1991), 256–61; Toscano, M., *Le origini diplomatiche del patto d'acciaio* (Florence, 1956), 28–32, 385, 388.

73 Ciano, *Diplomatic Papers*, 142–6.

74 Heineman, 159–63; Weinberg, G.L., *The Foreign Policy of Hitler's Germany: Starting World War II, 1937–1939* (Chicago and London, 1980), 35–42; Carr, *Hitler*, 75ff. See also Chapters 3–4 in this study.

75 Speer, A., *Erinnerungen* (Frankfurt am Main, 1969), 120.

76 Mason, T., 'Intention and Explanation. A Current Controversy about the Interpretation of National Socialism', in Hirschfeld, G. and Kettenacker, L. (eds), *Der 'Führerstaat': Mythos und Realität. Studien zur Struktur und Politik des Dritten Reiches* (Stuttgart, 1981), 33–4.

77 Quartararo, *Roma tra Londra e Berlino*, 365ff; Ciano, *Diplomatic Papers*, 164ff (report of talks between Grandi and Chamberlain); Muggeridge, *Ciano's Diaries*, 21 February 1938.

78 For the British attitude, see DGFP, D, 2, 88; and for the Italian, Santarelli, C., *Storia del movimento e del regime fascista* (Rome, 1967), 256–61. By contrast, the French government adopted a more anti-German policy (DGFP, D, 2, 98/204/647).

79 Freeman, M., *Atlas of Nazi Germany* (London and Sydney, 1987), 164–9.

80 DGFP, D, 1, 16; and Domarus, II, 1061ff; Muggeridge, *Ciano's Diaries*, 6 November 1937.

81 Wiskemann, *Rome–Berlin Axis*, 72–3; Quartararo, 375ff, 395ff.

82 Lowe and Marzari, 310–4; Morewood, 181–2.

83 Vigezzi, B., 'Mussolini, Ciano, la diplomazia italiana e la percezione della "politica dei potenza" al'inizio della seconda guerra mondiale', in Di Nolfo, Rainero and Vigezzi, *L'Italia e la politica di potenza in Europa*, 3–18.

84 Quoted in Lowe and Marzari, 291.

85 DGFP, D, 2, 611/661.

86 Lowe and Marzari, 312–4; Pastorelli, P. 'La politica estera', 112.

87 Ciano, *Diplomatic Papers*, 259–66 (conversations of Chamberlain with Ciano and Mussolini, 11/12 January, 1939); Quartararo, *Roma tra Londra e Berlino*, 413ff; Mack Smith, D., *Mussolini's Roman Empire* (London, 1982), 137–9.

88 Quartararo, 396ff; Toscano, *Le origini diplomatiche*, 46ff.

89 Pastorelli, P., 'La politica estera', 114; Mack Smith, 'Appeasement in Mussolini's Foreign Policy', in Mommsen, W. J. and Kettenacker, L. (eds), *The Fascist Challenge and the Policy of Appeasement* (London, 1983), 258–66.

90 DGFP, D, 1, 743 (Weizsäcker report, 19 March 1938); D, 6, 199 (Heydrich to Ribbentrop, 14 April 1939).

91 DGFP, D, 4, 374; D, 4, 421/454/462.

92 Lowe and Marzari, 326–31; and, in this study, Chapters 4–5.

93 Webster, R.A., *Industrial Imperialism in Italy 1908–1915* (Berkeley and Los Angeles, 1975), 316ff.

94 See Mussolini's irritation with the liquidation of the Czech state (DGFP, D, 6, 87/140).

95 Muggeridge, *Ciano's Diaries*, 10/11 February 1939.

96 DGFP, D, 1, 793.

97 Dülffer, J., 'Determinants of German Naval Policy, 1920–1939', in Dülffer, J. (ed.), *The German Military in the Age of Total War* (Leamington Spa, 1985), 152–70; Salewski, M., 'Navy and Politics in Germany and France in the Twentieth Century', in

NOTES

Müller, K.-J. (ed.), *The Military in Politics and Society in France and Germany in the Twentieth Century* (Oxford, 1995), especially 83ff.

98 Geyer, M., *Die Reichswehr und die Krise der Machtpolitik 1924–1936* (Wiesbaden, 1980).

99 Minniti, F., 'La politica industriale del Ministero dell'Aeronautica. Mercato, pianificazione, svillupo (1935–43)', *Storia Contemporanea*, 1 (1981), 5–55 and 271–312; Rochat, G. and Massobrio, C., *Breve storia del'esercito italiano dal 1861 al 1945* (Turin, 1978), 230–5.

100 DGFP, D, 6, 737; and Hitler's rejection of the idea, D, 7, 47. See also Lamb, R., *Ghosts of Peace, 1935–1943* (London, 1987), 93–120.

101 Vigezzi, B., *Politica estera e opinione pubblica in Italia dall'unità ai giorni nostri. Orientamenti degli studi e prospettiva della ricerca* (Milan, 1991), 106ff, 119.

102 Bosworth, R.J.B., *Italy, the Least of the Great Powers: Italian Foreign Policy Before the First World War* (Cambridge, 1979).

103 DBFP, 3rd, 1, 198–235; Douglas, R., 'Chamberlain and Appeasement', Mommsen, W.J. and Kettenacker, L. (eds), *The Fascist Challenge and the Policy of Appeasement* (London, 1983), 79–88.

104 Nuremberg Documents, 2949-PS, also in Noakes, J. and Pridham, G. (eds), *Nazism: A Documentary Reader*, vol. III: *Foreign Policy, War and Racial Extermination* (Exeter, 1988), 705.

105 De Felice, *Mussolini il duce*, II, 780ff; Wiskemann, *Rome–Berlin Axis*, 339–52, and chaps 5–13.

106 For Mussolini's initial 'realism', see De Felice, R., *Mussolini il duce*, I, 798ff; Quartararo, *Roma tra Londra e Berlino*, passim.

107 Bosworth, R.J.B., 'Italian foreign policy and its historiography', in Bosworth, R.J.B. and Rizzo, G. (eds), *Altro Polo: Intellectuals and their Ideas in Contemporary Italy* (Sydney, 1983), 65ff; Bosworth, R.J.B., *The Italian Dictatorship: Problems and Perspectives in the Interpretation of Mussolini and Fascism* (London and New York, 1998), 99–101.

108 Reynolds, C., *Modes of Imperialism* (Oxford, 1981), 160–6.

6 FASCIST EXPANSIONISM AND WAR

1 Arendt, H., *The Origins of Totalitarianism* (London 1967, 3rd edn), 389–459.

2 See for example DGFP, D, 6, 433; Toscano, M., *Le origini diplomatiche del patto d'acciaio* (Florence, 1956), 396ff.

3 Geyer, M., 'Restorative Elites, German Society and the Nazi Pursuit of Goals', in Bessel, R. (ed.), *Fascist Italy and Nazi Germany: Comparisons and Contrasts* (Cambridge, 1996), 139ff.

4 DGFP, D, 7, 192/193; Domarus, M. (ed.), *Hitler: Reden und Proklamationen*, vol. II: *Untergang (1939–1945)*, (Würzburg 1963), 1234–40. For a discussion of the speech see Baumgart, W., 'Zur Ansprache Hitlers von den Führern der Wehrmacht am 22. August 1939', *Vierteljahrshefte für Zeitgeschichte*, 16 (1968), 120–49.

5 Weinberg, G.L., *Germany, Hitler, and World War II: Essays in Modern German and World History* (Cambridge, 1995), 143–4.

6 DGFP, D, 6, 433; Domarus, II, 1196–1201, especially 1198–9.

7 DGFP, D, 6, 126; D, 7, 195/196.

8 See, for example, his reply of 14 August 1939 in Domarus, II, 1229; and his reply of 25 August in DGFP, D, 7, 205 (translation in Noakes, J. and Pridham, G. (eds), *Nazism: A Documentary Reader*, vol. III: *Foreign Policy, War and Racial Extermination* (Exeter, 1988), 746–7).

9 Weinberg, G.L., *A World at Arms: A Global History of World War II* (Cambridge, 1994), 43–7.

10 Domarus, II, 1312ff (1 September 1939).

11 Domarus, II, 1225 (translation in Noakes and Pridham, *Nazism*, III, 739).

12 Wiedemann, F., *Der Mann der Feldherr werden wollte* (Kettwig, 1964), 127ff.

13 Dilks, D., '"We must hope for the best and prepare for the worst": the Prime Minister, the Cabinet and Hitler's Germany, 1937–1939', *Proceedings of the British Academy*, 73 (1987), 309–52.

14 Weinberg, G.L., *The Foreign Policy of Hitler's Germany: Starting World War II, 1937–1939* (Chicago, 1980), 635ff; for its repercussions in Berlin see Jacobsen, H.-A. (ed.), *Generaloberst Halder: Kriegstagebuch* (Stuttgart 1962), I, 34ff.

15 On Italy's position see DDI, 8th, XIII, 147/154/167/182; DGFP, D, 7, 192/193. On Hitler's anticipation of Mussolini's help see Domarus, II, 1234–5; for Ribbentrop's confidence see DGFP, D, 6, enclosure to Doc. 185.

16 Robertson, E.M., 'German Mobilisation Preparations and the Treaties between Germany and the Soviet Union of August and September 1939', in Boyce, R. and Robertson, E.M. (eds), *Paths to War: New Essays on the Origins of the Second World War* (Basingstoke and London, 1989), 345ff.

17 Domarus, II, 1276–7.

18 DGFP, D, 7, 357.

19 DBFP, 3rd, 7, 538/539 (translated in Noakes and Pridham, *Nazism*, III, 748–9).

20 DGFP, D, 7, 477–8; Weinberg, *Starting World War II*, 645–8.

21 Weinberg, G.L., *Germany and the Soviet Union, 1939–1941* (Leyden, 1972); Weinberg, *Starting World War II*, 602ff; Weinberg, G.L., *Germany, Hitler, and World War II*, 168–81; Uldricks, T.J., 'Soviet Security Policy in the 1930s', in Gorodetsky, G. (ed.), *Soviet Foreign Policy, 1917–1991: A Retrospective* (London, 1994), 65–74.

22 Weinberg, *Germany, Hitler, and World War II*, 146–50, 156ff; Erickson, J., 'Threat Identification and Strategic Appraisal by the Soviet Union, 1930–1941', in Finney, P. (ed.), *The Origins of the Second World War* (New York and London, 1997), 338–9.

23 DGFP, D, 7, 228; 6, 325; Erickson, 336–7.

24 DGFP, D, 7, 56/70/75/79. For the demand to bring forward the date of the agreement, see DGFP, D, 7, 149.

25 DGFP, D, 7, 284 (translated in Noakes and Pridham, *Nazism*, III, 743–4).

26 Taylor, A.J.P., *The Origins of the Second World War* (London, 1961), 69ff.

27 Taylor, *Origins*, 277–8; and Taylor, A.J.P., 'War Origins Again', in Robertson, E.M. (ed.), *The Origins of the Second World War: Historical Interpretations* (London and Basingstoke, 1971), 136–41. See also the discussion in Noakes and Pridham (eds), *Nazism*, III, 750–4; Williamson, D.G., *The Third Reich* (Harlow 1995, 2nd edn), 59–60; Boyce, R., 'Introduction', in Boyce, R. and Robertson, E.M. (eds), *Paths to War: New Essays on the Origins of the Second World War* (Basingstoke and London, 1989), 1–32.

28 Michalka, W. (ed.), *Das Dritte Reich*, vol. I: *Volksgemeinschaft und Grossmachtpolitik* (Munich, 1985), 224ff; Domarus, II, 1196–1201 (speech to Generals, 23 May 1939); 1234–8 (speech to Generals, 22 August 1939).

29 Taylor, 'War Origins Again', 139–41; Mason, T.W., 'Some Origins of the Second World War', in Robertson, *Origins of the Second World War*, 107ff.

30 Taylor, *Origins*, 287ff. See Koch, H.W., 'Hitler and the Origins of the Second World War: Second Thoughts on the Status of Some of the Documents', *Historical Journal*, 11 (1968), 125–43.

31 DGFP, D, 6, 433 (conference with the Wehrmacht leadership and Göring, 23 May 1939).

32 Weinberg, *Starting World War II* (Chicago, 1980), 555–6.

33 Jacobsen, *Halder*, I, 7ff.

34 Eatwell, R., *Fascism: A History* (London, 1995), 136–7.

35 For example, his comments against Britain and France in 1937 in DGFP, D, 1, 19; Michalka (ed.), *Das Dritte Reich*, vol. I, 241–6. See also, in this study, Chapter 3.

36 Michalka, W., 'Die nationalsozialistische Aussenpolitik im Zeichen eines "Konzeptionen-Pluralismus" – Fragestellungen und Forschungsaufgaben', in

Funke, M. (ed.), *Hitler, Deutschland und die Mächte. Materialien zur Aussenpolitik des Dritten Reiches* (Düsseldorf, 1977), 59ff.

37 Robertson, 'German Mobilisation', 342–50. For the British reply see DBFP, 3rd, 7, 79/127/128/145. See also Aster, S., *1939: The Making of the Second World War* (London, 1973), ch. 9.

38 Domarus, II, 1299–1300.

39 Jacobsen (ed.), *Halder*, I, 46ff.

40 Wagner, E. (ed.), *Der Generalquartiermeister. Briefe und Tagebuchaufzeichnungen des Generalquartiermeisters des Heeres, General der Artillerie Eduard Wagner* (Munich, 1963), 98–109; Hill, L. (ed.), *Die Weizsäcker-Papiere, 1933–1950* (Frankfurt, 1974), 158–60.

41 Kershaw, I., *The 'Hitler-Myth': Image and Reality in the Third Reich* (Oxford, 1989), 132–9. For the attitude of the military during the Czech crisis see, in this study, Chapter 3.

42 DGFP, D, 7, 119.

43 Hill, *Weizsäcker-Papiere*, 157–8.

44 Wagner, *Generalquartiermeister*, 108–9.

45 Weinberg, *Hitler*, 144–5; Robertson, 'German Mobilisation', 356ff.

46 DDI, 8th, XIII, 10/67.

47 Weinberg, *Starting World War II*, ch. 14.

48 Kershaw, *Hitler-Myth*, 138–47.

49 Jäckel, E., 'Hitlers Kriegspolitik und ihre nationalen Voraussetzungen', in Hildebrand *et al.*, *1939: An der Schwelle zum Weltkrieg* (Berlin, 1990), 26–9.

50 Hill, *Weizsäcker-Papiere*, 180–1; Overy, R.J., *Goering: The 'Iron Man'* (London, 1984), 91–4.

51 Seraphin, H.G. (ed.), *Das Politische Tagebuch Alfred Rosenbergs 1934/5 und 1939/40* (Göttingen, Berlin and Frankfurt, 1956), 22 and 25 August 1939.

52 Steinert, M.G., *Hitler's War and the Germans: Public Mood and Attitude towards the Second World War* (Ohio, 1977), 49ff; Kershaw, *Hitler-Myth*, 143–57.

53 Mason, T., 'Innere Krise und Angriffskrieg 1938–9', in Forstmeier, F. and Volkmann, H.E. (eds), *Wirtschaft und Rüstung am Vorabend des Zweiten Weltkrieges* (Düsseldorf, 1975), 158–88; Mason, T., *Sozialpolitik im Dritten Reich* (Opladen, 1977); Mason, T., 'The Domestic Dynamics of Nazi Conquest', in Childers, T. and Caplan, J. (eds), *Reevaluating the Third Reich* (New York, London, 1993), 161–89; Mason, T., *Arbeiterklasse und Volksgemeinschaft. Dokumente und Materialen zur deutschen Arbeiterpolitik, 1936–1939* (Opladen, 1975).

54 Mason, T. and Overy, R., 'Debate: Germany, "Domestic Crisis" and War in 1939', *Past and Present*, 122 (1989), 205–40; 'Innere Krise', 186ff.

55 Mason, *Sozialpolitik*, 40ff; 'Debate', 219ff.

56 Mason, T., 'Intention. and Explanation: A Current Controversy about the Interpretation of National Socialism', in Hirschfeld, G. and Kettenacker, L. (eds), *Der 'Führerstaat'. Mythos und Realität. Studien zur Struktur und Politik des Dritten Reiches* (Stuttgart, 1981), 23–42.

57 Mason, *Arbeiterklasse*, 103ff; 'Debate', 215ff. For a discussion of these arguments see Hancock, E., *The National Socialist Leadership and Total War, 1941–5* (New York, 1991), 19ff.

58 Mason, 'Debate', 214ff; *Sozialpolitik*, 30ff.

59 For Overy's rejection of the notion of crisis, see Overy, R.J., 'Germany, "Domestic Crisis" and War in 1939', *Past and Present*, 116 (1987), 138–68; Overy, R.J., 'Hitler's War Plans and the German Economy', in Boyce and Robertson, *Paths to War*, especially 119–21; Mason and Overy, 'Debate', 205–40.

60 Orlow, D., *The History of the Nazi Party, 1919–1945*, vol. II: *1933–1945* (Pittsburgh, 1973), 230ff.

61 Overy, *The 'Iron Man'*, 80–108; Kube, A., 'Hermann Goering: The Second Man in the Reich', in Smelser, R. and Zitelmann, R. (eds), *The Nazi Elite* (Houndmills and London, 1993), 65ff.

62 Chamberlain, N., *In Search of Peace* (London, 1939), 276–7 (and the report of the speech in Germany in DGFP, D, 6, 23).

63 Domarus, II, 1236.

64 Domarus, II, 1299–1300 (Directive 1, 31 August 1939). This view is supported by Weinberg, *Starting World War II*, ch. 14.

65 Robertson, 'German Mobilisation', 355.

66 Mayer, S.L. (ed.), *Hitler's Wartime Picture Magazine* (London, 1979), Introduction.

67 Hill, *Weizsäcker-Papiere*, 207–8.

68 Burckhardt, C.J., *Meine Danziger Mission, 1937–1939* (Munich, 1962), 272–3 (22 August 1939); Domarus, II, 1236ff.

69 Schmidt, P., *Statist auf diplomatischer Bühne, 1923–1945* (Bonn, 1950), 462–4. Weinberg doubts the accuracy of the account; see his *Hitler, Germany and World War II*, 91–2.

70 Whittam, J., 'The Italian General Staff and the Coming of the Second World War', in Preston, A. (ed.), *General Staffs and Diplomacy Before the Second World War* (Totowa, 1978), 77–97; Rochat, G., 'Mussolini e le forze armate', in Aquarone, A. and Vernassa, M. (eds), *Il regime fascista* (Bologna, 1974), 127–32; Bottai, G., *Diario, 1935–1944* (Milan, 1994), 26 August 1939.

71 De Felice, R., *Mussolini il duce*, vol. II: *Lo Stato Totalitario, 1936–1940* (Turin, 1981), 618–40; Quartararo, R., *Roma tra Londra e Berlino. La politica estera fascista dal 1930 al 1940* (Rome, 1980), ch. 8.

72 De Felice, *Mussolini il duce*, II, passim; Quartararo, 519–66. For Mussolini's thoughts about breaking off the Pact of Steel, see DDI, 8th, XIII, 264.

73 Quartararo, 604ff.

74 De Felice, *Mussolini l'alleato*, vol. 1: *L'Italia in Guerra*, Part A: *Dalla guerra 'breve' alla guerra lunga, 1940–1943* (Turin, 1990), 92–105; Rochat, 'Mussolini e le forze armate', 127–32.

75 Mack Smith, D., *Mussolini's Roman Empire* (London, 1982), 216ff.

76 Knox, M., *Mussolini Unleashed, 1939–1941: Politics and Strategy in Fascist Italy's Last War* (Cambridge, 1982), 102; Knox, M., 'The Fascist Regime, its Foreign Policy and its Wars: an "anti-anti-fascist" orthodoxy?', in Finney, P. (ed.), *The Origins of the Second World War* (London and New York, 1997), 157–65; Knox, M., 'Conquest, Domestic and Foreign, in Fascist Italy and Nazi Germany', *Journal of Modern History*, 56 (1984), 1–57.

77 Rumi, G., 'Revisionismo' fascista ed espansione coloniale (1925–1935)', in Aquarone and Vernassa, *Il regime fascista*, 435–64.

78 Ceva, L., *Storia della società italiana: le forze armate* (Torise, 1981), ch. 13.

79 Knox, *Mussolini Unleashed*, 18–21.

80 Muggeridge, M. (ed.), *Ciano's Diary, 1937–1938* (London, 1952), 25/26/27 September 1938.

81 Bottai, *Diario*, 4 February 1939.

82 Bottai, *Diario*, 9 June 1939.

83 DGFP, D, 6, 52.

84 Ciano, G., *Europa verso il catastrofe* (Milan, 1948), 449–59; DDI, 8th, XIII, 1/4/21; DGFP, D, 7, 47; Siebert, F., *Italiens Weg in den Zweiten Weltkrieg* (Bonn, 1962), ch. 7.

85 For the proposal see DDI, 8th, XIII, 27. For Ciano's comments see Muggeridge, M. (ed.), *Ciano's Diaries, 1939–1943* (London and Toronto, 1947), 15 February 1939.

86 Muggeridge, *Ciano's Diaries*, 18 August 1939; DDI, 8th, XIII, 162.

87 Candeloro, G., *Storia dell'Italia moderna*, vol. 9: *Il fascismo e le sue guerre* (Milan, 1986), 487ff; Colarizi, S., *L'opinione degli italiani sotto il regime, 1929–1943* (Rome and Bari,

1991), 315–9; Bottai, *Diario*, 31 August 1939. On the earlier divisions within the PNF about the Axis see, in this study, Chapters 3 and 5.

88 Muggeridge, *Ciano's Diaries*, 15 August 1939; Bottai, *Diario*, 31 August 1939.

89 For the King's arguments, see DDI, 8th, XIII, 250/293/298; Mack Smith, D., *Italy and its Monarchy* (New Haven and London, 1989), 280ff. Mussolini's letter to Hitler is in DGFP, D, 7, 271.

90 Bottai, *Diario*, 7 September 1939; Muggeridge, *Ciano's Diaries*, 7 September 1939.

91 Marzari, F., 'Projects for an Italian-led Balkan Bloc of Neutrals, September–December 1939', *Historical Journal*, 13 (1970), 767–88; Quartararo, 527ff. For the abandonment of the plan see DGFP, D, 8, 266; DDI, 9th, II, 510.

92 DDI, 9th, III, 194; Morewood, S., 'Anglo-Italian Rivalry in the Mediterranean and Middle East 1935–1940', in Boyce and Robertson, *Paths to War*, 192.

93 Bottai, *Diario*, 8 December 1939.

94 Muggeridge, *Ciano's Diaries*, 16 December 1939; DDI, 9th, III, 40.

95 DDI, 9th, III, 33; Wiskemann, E., *The Rome-Berlin Axis* (London 1966, 2nd edn), 225ff; Quartararo, 572ff; Andrè, G., 'La politica estera fascista durante il seconda guerra mondiale', in De Felice, R. (ed.), *L'Italia fra tedeschi e alleati. La politica estera fascista e la seconda guerra mondiale* (Bologna, 1973), 118–20.

96 De Felice, R., *Mussolini il duce*, II, 669–85; 'Alcune osservazioni sulla politica estera mussoliniana', in De Felice (ed.), *L'Italia fra tedeschi e alleati. La politica estera fascista e la seconda guerra mondiale* (Bologna, 1973), 72–4.

97 Quartararo, 572–4.

98 Bottai, *Diario*, 23 January 1940.

99 Muggeridge, *Ciano's Diaries*, 7–8/20 February 1940; DDI, 9th, I, 328 and 3, 30; DGFP, D, 8, 627; Knox, *Mussolini Unleashed*, 70ff.

100 Bottai, *Diario*, 1 March 1940.

101 Muggeridge, *Ciano's Diaries*, 22 February 1940; Bottai, *Diario*, 1/2 March 1940.

102 On Hitler's reply see DGFP, D, 8, 663. On Ribbentrop's visit see Siebert, 403ff; Di Nolfo, E., 'Mussolini e la decisione italiana di entrare nella seconda guerra mondiale', in Di Nolfo, A., Rainero, R.H. and Vigezzi, B. (eds), *L'Italia e la politica di potenza in Europa (1938–1940)* (Milan, 1986), 33–8. For the talks see Ciano, *Europe verso il catastrofe*, 527–41.

103 Siebert, 417ff; Andrè, 'Politica estera fascista', 119–20.

104 DGFP, D, 8, 663/665. See also Andrè, G., *La guerra in Europa (1o settember–22 giugnio 1941)* (Milan, 1964), 370ff; Knox, *Mussolini Unleashed*, 82ff.

105 See Ciano's comments in Muggeridge, *Ciano's Diaries*, 12/13 March 1940; Bottai, *Diario*, 12 March 1940.

106 Bottai, *Diario*, 14 February 1940.

107 DDI, 9th, III, 689.

108 Bottai, *Diario*, 2 April 1940.

109 Bottai, *Diario*, 10 April 1940; Muggeridge, *Ciano's Diaries*, 10/11 April 1940.

110 Bottai, *Diario*, 1 April 1940; DDI, 9th, 4, 37.

111 *Ciano's Diaries*, 21 April 1940.

112 De Leonardis, M., 'La monarchia e l'intervento dell'Italia in guerra', in Di Nolfo, Rainero and Vigezzi, *L'Italia e la politica di potenza in Europa*, 39–67; Mack Smith, *Italy and its Monarchy*, 282ff.

113 Muggeridge, *Ciano's Diaries*, 14 March 1940; De Leonardis, 50–1; Mack Smith, *Italy and its Monarchy*, 287ff.

114 His resignation is obvious in *Ciano's Diaries*, see entries for 11/14/19 May 1940.

115 Grandi, D., *Il mio paese. Ricordi autobiografici*, ed. R. De Felice (Bologna, 1985), ch. 48.

116 Bottai, *Diario*, 23 April/7 May 1940. See also De Grand, A.J., *Bottai e la cultura fascista* (Rome and Bari, 1978), 238–9.

117 Segrè, *Italo Balbo: A Fascist Life* (Berkeley , Los Angeles and London, 1987), 375–91; De Felice, *Mussolini il duce*, II, 823ff.

118 De Leonardis, 39–60, 65–7; Muggeridge, *Ciano's Diaries*, 21/26 May 1940; Mack Smith, *Italy and its Monarchy*, 287–8.

119 Muggeridge, *Ciano's Diaries*, 22 April 1940.

120 For the letter see DDI, 9th, 4, 37. For the objections see Bottai, *Diario*, 28 March 1940; Knox, *Mussolini Unleashed*, 93–4.

121 Muggeridge, *Ciano's Diaries*, 10/11 May 1940; Anfuso, F., *Roma, Berlino, Salò* (Milan, 1970), 148ff.

122 Bosworth, R.J.B., *Italy and the Wider World, 1860–1960* (London and New York, 1996), 52–3.

123 Bottai, *Diario*, 25 May 1940; Jacomoni, F., *La politica dell'Italia in Albania* (Bologna, 1965), 225ff.

124 DDI, 9th, 4, 607.

125 Quartararo, 616ff; Anfuso, 147ff.

126 DDI, 9th, 5, 728.

127 Bosworth, *Italy and the Wider World*, 36–9.

128 Andrè, 'Politica estera fascista', 115ff.

129 For the first comment see Bottai, *Diario*, 28 August 1939. For the interpretation of the letter see Di Nolfo, 'Mussolini e la decisione italiana', 30–3.

130 Bottai, *Diario*, 12 May 1940.

131 Quoted in Bocca, G., *Storia d'Italia nella guerra fascista, 1940–1943* (Milan, 1997), 131–2.

132 Bottai, *Diario*, 8 December 1939.

133 Quartararo, ch. 14; DDI, 9th, 2, 217; and 3, 644.

134 Quartararo, 612–22; De Felice, R., *Mussolini il duce*, II, 762ff.

135 De Felice, *Mussolini l'alleato*, vol. Ia, 3ff. See also Andrè, 'Politica estera italiana', 114–15.

136 Quartararo, 624.

137 Di Nolfo, 'Mussolini e la decisione', 19–25. For the 'embarrassing' state of non-intervention in 1939 see Bottai, *Diario*, 31 August 1939.

138 Bottai, *Diario*, 1 September 1939; Pieri, P. and Rochat, G., *Pietro Badoglio* (Turin, 1974), 735ff.

139 Bosworth, R.J.B., 'Mito e linguaggio nella politica estera italiana', in Bosworth and Romano, *La politica estera italiana*, 59ff.

140 Araldi, V., *Dalla non-belligerenza all'intervento* (Rome, 1961), 116ff.

141 Bottai, *Diario*, 2 April 1940.

142 De Felice, *Mussolini il duce*, II, 807ff; Mussolini's comments in Bottai, *Diario*, 10 August 1940.

143 Quoted in Bocca, 133; Di Nolfo, 'Mussolini e la decisione', 36–8.

144 Muggeridge, *Ciano's Diaries*, 17 June 1940.

145 Mira, G. and Salvatorelli, L., *Storia d'Italia nel periodo fascista* (Turin, 1964), 1039–46; Mack Smith, *Mussolini's Roman Empire*, 221ff.

146 Rossi, F., *Mussolini e lo Stato Maggiore. Avvenimenti del 1940* (Rome, 1951), 168–75; De Felice, R., *Mussolini l'alleato*, vol. Ia, 118ff.

147 Quoted in Bocca, 161.

148 DDI, 9th, V, 76; and Mussolini's notice in 5, 83. See also Mack Smith, *Mussolini's Roman Empire*, 222–5.

149 For the text of the armistice see DDI, 9th, V, 95; for the French reactions see Rossi, *Stato Maggiore*, 70ff.

150 DDI, 9th, V, 200; DGFP, D, 10, 147.

151 Bottai, *Diario*, 4 July 1940. For Mussolini's assistance DDI, 9th, V, 109; DGFP, D, 10, 26.

152 DGFP, D, 10, 166; DDI, 9th, V, 242.
153 DDI, 9th, V, 274 conversation between Hitler and Ciano); and Ciano, *L'Europa verso il catastrofe*, 574–6.
154 DDI, 9th, V, 264.
155 Muggeridge, *Ciano's Diaries*, 18 August 1940.
156 Hitler's speech in Domarus, II, 1540–9 (speech to the Reichstag, 19 July 1940).
157 Knox, *Mussolini Unleashed*, 150f; Bocca, ch. 9.
158 DDI, 9th, V, 357/371/393/411.
159 For the attack on Egypt see DDI, 9th, V, 467. For Greece, see Bottai, *Diario*, 12 August 1940; Muggeridge, *Ciano's Diaries*, 12 August 1940; DDI, 9th, V, 386. See also Knox, *Mussolini Unleashed*, 167ff.
160 DDI, 9th, V, 431/490/506; DGFP, D, 10, 353.
161 Muggeridge, *Ciano's Diaries*, 27 August/1 September 1940.
162 DDI, 9th, V, 376/507/516.
163 Bottai, *Diario*, 29 August 1940. See also DDI, 9th, V, 516.
164 DDI, 9th, V, 602/617; DGFP, D, 11, 68/73/79/87; Hillgruber, A., *Hitlers Strategie. Politik und Kriegführung, 1940–1941* (Frankfurt, 1965), 167–78.
165 For the announcement of the postponement see DGFP, D, 10, 149; Muggeridge, *Ciano's Diaries*, 4 October 1940. For reports on 30 September, see DDI, 9th, V, 656.
166 USE, *Il Africa settentrionale. La preparazione al conflitto. L'avanzata di Sidi el-Baranni* (Rome, 1953); Armellini, Q., *Diario di guerra. Nove mesi al Comando Supremo* (Milan, 1946), 78ff.
167 Armellini, 98–9; Muggeridge, *Ciano's Diaries*, 17 September/2 October 1940.
168 DDI, 9th, V, 609/634/665; Craveld, L. van, *Hitler's Strategy 1940–1941: The Balkan Clue* (London, 1973), 26ff.
169 Muggeridge, *Ciano's Diaries*, 30 September 1940; Armellini, 90ff.
170 DGFP, D, 11, 107/149; DDI, 9th, V, 677.
171 For doubts over Gibraltar see DGFP, D, 11, 79; Muggeridge, *Ciano's Diaries*, 24 September, 1940. For doubts over Spain see DGFP, D, 11, 149 and 166–7.
172 Muggeridge, *Ciano's Diaries*, 2 October 1940.
173 DGFP, D, 11, 192; DDI, 9th, V, 707/724; Bottai, *Diario*, 12 October, 1940; Muggeridge, *Ciano's Diaries*, 12 October 1940. For Mussolini's fears of German expansion in the Balkans see DDI, 9th, V, 506/557; Muggeridge, *Ciano's Diaries*, 6 September 1940.
174 Bocca, 214ff; DDI, 9th, V, 728. Cf. DGFP, D, 11, 135.
175 Muggeridge, *Ciano's Diaries*, 12 October 1940.
176 Bocca, 258ff; Muggeridge, *Ciano's Diaries*, 16 October 1940.
177 DDI, 9th, V, 753/ DGFP, D, 11, 199.
178 Muggeridge, *Ciano's Diaries*, 12 October 1940 (and also 29 October); Bottai, *Diario*, 12 October 1940.
179 DGFP, D, 11, 199, 332; Bottai, *Diario*, 19 October 1940. See also Knox, 'The Fascist Regime', 164–5; Mack Smith, *Mussolini's Roman Empire*, 216ff; Hoggan, D.L., *Der erzwungene Krieg* (Tübingen, 1964), especially 611ff.
180 Knox, *Mussolini Unleashed*, 289ff. The quote is from *Ciano's Diaries*, 30 January 1940.
181 Quartararo, *Roma tra Londra e Berlino*, ch. 8. See also De Felice, *Mussolini il duce*, vol. I: *Gli anni del consenso, 1929–1936* (Turin, 1974), 800–2.
182 Bocca, 259–60; USE, *La prima offensive britannica in Africa settentrionale (ottobre 1940 – febbraio 1941)* (Rome, n.d.), vol. I, 45ff; Bottai, *Diario*, 24 October 1940.
183 Knox, *Mussolini Unleashed*, 166–7, 191–2, 204–5; Muggeridge, *Ciano's Diaries*, 18 October 1940.
184 Muggeridge, *Ciano's Diaries*, 22 October 1940; Cervi, M., *Storia della guerra di Grecia* (Milan, 1965), 150–1; DDI, 9th, V, 803. For a good account of the events see We-

inberg, G.L., *A World at Arms: A Global History of World War II* (Cambridge 1994), 208ff.

185 DGFP, D, 11, 246, 418; DDI, 9th, V, 807.

186 Domarus, II, 1600 (meeting at Florence, 28 October 1940); von Kotze, H., (ed.), *Heeresadjutant bei Hitler, 1938–1943. Aufzeichnungen des Majors Engel* (Stuttgart, 1974), 88 (Hitler's anger).

187 Sadkovich, J.J., 'The Italo-Greek War in Context: Italian Priorities and Axis Diplomacy', *Journal of Contemporary History*, 28 (1993), 493–64.

188 Sadkovich, 'The Italo-Greek War', 440ff; Sadkovich, J.J., 'Of Myths and Men: Rommel and the Italians in North Africa, 1940–42', *International History Review*, 13 (1991), 287–301.

189 De Felice, R., *Mussolini l'alleato*, vol. 1a, 28ff; Sadkovich, J.J., 'Understanding Defeat: Reappraising Italy's Role in World War II', *Journal of Contemporary History*, 24 (1989), 27–61.

190 USM, *La marina italiana nella seconda guerra mondiale*, vol. 4: *La guerra nel Mediterraneo* (Rome, 1959), 200ff; Knox, *Mussolini Unleashed*, 236ff; Muggeridge, *Ciano's Diaries*, 12 November 1940; Bottai, *Diario*, 14 November 1940.

191 Bocca, 261–9; Knox, *Mussolini Unleashed*, 251ff; USE, *La prima offensiva britannica in Africa settentrionale*, I.

192 Bocca, ch. 14 (Africa), and 295–304; Weinberg, *World at Arms*, 225–34 (attack on the Balkans), 348–63 (German offensive in north Africa); Sadkovich, 'Of Myths and Men', 287ff.

193 Segrè, *Balbo*, 340–1.

194 Rochat, 'Mussolini e forze armate', 130–2; Ceva, L., 'Appunti per una storia dello Stato Maggiore Generale fino alla vigilia della "non-belligerenza" (giugnio 1925–luglio, 1939)', *Storia Contemporanea*, 2 (1979), 207–52.

195 Muggeridge, *Ciano's Diaries*, 21/22/27 November 1940; Bottai, *Diario*, 30 November 1940.

196 Andrè, G., 'Politica estera fascista', 122–6.

197 Colarizi, *Opinione pubblica*, 345–8.

198 Knox, *Mussolini Unleashed*, 245ff; Muggeridge, *Ciano's Diaries*, 7/18 December 1940, 16 January 1941.

199 Bottai, *Diario*, 13 December 1940.

200 DGFP, D, 12, 379/510.

201 Domarus, II, 1672–3 (Directive 24, 4 March 1941).

202 Muggeridge, *Ciano's Diaries*, 1 July 1941. On Italy's participation in the operation, see Weinberg, *A World at Arms*, 276–7; Clark, M., *Modern Italy, 1860–1995* (London, 1996), 285–9. See also Ciano's and Mussolini's desperate attempt to persuade Hitler to include more Italian forces in 'Barbarossa', in DGFP, D, 13/424/522.

203 Muggeridge, *Ciano's Diaries*, 30 September 1941.

204 Muggeridge, *Ciano's Diaries*, 17 October 1941.

205 Thompson, D., *State Control in Fascist Italy: Culture and Conformity, 1925–43* (Manchester and New York 1991), 146–8; Aquarone, *Stato Totalitario*, 310–2, and 'Public Opinion in Italy before the Outbreak of World War II', in Sarti, R. (ed.), *The Ax Within: Italian Fascism in Action* (New York, 1974), 209–20.

206 Aga-Rossi, E., 'La politica degli Alleati verso l' Italia nel 1943', *Studi Storici*, 3 (1972), 843–95.

207 De Felice, R., *Mussolini l'alleato*, vol. 1b: *Crisi e agonia del regime* (Turin, 1990), 1089–1410.

208 Collotti, E., *L'amministrazione tedesca dell'Italia occupata 1943–1945* (Milan, 1963); Schröder, J., 'La caduta di Mussolini e la contromisure tedesche nell' Italia centrale fino alla formazione della Repubblica Sociale Italiana', in De Felice, *Italia fra Tedeschi e Alleati*, 137–70.

209 DDI, 9th, VIII, 169.
210 Muggeridge, *Ciano's Diaries*, 30 June 1941.
211 Muggeridge, *Ciano's Diaries*, 8 February 1943.
212 Domarus, II, 1354–66 (speech to Gauleiters, 19 September 1939). For a detailed and interesting history of the German war against Poland see Bethell, N., *The War Hitler Won: The Fall of Poland, September 1939* (New York, 1972).
213 Jacobsen, *Halder*, I, 89–91.
214 Domarus, II, 1394ff; Noakes and Pridham, *Nazism*, III, 762.
215 Jacobsen, H.-A. (ed.), *Dokumente zur Vorgeschichte des Westfeldzuges, 1939–1940* (Göttingen, 1956), 5–7.
216 Weinberg, *World at Arms*, 107ff.
217 Domarus, II, 1426–7 (speech to the generals, 23 November 1939).
218 Müller, K.-J., *Das Heer und Hitler, 1933–1940* (Stuttgart, 1969), 675ff.
219 On Admiral Raeder's objections see Domarus, II, 1348 (7 September 1939), 1450 (27 January 1940).
220 Domarus, II, 1471ff; Weinberg, *World at Arms*, 113ff. On Raeder's importance for the prioritisation of this operation see Gemzell, C.-A., *Raeder, Hitler und Skandinavien* (Lund, 1965).
221 Domarus, II, 1511–12 (Directive for Operation Yellow); and 1502–3 (Proclamation to the soldiers of the Western Front, 9 May 1940).
222 Seraphin, *Politische Tagesbuch Alfred Rosenbergs*, 23 March/17 June 1940; Cecil, R., *The Myth of the Master Race: Alfred Rosenberg and Nazi Ideology* (London, 1972), 184–5.
223 Domarus, II, 1540–58.
224 Domarus, II, 1354ff. The second peace offer in ibid., II, 1540ff (speech to the Reichstag, 19 July 1940), and the British rejection, 1562.
225 DGFP, D, 10, 177; Domarus, II, 1538–9 (16 July 1940). See also Wheatley, R., *Operation 'Sea Lion': German Plans for the Invasion of England 1939–1942* (Oxford, 1958), 1–15.
226 Jacobsen, *Halder*, II, 31–50; Domarus, II, 1564–5; Robertson, E.M., 'Hitler Turns from the West to Russia', in Boyce and Robertson, *Paths to War*, 367–72.
227 Weinberg, *Hitler, Germany and World War*, II, 158ff; *World at Arms*, 170ff; Hill (ed.), *Weizsäcker-Papiere*, 204ff; Jacobsen, *Halder*, 30–1.
228 Jacobsen, *Halder*, 46–8; Craig, G.A., *Germany 1866–1945* (Oxford, 1978), 721ff.
229 Jacobsen, *Halder*, 43ff; Robertson, 'Germany Turns', 373–4; Craig, *Germany*, 722.
230 Domarus, II, 1566 (Directive no.17); Trevor-Roper, H.R. (ed.), *Blitzkrieg to Defeat: Hitler's War Directives, 1939–1945* (New York, 1964), 36ff.
231 Collier, B., *The Battle of Britain* (London, 1962), 111ff.
232 Domarus, II, 1575ff (4 September 1940). See Ciano's comments in Muggeridge, *Ciano's Diaries*, 5 September 1940.
233 Klee, K., *Das Unternehmen 'Seelöwe'* (Göttingen, 1948), 204ff.
234 Schreiber, G., 'The Mediterranean in Hitler's Strategy in 1940: "Programme" and Military Planning', in Deist, W. (ed.), *The German Military in the Age of Total War* (Leamington Spa, 1985), 254ff; Robertson, 'Hitler Turns', 376ff.
235 Noakes and Pridham, *Nazism*, III, 794–5; and an analysis in Schreiber, 256–8.
236 Weinberg, G.L., 'Der deutsche Entschluss zum Angriff auf die Sowjetunion', *Vierteljahrshefte für Zeitgeschichte*, 1 (1953), 301–18; *World at Arms*, ch. 4; Hillgruber, A., *Hitlers Strategie und Kriegführung, 1940–41* (Frankfurt, 1965); Hildebrand, *The Foreign Policy of the Third Reich*; Hildebrand, *Deutsche Aussenpolitik, 1939–1945. Kalkul oder Dogma?* (Stuttgart, 1970).
237 Michalka, W., 'From the Anti-Comintern Pact to the Euro-Asiatic Bloc: Ribbentrop's Alternative Concept to Hitler's Foreign Policy Programme', in Koch, *Aspects of the Third Reich*, 267–84; and Koch, 'Die nationalsozialistische Aussenpolitik im Zeichen eines "Konzeptionen-Pluralismus"', 59–62.

238 Koch, H.W., 'Hitler's Programme and the Genesis of Operation "Barbarossa" ', in Koch, *Aspects of the Third Reich* (Houndmills and London 1985), 285–322; Craveld, 28f, 92ff, 179ff. See also Broszat, M., 'Soziale Motivation und Führer-Bindung der Nationalsozialismus', *Vierteljahrshefte für Zeitgeschichte*, 18 (1970), 392–400.
239 DGFP, D, 11, 70/87; Koch, 'Barbarossa', 307–8.
240 DGFP, D, 11, 220/207/227/246.
241 Domarus, II, 1609ff (Directive no. 18); DGFP, D, 11, 323. The talks with Suner in D, 11, 352/357.
242 Jacobsen, H.-A., (ed.), *Kriegstagebuch des Oberkommandos der Wehrmacht*, vol. I: *1 August 1940–31 Dezember 1941* (Frankfurt, 1965), 5 December 1940 (henceforward, *OKW*).
243 DGFP, D, 11, 476/491; Schreiber, 267–8; Hillgruber, *Hitlers Strategie*, 178ff.
244 Weinberg, *World at Arms*, 207–8; DGFP, D, 12, 46/73.
245 DGFP, D, 11, 532. See also Schreiber, 268–9; Weinberg, *World at Arms*, 187ff.
246 Funke, M., 'Die deutsche-italienische Beziehungen: Anti-bolschevismus und aussenpolitische Interessenkonkurrenz als Strukturprinzip der "Achse"', in Funke, M. (ed.), *Hitler, Deutschland und die Mächte. Materialien zur Aussenpolitik des Dritten Reiches* (Düsseldorf, 1977), 828–30; Lowe and Marzari, 326.
247 DGFP, D, 11, 192.
248 Jacobsen, *OKW*, 8/9 January 1941; DGFP, D, 11, 643.
249 DGFP, D, 11, 487.
250 Jacobsen, *Halder*, II, 45ff.
251 Raeder's analysis is in Noakes and Pridham, *Nazism*, III, 794–5. For General Thoma's report see DGFP, D, 11, 462.
252 Domarus, II, 1609ff; DGFP, D, 11, 323. See also Jacobsen, *Halder*, II, 160–1.
253 Hitler's orders in DGFP, D, 11, 642; Muggeridge, *Ciano's Diaries*, 18/19 November 1940.
254 Knox, *Mussolini Unleashed*, 282ff; Bosworth, R.J.B., *Italy and the Wider World*, 108–9; Bocca, ch. 16; Muggeridge, *Ciano's Diaries*, 30 May 1941.
255 Weinberg, *World at Arms*, 187ff. For the strategic importance of Rumania in Hitler's strategic plans for Barbarossa see his Directives 18 and 21 in DGFP, D, 11, 323/899.
256 DGFP, D, 11, 325/511.
257 Hancock, E., *The National Socialist Leadership and Total War, 1941–5* (New York, 1991), ch. 2; Hillgruber, A., 'Das Russlandbild der führenden deutschen Militärs vor Beginn des Angriffs auf die Sowjetunion', in Hillgruber, A. (ed.), *Die Zerstörung Europas. Beiträge zur Weltkriegsepoche, 1914 bis 1945* (Berlin, 1988), 256–72.
258 Koch, 'Barbarossa', 291ff.
259 Jacobsen, *Halder*, II, 3ff.
260 Jacobsen, *Halder*, II, 30ff; and Domarus, II, 1652–3 (Hitler's speech to Generals, 8–9 January 1941).
261 DGFP, D, 11, 325–6/328–9; Craig, *Germany*, 727ff; Hillgruber, *Hitlers Strategie*, 356ff; Schreiber, 263ff; Noakes and Pridham, *Nazism*, III, 799ff.
262 Koch, 'Barbarossa', 292ff.
263 DGFP, D, 11, 404/405; Koch, 'Barbarossa', 318–19.
264 Domarus, II, 1609f (Directive 18, 12 November 1940).
265 Koch, 'Barbarossa', 301–7; Weinberg, *World at Arms*, 183–5; Weinberg, *Germany and the Soviet Union*, 134ff.
266 Koch, 'Barbarossa', 312–13.
267 Erickson, 'Threat identification', 342–4; Jacobsen, *Halder*, II, 113ff; DGFP, D, 12, 423.
268 DGFP, D, 11, 88/166/170.
269 DGFP, D, 11, 568, and 636 for the text of the agreement.
270 DGFP, D, 12, 423/468/505/547/628.

271 Domarus, II, 1683–4 (Directive for the Liquidation of Russian Commissars, 30 March 1941); Jacobsen (ed.), *Halder*, II, 320–37. See also Weinberg, *World at Arms*, 190ff; Wippermann, W., *Wessen Schuld? Vom Historikerstreit zur Goldhagen-Kontroverse* (Berlin, 1997), 59–79.

272 DGFP, D, 11, 323, 527; Weinberg, *World at Arms*, ch. 4.

273 Schreiber, 268–70; Weinberg, *World at Arms*, 190–3; Hassell, U. von, *The von Hassell Diaries* (London, 1948), 1 September 1939; Schöllgen, G., *A Conservative against Hitler. Ulrich von Hassell, Diplomat in Imperial Germany, the Weimar Republic and the Third Reich, 1881–1944* (Basingstoke and London, 1991), 67ff. For Weizsäcker's memorandum containing strong critical comments see DGFP, D, 12, 419. For Canaris's objections see Streit, C., *Keine Kameraden. Die Wehrmacht und die sowjetischen Kriegsgefangenen, 1941–1945* (Stuttgart, 1978).

274 See, for example, Jacobsen, *Halder*, II, 257–261.

275 Michalka, 'From the Anti-Comintern Pact', 283–4.

276 Michalka, 'Die nationalsozialistische Aussenpolitik im Zeichen eines "Konzeptionen-Pluralismus"', 55–62.

277 Overy, *'Iron Man'*, ch. 5, especially 190–1.

278 See Rosenberg's plans for the administration of the eastern provinces in DGFP, D, 12, 649; Wegner, B., '"My Honour is Loyalty": the SS as a Military Factor in Hitler's Germany', in Deist, W., (ed.), *The German Military in the Age of Total War* (Leamington Spa, 1985), 220–39; Ackermann, J., 'Heinrich Himmler: Reichsführer – SS', in Smelser, R. and Zitelmann R. (eds), *The Nazi Elite* (Houndmills and London, 1993), 98–112.

279 Seraphin (ed.), *Tagesbuch Rosenbergs*, entries for 29 May/21 June 1941.

280 Manvell, R. and Fraenkel, H., *Heinrich Himmler* (London, 1965), 113ff.

281 Quoted in Rhodes, J.M., *The Hitler Movement* (Stanford, 1980), 119.

282 DGFP, D, 12, 660; Muggeridge, *Ciano's Diaries*, 22 June 1941.

283 Domarus, II, 1967ff (address to the nation, 1 January 1943).

284 Seabury, P., *The Wilhelmstrasse: A Study of German Diplomats under the Nazi Regime* (Berkeley 1954), 123–4, 126ff; Orlow, II, 403–4.

285 Berghahn, V.R., 'NSDAP und "Geistige Führung" der Wehrmacht', *Vierteljahrshefte für Zeitgeschichte*, 17 (1969), 49ff.

286 Broszat, M., *The Hitler State: The Foundation and Development of the Internal Structure of the Third Reich* (London and New York 1981), 294ff; Hancock, 190, where Guderian's criticism is also stated; Geyer, 'Restorative Elites', 144.

287 See Hitler's comments as recorded in Goebbels' Diaries in Lochner, 20 March 1942, 9 March 1943, 10 May 1943.

288 Geyer, 'Restorative Elites', 157ff; Bartov, O., 'Savage War', in Burleigh, M. (ed.), *Confronting the Nazi Past: New Debates on Modern German History* (London, 1996), 129ff.

289 Jacobsen, *OKW*, 1062–3; DDI, 9th, VIII, 211.

290 Domarus, II, 1812–6 (19 December 1941); Noakes and Pridham, *Nazism*, III, 827–8; Weinberg, *World at Arms*, chaps 5–6.

291 Weinberg, *World at Arms*, 431–47; Howe, G.F., *Northwest Africa: Seizing the Initiative in the West* (Washington, 1957).

292 Ziemke, E.F., *Moscow to Stalingrad: Decision in the East* (Washington, 1987), 430ff; Weinberg, *World at Arms*, 447–64.

293 Klink, E., *Das Gesetz des Handels. Die Operation 'Zitadelle', 1943* (Stuttgart, 1966), and Noakes and Pridham, *Nazism*, III, ch. 33.

294 Jacobsen, H.-A. (ed.), *1939–1945: Der Zweite Weltkrieg in Chronik und Dokumenten* (Darmstadt 1962), 474; Noakes, J. and Pridham, G. (eds), *Documents on Nazism, 1919–1945* (London, 1974), 676–7. On Hitler's insistence to fight all wars till the very end, see Domarus, II, 2022 (Proclamation for Operation 'Citadel', 4 July 1943).

NOTES

295 Speer, A., *Inside the Third Reich* (London, 1970), 404–5.
296 Goebbels himself had acknowledged that there is no chance for active opposition to Hitler in the framework of the regime (Trevor-Roper, H., *The Goebbels Diaries: Final Entries, 1944–1945* (London 1988), 2 June 1944).
297 Speer, *Inside the Third Reich*, 485–7; Hansen, R., 'Aussenpolitik im Zusammenbruch des Dritten Reiches', in Funke, M. (ed.), *Hitler, Deutschland und die Mächte. Materialien zur Aussenpolitik des Dritten Reiches* (Düsseldorf, 1977), 128ff.

CONCLUSIONS

1 Eatwell, R., *Fascism: A History* (London, 1996), 279.
2 Kershaw, I., *The Nazi Dictatorship: Problems and Perspectives of Interpretation* (London 1989, 2nd edn), 168–91; Kühnl, R. (ed.), *Vergangenheit, die nicht vergeht* (Cologne, 1987); Maier, C., *The Unmasterable Past: History, Holocaust, and German National Identity* (Munich, 1988); Knowlton, J., Cates, T. (eds), *Forever in the Shadow of Hitler? Original Documents of the Historikerstreit, the Controversy concerning the Singularity of the Holocaust* (Princeton, 1993).
3 Azzi, S.C., 'The Historiography of Fascist Foreign Policy', *The Historical Journal*, 1 (1993), 203.
4 De Felice, R., *Mussolini il duce*, vol. I: *Gli anni del consenso, 1929–1936* (Turin, 1974), 320ff.
5 Cassels, A., *Mussolini's Early Diplomacy* (Princeton, 1970).
6 See the discussion in Kershaw, *The Nazi Dictatorship*, 122–5; Azzi, 'Historiography of Fascist Foreign Policy', 187–90.
7 Mosse, G.L., 'Towards a General Theory of Fascism', in Mosse, G.L. (ed.), *International Fascism: New Thoughts and New Approaches* (London and Beverly Hills, 1979), 1–41.
8 O'Sullivan, N., *Fascism* (London and Melbourne, 1983), chaps 2–4.
9 See the detailed analysis of the *Dopolavoro* in De Grazia, V., *The Culture of Consent: Mass Organisation of Leisure in Fascist Italy* (Cambridge, 1981), especially 220ff.
10 De Felice, R., *Mussolini il duce*, vol. 1: *Gli anni del consenso*, passim.
11 Kershaw, I., *The 'Hitler-Myth': Image and Reality in the Third Reich* (Oxford, 1989), ch. 5.
12 Bottai, G., *Vent'anni e un giorno (24 luglio 1943)* (Milan, 1977), 79–91.
13 Bottai, *Vent'anni*, 64–7.
14 Colarizi, S., *L'opinione degli italiani sotto il regime, 1929–1943* (Rome and Bari, 1991), 327ff, 399–404.
15 For the attitudes of German public opinion in 1941–5 see Kershaw, *The 'Hitler-Myth'*, 149–225.
16 Knox, M., 'Expansionist Zeal, Fighting Power, and Staying Power in the Italian and German Dictatorships', in Bessel, R. (ed.), *Fascist Italy and Nazi Germany: Comparisons and Contrasts* (Cambridge, 1996), 115–33.
17 Payne, S.G., *A History of Fascism, 1914–45* (London, 1997), 462–70; Griffin, R., *The Nature of Fascism* (London and New York, 1994), 245–8.
18 Steinberg, J., *All or Nothing: The Axis and the Holocaust, 1941–42* (London, 1990).
19 Germino, D.L., *The Italian Fascist Party in Power: A Study in Totalitarian Rule* (New York, 1971), 141–4.
20 Perfetti, F., *Il dibattito sul fascismo* (Rome, 1984), 10–13.
21 De Felice, R., *Mussolini il fascista*, vol. 1: *La conquista del potere, 1921–1925* (Turin, 1966), 470.
22 Mack Smith, D., *Mussolini's Roman Empire* (London, 1976), 252ff.
23 On the last issue see Capogreco, C.S., 'I campi di internamento fascista per gli ebrei (1940–1943)', *Storia Contemporanea*, 22 (1991), 663–82.

24 Vivarelli, R., 'Interpretations of the Origins of Fascism', *Journal of Modern History*, 63 (1991), 29–43; De Felice, *Intervista sul fascismo* (Bari, 1975), 11ff.
25 Griffin, R., 'Three Faces of Fascism', *Patterns of Prejudice*, 30 (1996), 69–70.
26 Bosworth, R.J.B., *The Italian Dictatorship: Problems and Perspectives in the Interpretation of Mussolini and Fascism* (London, 1998), ch. 9, especially 229–30.

SELECT BIBLIOGRAPHY

Primary sources

Documents

Documenti Diplomatici Italiani (published by Libreria dello Stato, Rome), Series 6–9.
Documents on British Foreign Policy (published by Her Majesty's Stationery Office, London), Series 5.
Documents on German Foreign Policy (published by Her Majesty's Stationery Office, London), Series B–D.

Speeches and writings of Mussolini and Hitler

Baynes, N.H. (ed.), *The Speeches of Adolf Hitler: April 1922 – August 1939* (London, New York, Toronto, 1942), 2 vols.
Bernardo Quaranta di San Severino, Baron (ed.), *Mussolini as Revealed in his Political Speeches (November 1914 – August, 1923)* (London and Toronto, 1923).
Domarus, M. (ed.), *Hitler: Reden und Proklamationen 1932–1945*, (Würzburg 1962–3), 2 vols.
Hitler, A., *Mein Kampf*, trans. R. Mannheim (London, 1972).
Jäckel, E. and Kuhn, A. (eds.), *Hitler: Sämtliche Aufzeichnungen, 1905–1924* (Stuttgart, 1980).
Mussolini, B., *Scritti e Discorsi*, 12 vols (Milan 1934–9).
Phelps, R., 'Hitler als Parteiredner in Jahre 1920', *Vierteljahrshefte für Zeitgeschichte*, 11 (1963), 274–330.
Santarelli, E. (ed.), *Scritti politici di Benito Mussolini* (Milan, 1979).
Susmel, E. and Susmel, D. (eds.), *Opera Omnia di Benito Mussolini* (Florence and Rome 1951–78).
von Kotze, H. and Krausnick, H. (eds.), *'Es spricht Hitler'. Sieben exemplariche Hitler-Reden* (Gütersloh, 1966).

Diaries, memoirs and autobiographies

Aloisi, P., *Journal, 25 juin–14 juillet 1936* (Paris, 1957).
Armellini, Q., *Diario di guerra. Nove mesi al Comando Supremo* (Milan, 1946).

Bottai, G., *Vent'anni e un giorno (24 luglio 1943)* (Milan, 1977).

Burckhardt, C.J., *Meine Danziger Mission 1937–1939* (Munich, 1962).

Cantalupo, R., *Fu la Spagna. Ambasciata presso Franco, febbraio–aprile 1937* (Milan, 1948).

Ciano, G., *Diplomatic Papers* (London, 1948).

Giurati, G., *La parabola di Mussolini nelle memorie di un gerarca*, ed. E. Gentile (Rome and Bari, 1981).

Grandi, D., *Il mio paese. Ricordi autobiografici*, ed. R. De Felice (Bologna, 1985).

Guariglia, R., *Ricordi* (Naples, 1950).

Hill, L. (ed.), *Die Weizsäcker-Papiere, 1933–1950* (Frankfurt, 1974).

Hossbach, F., *Zwischen Wehrmacht und Hitler, 1934–1938* (Wolfenbüttel and Hannover, 1949).

Jacobsen, H.-A. (ed.), *Generaloberst Halder: Kriegstagebuch* (Stuttgart, 1962), 2 vols.

—— (ed.), *Kriegstagebuch des Oberkommandos der Wehrmacht, vol. I: 1 August 1940 – 31 Dezember 1941* (Frankfurt, 1965).

Lochner, L.P. (ed.), *The Goebbels Diaries* (London, 1948).

Muggeridge, M. (ed.), *Ciano's Diaries, 1939–1943* (London and Toronto, 1947).

—— *Ciano's Diary, 1937–1938* (London, 1952).

Seraphin, H.G. (ed.), *Das Politische Tagebuch Alfred Rosenbergs 1934/5 und 1939/40* (Göttingen, Berlin and Frankfurt, 1956).

Speer, A., *Erinnerungen* (Frankfurt am Main, 1969).

—— *Inside the Third Reich* (London, 1970).

Suvich, F., *Memorie, 1932–1936* (Milan, 1984).

Trevor-Roper, H.R. (ed.), *The Table Talk of Adolf Hitler, 1941–1944* (London, 1953).

—— *The Testament of Adolf Hitler: The Hitler-Bormann Documents, February–April 1945* (London, 1961).

—— *Final Entries 1945: The Diaries of Joseph Goebbels* (New York, 1978).

von Kotze, H. (ed.), *Heeresadjutant bei Hitler, 1938–1943. Aufzeichnungen des Majors Engel* (Stuttgart, 1974).

Wagner, E. (ed.), *Der Generalquartiermeister. Briefe und Tagebuchaufzeichnungen des Generalquartiermeisters des Heeres, General der Artillerie Eduard Wagner* (Munich, 1963).

Wiedemann, F., *Der Mann der Feldherrwerden wollte* (Kettwig, 1964).

Contemporary studies and interpretations

Ciano, G., *Europa verso il catastrofe* (Milan, 1948).

Gentile, G, 'The Philosophical Basis of Fascism', *Foreign Affairs*, 6 (1928), 290–304.

—— *Origini e dottrina del fascismo* (Rome, 1929).

—— *I Profeti del Risorgimento* (Florence 1944, 3rd edn).

Goebbels, J., *Vom Kaiserhof zum Reichskanzlei* (Munich, 1938).

Göring, H., *Aufbau einer Nation* (Berlin, 1934).

Juenger, E., *Der Kampf als inneres Erlebnis* (Berlin, 1922).

—— 'Die Totale Mobilmachung', in Jünger, E. (ed.), *Krieg und Krieger* (Berlin, 1930).

—— *Der Arbeiter. Herrschaft und Gestalt* (Hamburg 1932, 2nd edn).

Malaparte, C., *Technique du coup d'état* (Paris, 1948), 161–72.

Missiroli, M., *Una battaglia perduta* (Milan, 1924).

Moeller van den Bruck, *Germany's Third Empire* (New York, 1971).

Mussolini, B., 'Political and Social Doctrine of Fascism', in Oakeshott, M. (ed.), *The Social and Political Doctrines of Contemporary Europe* (New York, 1949), 164–79.

Neumann, F., *Behemoth: The Structure and Practice of National Socialism* (New York, 1963).

Papini, G., *Italia mia* (Florence, 1941).

Rauschning, H., *The Revolution of Nihilism* (New York, 1939).

—— *Voice of Destruction* (New York, 1940).

—— *Men of Chaos* (New York, 1942).

Rosenberg, A., *Pest in Russland* (Munich, 1922).

Salvemini, G., *Dal Patto di Londra alla Pace di Roma* (Turin, 1925).

—— *Mussolini Diplomatico* (Bari, 1952).

—— *Preludio alla seconda guerra mondiale* (Milan, 1967), also translated in English as *Prelude to the Second World War* (London, 1953).

—— *Opere*, Part 6: *Scritti sul fascismo*, ed. R. Vivarelli, (Milan, 1974), 3 vols.

Schacht, H., 'Germany's Colonial Demands', *Foreign Affairs*, 15 (1937), 223–34.

Spengler, O., *The Decline of the West* (London, 1926).

—— *Jahre der Entscheidung* (Berlin, 1933).

Strasser, O., *Aufbau des Sozialismus* (Prague, 1936).

Secondary sources

General works on fascism

Allardyce, G., 'What Fascism is Not: Thoughts on the Deflation of a Concept', *American Historical Review*, 84 (1979), 367–88.

Andreski, S., 'Fascists as Moderates', in Larsen, S.U., Hagtvet, B. and Myklebust, J.P. (eds), *Who Were the Fascists? Social Roots of European Fascism* (Bergen, Oslo and Tromso, 1980), 52–5.

Bracher, K.D., *The Age of Ideologies: A History of Political Thought in the Twentieth Century* (London, 1982).

Brooker, P., *The Faces of Fraternalism: Nazi Germany, Fascist Italy and Imperial Japan* (Oxford, 1991).

De Grand, A.J., *Fascist Italy and Nazi Germany: The 'Fascist' Style of Rule* (London and New York, 1995).

Deakin, F.W., *The Brutal Friendship: Mussolini, Hitler and the Fall of Italian Fascism* (London, 1962).

Eatwell, R., 'Towards a New Model of Generic Fascism', *Journal of Theoretical Politics*, 4 (1992), 161–94.

—— *Fascism: A History* (London, 1995).

Griffin, R., *The Nature of Fascism* (London and New York, 1994).

—— (ed.), *Fascism* (Oxford and New York, 1995).

Hamilton, A., *The Appeal of Fascism: A Study of Intellectuals and Fascism 1919–1945* (London, 1971).

Hayes, P.M., *Fascism* (London, 1973).

—— 'The Triumph of Caesarism: Fascism and Nazism', in Hayes, P.M. (ed.), *Themes in Modern European History, 1890–1945* (London and New York, 1992), 174–204.

Linz, J.J., 'Some Notes Towards a Comparative Study of Fascism in Sociological Historical Perspective', in Laqueur, W. (ed.), *Fascism: A Reader's Guide. Analyses, Interpretations, Bibliography* (Harmondsworth, 1979), 29–39.

—— 'Political Space and Fascism as Late-Comer', in Larsen, S.U., Hagtvet, B. and Myklebust, J.P. (eds), *Who Were the Fascists? Social Roots of European Fascism* (Bergen, Oslo and Tromso, 1980), 153–89.

Maier, C., *Recasting Bourgeois Europe: Stabilisation in France, Germany, and Italy in the Decade after World War I* (Princeton, 1975).

Mason, T., 'Whatever Happened to "Fascism"', in Childers, T. and Caplan, J. (eds), *Reevaluating the Third Reich* (New York, London, 1993), 253–62.

Mosse, G.L., 'Towards a General Theory of Fascism', in Mosse, G.L. (ed.), *International Fascism: New Thoughts and New Approaches* (London and Beverly Hills, 1979), 1–41.

—— 'Two World Wars and the Myth of the War Experience', *Journal of Contemporary History*, 21 (1986), 491–514.

Neocleous, M., *Fascism* (London, 1997).

Noakes, J. and Pridham, G. (eds), *Documents on Nazism, 1919–1945* (London, 1974).

—— (eds), *Nazism: A Documentary Reader* (Exeter 1983–1988), 3 vols.

Nolte, E., *Three Faces of Fascism: Action Française, Italian Fascism, National Socialism* (London, 1965).

O'Sullivan, N., *Fascism* (London and Melbourne, 1983).

Payne, S.G., *Fascism: Comparison and Definition* (Madison, 1980).

—— *A History of Fascism, 1914–45* (London, 1997).

Petersen, J., *Hitler und Mussolini. Die Entstehung der Achse Berlin-Rom 1933–1936* (Tübingen, 1973).

Schieder, W., 'Fascismo e nazionalsocialismo nei primi anni Trenta' in Del Boca, A., Legnani, M. and Rossi, M.G. (eds), *Il regime fascista. Storia e storiografia* (Rome and Bari, 1995), 45–56.

Steinberg, J., *All or Nothing: The Axis and the Holocaust, 1941–42* (London, 1990).

Sternhell, Z., 'Fascist Ideology', in Laqueur, W. (ed.), *Fascism: A Reader's Guide. Analyses, Interpretations, Bibliography* (Harmondsworth, 1979), 325–406.

—— *The Birth of Fascist Ideology: From Cultural Rebellion to Political Revolution* (Princeton, 1994).

Weber, E., 'Revolution? Counter-revolution? What Revolution?', in Laqueur, W. (ed.), *Fascism: A Reader's Guide. Analyses, Interpretations, Bibliography* (Harmondsworth, 1979), 488–531.

Biographies

Ackermann, J., *Himmler als Ideologe* (Göttingen, 1970).

—— 'Heinrich Himmler: Reichsführer-SS', in Smelser, R. and Zitelmann R. (eds), *The Nazi Elite* (Houndmills and London, 1993), 98–112.

Bullock, A., *Hitler: A Study in Tyranny* (Harmondsworth, 1962).

Carr, W., *Hitler: A Study in Personality and Politics* (London, 1978).

Casmirri, S., 'Luigi Federzoni', in Cordova, F. (ed.), *Uomini e volti del fascismo* (Rome, 1980), 281–99.

Cecil, R., *The Myth of the Master Race: Alfred Rosenberg and Nazi Ideology* (London, 1972).

Cordova, F. (ed.), *Uomini e volti del fascismo* (Rome, 1980).

De Felice, R., *Mussolini il rivoluzionario* (Turin, 1965).

—— *Mussolini il fascista*, vol. 1: *La conquista del potere, 1921–1925* (Turin, 1966); vol. 2: *L'organizzazione dello Stato Fascista, 1925–1929* (Turin, 1968).

—— *Mussolini il duce*, vol. 1: *Gli anni del consenso, 1929–1936* (Turin, 1974); vol. 2: *Lo Stato Totalitario, 1936–1940* (Turin, 1981).

—— *Mussolini l'alleato*, vol. 1a/b: *L'Italia in guerra, 1940–1943* (Turin, 1990).

Fischer, C., 'Ernst Julius Röhm: Chief of Staff of the SA and Indispensible [sic] Outsider', in Smelser, R. and Zitelmann, R. (eds), *The Nazi Elite* (Houndmills and London, 1993), 173–82.

Froehlich, E., 'Joseph Goebbels: The Propagandist', in Smelser, R. and Zitelmann, R. (eds), *The Nazi Elite* (Houndmills and London, 1993), 48–61.

Guerri, G.B. (ed.), *Giuseppe Bottai: Diario, 1935–1944* (Milan 1996, 3rd edn).

—— *Galeazzo Ciano. Una vita, 1903/1944* (Milan, 1979).

Heiber, H., *Goebbels* (New York, 1972).

Hibbert, C., *Benito Mussolini* (London, 1975).

Kershaw, I., *Hitler. 1889–1936: Hubris* (London, 1998).

Kirkpatrick, I.S., *Mussolini: Study of a Demagogue* (London, 1964).

Kube, A., 'Hermann Goering: The Second Man in the Reich', in Smelser, R. and Zitelmann, R. (eds), *The Nazi Elite* (Houndmills and London, 1993), 62–73.

Longerich, P., 'Joseph Goebbels und der totale Krieg: eine unbekannte Denkschrift des Propagandministers vom 18. Juli 1944', *Vierteljahrshefte für Zeitgeschichte*, 35 (1987), 289–314.

Mack Smith, D., *Mussolini* (London, 1981).

Manvell, R. and Fraenkel, H., *Heinrich Himmler* (London, 1965).

Michaelis, M., 'Il Maresciallo dell'aria Italo Balbo e la politica mussoliniana', *Storia Contemporanea*, 14 (1983), 330–61.

Michalka, W., *Ribbentrop und die deutsche Weltpolitik 1933–1940. Aussenpolitische Konzeptionen und Entscheidungsprozesse im Dritten Reich* (Munich, 1980).

Mosse, G.L., 'The Poet and the Exercise of Political Power: Gabriele D'Annunzio', in Mosse, G.L. (ed.), *Masses and Man* (New York, 1980), 35–61.

Müller, K.-J, *General Ludwig Beck. Studien und Dokumente zur politisch-militärischen Vorstellungswelt und Tätigkeit des Generalstabchefs des deutschen Heers 1933–1938* (Boppard, 1980).

Nello, P. (ed.), *Dino Grandi: la politica estera dell'Italia dal 1929 al 1932 (Rome, 1985) – Un fedele disubbidiente. Dino Grandi dal palazzo Chigi al 25 luglio* (Bologna, 1993).

Overy, R.J., *Göring: The 'Iron Man'* (London, Boston, Melbourne and Henley, 1984).

Padfield, P., *Himmler: Reichsführer-SS* (London and Basingstoke, 1990).

Pieri, P. and Rochat, G., *Pietro Badoglio* (Turin, 1974).

Rochat, G., *Italo Balbo. Aviatore e ministro dell'aeronautica, 1926–1933* (Ferrara, 1979).

Schwarz, P., *This Man Ribbentrop: His Life and Times* (New York, 1943).

Segrè, C.C., *Italo Balbo: A Fascist Life* (Berkeley, Los Angeles and London, 1987).

Zitelmann, R., *Hitler: Selbstverständnis eines Revolutionärs* (Hamburg, Leamington Spa and New York, 1987).

Works on Germany and Nazism

General works

Berghahn, V.R., *Modern Germany: Society, Economy and Politics in the 20th Century* (Cambridge 1987, 2nd edn).

Blackbourn, D. and Eley, G. (eds), *The Peculiarities of German History* (Oxford, 1984).

Bracher, K.D., *The Nazi Dictatorship* (London, 1970).
—— *The Making of the Nazi Revolution* (New York, 1973).
Craig, G.A., *Germany 1866–1945* (Oxford, 1978).
Fest, J., *The Face of the Third Reich* (London, 1970).
Hiden, J. and Farquharson, J., *Explaining Hitler's Germany* (Totowa, 1983).
Hildebrand, K., *The Third Reich* (London, 1984).
Hughes, M., *Nationalism and Society: Germany, 1800–1945* (London, 1988).
Kershaw, I., *The Nazi Dictatorship: Problems and Perspectives of Interpretation* (London 1989, 2nd edn).
Kershaw, I. and Lewin, M. (eds), *Stalinism and Nazism: Dictatorships in Comparison* (Cambridge, 1997).
Mason, T., 'Intention and Explanation. A Current Controversy about the Interpretation of National Socialism', in Hirschfeld, G. and Kettenacker, L. (eds), *Der 'Führerstaat'. Mythos und Realität. Studien zur Struktur und Politik des Dritten Reiches* (Stuttgart, 1981), 23–42.
Mommsen, H., 'National Socialism: Continuity and Change', in Laqueur, W. (ed.), *Fascism: A Reader's Guide. Analyses, Interpretations, Bibliography* (Harmondsworth, 1979), 151–92.
Nipperdey, T., '1933 and Continuity of German History', in Koch, H.W. (ed.), *Aspects of the Third Reich* (Houndmills and London, 1985), 489–508.
Nolte, E., *Das Europäische Bürgerkrieg, 1917–1945. Nationalsozialismus und Bolschevismus* (Berlin, 1987).
Peukert, D.J.K., *Inside Nazi Germany: Conformity, Opposition and Racism in Everyday Life* (Harmondsworth, 1989).
Remak, J. (ed.), *The Nazi Years: A Documentary History* (Englewood Cliffs, 1969).
Schieder, T., 'Das deutsche Reich in seinen nationalen und universalen Beziehungen: 1871 bis 1945', in Schieder, T. and Dauerlein, E. (eds), *Reichsgründung 1870/71. Tatsachen, Kontroversen, Interpretationen* (Stuttgart, 1970), 422–54.
Williamson, D.G., *The Third Reich* (Harlow, 1995, 2nd edn).

Bismarckian and Wilhelminian Reich (1871–1918)

Breuilly, J., *The Formation of the First German Nation-State, 1800–1871* (Basingstoke and London, 1996).
Chickering, R., *We Men Who Feel Most German: A Cultural Study of the Pan-German League, 1886–1914* (Boston, 1984).
Eley, G., *Reshaping the German Right: Radical Nationalism and Political Change after Bismarck* (New Haven and London, 1980).
Evans, R.J., *Society and Politics in Wilhelmine Germany* (New York, 1978).
Fischer, F., *Germany's Aims in the First World War* (New York, 1967).
—— *War of Illusions: German Policies from 1911 to 1914* (London, 1975).
—— *From Kaiserreich to Third Reich* (London, 1979).
Fletcher, R., *Revisionism and Empire: Social Imperialism in Germany, 1897–1914* (London, 1984).
Geiss, I., *German Foreign Policy, 1871–1914* (Boston, 1976).
Henderson, W.O., *The German Colonial Empire, 1884–1919* (London, 1993).
Kaiser, D.E., 'Germany and the Origins of the First World War', *Journal of Modern History*, 55 (1983), 442–74.
Kruck, A., *Geschichte des alldeutschen Verbandes, 1890–1939* (Wiesbaden, 1954).

Mommsen, W.J., 'Domestic Factors in German Foreign Policy before 1914', in Sheehan, J.J. (ed.), *Imperial Germany* (New York and London, 1976), 223–68.

Moses, J.A., *The Politics of Illusion: The Fischer Controversy in German Historiography* (London, 1975).

Stegmann, D., *Die Erben Bismarcks. Parteien und Verbände in der Spätphase des Wilhelminischen Deutschlands. Sammlungspolitik 1897–1918* (Cologne, 1970).

Stone, N., *The Eastern Front 1914–1917* (London, Sydney, Auckland and Toronto, 1975).

Wehler, H.-U., *Bismarck und der Imperialismus* (Cologne, 1969).

—— *Das deutsche Kaiserreich 1871–1918* (Göttingen, 1975), translated as *The German Empire 1871–1918* (Leamington Spa, 1985).

—— 'Bismarck's Imperialism, 1862–1890', in Sheehan, J.J. (ed.), *Imperial Germany* (New York and London, 1976), 180–222.

Wertheimer, M.S., *The Pan-German League, 1890–1914* (New York, 1924).

The Weimar Period (1918–33)

Bretton, H.L., *Stresemann and the Revision of Versailles* (Stanford, 1953).

Eley, G., 'Conservatives and Radical Nationalists in Germany: The Production of Fascist Potentials, 1912–1928', in Blinkhorn, M. (ed.), *Fascists and Conservatives: The Radical Right and the Establishment in Twentieth-Century Europe* (London, 1990), 50–70.

Gatske, H.W., *Stresemann and the Rearmament of Germany* (Baltimore, 1954).

Geyer, M., 'The Dynamics of Military Revisionism in the Interwar Years: Military Policy between Rearmament and Diplomacy', in Deist, W. (ed.), *The German Military in the Age of Total War* (Leamington Spa, 1985), 100–51.

Howard, M., 'The Legacy of the First World War', in Boyce, R. and Robertson, E.M. (eds), *Paths to War: New Essays on the Origins of the Second World War* (Houndmills and London, 1989), 33–54.

Jacobson, J., *Locarno Diplomacy* (Princeton, 1972).

Lee, M.M. and Michalka, W., *German Foreign Policy 1917–1933* (Leamington Spa, Hamburg and New York, 1987).

Matthias, E., 'The Influence of the Versailles Treaty on the Internal Development of the Weimar Republic', in Nicholls, A. and Matthias, E. (eds), *German Democracy and the Triumph of Hitler* (London, 1971), 13–28.

Sharp, A., *The Versailles Settlement: Peacemaking in Paris, 1919* (London, 1991).

Strandmann, H.P. von, 'Imperialism and Revisionism in Interwar Germany', in Mommsen, W.J. and Osterhammel, J. (eds), *Imperialism and After: Continuities and Discontinuities* (London, Boston and Sydney, 1986), 90–119.

Ideology and foreign policy

Birken, L., *Hitler as Philosophe. Remnants of the Enlightenment in National Socialism* (Westport and London, 1995).

Jäckel, E., *Hitlers Weltanschauung. Entwurf einer Herrschaft* (Tübingen, 1969), translated as *Hitler's Weltanschauung: A Blueprint for Power* (Middletown, 1972).

Koch, H.W., 'Die Rolle des Sozialdarwinismus als Faktor im Zeitalter des neuen Imperialismus um die Jahrhundertwende', *Zeitschrift für Politik*, 17 (1970), 51–70.

Mosse, G.L., *The Crisis of German Ideology* (London, 1966).

—— *The Nationalisation of the Masses: Political Symbolism and Mass Government in Germany from the Napoleonic Years through the Third Reich* (Ithaca and London, 1991).

Pese, W.W., 'Hitler und Italien, 1920–1928', *Vierteljahrshefte für Zeitgeschichte*, 3 (1955), 113–26.

Smith, W.D., *The Ideological Origins of Nazi Imperialism* (Oxford, 1986).

Stern, F., *The Politics of Cultural Despair* (Berkeley, 1961).

Stoakes, G., 'The Evolution of Hitler's Ideas on Foreign Policy, 1919–1925', in Stachura, P.D. (ed.), *The Shaping of the Nazi State* (London, 1978), 22–47.

Struve, W., *Elites against Democracy: Leadership Ideals in Bourgeois Political Thought in Germany, 1890–1933* (Princeton, 1973).

Foreign policy (1933–39)

Abendroth, H.-H., 'Deutschlands Rolle im Spanischen Bürgerkrieg', in Funke, M. (ed.), *Hitler, Deutschland und die Mächte. Materialien zur Aussenpolitik des Dritten Reiches* (Düsseldorf, 1977), 471–88.

Aigner, D., 'Hitler's Ultimate Aims: A Programme of World Domination?', in Koch, H.W. (ed.), *Aspects of the Third Reich* (Houndmills and London, 1985), 235–50.

Bracher, K.D., 'Das Anfangsstadium der Hitlerischen Aussenpolitik', *Vierteljahrshefte für Zeitgeschichte*, 5 (1957), 113–48.

Carr, W., *Arms, Autarky and Aggression: A Study in German Foreign Policy 1933–1939* (London, 1972).

—— 'National Socialism: Foreign Policy and Wehrmacht', in Laqueur, W., *Fascism: A Reader's Guide. Analyses, Interpretations, Bibliography* (Harmondsworth, 1979), 115–50.

Craig, G.A., 'The German Foreign Office from Neurath to Ribbentrop', in Gilbert, F. and Craig, G.A. (eds), *The Diplomats* (Princeton, 1953), 406–36.

Funke, M., *Sanktionen und Kanonen. Hitler, Mussolini und der nationale Abessinienkonflikt 1935–1936* (Düsseldorf, 1970).

—— 'Die deutsche-italienische Beziehungen: Anti-bolschevismus und aussenpolitische Interessenkonkurrenz als Strukturprinzip der "Achse"', in Funke, M. (ed.), *Hitler, Deutschland und die Mächte. Materialien zur Aussenpolitik des Dritten Reiches* (Düsseldorf, 1977), 823–46.

—— *Nazionalsozialistische Aussenpolitik* (Darmstadt, 1978), 277–324.

Hauner, M., 'The Professionals and the Amateurs in National Socialist Foreign Policy: Revolution and Subversion in the Islamic and Indian World', in Hirschfeld, G. and Kettenacker, L. (eds), *Der 'Führerstaat'. Mythos und Realität* (Stuttgart, 1981), 305–28.

Heineman, J.L., *Hitler's First Foreign Minister: Constantin Freiherr von Neurath, Diplomat and Statesman* (Berkeley, Los Angeles and London, 1979).

Hildebrand, K., *Vom Reich zum Weltreich. Hitler, NSDAP und die koloniale Frage 1919–1945* (Munich, 1969).

—— *The Foreign Policy of the Third Reich* (London, 1972).

Hillgruber, A., *Kontinuität und Diskontinuität in der deutschen Aussenpolitik von Bismarck bis Hitler* (Düsselfdorf, 1969).

Jacobsen, H.-A., *Nazionalsozialistische Aussenpolitik 1933–1945* (Frankfurt, 1968).

Jarausch, K.H., '"From Second to Third Reich": The Problem of Continuity in German Foreign Policy', *Central European History*, 12 (1979), 68–82.

Koch, H.W., 'Hitler and the Origins of the Second World War: Second Thoughts on the Status of Some of the Documents', *Historical Journal*, 11 (1968), 125–43.

Kuhn, A., *Hitlers Aussenpolitisches Programm* (Stuttgart, 1970).

Louis, W.M.R., (ed.), *The Origins of the Second World War: A.J.P. Taylor and His Critics* (New York, 1972).

Maser, W., *Hitler's Mein Kampf: An Analysis* (London, 1970).

Mason, T., 'Some Origins of the Second World War', in Robertson (ed.), *The Origins of the Second World War: Historical Interpretations* (London and Basingstoke, 1971), 105–35.

—— 'Innere Krise und Angriffskrieg 1938–9', in Forstmeier, F. and Volkmann, H.E. (eds), *Wirtschaft und Rüstung am Vorabend des Zweiten Weltkrieges* (Düsseldorf, 1975), 158–88.

—— 'The Domestic Dynamics of Nazi Conquest', in Childers, T. and Caplan, J. (eds), *Reevaluating the Third Reich* (New York, London, 1993), 161–89.

Mason, T. and Overy, R., 'Debate: Germany, "Domestic Crisis" and War in 1939', *Past and Present*, 122 (1989), 205–40.

Michaelis, M., 'World Power Status or World Domination?', *Historical Journal*, 15 (1972), 331–60.

Michalka, W., 'Die nationalsozialistische Aussenpolitik im Zeichen eines "Konzeptionen-Pluralismus": Fragestellungen und Forschungsaufgaben', in Funke, M. (ed.), *Hitler, Deutschland und die Mächte. Materialien zur Aussenpolitik des Dritten Reiches* (Düsseldorf, 1977), 46–62.

—— 'From Anti-Comintern Pact to the Euro-Asiatic Bloc: Ribbentrop's Alternative Concept to Hitler's Foreign Policy Programme', in Koch, H.W. (ed.), *Aspects of the Third Reich* (Houndmills and London, 1985), 267–84.

Michalka, W. (ed.), *Das Dritte Reich*, vol. I: *Volksgemeinschaft und Grossmachtpolitik* (Munich, 1985).

Müller, K.-J., 'The Structure and Nature of the National Conservative Opposition in Germany up to 1940', in Koch, H.W. (ed.), *Aspects of the Third Reich* (London, 1985), 133–78.

Murray, W., *The Change in the European Balance of Power, 1938–1939: The Path to Ruin* (Princeton, 1984).

Rich, N., *Hitler's War Aims*, vol. 1: *Ideology, the Nazi State and the Course of Expansion* (London, 1973).

Roberts, H.L., 'The Diplomacy of Colonel Beck', in Craig, G.A. and Gilbert, F. (eds), *The Diplomats, 1919–1939* (Princeton, 1953), 579–614.

Robertson, E.M., 'German Mobilisation Preparations and the Treaties between Germany and the Soviet Union of August and September 1939', in Boyce, R. and Robertson, E.M. (eds), *Paths to War: New Essays on the Origins of the Second World War* (Basingstoke and London, 1989), 330–66.

—— 'Hitler turns from the West to Russia, May–December 1940', in Boyce, R. and Robertson, E.M. (eds), *Paths to War: New Essays on the Origins of the Second World War* (London, 1989), 330–66.

Schieder, W., 'Spanischer Bürgerkrieg und Vierjahresplan. Zur Struktur der national-sozialistischen Aussenpolitik', in Michalka, W. (ed.), *Nationalsozialistische Aussenpolitik* (Darmstadt, 1978), 325–59.

Schmokel, W.W., *Dream of Empire: German Colonisation, 1919–1945* (New Haven and London, 1964).

Schubert, G., *Anfänge nationalsozialistischer Aussenpolitik* (Cologne, 1961).

Seabury, P., *The Wilhelmstrasse: A Study of German Diplomats under the Nazi Regime* (Berkeley, 1954).

Stoecker, H., *German Imperialism in Africa* (London, 1986).

Watt, D.C., 'The Anglo-German Naval Agreement of 1935. An Interim Judgment', *Journal of Modern History*, 28 (1956), 155–75.

Weinberg, G.L., *The Foreign Policy of Hitler's Germany: Diplomatic Revolution in Europe, 1933–1936* (Chicago, 1970).

—— *The Foreign Policy of Hitler's Germany: Starting World War II, 1937–1939* (Chicago, 1980).

—— *Germany, Hitler, and World War II: Essays in Modern German and World History* (Cambridge, 1995).

Wheeler-Bennett, J.W., *Munich: Prologue to Tragedy* (London, 1962).

Wollstein, G., *Von Weimarer Revisionismus zu Hitler. Das deutsche Reich und die Grossmächte in der Anfangsphäse der nationalsozialistische Herrschaft in Deutschland* (Bonn and Bad Godesberg, 1973).

Armed forces and foreign policy

Berghahn, V.R., 'NSDAP und "Geistige Führung" der Wehrmacht, 1939–1943', *Vierteljahrshefte für Zeitgeschichte*, 17 (1969), 17–71.

Carsten, F.L., *The Reichswehr and Politics, 1918–1933* (Oxford, 1966).

Craig, G.A., *The Politics of the Prussian Army, 1640–1945* (Oxford, 1955).

Deist, W., 'Die Aufrüstung der Wehrmacht', in Deist, W. *et al.* (eds), *Das Deutsche Reich und der Zweite Weltkrieg*, vol. I: *Ursachen und Vorraussetzungen der deutschen Kriegspolitik* (Stuttgart, 1979), 400–532.

—— *The Wehrmacht and German Rearmament* (London and Basingstoke, 1981).

Düllfer, J., *Weimar, Hitler und die Marine. Reichspolitik und Flottenbau, 1920 bis 1939* (Düsseldorf, 1973).

—— 'Determinants of German Naval Policy, 1920–1939', in Düllfer (ed.), *The German Military in the Age of Total War* (Leamington Spa, 1985), 152–70.

Geyer, M., *Aufrüstung oder Sicherheit? Die Reichswehr und die Krise der Machtpolitik 1924–1936* (Wiesbaden, 1980).

Gordon, H.J., *The Reichswehr and the German Republic* (Princeton, 1957).

Herbst, L., 'Die Krise des nationalsozialistichen Regimes am Vorabend des Zweiten Weltkrieges und die forcierte Aufrüstung', *Vierteljahrshefte für Zeitgeschichte*, 26 (1978), 347–92.

Meinck, G., *Hitler und die deutsche Aufrüstung* (Wiesbaden, 1959).

Messerschmidt, M., *Die Wehrmacht im nationalsozialistischen Staat. Zeit der Indoktrination* (Hamburg, 1969).

—— 'Reichswehr und die Röhm-Affäre', *Militärgeschichtliche Mitteilungen*, 3 (1986), 107–44.

Michalka, W., 'Conflicts within the German Leadership on the Objectives and Tactics of German Foreign Policy, 1933–1939', in Mommsen, W.J. and Kettenacker, L. (eds), *The Fascist Challenge and the Policy of Appeasement* (London, 1983), 48–60.

Müller, K.-J., *Das Heer und Hitler. Armee und nationalsozialistisches Regime, 1933–1944* (Stuttgart, 1956).

—— 'The German Military Opposition before the Second World War', in Mommsen, W.J. and Kettenacker, L. (eds), *The Fascist Challenge and the Policy of Appeasement* (London, 1983), 65–75.

—— *The Army, Politics and Society in Germany, 1933–45: Studies in the Army's Relation to Nazism* (Manchester, 1987).

O'Neill, R.J., *The German Army and the Nazi Party, 1933–1939* (London, 1966).

Rosinski, H., *The German Army* (New York, 1966).

Vogelsang, T., *Reichswehr, Staat und NSDAP. Beiträge zur deutschen Geschichte, 1930–1932* (Stuttgart, 1962).

Wegner, B., 'My Honour is Loyalty: the SS as a Military Factor in Hitler's Germany', in Deist, W., (ed.), *The German Military in the Age of Total War* (Leamington Spa, 1985), 220–39.

Second World War (1939–45)

Bartov, O., 'Soldiers, Nazis and War in the Third Reich', *Journal of Modern History*, 63 (1991), 44–60.

—— 'Savage War', in Burleigh, M. (ed.), *Confronting the Nazi Past: New Debates on Modern German History* (London, 1996), 125–39.

Bethell, N., *The War Hitler Won: The Fall of Poland, September 1939* (New York, 1972).

Clark, A., *Barbarossa: the Russian-German Conflict, 1941–1945* (Harmondsworth, 1966).

Craveld, L. van, *Hitler's Strategy 1940–1941: The Balkan Clue* (London, 1973).

Hancock, E., *The National Socialist Leadership and Total War, 1941–5* (New York, 1991).

Hansen, R., 'Aussenpolitik im Zusammenbruch des Dritten Reiches', in Funke, M. (ed.), *Hitler, Deutschland und die Mächte. Materialien zur Aussenpolitik des Dritten Reiches* (Düsseldorf, 1977), 115–34.

Hillgruber, A., *Hitlers Strategie. Politik und Kriegführung, 1940–1941* (Frankfurt, 1965).

—— 'Das Russlandbild der führenden deutschen Militärs vor Beginn des Angriffs auf die Sowjetunion', in Hillgruber, A. (ed.), *Die Zerstörung Europas. Beiträge zur Weltkriegsepoche, 1914 bis 1945* (Berlin, 1988), 256–72.

Jacobsen, H.-A., (ed.), *1939–1945: Der Zweite Weltkrieg in Chronik und Dokumenten* (Darmstadt, 1962).

Kitchen, M., *Nazi Germany at War* (London and New York, 1995).

Koch, H.W., 'Hitler's Programme and the Genesis of Operation "Barbarossa"', in Koch, H.W. (ed.), *Aspects of the Third Reich* (Houndmills and London, 1985), 285–322.

Leach, B.A., *German Strategy against Russia, 1939–1941* (Oxford, 1973).

Leitz, C., *Economic Relations between Nazi Germany and Franco's Spain, 1936–1945* (Oxford, 1996).

Milward, A., 'Der Einfluss ökonomischer und nicht-ökonomischer Faktoren auf die Strategie des Blitzkriegs', in Forstmeier, F. and Volkmann, H.E. (eds), *Wirtschaft und Rüstung am Vorabend des Zweiten Weltkrieges* (Düsseldorf, 1975), 96–122.

Overy, R.J., 'Hitler's War and the German Economy. A Reinterpretation', *The Economic History Review*, 35 (1982), 272–91.

—— 'Germany, "Domestic Crisis" and War in 1939', *Past and Present*, 116 (1987), 138–68.

—— 'Hitler's War Plans and the German Economy', in Boyce, R. and Robertson, E.M. (eds), *Paths to War: New Essays on the Origins of the Second World War* (London, 1989), 96–127.

—— 'Debate: Germany, "Domestic Crisis" and War in 1939', *Past and Present*, 122 (1989), 200–40.

Roskill, S.W., *The War at Sea* (London, 1954).

Schramm, P. (ed.), *Kriegshandbuch des Oberkommandos der Wehrmacht 1940–1941* (Munich, 1982).

Schreiber, G., 'The Mediterranean in Hitler's Strategy in 1940: "Programme" and Military Planning', in Deist, W. (ed.), *The German Military in the Age of Total War* (Leamington Spa, 1985), 240–81.

Steinert, M.G., *Hitler's War and the Germans: Public Mood and Attitude towards the Second World War* (Ohio, 1977).

Streit, C., *Keine Kameraden. Die Wehrmacht und die sowjetischen Kriegsgefangenen, 1941–1945* (Stuttgart, 1978).

Taylor, A.J.P., *The Origins of the Second World War* (London, 1961).

—— 'War Origins Again', in Robertson, E.M. (ed.), *The Origins of the Second World War: Historical Interpretations* (London and Basingstoke, 1971), 136–41.

Trevor-Roper, H.R., 'Hitlers Kriegsziele', *Vierteljahrshefte für Zeitgeschichte*, 8 (1960), 121–33.

—— (ed.), *Blitzkrieg to Defeat: Hitler's War Directives, 1939–1945* (New York, 1964).

—— 'A.J.P. Taylor, Hitler and the War', in Robertson, E.M. (ed.), *The Origins of the Second World War: Historical Interpretations* (London and Basingstoke, 1971), 83–99.

—— 'Hitler's War Aims', in Koch, H.W. (ed.), *Aspects of the Third Reich* (London, 1985), 235–50.

Uldricks, T.J., 'Soviet Security Policy in the 1930s', in Gorodetsky, G. (ed.), *Soviet Foreign Policy, 1917–1991: A Retrospective* (London, 1994), 65–74.

Weinberg, G.L., 'Der deutsche Entschluss zum Angriff auf die Sowjetunion', *Vierteljahrshefte für Zeitgeschichte*, 1 (1953), 301–18.

—— 'German Colonial Plans and Policies 1938–1942', in Besson, W. and von Gärtringer, F. Freiherr (ed.), *Geschichte und Gegenwartsbewusstsein. Historische Betrachtungen und Untersuchungen. Festschrift für Hans Rothfels* (Göttingen, 1963), 465–503.

—— *A World at Arms: A Global History of World War II* (Cambridge, 1994).

Wheatley, R., *Operation 'Sea Lion': German Plans for the Invasion of England 1939–1942* (Oxford, 1958).

Ziemke, E.F., *Moscow to Stalingrad: Decision in the East* (Washington, 1987).

Nazi society and domestic organisation

Broszat, M., 'Soziale Motivation und Führer-Bindung der Nationalsozialismus', *Vierteljahrshefte für Zeitgeschichte*, 18 (1970), 392–400.

—— *The Hitler State: The Foundation and Development of the Internal Structure of the Third Reich* (London and New York, 1981).

Burleigh, M. and Wippermann, W., *The Racial State. Germany 1933–1945* (Cambridge, 1991).

Caplan, J., *Government without Administration: State and Civil Service in Weimar and Nazi Germany* (Oxford, 1988).

—— 'National Socialism and the Theory of the State', in Childers, T. and Caplan, J. (eds), *Reevaluating the Third Reich* (New York and London, 1993), 98–113.

Diehl-Thiele, P., *Partei und Staat im Dritten Reich. Untersuchung zum Verhältnis von NSDAP und allgemeiner innerer Staatsverwaltung, 1933–1945* (Munich, 1971).

Frei, N., *National Socialism Rule in Germany. The Führer-State 1933–1945* (Oxford and Cambridge, MA, 1993).

Geyer, M., 'The State in National Socialist Germany', in Bright, C. and Harding, S. (eds), *Statemaking and Social Movements* (Ann Arbor, 1984), 132–66.

—— 'Restorative Elites, German Society and the Nazi Pursuit of Goals', in Bessel, R. (ed.), *Fascist Italy and Nazi Germany: Comparisons and Contrasts* (Cambridge, 1996), 134–64.

Goldhagen, D., *Hitler's Willing Executioners: Ordinary Germans and the Holocaust* (London, 1996).

Herf, G., *Reactionary Modernism: Technology, Culture and Politics in Weimar and the Third Reich* (Cambridge, 1984).

Hildebrand, K., 'Hitlers Ort in der Geschichte der preussisch-deutschen Nationalstaates', *Historische Zeitschrift*, 217 (1973), 584–632.

—— 'Monokratie oder Polykratie? Hitlers Herrschaft und das Dritte Reich', in Hirschfeld, G. and Kettenacker, L. (eds), *Der 'Führerstaat'. Mythos und Realität* (Stuttgart, 1981), 73–97.

Kershaw, I., *The 'Hitler-Myth'. Image and Reality in the Third Reich* (Oxford, 1989).

Kettenacker, L., 'Social and Psychological Aspects of the Führer's Rule', in Koch, H.W. (ed.), *Aspects of the Third Reich* (Houndmills and London, 1985), 96–132.

Koehl, R., 'Feudal Aspects of National Socialism', in Turner, H.A., Jr. (ed.), *Nazism and the Third Reich* (New York, 1972), 151–74.

Krausnick, H., Buchheim, H., Broszat, M. and Jacobsen, H.-A. (eds), *Anatomy of the SS State* (London, 1968).

Mason, T., *Sozialpolitik im Dritten Reich* (Opladen, 1977).

—— 'The Primacy of Politics – Politics and Economics in National Socialist Germany', in Woolf, S.J. (ed.), *The Nature of Fascism* (London, 1968), 165–95.

Merkl, P.H., *Political Violence under the Swastika: 581 Early Nazis* (Princeton, 1975).

Mommsen, H., *Beamtentum im Dritten Reich. Mit ausgewählten Quellen zur nationalsozialistischen Beamtenpolitik* (Stuttgart, 1966).

—— 'Reflections on the Position of Hitler and Göring in the Third Reich', in Childers, T. and Caplan, J. (eds), *Reevaluating the Third Reich* (New York and London, 1993), 94–5.

—— 'Ausnahmezustand als Herrschaftstechnik des Nationalsozialistischen-Regimes', in Funke, M. (ed.), *Hitler, Deutschland und die Mächte. Materialien zur Aussenpolitik des Dritten Reiches* (Düsseldorf, 1977), 30–45.

Noakes, J., 'German Conservatives and the Third Reich: an Ambiguous Relationship', in Blinkhorn, M. (ed.), *Fascists and Conservatives: The Radical Right and the Establishment in the Twentieth Century Europe* (London, 1990), 71–97.

Orlow, D., *The History of the Nazi Party, 1919–1945* (Pittsburgh 1969–73), 2 vols.

Petzina, D., *Autarkiepolitik im Dritten Reich. Der Nationalsozialistische Vierjahresplan, 1936–1941* (Stuttgart, 1968).

Pulzer, P.G.J., *Jews and the German State: The Political History of a Minority* (Oxford, 1992).

Schoenbaum, D., *Hitler's Social Revolution: Class and Status in Nazi Germany, 1933–1939* (New York and London, 1980).

Stephenson, J., *The Nazi Organisation of Women* (London, 1981).

Theweleit, K., *Male Fantasies*, vol. II: *Male Bodies: Psychoanalyzing the White Terror* (Cambridge, 1989).

Weindling, P., 'Understanding Nazi Racism: Precursors and Perpetrators', in Burgleigh, M. (ed.), *Confronting the Nazi Past: New Debates on Modern German History* (London, 1996), 66–83.

Works on Italy and Italian Fascism

General works on Italian history and fascism

Bosworth, R.J.B., *Italy and the Wider World, 1860–1960* (London and New York, 1996).
—— *The Italian Dictatorship: Problems and Perspectives in the Interpretation of Mussolini and Fascism* (London and New York, 1998).
Candeloro, G., *Storia dell'Italia moderna*, vol. 9: *Il fascismo e le sue guerre* (Milan 1998, 8th edn).
Carocci, G., *Storia del fascismo* (Milan, 1972).
—— *Storia d'Italia dall'unità ad oggi* (Milan, 1975).
Chabod, F., *A History of Italian Fascism* (London, 1963).
Clark, M., *Italy 1860–1995* (London 1996, 2nd edn).
Delzell, C.F. (ed.), *Mediterranean Fascism, 1919–1945* (New York, Evanston and London, 1970).
Lyttelton, A., *The Seizure of Power: Fascism in Italy 1919–1929* (London 1987, 2nd edn).
—— 'Italian Fascism', in Laqueur, W. (ed.), *Fascism: A Reader's Guide. Analyses, Interpretations, Bibliography* (Harmondsworth, 1979), 81–114.
Mack Smith, D., *Italy: A Modern History* (Ann Arbor, 1969).
Morgan, P., *Italian Fascism, 1919–1945* (Basingstoke, 1995).
Saladino, S., 'Italy', in Rogger, H. and Weber, E. (eds), *The European Right: A Historical Profile* (London, 1965), 209–58.
Salvatorelli, L. and Mira, G., *Storia dell'Italia nel periodo fascista* (Turin, 1957).
Santarelli, C., *Storia del movimento e del regime fascista* (Rome, 1967), 2 vols.
Sarti, R. (ed.), *The Ax Within: Italian Fascism in Action* (London, 1974).
—— 'Italian Fascism: Radical Politics and Conservative Goals', in Blinkhorn, M. (ed.), *Fascists and Conservatives: The Radical Right and the Establishment in Twentieth Century Europe* (London, 1990), 14–30.
Tannenbaum, E.R., *Fascism in Italy: Society and Culture 1922–1945* (London, 1973).
Thompson, D., *State Control in Fascist Italy: Culture and Conformity, 1925–43* (Manchester and New York, 1991).
Vivarelli, R., 'Interpretations of the Origins of Fascism', *Journal of Modern History*, 63 (1991), 29–43.
Wiskemann, E., *Fascism in Italy* (London and Basingstoke 1970, 2nd edn).

Italy from unification to the March on Rome (1860–1922)

Adamson, W., 'The Language of Opposition in Early Twentieth-Century Italy: Rhetorical Continuities between Prewar Florentine Avant-garde and Mussolini's Fascism', *Journal of Modern History*, 64 (1992), 22–51.
—— 'Avant-Garde Political Rhetorics: Pre-War Culture in Florence as a Source of Post-War Fascism', *Journal of European Ideas*, 16 (1993), 753–7.
Bosworth, R.J.B., *Italy, the Least of the Great Powers: Italian Foreign Policy Before the First World War* (Cambridge, 1979).
—— *Italy and the Approach of the First World War* (New York, 1983).
Cunsolo, R.S., 'Italian Nationalism in Historical Perspective', *History of European Ideas*, 16 (1993), 759–66.

De Grand, A.J., *The Italian Nationalist Association and the Rise of Fascism in Italy* (Lincoln and London, 1978).

Gaeta, F., 'L' Associazione Nazionalista Italiana', in Gentile, E. (ed.), *L'Italia giolittiana. La storia e la critica* (Rome and Bari, 1977), 253–68.

Lotti, L., 'L'età giolittiana', in Spadolini, G. (ed.), *Nazione e nazionalità in Italia. Dall'alba del secolo ai nostri giorni* (Rome and Bari, 1994), 45–64.

Thayer, J.A., *Italy and the Great War: Politics and Culture 1870–1915* (Madison and Milwaukee, 1964).

Vivarelli, R., *Il fallimento del liberalismo. Studi sulle origini del fascismo* (Bologna 1981).

Webster, R.A., *Industrial Imperialism in Italy 1908–1915* (Berkeley and Los Angeles, 1975).

Ideology and foreign policy

Alatri, P., *Le origini del fascismo* (Rome, 1963).

Gentile, E., *Le origini dell'ideologia fascista, 1918–1925* (Roma and Bari, 1975).

Gregor, A.J., *The Ideology of Fascism: The Rationale of Totalitarianism* (New York, 1969).

Simonini, A., *Il linguaggio di Mussolini* (Milan, 1978).

Vivarelli, R., 'Benito Mussolini dal socialismo al fascismo', *Rivista storica italiana*, 79 (1967), 438–58.

Zapponi, N., 'Futurismo e fascismo', in De Felice, R. (ed.), *Futurismo, cultura e politica* (Turin, 1986), 161–76.

Foreign policy (1922–39)

Azzi, S.C., 'The Historiography of Fascist Foreign Policy', *The Historical Journal*, 1 (1993), 187–203.

Baer, G.W., *The Coming of the Italo-Ethiopian War* (Cambridge, MA, 1967).

Barros, J., *The Corfu Incident of 1923* (Princeton, 1966).

Bianchini, S., 'L'idea fascista dell' impero nell' area danubiano-balcanica', in Di Nolfo, A., Rainero, R.H. and Vigezzi, B. (eds), *L'Italia e la politica di potenza in Europa (1938–1940)* (Milan, 1986), 173–86.

Bosworth, R.J.B, 'Italian Foreign Policy and its Historiography', in Bosworth, R.J.B. and Rizzo, G. (eds), *Altro Polo: Intellectuals and their Ideas in Contemporary Italy* (Sydney, 1983), 52–96.

—— 'Mito e linguaggio nella politica estera italiana', in Bosworth, R.J.B. and Romano, S. (eds), *La politica estera italiana, 1860–1985* (Bologna, 1991), 35–67.

Braddick, H., 'The Hoare-Laval Plan: A Study in International Politics', *Review of Politics*, 24 (1962), 69–78.

Carocci, G., *La politica estera dell'Italia fascista 1925–1928* (Bari, 1969).

Casella, F. 'L'immagine fascista dell' impero: quale ruolo all' Adriatico', in Di Nolfo, A., Rainero, R.H. and Vigezzi, B. (eds), *L'Italia e la politica di potenza in Europa (1938–1940)* (Milan, 1986), 187–204.

Cassels, A., *Mussolini's Early Diplomacy* (Princeton, 1970).

Catalano, F., *L'economia italiana di guerra. La politica economico-finanziaria del fascismo dalla guerra d'Etiopia alla caduta del regime, 1935–1943* (Milan, 1969).

Coverdale, J.F., *Italian Intervention in the Spanish Civil War* (Princeton, 1975).

272

De Felice, R., 'Alcune osservazioni sulla politica estera mussoliniana', in De Felice, R. (ed.), *L'Italia fra Tedeschi e Alleati. La politica estera fascista e la seconda guerra mondiale* (Bologna, 1973), 57–74.

Di Nolfo, E., *Mussolini e la politica estera italiana 1919–1933* (Padova, 1960).

Gilbert, F., 'Ciano and his Ambassadors' in Craig, G. and Gilbert, F. (eds), *The Diplomats* (Princeton, 1953), 512–36.

Hildebrand, K., 'Hitlers "Programm" und seine Realisierung', in Funke, M. (ed.), *Hitler, Deutschland, und die Mächte. Materialien zur Aussenpolitik des Dritten Reiches* (Düsseldorf, 1977), 63–93.

Hughes, S., 'The Early Diplomacy of Italian Fascism: 1922–1932', in Craig, G. and Gilbert, F.A. (eds), *The Diplomats 1919–1939* (Princeton, 1953), 210–33.

Knox, M., 'Conquest, Domestic and Foreign, in Fascist Italy and Nazi Germany', *Journal of Modern History*, 56 (1984), 1–57.

—— 'Il fascismo e la politica estera italiana', in Bosworth, R.J.B. and Romano, S. (eds), *La politica estera italiana (1860–1985)* (Bologna, 1991), 287–330.

—— 'Expansionist Zeal, Fighting Power, and Staying Power in the Italian and German Dictatorships', in Bessel, R. (ed.), *Fascist Italy and Nazi Germany: Comparisons and Contrasts* (Cambridge, 1996), 115–33.

Labanca, N., 'L'amministrazione coloniale fascista. Stato, politica e società', in Del Boca, A., Legnani, M. and Rossi, M.C. (eds), *Il regime fascista. Storia e storiografia* (Rome and Bari, 1995), 352–95.

Laurens, F.D., *France and the Italo-Ethiopian Crisis 1935–1936* (The Hague, 1967).

Ledeen, M.A., *The First Duce: D'Annunzio at Fiume* (Baltimore, 1977).

Lowe, C.J. and Marzari, F., *Italian Foreign Policy 1870–1940* (London and Boston, 1975).

Mack Smith, D., *Le guerre di Duce* (Bari and Rome 1976, 2nd edn), translated as *Mussolini's Roman Empire* (London, 1982).

Marzari, F., 'Projects for an Italian-led Balkan Bloc of Neutrals, September-December 1939', *Historical Journal*, 13 (1970), 767–88.

Morewood, S., 'Anglo-Italian Rivalry in the Mediterranean and Middle East 1935–1940', in Boyce, R. and Robertson, E.M. (eds), *Paths to War: New Essays on the Origins of the Second World War* (London, 1989), 167–98.

Orsini, F.G., 'La diplomazia', in Del Boca, A., Legnani, M. and Rossi, M.C. (eds), *Il regime fascista. Storia e storiografia* (Rome and Bari, 1995), 277–328.

Pastorelli, L., 'La storiografia italiana del dopoguerra sulla politica estera', *Storia e Politica*, 10 (1971), 603–49.

Pastorelli, P., 'La politica estera fascista dalla fine del conflitto etiopico alla seconda guerra mondiale', in de Felice, R. (ed.), *L'Italia fra tedeschi e alleati. La politica estera fascista e la seconda guerra mondiale* (Bologna, 1973), 103–14.

Petersen, J., 'La politica estera del fascismo come problema storiografico', in De Felice, R. (ed.), *L'Italia fra tedeschi e alleati. La politica estera fascista e la seconda guerra mondiale* (Bologna, 1973), 11–56.

Quartararo, R., 'Appendice a Inghilterra e Italia. Dal Patto di Pasqua a Monaco', *Storia Contemporanea*, 7 (1976), 648–716.

—— 'L'Italia e lo Yemen. Uno studio sulla politica di espansione italiana nel Mar Rosso', *Storia Contemporanea*, 10 (1979), 811–67.

—— *Roma tra Londra e Berlino. La politica estera fascista dal 1930 al 1940* (Rome, 1980).

Robertson, E.M., 'Hitler and Sanctions. Mussolini and the Rhineland', *European Studies Review*, 7 (1977), 409–35.

—— *Mussolini as Empire-Builder: Italy and Africa 1932–1936* (London and Basingstoke, 1979).

Rochat, G., *Il colonialismo italiano* (Turin, 1973).

Rumi, G., *Alle origini della politica estera fascista (1918–1923)* (Bari, 1968).

—— '"Revisionismo" fascista ed espansione coloniale (1925–1935)', in Aquarone, A. and Vernassa, M. (eds), *Il regime fascista* (Bologna, 1974), 435–64.

Santoro, C.M., *La politica estera di una media potenza. L'Italia dall'Unità ad oggi* (Bologna, 1991).

Sechi, S., 'Imperialismo e politica fascista', in Aquarone, A. and Vernassa, M. (eds), *Il regime fascista* (Bologna, 1974), 464–83.

Segrè, C.G., *Fourth Shore: The Italian Colonization of Libya* (Chicago and London, 1974).

—— 'Il colonialismo e la politica estera: variazioni liberali e fasciste', in Bosworth, R.J.B. and Romano, S. (eds), *La politica estera italiana, 1860–1985* (Bologna, 1991), 121–46.

Serra, E., *La diplomazia in Italia* (Milan, 1984).

—— 'La burocrazia della politica estera italiana', in Bosworth, R.J.B. and Romano, S. (eds), *La politica estera italiana (1860–1985)* (Bologna, 1991), 81–3.

Toscano, M., *Le origini diplomatiche del patto d'acciaio* (Florence, 1956).

—— *Alto Adige, South Tyrol: Italy's Frontier with the German World* (Baltimore, 1975).

Vedovato, G., *Gli accordi Italo-Etiopici dell'agosto 1928* (Florence, 1956).

Vigezzi, B., 'Mussolini, Ciano, la diplomazia italiana e la percezione della "politica dei potenza" al' inizio della seconda guerra mondiale', in di Nolfo, E., Rainero, R.H. and Vigezzi, B. (eds), *L'Italia e la politica di potenza in Europa (1938–1940)* (Milan, 1986), 3–18.

—— *Politica estera e opinione pubblica in Italia dall'unità ai giorni nostri. Orientamenti degli studi e prospettiva della ricerca* (Milan, 1991).

Wiskemann, E., *The Rome-Berlin Axis* (London 1966, 2nd edn).

Zapponi, N., 'Fascism in Italian Historiography, 1986–93: A Fading National Identity', *Journal of Contemporary History*, 29 (1994), 547–68.

Armed forces and foreign policy

Ceva, L., *Storia della società italiana: le forze armate* (Torise, 1981).

Ceva, L. and Curami, A., *La mecchanizzazione dell'esercito italiano dalle origini al 1943* (Rome, 1989), 2 vols.

Rochat, G., *L'esercito italiano da Vittorio Veneto a Mussolini (1919–1925)* (Bari, 1967).

—— *Militari e politici nella preparazione della campagna d'Etiopia* (Milan, 1971).

—— 'Il ruolo delle forze armate nel regime fascista: conclusioni provvisorie e ipotesi di lavoro', *Rivista di Storia Contemporanea*, 1 (1972), 188–99.

—— 'Mussolini e le forze armate', in Aquarone, A. and Vernassa, M. (eds.), *Il regime fascista* (Bologna, 1974), 113–32.

—— 'Il fascismo e la preparazione militare al conflitto mondiale', in Del Boca, A., Legnani, M. and Rossi, M.G. (eds), *Il regime fascista. Storia e storiografia* (Rome and Bari, 1995), 151–65.

Rochat, G. and Massobrio, C., *Breve storia dell'esercito italiano dal 1861 al 1945* (Turin, 1978).

Rossi, F., *Mussolini e lo Stato Maggiore. Avvenimenti del 1940* (Rome, 1951).

Whittam, J., 'The Italian General Staff and the Coming of the Second World War', in Preston, A. (ed.), *General Staffs and Diplomacy Before the Second World War* (Totowa, 1978), 77–97.

Italy in the Second World War (1939–43)

Andrè, G., *La guerra in Europa (1o settember–22 giugnio, 1941)* (Milan, 1964).
—— 'La politica estera fascista durante il seconda guerra mondiale', in De Felice, R. (ed.), *L'Italia fra tedeschi e alleati. La politica estera fascista e la seconda guerra mondiale* (Bologna, 1973), 115–26.
Bocca, G., *Storia d'Italia nella guerra fascista, 1940–1943* (Milan, 1997).
Cervi, M., *Storia della guerra di Grecia* (Milan, 1965).
De Leonardis, M., 'La monarchia e l'intervento dell'Italia in guerra', in Di Nolfo, E., Rainero, R.H. and Vigezzi, B. (eds), *L'Italia e la politica di potenza in Europa (1938–1940)* (Milan, 1986), 39–67.
Di Nolfo, E., 'Mussolini e la decisione italiana di entrare nella seconda guerra mondiale', in Di Nolfo, A., Rainero, R.H. and Vigezzi, B. (eds), *L'Italia e la politica di potenza in Europa (1938–1940)* (Milan, 1986), 19–38.
Faldella, E., *L'Italia e la seconda guerra mondiale. Revisione di giudizi* (Bologna 1960, 2nd edn).
Knox, M., *Mussolini Unleashed, 1939–1941: Politics and Strategy in Fascist Italy's Last War* (Cambridge, 1982).
Minniti, F., 'Aspetti della politica fascista degli armamenti dal 1935 al 1943', in de Felice, R. (ed.), *L'Italia fra tedeschi e alleati. La politica estera fascista e la seconda guerra mondiale* (Bologna, 1973).
—— 'Il problema degli armamenti nella preparazione militare italiana dal 1935 al 1943', *Storia Contemporanea*, 2 (1978), 1–56.
Pelagalli, S., 'Il generale Pietro Gàzzera al ministero della guerra (1928–1933)', *Storia Contemporanea*, 20 (1989), 1040–50.
Sadkovich, J.J., 'Understanding Defeat: Reappraising Italy's role in World War II', *Journal of Contemporary History*, 24 (1989), 27–61.
—— 'Of Myths and Men: Rommel and the Italians in North Africa, 1940–42', *International History Review*, 13 (1991), 284–313.
—— 'The Italo-Greek War in Context: Italian Priorities and Axis Diplomacy', *Journal of Contemporary History*, 28 (1993), 493–64.
Siebert, F., *Italiens Weg in der Zweiten Weltkrieg* (Frankfurt, 1962).
USE, *Il Africa settentrionale. La preparazione al conflitto. L'avanzata di Sidi el-Baranni* (Rome, 1953).
—— *La prima offensiva britannica in Africa settentrionale (ottobre 1940 – febbraio, 1941)* (Rome, no date), 2 vols.
—— *La marina italiana nella seconda guerra mondiale*, vol. 4: *La guerra nel Mediterraneo* (Rome, 1959).

Fascist society and domestic organisation

Aquarone, A., *L'organizzazione dello Stato Totalitario* (Turin, 1965).
—— 'La milizia volontaria nello stato fascista', in Aquarone, A. and Vernassa, M. (eds), *Il regime fascista* (Bologna, 1974), 85–111.
—— 'The Totalitarian State and Personal Dictatorship', in Menze, E.A. (ed.), *Totalitarianism Revisited* (Port Washington and New York, 1981), 84–103.
Bernardini, G., 'The Origins and Development of Racial Anti-Semitism in Fascist Italy', *Journal of Modern History*, 49 (1977), 431–53.
Binchy, D.A., *Church and State in Fascist Italy* (Oxford 1970, 2nd edn).

Borchardt, K., 'Germany', in Cipolla, C. (ed.), *Fontana Economic History of Europe*, vol. 4: *The Emergence of Industrial Societies* (Part 1) (London and Glasgow, 1973), 76–160.

—— *Perspectives on Modern German Economic History and Policy* (Cambridge, 1982).

Bracher, K.D., 'The Role of Hitler: Perspectives of Interpretation', in Laqueur, W., *Fascism: A Reader's Guide. Analyses, Interpretations, Bibliography* (Harmondsworth, 1979), 193–212.

Caldwell, L., 'Reproducers of the Nation: Women and the Family in Fascist Policy', in Forgacs, D. (ed.), *Rethinking Italian Fascism: Capitalism, Populism and Culture* (London, 1986), 110–41.

Colarizi, S., *L'opinione degli italiani sotto il regime, 1929–1943* (Rome and Bari, 1991).

De Felice, R., *Storia degli ebrei sotto il fascismo* (Turin, 1972).

Gentile, E., 'The Problem of the Party in Italian Fascism', *Journal of Contemporary History*, 19 (1984), 251–74.

—— 'Partito, Stato e Duce nella mitologia e nella organizzazione del fascismo', in Bracher, K.D. and Valiani, L. (eds), *Fascismo e nazionalsocialismo* (Bologna, 1986), 265–94.

—— *Storia del Partito Fascista, 1919–1922. Movimento e militia* (Rome and Bari, 1989).

—— *Il culto del littorio. La sacralizzazione della politica nell'Italia fascista* (Rome and Bari, 1993).

—— 'La nazione del fascismo. Alle origini del declino dello stato nazionale', in Spadolini, G. (ed.), *Nazione e nazionalita in Italia. Dall'alba del secolo ai nostri giorni* (Rome and Bari, 1994), 65–124.

Germino, D.L., *The Italian Fascist Party in Power: A Study in Totalitarian Rule* (New York, 1971).

Goglia, L., 'Note sul razzismo coloniale fascista', *Storia Contemporanea*, 19 (1988), 1223–66.

Ipsen, C., *Dictating Demography: The Problem of Population in Fascist Italy* (Cambridge, 1996).

Mack Smith, D., *Italy and its Monarchy* (New Haven and London, 1989).

Melograni, P., 'The Cult of the *Duce* in Mussolini's Italy', in Mosse, G.L. (ed.), *International Fascism: New Thoughts and New Approaches* (London and Beverly Hills, 1979), 73–90.

Michaelis, M., *Mussolini and the Jews: German-Italian Relations and the Jewish Question in Italy 1922–1945* (Oxford, 1978).

Pombeni, P., *Demagogia e tirannide. Uno studio sulla forma-partito del fascismo* (Bologna, 1984).

—— 'La forma partito del fascismo e del nazismo', in Bracher, K.D. and Valiani, L. (eds), *Fascismo e nazionalsocialismo* (Bologna, 1986), 219–64.

Scopolla, P., 'La Chiesa e il fascismo durante il pontificato di Pio XI', in Bosworth, R.J.B. and Romano, S. (eds), *La politica estera italiana (1860–1985)* (Bologna, 1991), 195–232.

Unger, A.L., *The Totalitarian Party: Party and People in Nazi Germany and Soviet Russia* (London, 1974).

Zuccotti, S., *The Italians and the Holocaust: Persecution, Rescue, Survival* (New York, 1987).

INDEX